Global Ocean of Knowledge, 1660–1860

Global Ocean of Knowledge, 1660–1860

Globalization and Maritime Knowledge in the Atlantic World

Karel Davids

BLOOMSBURY ACADEMIC
LONDON • NEW YORK • OXFORD • NEW DELHI • SYDNEY

BLOOMSBURY ACADEMIC
Bloomsbury Publishing Plc
50 Bedford Square, London, WC1B 3DP, UK
1385 Broadway, New York, NY 10018, USA
29 Earlsfort Terrace, Dublin 2, Ireland

BLOOMSBURY, BLOOMSBURY ACADEMIC and the Diana logo are trademarks of
Bloomsbury Publishing Plc

First published in Great Britain 2020
This paperback edition published in 2021

Copyright © Karel Davids, 2020

Karel Davids has asserted his right under the Copyright, Designs and
Patents Act, 1988, to be identified as Author of this work.

Cover image: Gulf Stream and Drift. Plate from the first edition of
The Physical Geography of the Sea (1855) by Matthew Fontaine Maury.
(© Granger Historical Picture Archive / Alamy Stock Photo)

All rights reserved. No part of this publication may be reproduced or transmitted
in any form or by any means, electronic or mechanical, including photocopying,
recording, or any information storage or retrieval system, without prior
permission in writing from the publishers.

Bloomsbury Publishing Plc does not have any control over, or responsibility for,
any third-party websites referred to or in this book. All internet addresses given in
this book were correct at the time of going to press. The author and publisher
regret any inconvenience caused if addresses have changed or sites have
ceased to exist, but can accept no responsibility for any such changes.

Every effort has been made to trace copyright holders and to obtain their
permissions for the use of copyright material. The publisher apologizes for any
errors or omissions and would be grateful if notified of any corrections that should
be incorporated in future reprints or editions of this book.

A catalogue record for this book is available from the British Library.

A catalog record for this book is available from the Library of Congress.

ISBN: HB: 978-1-3501-4213-8
PB: 978-1-3502-4043-8
ePDF: 978-1-3501-4214-5
eBook: 978-1-3501-4215-2

Typeset by Deanta Global Publishing Services, Chennai, India

To find out more about our authors and books visit www.bloomsbury.com and
sign up for our newsletters.

Contents

List of figures	vii
Preface	viii
Introduction: Globalization, knowledge and the Atlantic world	1
Key issues	2
Globalization	6
Knowledge	7
The Atlantic world, c. 1660–1860	10
Globalizing forces	13
Approach and argument	19

Part I Globalizing forces and the growth of maritime knowledge in the Atlantic world, c. 1660–1730

Introduction: Globalization between c. 1660 and 1730	25
1 Globalizing forces and the growth of maritime knowledge	32
Machines and the making of infrastructure	32
Self-organization and social networks	50
2 Growing maritime knowledge and globalization	58
Designing ships, navigating the ocean and probing the depths	58
Observing living creatures in and above the water	66
Keeping the humans on board alive	69
Conclusion	74
Capabilities and limitations	74
Changes	77

Part II Maritime knowledge and globalization in the Atlantic world, c. 1730–1800

Introduction: Globalization between c. 1730 and 1800	83
3 The maritime knowledge supporting globalization	89
Faster ships	90
Improving the chances of survival: Mortality and health care	99

4	The globalizing forces supporting maritime knowledge	110
	Imperial and commercial machines and the growth of infrastructure for maritime knowledge	110
	Self-organized networks and the circulation of maritime knowledge	130
Conclusion		139
	Capabilities and limitations	139
	Changes	147

Part III The reshaping of the Atlantic world and the collectivization of maritime knowledge, *c.* 1800–60

Introduction: Globalization between *c.* 1800 and 1860		153
5	Maritime knowledge and globalization: Advances and lags	162
	Increasing speed, lagging safety	162
	Improving the chances of survival: Mortality and health care	175
	Growing harvests from the sea: Fishing, sealing and whaling	181
6	Globalizing forces and the collectivization of maritime knowledge	185
	Imperial machines, infrastructure and the circulation of maritime knowledge	185
	Self-organization, infrastructure and the circulation of maritime knowledge	208
Conclusion		217
	Capabilities and limitations	217
	Changes	221
Conclusion		226
Notes		233
Sources and bibliography		268
Index		316

Figures

1 Map and description of Cartagena on the Spanish Main, from Arent Roggeveen, *La primera parte de monte de turba ardiente* (Amsterdam 1680). Special Collections Vrije Universiteit Amsterdam   26
2 Portrait of Michel Sarrazin (1659–1734), *médecin du roi* and botanist in Canada, by Pierre Mignard. Wikimedia Commons   40
3 Title page of Jorge Juan, *Compendio de navegación* (Cádiz: 1757). Wikimedia Commons   97
4 Hales's ventilation apparatus, from Stephen Hales, 'An Account of the Great Benefit of Ventilators', *Philosophical Transactions of the Royal Society* (1755–6). Wikimedia Commons   107
5 An Inuit and his canoe, pictured in Cornelis Gijsbertsz. Zorgdrager, *Bloeijende opkomst der aloude en hedendaagsche Groenlandsche visschery* (The Hague 1727²). Het Scheepvaartmuseum, Amsterdam   138
6 Diagonal braces for ships, from Robert Seppings, 'On the Great Strength Given to Ships of War by the Application of Diagonal Braces', *Philosophical Transactions of the Royal Society* (1818). Royal Society London, Public domain   164
7 Stevens on the density of seawater in different seas of the world, in proportion to the quantity of salt, and its implications for the draft of ships, from Robert White Stevens, *On the Stowage of Ships and Their Cargoes* (London 1850). Koninklijke Bibliotheek, The Hague   167
8 Map showing the patterns of winds across the globe and optimal routes for sailing ships, from Matthew Fontaine Maury, *Explanations and Sailing Directions to Accompany the Wind and Current Charts* (Philadelphia, 8th edn. 1858). Het Scheepvaartmuseum, Amsterdam   169
9 Minutes of the first meeting of the Bureau des Longitudes in Paris, 6 July 1795, from http://bdl.ahp-numerique.fr, Public domain   192

Preface

This book is the concluding piece of a trilogy on the history of knowledge. All three books are concerned with the context and impact of the development of knowledge before the middle of the nineteenth century, each taking a different perspective and a different approach. The first book, published in 2008, investigates the rise and fall of technological leadership by means of a case study of technology, economy and culture in the Netherlands between about 1350 and 1800. The second one, published in 2013, offers a long-term comparative analysis of the relationship between religious contexts and technological development in China and Europe between about 700 and 1800. This work, which concludes the trilogy, is a synthesis on the relation between globalization and the growth of maritime knowledge, centred on the Atlantic world between about 1660 and 1860, which makes comparisons as well as examines connections.

Sections of chapters of this book have been presented as papers at workshops held at the Institut d'Estudis Catalans in Barcelona in 2009, the National Maritime Museum in Greenwich in 2012, the Maison des Sciences de l'Homme in Nancy in 2013 and the Max Planck Institut für Wissenschaftsgeschichte in Berlin in 2014, in panels at the World Economic History Congress in Stellenbosch in 2012 and the European Conferences on World and Global History in London in 2011 and in Paris in 2014 and at a conference on 'The Global Lowlands in the Early Modern Period, 1300-1800' which took place at Brown University, Providence (RI), in 2014. A substantial part of the book has been written during a stay at the Netherlands Institute for Advanced Study in Wassenaar, with support from the Netherlands Organization for Scientific Research (NWO). I am grateful to all those present at these meetings for their stimulating comments on my work. I also thank three anonymous reviewers, whose thoughtful and stimulating remarks helped to improve the text. Finally, I would once again like to thank Dr Vivienne Collingwood for her excellent editing of the manuscript.

Heemstede, September 2019

Introduction

Globalization, knowledge and the Atlantic world

The story of John Harrison is well known. In the summer of 1773, the British Parliament awarded this brilliant carpenter and clockmaker from Foulby, Yorkshire, the sum of £8,750 for constructing the first reliable timekeeper for determining longitude at sea. Added to the large amounts of money that he had received from the Board of Longitude in the previous ten years, Harrison's total remuneration for his efforts exceeded the £20,000 reward set by an Act of Parliament in 1714 for the best method for calculating longitude at sea.[1] Harrison was hence known to posterity as the lone genius who had finally solved the most vexing problem in navigation. He was hailed as 'the man who found longitude'.

Determining longitude at sea is of course an important aid in an age of advancing globalization. Once you are able to calculate your exact position at sea at all times, it becomes much safer, easier and cheaper to cross the oceans and to maintain regular maritime connections between different parts of the world. The story of Harrison's timekeeper is thus a perfect illustration of the relationship between globalization, knowledge and seafaring.

Yet, this familiar tale about the Yorkshire master craftsman represents merely a fraction of a much more complex web of relations between changing global connections, the expansion of knowledge and developments in oceanic shipping. For one thing, John Harrison was not the only pioneer to offer a successful solution to the problem of determining longitude. Pierre Le Roy and Ferdinand Berthoud pulled off the same feat in France at more or less the same time. During trials at sea, the marine chronometers made by these French craftsmen proved to be as reliable as Harrison's timekeeper.[2] In addition to the chronometer method, in this period the method of finding longitude by observing lunar distances became practicable as well, thanks to the combined efforts of scholars in Britain, France and other European countries. What is more, solutions to the problem of longitude were not the only advances in navigation technology nor were advances in knowledge limited to navigation technology or to the second half of the eighteenth century. The story of the relationship between globalization, knowledge and seafaring involves a wide range of countries, includes a variety of 'bodies of knowledge' and evolves over a prolonged period of time; and it is the story that lies at the heart of this book.

Key issues

Global Ocean of Knowledge is about the relationship between globalization and the growth of knowledge related to the ocean. How did globalization influence the growth of maritime knowledge? What was the impact of maritime knowledge on globalization? How did this relationship change, and how can it be explained?

Historians have addressed the question of the relationship between globalization and knowledge in a number of ways. The most comprehensive and groundbreaking efforts to tackle this question include the Berlin-based Max Planck Institut für Wissenschaftsgeschichte's project on 'The Globalization of Knowledge' and Daniel Headrick's analysis of the relationship between global hegemonies and technological change. In a sense, these studies represent contrasting approaches to the same problem.

The Berlin project, carried out under the supervision of Jürgen Renn, aimed to move beyond economic aspects of globalization, which seemed to dominate the perception of globalization as such. Instead of viewing globalization primarily as the integration of markets for goods, capital and labour, the Berlin authors argued that globalization should rather be conceived as a 'superposition of various layers, such as the migration of populations, the spread of technologies, the dissemination of religious ideas or the emergence of multilingualism', each of which had 'their own dynamics and history'. 'Knowledge' is involved in globalization processes in each of these various layers, but not just as one ingredient among many. It should be considered 'a critical element' of globalization as such. According to the Berlin-based researchers, 'the globalization of knowledge as a historical process with its own dynamics ... orchestrates the interaction of all the underlying layers of globalization.' Thus, they claim, studying the globalization of knowledge is the key to studying globalization as such.[3]

The result of this project was a massive overview of the globalization of knowledge ranging from Antiquity until the present day, surveying many fields of science and covering large parts of the world. The thrust of the argument was that scientific knowledge originally emerged as a 'by-product of socio-cultural evolution' in various places in Eurasia, then spread over a wider area as a 'fellow traveller' with the growth of trade, the rise of empires and the diffusion of religious belief systems, and finally acquired a self-organizing quality after the production of scientific knowledge had become connected with economic globalization. This linkage between 'globalization processes of science and economy' first emerged in early modern Europe.[4] Renn and colleagues argue that the development of knowledge was generally driven by an interplay of 'extrinsic' and 'intrinsic' dynamics. 'Extrinsic' (societal) contexts, such as colonization processes, could be transformed into conditions for the intrinsic (cognitive) development of knowledge systems, such as the growth of medical knowledge, and 'the intrinsic evolution of knowledge systems', such as the development of astronomy, could turn into an extrinsic factor of knowledge globalization, such as colonization.[5] Although the combination of the globalization of scientific knowledge and economic globalization first occurred in Europe, the Berlin-based researchers insisted that globalized science did not result from a 'single dominant Western model', but from a 'synthesis of many local traditions'. Given the variety of local conditions, knowledge will continue to diversify at a local level.[6]

For all its breadth in time, space and fields of inquiry, and for all the subtlety of its conceptual distinctions, however, the Berlin project still only partially addressed the complex question of the relationship between globalization and the growth of knowledge. The desire to move beyond the prevalent focus on *economic* globalization appears to have been carried so far in this project that the analysis of economic developments was largely relegated to the background. Economic processes hardly received any attention at all. The connections between the cognitive and economic layers remained unclear. How exactly did knowledge affect globalization? What were the mechanisms by which its influence was transmitted? Under what conditions could the influence of knowledge on globalization be more, or less, effective? In these respects, the Berlin project stopped short of opening the black box of the relationship between globalization and the growth of knowledge.

Moreover, 'knowledge' was conceived in a rather limited sense. Although the starting point of the Berlin project was a broad conception of knowledge as 'problem-solving potential' – the spectrum of which ranged from 'intuitive knowledge' and 'practitioners' knowledge', via 'symbolically represented knowledge' and 'technological knowledge', to 'scientific knowledge' and 'second- and higher-order knowledge'[7] – in practice, the research largely focused on the latter end of the spectrum. Knowledge was narrowed down to mean 'scientific' or 'higher-order' knowledge. As a result, the project dealt mainly with the rise of science. The decision to concentrate on 'higher' forms of knowledge implied that a substantial part of the potential relationship between knowledge and economic globalization remained out of sight.

By contrast, Daniel Headrick's studies on global hegemonies and technological change, conducted between 1980 and 2010, addressed this very relationship. Headrick examined the effects of technological change in what he called the 'global expansion of Western societies' over the past six centuries. He defined technology as 'all the ways in which humans use the materials and energy in the environment for their own ends'. This concept covers both hardware and software technologies, and includes 'not only artifacts and domesticated plants and animals but also the skills needed to use them and the systems in which they are embedded'.[8] Information systems can be conceived as 'technology', too. Information systems are described as 'methods and techniques by which people organized and manage information' – that is to say, data on 'patterns of matter and energy that humans understand'.[9]

By examining a broad range of technologies and looking at a variety of imperial ventures spread widely across time and space, Headrick demonstrated both the potential and the limits of Western technological innovations in global expansion. In the early modern period, sailing ships, cannon, navigation techniques and horses allowed Europeans to dominate the oceans and conquer part of the Americas. In the nineteenth century, steamships, railroads, quinine, fast-firing guns and rapid telecommunication systems allowed Westerners to conquer most of the rest of the world, and aircraft made it possible to extend their control still further in the twentieth century.[10] The transfer of hydraulic technologies, science-based agriculture and technologies for mining and steel-making opened up unprecedented possibilities to exploit the resources of colonial possessions.[11] Headrick insisted that technologies 'are always environment-specific', however. What works effectively in environment A (sailing ships, cannon) does not necessarily work effectively in environment B. Moreover, mastery over nature does not always guarantee control over peoples; people with less advanced technologies can sometimes successfully resist powers with more sophisticated ones.[12] Thus, the relationship between technical knowledge and globalization was, and is, a contingent one; whether technological innovations aid globalization, and in what ways and to what extent, depends on particular conditions and circumstances. While Headrick discussed the effects of technological change on Western expansion at length, however, he treated the knowledge embodied in technologies more or less as given. In contrast to the researchers based in Berlin, he did not analyse cognitive developments as such, and he discussed only briefly the effects of globalization on the growth of knowledge.

Global Ocean of Knowledge is inspired by both of these perspectives, but it takes a different approach in several respects. This book investigates *both* the effects of globalization on the growth of maritime knowledge *and* the impact of the development of maritime knowledge on globalization. The concept of knowledge that I will use in this book includes elements from the Berlin project as well as from Headrick's work. Like those studies, this book covers a long period of time, but it concentrates on bodies of knowledge related to a specific geographical region, namely the Atlantic world. In this way, *Global Ocean of Knowledge* aims to contribute to filling in what the maritime historian Ingo Heidbrink called the 'blue hole' in our understanding of global history.

Heidbrink argued that almost all global history should 'incorporate elements of maritime history, if its contributions are to be valid', for the self-evident reason that 'all kinds of transoceanic interaction between people and societies depended on the maritime industries for nearly all periods of history'. In his view, the main difficulty with this approach is that 'many historians' have a 'lack of knowledge about the oceans'.[13] Heidbrink contends that for most of the 'scholarly community', as for humankind in general, 'the oceans are an unknown and hostile environment, a mysterious place beyond the horizon', and that this has led to the 'blue hole' in their understanding.[14] Heidbrink's point was unintentionally underscored in recent work on the increasing speed of ships under sail between 1750 and 1830 by economic historians, who were surprised to note what maritime historians had already known for a long time: that shipping technology in this period showed significant advances.[15] A study about the relationship between globalization and the growth of maritime knowledge, focused on the Atlantic world, will thus bring global history, maritime history and economic history closer together.

A number of studies, in various ways, have already made a contribution to that very goal. Heidbrink himself singled out Lincoln Paine's *The Sea and Civilization* and Charles Mann's books about the 'Columbian Exchange' as examples of recent studies that bring global history and maritime history closer together.[16] More specifically concerning the connection between globalization and knowledge in relation to the oceans, fruitful perspectives and approaches can be found in Felipe Fernández-Armesto's various books on the history of exploration, for example, or a recent collective volume on navigational enterprises in Europe and European empires in the eighteenth and early nineteenth centuries.[17]

By addressing the relationship between globalization and knowledge related to the ocean, *Global Ocean of Knowledge* forms part of this expanding body of literature on globalization and maritime knowledge. As such, it is *not* a study of 'Atlantic science' or a book about 'knowledge and colonialism', both of which have been the subject of a host of other works published in the past few decades.[18] Although studies on these topics are certainly relevant for the issues examined in this book (and some of them will be passed in review shortly), *Global Ocean of Knowledge* does not aim to contribute to those bodies of literature as such.

Before explaining the argument in more detail, I will first discuss the concepts of globalization, knowledge, the Atlantic world and globalizing forces, which form the core elements of this book.

Globalization

People who use the term 'globalization' generally agree on two things: that 'globalization' implies growing interconnectedness and that it has a spatial dimension. Beyond this point, however, opinions diverge. For the sake of clarity, we may usefully borrow the distinction made by Jan de Vries between globalization as an outcome and globalization as a process, or between 'hard' and 'soft' forms of globalization. Globalization-as-outcome, according to De Vries, usually refers to the integration of markets across space through trade, foreign investment and international flows of labour and technology. These economic aspects of globalization, which lend themselves more readily to measurement than other dimensions, may be characterized as 'hard' globalization. 'Soft' globalization concerns processes rather than (economic) outcomes, and refers to various sorts of contact, interaction and exchange (economic, social, political, cultural or otherwise) leading to greater interdependence between different parts of the world.[19]

This book conceives of globalization in the 'soft', processual sense, as this definition is much more sensitive to historical variations and divergences than the narrow, outcome-oriented perspective that underlies the purely 'hard' way of defining the phenomenon. This view of globalization thus includes the economic elements of globalization, but it covers a range of other aspects as well. Globalization is more than a purely economic process of integration. Following the framework used by David Held et al., this book takes several spatial–temporal dimensions of globalization into account. It looks at the intensity of interconnectedness and the extensity of networks, as well as the velocity of flows of ships, people and goods.[20]

Unlike some economic historians, who insist that globalization only began when interconnections were established that embraced the entire world,[21] I do not view globalization as a single, unique movement in time, but rather as a recurring process. As Chris Bayly and others have argued, globalization can occur in different periods of history and can take place at different scales (continents, oceans, macro-regions).[22] Geoffrey Gunn situated the 'first age of globalization' in Eurasia between the fifteenth and nineteenth centuries, presenting it as a process of cultural crossover and exchange of ideas, philosophies and languages.[23] This book focuses on a globalization process in another region of the globe, namely the Atlantic world between the middle of the seventeenth century and the middle of the nineteenth century, and examines its relationship with the development of knowledge.

Knowledge

The concept of 'knowledge' is no less complex than that of 'globalization'. The Berlin project conceived of knowledge in a seemingly straightforward way, as 'the capacity of an individual, a group, or a society to solve problems and to mentally anticipate the necessary actions'.[24] The authors then proceeded to introduce distinctions that made the concept more varied and stratified. They distinguished a range of 'forms' of knowledge, varying from the universal to the individual, from separate bits to coherent systems, and from concrete data grasped by intuition to symbolically expressed reflections on knowledge itself.[25]

Cultural historians and historians of science and technology have likewise made a series of subtle distinctions when defining 'knowledge'. According to Peter Burke, knowledge is a plural concept; it can be differentiated by use (technical, scientific, everyday practice, etc.), for example, or by social group, such as artisans or scholars. Burke's *Social History of Knowledge* mainly addresses a particular subcategory, namely subjects that were considered 'academic' knowledge in the past.[26] Harold Cook distinguishes two modes of knowledge, which in Dutch are called *kennen* and *weten*, and in French as *connaître* and *savoir*. *Kennen/connaître* is knowledge by acquaintance with objects, namely from the senses by taste and experience; *weten/savoir* is knowledge of causal explanation by reasoning.[27] Ian Inkster and Joel Mokyr coined the concept of 'useful knowledge'.

In Inkster's view, 'useful and reliable' knowledge 'embraced the knowledge that was brought to bear at points of significant technological advancement'. Mokyr conceives of 'useful knowledge' as 'knowledge of natural phenomena and regularities that had the potential to affect technology'.[28] In Mokyr's model, techniques can be described as knowledge of *how*, or *prescriptive* knowledge. Prescriptive knowledge can be distinguished from *propositional* knowledge, or knowledge of *what*. Knowledge in the latter category comprises observation, classification, measurement and the cataloguing of natural phenomena, as well as the establishment of the regularities, principles and 'natural laws' that govern these occurrences.[29]

The concept of 'knowledge' is closely related to the concepts of 'information' and 'data'. In his book *Imperium und Empirie*, on the relationship between power and knowledge (*Wissen*) in the Spanish empire, Arndt Brendecke uses the terms 'knowledge' and 'information' almost interchangeably.[30] Brendecke examines how knowledge was acquired and employed in the administration of the empire ruled by the Spanish Habsburgs in the sixteenth and early seventeenth centuries. Following contemporary Spanish usage, Brendecke conceives of knowledge concretely as empirical data on spaces, places, peoples and politics. In this context, knowledge primarily meant 'being informed'. Brendecke's research on the relationship between power and knowledge likewise takes place at a fairly concrete level. He focuses on specific contemporary practices, discourses and interest groups, rather than on general theoretical debates about state-formation, empire-building, decision making or the accumulation and circulation of knowledge.[31] *Imperium und Empirie* contains a detailed examination of communication and information flows at court, the Casa de la Contratación and the Council of the Indies, and the kind of data that were recorded in inspectors' reports and in replies to questionnaires sent to the Americas.

Jacob Soll and Chris Bayly hardly distinguish between 'information' and 'knowledge', either. In his study on the information system built by Louis XIV's minister Jean-Baptiste Colbert, Soll uses the term 'information' to denote fiscal, economic and political data, as well as legal, historical, natural and religious knowledge. Bayly's concept of an 'information order' comprises both information systems and 'groups of knowledge-rich communities'.[32]

Other authors prefer to keep the terms 'information' and 'knowledge' separate, despite being aware that 'the distinction is only a relative one'. Peter Burke uses 'information' to denote 'what is relatively "raw", specific and practical', and 'knowledge' for 'what has been "cooked", processed or systematized'.[33] Ann Blair takes the view that 'knowledge' implies an individual owner, whereas 'information' 'typically takes the form of discrete and small-sized items that have been removed from their original context and made available as "morsels" ready to be rearticulated', and can be used by many people in many different ways.[34] Taken in this sense, 'information' is identical to 'data'.

Given the complexity of the phenomenon of 'knowledge', we would be ill-advised to take a limited definition as our starting point here. Using a narrow concept of knowledge would not adequately reflect the variety of history and would unduly restrict one's research possibilities. After all, there is no logical reason to assume that globalization was exclusively related to a specific category of knowledge, such as 'technological knowledge' or 'scientific knowledge', however important these may have been. It is more fruitful, to my mind, to take the very diversity of notions of 'knowledge' as our starting point. Knowledge could mean different things to different people, and the relations between these different meanings could change in the course of time. In this book, the interplay between different notions of 'knowledge' through time is part of the inquiry itself. It goes without saying, however, that the investigation does not aim to cover the entire range of possible bodies of knowledge in the past. *Global Ocean of Knowledge* will focus on specific *fields* of knowledge that are closely related to the space that forms the focal point of this study, the Atlantic Ocean. We shall reflect on this choice in more detail shortly.

Nowadays, one central issue in the history of knowledge is that of the circulation of knowledge, which James Secord captures as follows: 'How and why does knowledge circulate? How does knowledge cease to be the exclusive property of a single individual or group and become part of the taken-for-granted understanding of much wider groups of people?'[35] The other side of this issue is the 'localization' of shared knowledge, or what the authors of the Berlin project called the 'local appropriation" of globalized knowledge.[36] How does the taken-for-granted knowledge belonging to wider groups of people become the 'property' of a single individual or group?

When tackling such questions, Bruno Latour's conceptual framework of 'centres of accumulation', 'centres of calculation', 'immutable and combinable mobiles' and so forth has proved to be a useful tool,[37] but it has also been shown to suffer from serious limitations. Today's historians of science often consider Latour's model to be teleological, Eurocentric and overly focused on simple centre-periphery relations.[38] Historians still take some inspiration from Latour's example, but they have also moved in new directions. Even when they analyse the growth of knowledge in a Latourian vein, they usually address the *how* and the *why* as an open-ended question. On closer inspection, for instance, the 'travel' process of 'facts' turns out to be 'quite unpredictable: it is dynamic, extended and interactional'. Facts *do* have a certain hardness and integrity, but when travelling they may become more or less complex, they may lose or gain information, and they may undergo different interpretations and alterations.[39]

The local appropriation of knowledge is a contingent and variable process as well. 'Specific geographies, histories, and languages' clearly matter, even though these, too, are affected by processes of globalization.[40] Mixtures of local, regional and global cultural elements have been in evidence for centuries. Awareness of the wider world can lead people to view their own immediate environment with new eyes. Since the 'Columbian Encounter', for instance, descriptions of 'indigenous' nature in Europe have often been 'framed … in relation to "exotic counterparts"'. 'Local' knowledge was thus created in relation to growing knowledge about the wider world.[41]

In this book, I take account of these contingent and variable aspects of the 'universalization' and 'localization' of knowledge as much as possible. Although I borrow some notions from existing theories (such as Latour's model) when appropriate, I do not rely on any of these larger theoretical constructions as an overall framework. I prefer to take an open-ended approach to investigating the relationship between globalization and the growth of knowledge.

The Atlantic world, c. 1660–1860

Global Ocean of Knowledge focuses on the Atlantic world between the mid-seventeenth and mid-nineteenth centuries. Why the Atlantic, and why this period? The Atlantic, to begin with, is one of the main battlefields in the debate about globalization. It lies at the heart of historians' discussions about the beginnings, forms, phases, driving forces and limits of globalization processes between 1500 and the present day.[42] The period from c. 1660 to 1860 is especially promising when examining these questions, because – to paraphrase David Held – it witnessed remarkable variations in the extensity of networks as well as the intensity of interconnectedness and velocity of flows. These 200 years encompass both the heyday of the Atlantic world as – according to some scholars – a 'distinct regional entity' or even an 'Atlantic system'[43] and the age of its sweeping transformation, all of which took place at a time when ocean-going shipping was still almost exclusively powered by wind. Bernard Bailyn, Nicholas Canny, Philip Morgan, Horst Pietschmann and others have forcefully argued that the eighteenth century saw a higher degree of integration in the Atlantic world than ever before, 'not only economically, but socially, culturally, demographically'. This was presumably the time, more than any other, when the Atlantic could most accurately be described as a 'system'.

This integration process began to accelerate from around the mid-seventeenth century onwards, in particular because of the expansion of commercial and imperial networks across the Atlantic from Britain, France and the Dutch Republic. By the 1660s, all three powers had established a lasting presence on both sides of the ocean. The 1660s thereby marked a kind of watershed. Admittedly, transatlantic networks as such were not a new phenomenon. From the ninth century onwards, the Norsemen had created a maritime 'empire' of sorts in the North Atlantic, stretching via Shetland, the Faroes and Iceland to Greenland and Newfoundland.[44] The Spaniards and the Portuguese had established footholds on the African coast and offshore islands from the early fifteenth century, and then ventured across the ocean, colonizing parts of the Caribbean and Central and South America from 1500.[45] But the Norse network beyond Iceland withered in the mid-fifteenth century, and before 1660 the Spanish and Portuguese maritime empires forged stronger connections in the Middle Atlantic than in the northern or southern parts of the ocean. Tellingly, Brazilian ports did not begin to play a significant role in Portuguese shipping to and from Asia until after 1664.[46] The Dutch, meanwhile, had established a port of call at the southernmost tip of Africa, the Cape of Good Hope. As the great French historian Pierre Chaunu insisted, there was a significant difference between the 'second' Atlantic of the late seventeenth century and the 'first' Atlantic of the Spaniards and Portuguese.[47]

In the early decades of the nineteenth century, the Atlantic world underwent another radical transformation. Empires disintegrated into nation states, which went their separate ways; slavery and the slave trade no longer functioned as a common link.[48] Old connections dissolved, new ones were forged. The 1860s mark a clear endpoint, as the Age of Sail made way for the Age of Steam. Steam changed shipping more fundamentally than ever before. The use of steam power in ocean shipping not only demanded a new set of skills but also had a deep impact on speed, safety and navigational routes. Notably, the rise of steam led to a sharp fall in transport costs, which helped to trigger a new wave of globalization.[49] With steam, we enter a different era.

The Atlantic Ocean was already an ocean before it became 'the Atlantic', of course; it loomed as a tempestuous, dangerous place, and served as a communication highway long before it came to be conceived as a single space covering the entire expanse between Europe, Africa and the Americas. An 'Atlantic identity' may have arisen on the western rim of Europe as early as 8000–4000 BC, in the sense that communities living in coastal areas may have developed a somewhat distinctive 'mindset', dominated 'by the need to maintain an equilibrium with the fearsome natural force by competition and propitiation'.[50] Yet, the view of the oceanic expanse as having an identity of its own took much longer to develop. Before the eighteenth century, Europeans did not use a single name for the entire ocean, but employed separate labels for its various parts, such as the 'Western Ocean', 'Mar del Norte', 'Southern Ocean' or 'Ethiopian Sea'. The name 'Atlantic' as a common denominator came into usage among English seamen after about 1700, and became more widely accepted after the Seven Years' War.[51]

Paradoxically, the Atlantic acquired a more clear-cut identity as a nautical space at the very time when it seems to have lost its former coherence as an overlapping set of economic, sociocultural and imperial bonds. Michael Reidy and Helen Rozwadowski have claimed that it was not until the nineteenth century that scientists started to envisage the ocean as an object of study in its own right. It finally became the subject of sustained, extensive and systematic exploration. Scientists fixed their gaze on the physical and biological properties of the sea itself, and oceanography and biogeography began to take shape as distinct scientific fields. 'The ocean transformed from highway to destination,' as Reidy and Rozwadowski succinctly put it.[52]

Although Pierre Chaunu and Frédéric Mauro put the Atlantic Ocean right at the heart of their economic histories of the Spanish and Portuguese maritime empires as early as the 1950s, it was only recently that the idea that the ocean itself could be a relevant unit of study became widely shared among historians.[53] Just a decade ago, critical voices pointed out that 'one area of inquiry remain[ed] largely absent from Atlantic history: the ocean itself', and that 'it [was] time to restore the ocean to Atlantic history'.[54] The 'blue hole' had long troubled Atlantic historians, too. Slowly, the nautical turn has begun to have an effect on their sub-field of history. Likewise, historians of science, historical geographers and anthropologists have recently discovered the relevance of the ocean for their disciplines.[55] *Global Ocean of Knowledge* aims to make a further contribution to this trend of putting the ocean at the forefront of the study of the Atlantic world. The maritime environment lies at the heart of this book. In the following chapters, the Atlantic world encompasses the entire maritime area, including its rims, between Greenland, Spitsbergen and Norway in the north to Tierra del Fuego, South Georgia and the Cape of Good Hope in the south, and between the British Isles, the Iberian Peninsula and Africa in the east to New England, Mexico and Brazil in the west. The Indian Ocean and the Pacific will occasionally appear in this book as well, because of the links with the Atlantic, but they do not take centre stage.

Global Ocean of Knowledge is not just concerned with the views of those whom we now designate as 'scientists'. After all, as I argued earlier, 'knowledge' covers a broader area than 'science', and there are more bodies of knowledge in existence than 'scientific' knowledge alone. Knowledge about the Atlantic Ocean was in fact collected, ordered and disseminated in various social communities long before scientists visualized the ocean as an object of inquiry in its own right. Knowledge and globalization influenced each other before maritime research was ultimately recognized as a legitimate and important field of scientific study. These discrepancies between developments in different spheres of knowledge, and their possible links to changes in other dimensions of the Atlantic world, should make the Atlantic between the late seventeenth and mid-nineteenth centuries an even more fascinating and important object of study.

To analyse the relationship between globalization and knowledge in the Atlantic orbit, I concentrate on those bodies of knowledge that are closely related to the ocean itself, and refer to these in short as 'maritime knowledge'. Some of the bodies of knowledge examined here relate to ways in which humans coped with the natural environment for their own ends, such as knowledge on ship construction, map-making, navigation, medicine, stowage, fishing or whaling. Other bodies of knowledge concern the maritime environment as such: knowledge about its geography and physical features, knowledge about winds, tides, currents, the weather and the climate, and knowledge about the fish, birds and other creatures living in, above and around the waters. The 'how' and 'what' forms of knowledge were, of course, interlinked in many ways. Ship construction, map-making, navigation technology or fishing or whaling techniques presupposed a certain amount of knowledge about features of the maritime environment, while the accumulation of experiences and observations made by humans at sea could add to the stock of knowledge about the environment itself.

Globalizing forces

How did the relationship between globalization and knowledge take shape and why did it change over time? Globalization itself was driven by a variety of forces. This book contends that in order to understand the relationship between globalization and knowledge, it is essential to examine the impact of all of these globalizing forces. Globalizing forces mediate between globalization and the growth of knowledge. The existing literature on Atlantic history, global history and the histories of science, technology and knowledge offers several models that may help us to analyse the operation of these forces. In the following chapters, I will refer to these models as the imperial machine, the commercial machine, the religious machine and self-organization. 'Machines' and 'self-organization' describe the various kinds of globalizing forces that were at work in the Atlantic world between 1660 and 1860. These globalizing forces are distinct from the four 'carriers' of early modern economic globalization discussed by the economic historians Van Zanden and De Zwart: the European competitive state system, technological and institutional innovations, European surplus income and demand, and American silver and gold deposits.[56] In contrast with these 'carriers', which in fact appear to be 'factors' or 'conditions', in this book the term 'globalizing forces' refers to the driving forces that actually make globalization happen.

Traditionally, the history of the Atlantic world prior to the nineteenth century has often been told as a story of the expansion of empires and their recurrent mutual rivalries. It is a tale about the rise (and demise) of different 'Atlantics' divided by states, nations or empires, such as those belonging to the Spanish, Portuguese, French, British or Dutch.[57] Much of this literature saw the making of the Atlantic world primarily as a product of the overwhelming power of centralizing forces 'from above'.

Likewise, the growth of knowledge, in particular scientific knowledge, in the Atlantic world is sometimes described as an element in the expansion orchestrated by institutions and organizations based in capitals or port cities in Europe. McClellan and Regourd's description of the French 'colonial machine' in the late seventeenth and eighteenth centuries, which puts particular emphasis on the role of the state, is the most elaborate and vivid version of this linking of 'knowledge and empire'. This perspective also figures prominently in Brendecke's book on the functions of knowledge in the Spanish empire in the sixteenth century. Richard Drayton, Claudia Swan, Londa Schiebinger and others also have portrayed the collection, transmission and application of knowledge as a coordinated set of actions by state agencies and state-sponsored institutions in the metropole.[58]

McClellan and Regourd introduced the term 'machine' as a tool in their historical study on colonialism and science in the early modern period. They coined the concept of the 'colonial machine' to denote the 'coordinated whole [of] state-supported institutions incorporating experts and expert knowledge [which] functioned collectively to support French overseas colonial expansion and colonial development' since the time of Colbert. The nucleus of this system was formed by the Académie Royale des Sciences, the Royal Observatory, the Jardin du Roi and the navy.[59] Other components, added after 1700, included the Académie Royale de Marine at Brest, the Société Royale de Médecine and the Société Royale d'Agriculture. The growth and operation of this set of institutions, which achieved a much greater degree of complexity than its precursor in Spain, was primarily driven by the 'perceived utility of science and expert knowledge' for the state-sponsored colonial enterprise.[60] McClellan and Regourd argue that all of these centres of expertise worked together to further French colonial development by expanding the mastery of space (e.g. by improving cartography and navigation), by promoting the health and welfare of colonists, sailors and slaves, and by enhancing the economic value of colonial possessions.[61] But the colonial machine brought benefits for the experts themselves, too: it offered them career opportunities, extended their horizons and made a mighty contribution to the advance of French science under the Old Regime. The experts were not mere slaves of the machine. McClellan and Regourd point out that scientific experts also could maintain relations outside the colonial machine with private correspondents in the Republic of Letters, for instance, religious organizations or scientific institutions in other countries.[62]

McClellan and Regourd acknowledge the metaphorical nature of this 'machine', but maintain that the term neatly reflects eighteenth-century usage and aptly describes the way the contemporary bureaucratic fabric actually worked: 'The crazy whole of our Colonial Machine functioned something like a machine, albeit a creaky one.'[63] Critics have argued that this picture overestimates the capacity of early modern states to coordinate human resources for their own goals. Even the supposedly powerful French state in the eighteenth century lacked the ability to do so in practice. If 'positive feedback' between the production of scientific knowledge and its application in colonial projects did in fact take place on occasions, it was 'more a matter of chance than of design'. Moreover, centres of accumulation of knowledge were to be found not only in the metropolis but also in outlying places such as Isle de France in the Indian Ocean. Coordination was a multi-centred rather than single-centred phenomenon.[64]

Yet, the metaphor of the 'machine' is a fruitful one in historical inquiry. The image of a 'machine' suggests deliberate construction, intentional linkages between different parts and a certain degree of steering. The 'machine' metaphor can serve as a lens to observe such phenomena in historical reality. My intention in this book is thus not to deconstruct or discard the metaphor but rather to modify and extend it. In this sense, the notion of a 'machine' as used in this book should be distinguished from familiar concepts such as 'mechanics', 'mechanistic' or the 'mechanization of the world picture', which refer to concepts and conceptual changes in science, rather than to a complex of coordinating human institutions.

However, the adjective 'colonial' suggests that the functioning of such an apparatus is invariably linked to the acquisition and exploitation of colonies. Although the machines that supposedly existed in France, Spain or Britain no doubt *could* be connected to colonial expansion, there is no logical reason to expect that such machines were only able to act in a colonial context. After all, the state-supported institutions incorporating expertise may also have used their resources to engineer flows of knowledge from areas beyond colonial control, for example, by undertaking scientific tours of Europe or by organizing voyages of discovery to the Pacific. Le Turc's espionage trip to the Dutch Republic and England, and Cook's, Bougainville's and Malaspina's expeditions to the Pacific in the late eighteenth century readily come to mind.[65] And the same institutions also could devote their expertise to the metropolis itself. The Académie Royale and the Royal Observatory owed their raison d'être in part to their usefulness in executing the vast, long-lasting project of mapping the entire territory of France.[66] Thus, it would perhaps be more accurate to speak of an 'imperial' rather than a 'colonial' machine.

Imperial machines were not the only kind of 'machines' that could act as a coordinating force in the global dissemination of knowledge. The machine metaphor has also been used for trading companies and religious organizations operating at a long distance from the metropole. Steven Harris, notably, has called these long-distance corporations 'twin engines' for the 'expansion of the scales of scientific practices' in the early modern period.[67] As well as imperial machines, we can thus identify commercial and religious machines.

As long-distance corporations, commercial and religious machines had a number of features in common. Harris defines a long-distance corporation as a 'legally constituted corporation established by the sovereign authority of Crown, Parliament or papacy', which was empowered to undertake activities in a specific domain in far-flung areas of the globe, and which had the jurisdiction to manage its own affairs and make regulations concerning the behaviour of its members. The concept covers both trading companies such as the Hudson's Bay Company, chartered by the king of England in 1670, and the Dutch East India Company (VOC), chartered by the States General of the United Provinces in 1602, and religious organizations such as the Society of Jesus, approved by

Pope Paul III in 1540, or the Missions Étrangères de Paris, whose statutes were endorsed by Rome in 1664. Long-distance corporations, Harris explains, were normally organized in a hierarchical way, 'with a centralized administrative apparatus and fixed headquarters'. Furthermore, these organizations had in common that they 'had to recruit and train reliable agents, send them to remote regions to undertake corporate business, and maintain cycles of correspondence that consisted primarily of directives from headquarters and intelligence reports from the field'. For this very reason, long-distance corporations were interested in the collection and transmission of knowledge about all sorts of matters and practices that could help to keep their operations going and their personnel fit for missions. They also had to devise ways 'to keep their members healthy, motivated, and loyal when stationed in remote and often hostile environments'.[68] Commercial machines and religious machines may thus be viewed alongside imperial machines as models that can help us to understand the relationship between globalization and the growth of knowledge.

There were also differences between commercial machines and religious machines, of course. Harris himself and other specialists in the history of trading companies and religious organizations, such as Ted Binnema, Luke Clossey and Helge Wendt, have highlighted salient features of both sorts of long-distance corporations.[69] Commercial machines aimed to make profits; religious machines strove to save souls. Commercial machines needed to attract capital to finance their operations, religious ones relied heavily on income from legacies, gifts or levies. Commercial machines invested heavily in logistics (ships, stores, trading posts), religious ones spent a great deal on fixed property (land, churches, schools, orphanages). And while the area of operations of chartered trading companies mostly lay outside the metropole, the sphere of action of religious machines lay both in Europe and in other parts of the world. Given such dissimilarities of purpose, income, assets and geographical scope, we might expect that the role of these organizations in the global dissemination of knowledge differed in several respects as well.

The 'machine' metaphor suggests a high degree of design and coordination. In the three models discussed so far, this coordination is largely provided by institutional arrangements. Whether, following Douglas Allen, one conceives of institutions as 'bundles of rules' or, following Douglass North, one defines institutions slightly more elaborately as 'the rules of the game in a society, or more formally, ... the humanly devised constraints that shape human interaction ... [and thus] structure incentives in human exchange',[70] imperial, commercial and religious machines can all be said to display clear institutional features, and rather formalized ones at that. Moreover, all three models emphasize the prominence of steering mechanisms from above.

By contrast, another view of the Atlantic world has recently emerged that stresses the importance of the agency of individuals and small groups, and the networks in which they worked and flourished. The growing literature on 'bottom-up' Atlantic history considers particular actors, groups and localities and their self-organized, decentralized networks, which criss-crossed the borders between states and empires.[71] Historians of Africa have argued that from the sixteenth and seventeenth centuries onwards, people from West Africa and West Central Africa formed their own pan-Atlantic networks connecting Africa and the Americas. Africans showed 'autonomous mobility' both inside and outside the structures of empires and trading companies. Communities on the Cape Verde islands and the coast of Upper Guinea acted as brokers in networks that ranged all the way from West Africa to the Bight of Benin, the Caribbean and the Americas. Residents of Annamaboe on the Gold Coast not only acted as middlemen in trading operations within Africa but also travelled the Atlantic Ocean as sailors, apprentices, students and diplomats.[72] Maritime historians have uncovered a sprawling, 'multi-ethnic' world of sailors, slaves, pirates, urban labourers and other groups of 'commoners', which extended across a large part of the Atlantic in the course of the eighteenth century.[73] Steven Harris has suggested that, in addition to trading companies and religious organizations, a loosely connected 'consortium of overlapping correspondence networks' consisting of 'scholars and experts from various countries and disciplines' may have been a powerful force in the globalization of knowledge in the Atlantic world, too.[74] The Atlantic world is thus studied from a networked, cross-imperial, 'entangled' perspective, with substantial attention given to individual agency.[75]

This bottom-up process can be called 'self-organization'. 'Self-organization' refers to the emergence of patterns through numerous interactions between individual entities without any form of direct, centralized control. Self-organization is a well-known concept in the life sciences that has also fruitfully been applied in various social scientific disciplines in recent years, such as sociology, economics, regional geography and political science.[76] Likewise, flows of knowledge in the Atlantic world were presumably moved not only by coordinating forces from above but also by forces from below, which could show a growing degree of regularity but did not entail a high measure of control.

Self-organization could arise both *inside* and *outside* imperial, commercial or religious machines. Networks based on private initiative and the 'restless enthusiasm of the volunteer', as Richard Drayton has argued, could not only serve to strengthen national or imperial expansion[77] but also help to forge links between people that transcended the official borders between states or empires. Within every machine, personnel in the field could take the initiative to enter into communication with correspondents in the metropole or in other parts of the world, who might not form part of the machine at all. The members, servants or employees of such machines were often not exclusively committed to the organization to which they formally belonged. In the mid-eighteenth century, for example, the cartographers of the Compagnie des Indes (part of the French imperial machine) and the British East India Company (EIC) exchanged maps from the collections of their own corporations. Jesuit missionaries in China corresponded not only with more senior members of their society in Rome, Lisbon or Paris but also with fellow Jesuits in Mexico, with the Royal Society in London, and with Gottfried Wilhelm Leibniz in Brandenburg.[78]

These four models of globalizing forces can help us to analyse how the relations between knowledge and globalization in the Atlantic world actually worked and why these relations changed over time. Having explained the key concepts of *Global Ocean of Knowledge*, let me now turn to the overall argument of this book.

Approach and argument

Global Ocean of Knowledge covers the era between 1660 and 1860. It consists of three parts, which address the periods 1660–1730, 1730–1800 and 1800–60, respectively. This division corresponds to major transformations in globalization in the Atlantic world, as the introductions to Parts I, II and III explain.

In accordance with the 'soft', processual view of globalization and the framework of different spatial–temporal dimensions described by David Held et al., these introductions outline changes in the intensity of interconnectedness, the extensity of networks and the velocity of flows of ships, people and goods. Globalization in the Atlantic world advanced throughout the period between the mid-seventeenth century and the mid-nineteenth century, but not in a uniform, straightforward way. Changes to the different dimensions did not always proceed at the same pace – intensity, for example, could increase more than velocity – and the nature of the interconnectedness or the structure of networks could vary over time. After 1800, the Atlantic world assumed a very different shape from that of previous centuries.

The focus of the analysis is on the relationship between globalization and the growth of maritime knowledge, mediated by globalizing forces 'from above' and 'from below'. The origin of these forces as such – including imperial, commercial and religious machines and self-organization – and the ways in which they influenced the process of globalization are not a subject of investigation. What is at issue here is the impact that these globalizing forces had on the growth of maritime knowledge, and the effects of the growth of maritime knowledge on globalization. The analysis of these connections forms the heart of each part of this book.

The impact of globalizing forces on the growth of maritime knowledge will be examined by looking at the infrastructure and social networks that facilitated the circulation of knowledge concerning the maritime environment. The term 'infrastructure of knowledge' refers to a set of institutions, regulations and facilities for the creation, certification and dissemination of knowledge. A 'social network of knowledge' is the network of a social group in which knowledge is communicated and created, such as scholars or practitioners of particular trades or crafts (e.g. artisans, seamen or fishermen). Parts I, II and III of this book analyse how and to what extent globalizing forces 'from above' and 'from below' influenced the development of infrastructures of knowledge and the ways in which knowledge was exchanged between social networks in successive periods, namely 1660–1730, 1730–1800 and 1800–60. The analysis thus covers the role played by imperial, commercial and religious machines, as well as the functioning of self-organized, decentralized networks, and thereby helps us to understand how knowledge related to the maritime environment could become 'universalized' or 'localized'.

To assess the impact of the various globalizing forces over time, it is insufficient to study developments in the British or the Spanish Atlantic alone, however important a role these countries' empires may have played in the Atlantic in the early modern period. The British and Spanish Atlantics cover but a part of the different forces 'from above' and 'from below' that constituted historical reality between the mid-seventeenth and mid-nineteenth centuries. A broader comparison will allow us to make a better appraisal of the impact of these different forces than by focusing on two cases alone. *Global Ocean of Knowledge* therefore not only looks at what happened in the British and Spanish Atlantic worlds but also examines developments in the French and Dutch spheres of activity and, after *c.* 1800, at developments in the American Atlantic, too. This comprehensive perspective is all the more necessary because globalizing forces did not function independently in separate national orbits, but were also interlinked across national boundaries, and increasingly so as the circulation of knowledge grew. The British, Spanish, French, Dutch and American Atlantics thus became more and more entangled over time. By including all of these spheres in the investigation, this book applies both a comparative and an entangled perspective on the impact of globalizing forces on the development of knowledge. Comparisons with the Portuguese Atlantic do not form a subject of this book, although there are frequent references to the role played by Portugal and Brazil.

The other side of the analysis addresses the effects of the growth of maritime knowledge on globalization. In order to estimate these effects, it is necessary to inquire how and to what extent changes in maritime knowledge influenced the intensity of interconnectedness, the extensity of networks and the velocity of flows of ships, people and goods in the Atlantic world. For that purpose, this book examines a wide range of bodies of knowledge concerning the ocean, which became interlinked to some extent. Each of the three parts of the book addresses questions such as: What changes occurred in the means and methods that were used to cross the ocean, to keep human bodies healthy at sea, to store and preserve goods during transatlantic passages or to harvest resources from the maritime environment? Did advances in knowledge make it possible for ships to sail faster or more regularly? Did they improve the chances of survival of those on board? Did they have an impact on patterns of commodity flows or lead to changes in the intensity or geographical spread of whale hunting or fisheries? In a similar way to the first part of the analysis discussed earlier, this multifaceted approach examines the impact of the growth of knowledge on globalization both from a comparative and an entangled perspective.

As globalization advanced between 1660 and 1860, the relationship between globalization, maritime knowledge and globalizing forces changed in several ways, too. One of these changes is reflected in the structure of the book itself: Part I on the period 1660–1730 first describes the impact of globalizing forces on the growth of maritime knowledge (Chapter 1) before discussing the effects of growing knowledge on globalization (Chapter 2), while Parts II and III on the periods 1730–1800 and 1800–60 follow the reverse order.

Chapters 1 and 2 in part I argue that between 1660 and 1730, imperial, religious and commercial 'machines' and self-organizing networks together created the basic infrastructure of knowledge in the Atlantic world and facilitated its circulation, but that the development of knowledge as such remained highly uneven and had only a minor impact on globalization itself. After 1730, as Chapters 3 and 4 in Part II show, changes in knowledge *did* increasingly have a marked effect on globalization, while globalizing forces, especially imperial machines and self-organizing networks, continued to extend the infrastructure of knowledge and facilitate its circulation. After 1800, additions to existing bodies of knowledge concerning the maritime environment were so broadly shared that one can rightly speak of the 'collectivization' of knowledge, and this phase forms the focus of Chapters 5 and 6 in Part III.

Globalization and the growth of maritime knowledge did not necessarily occur in sync, however; discrepancies and mismatches occurred more than once. After the Napoleonic Wars, in particular, globalization clearly exceeded the expansion of knowledge for a while, as Chapter 5 will show. Contemporary observers' increasing concerns about this glaring disparity and its impact on subsequent developments will be examined in detail.

All three parts of the book end with a conclusion, which first discusses shifts in capabilities and limitations in the development of knowledge in the period at hand, and then summarizes the most important changes in the relationship between globalization and maritime knowledge at that time. Generally speaking, the ability to develop knowledge, in terms of techniques, instruments and resources for collecting, classifying and interpreting data and for reproducing and transmitting information, improved over time in many respects. The limitations that existed before the mid-eighteenth century were largely overcome in the hundred years thereafter. The balance between capabilities and limitations shifted visibly in favour of the former. And yet, when the Age of Sail after 1860 gave way to the Age of Steam, there was still a vast ocean of knowledge to be discovered.

Finally, the conclusion to *Global Ocean of Knowledge* provides an overview of the main changes in the relationship between globalization and maritime knowledge during the whole period from 1660 to 1860, reflects on the shifting balance between capabilities and limitations and the causes of discrepancies between globalization and the growth of ocean-related knowledge, and offers some suggestions for further research that might forge closer connections between global history, the history of knowledge and maritime history.

Part I

Globalizing forces and the growth of maritime knowledge in the Atlantic world, *c.* 1660–1730

Introduction

Globalization between c. 1660 and 1730

In 1675, Arent Roggeveen from Middelburg and the publisher Pieter Goos from Amsterdam published a new sea atlas called *Het eerste deel van het Brandende Veen*. This sea atlas covered the entire western part of the North Atlantic between the Amazon and the banks of Newfoundland. Besides a small-scale survey chart of the Atlantic to the north of the equator, the atlas contained twenty-nine large-scale charts of the eastern coastline of the Americas and the principal islands in the Caribbean, interspersed with sailing directions, coastal views and other pieces of useful information on particular places, such as the location of shallows, anchorages and wells.[1] All the charts had been drawn by Roggeveen and the written materials bore his name, too.

Neither Roggeveen nor Goos had ever sailed the ocean themselves. Roggeveen was a surveyor, gauger and teacher of mathematics, astronomy and navigation by trade. Between about 1670 and his death in 1679, he also held the position of examiner of pilots at the Zeeland Chamber of the VOC.[2] Roggeveen claimed that he had collected the data for his atlas not by copying from existing works, but by carefully gathering information from experienced 'shipmasters and pilots' – an enterprise that had taken him about ten years.[3] A second part of Roggeveen's atlas, containing twenty-five charts of the coast of West Africa, was brought out by another Amsterdam publisher, Jacobus Robijn, in 1685. This part was dedicated to the Elector of Brandenburg, who together with a number of merchants from the Dutch Republic had just founded a company to trade in this very region. English, Spanish and French editions were soon published in Amsterdam, too (Figure 1).[4]

Separate printed charts of the Atlantic Ocean, or parts of it, had been produced before. A Mercator chart of the northern part of the Atlantic, for example, had been published by the Amsterdam firm Blaeu in the late 1620s and had been reprinted many times. Roggeveen's *Brandende Veen* (aka *The Burning Fen*, *El Monte de turba ardiente*, *La Tourbe ardante*), however, stands out for being the first printed atlas of the North Atlantic to have appeared in any European language. It comprised a huge amount of data, both visual and verbal, on a large

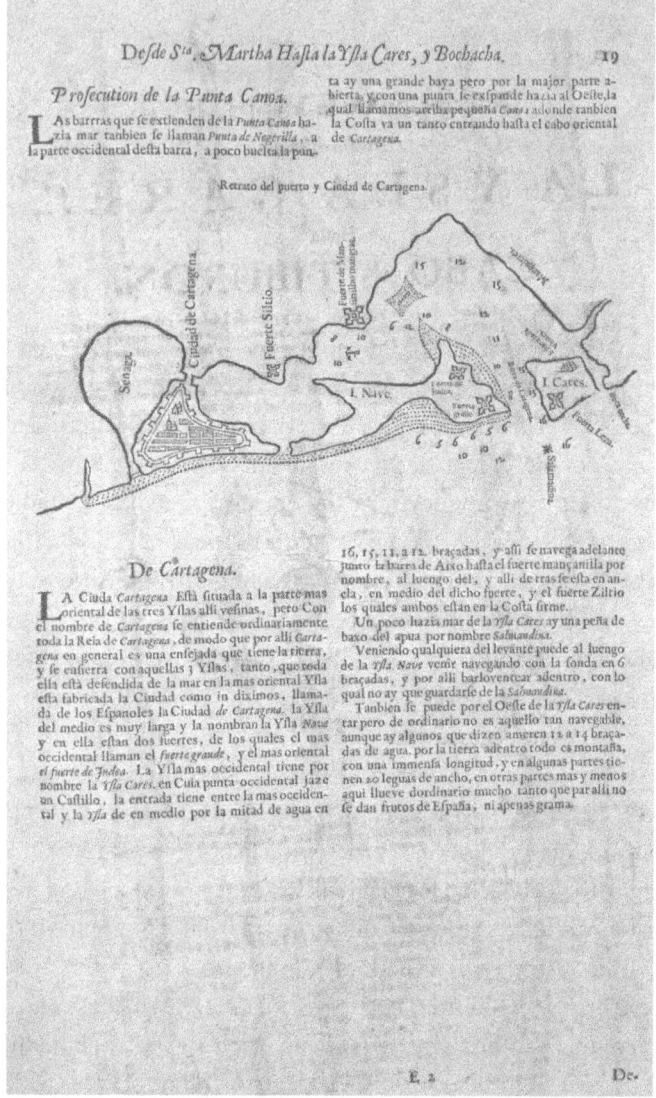

Figure 1 Map and description of Cartagena on the Spanish Main, from Arent Roggeveen, *La primera parte de monte de turba ardiente* (Amsterdam 1680). Special Collections Vrije Universiteit Amsterdam.

part of the North Atlantic, and this state-of-the-art overview was freely available for anyone who was prepared to pay for it. The atlas thus constituted a striking leap in the circulation of maritime knowledge.

The appearance of the *Brandende Veen* was an outcome of the globalization that had taken place in the Atlantic orbit from the early sixteenth century onwards. As a synthesis of knowledge on spatial features of the ocean, it could serve, in turn, as an aid to globalization. After all, the *Brandende Veen* was a useful device to help seamen to find their way more easily and safely across the ocean, and thus to assist the growth of shipping. And the more oceanic shipping grew, the denser the connections between different parts of the Atlantic world became and the further globalization advanced.

Remarkably, this innovative sea atlas was produced on the initiative of private entrepreneurs in a country that had just been forced to abandon most of its colonial empire in the Atlantic – namely, the Dutch Republic. At this point, self-organization, linked to the rise of a new trading company (the Brandenburg African Company), was clearly beyond what imperial or religious machines were able to achieve. It is a telling example of the new ways in which globalizing forces and the growth of maritime knowledge became connected from the late seventeenth century onwards. As this chapter argues, from this time onwards, self-organization as a globalizing force became an important ingredient in the growth of maritime knowledge in the Atlantic. The *Brandende Veen* exemplified this momentous change.

The *Brandende Veen* appeared when globalization began to gather speed in the Atlantic world. Contacts, interactions and exchanges between different parts of the Atlantic orbit became more frequent, leading to greater interdependence. The Atlantic Ocean became more crowded with ships, and ships carried more and more people and goods across the ocean.

The changes in the numbers of ships, the spread of sailings throughout the year and the density of connections between different locations in the Atlantic between the 1660s and the 1730s have been extensively documented for the English Atlantic. Ian Steele has shown that 'the number of English transatlantic and inter-colonial voyages accomplished in any one year rose dramatically in the lifetime before 1740'.[5] As shipping expanded, the average passage time on transatlantic routes decreased. For example, the average length of voyages in the tobacco trade between Virginia and Britain fell from eight months in the 1680s to seven months in the 1720s. The speed and frequency of communication also improved, because more and more ships sailed outside the common, '"optimum" shipping seasons'.[6] One by-product of the expansion of transatlantic shipping was a shift in the regional spread of lighthouses in the British Isles. While the biggest concentration of lighthouses before the end of the seventeenth century could be found on the east coast between the Firth of Forth and North Foreland, more and more structures now arose on the south-west and west coasts of England and Scotland. Although some of the lighthouses were erected and maintained by the corporation of Trinity House of Deptford (London), many new structures were built and exploited by private entrepreneurs through leases from Trinity House or patents from the Crown.[7]

Moreover, postal services were introduced in England and the colonies overseas during the War of the Spanish Succession. Regular packet boat services began to operate between England, the West Indies and New York, which showed that sailings to schedule were a feasible option. Once shipping and trade between West Indies and North American colonies expanded, the flow of news between these parts of the English empire increased, too. All of these changes helped to 'shrink' the Atlantic,[8] and thus contributed to globalization.

In the French Atlantic, many more ships from France or the French colonies were arriving in Quebec or Martinique in the 1730s than twenty years before. Most of these arrivals in colonial ports were merchantmen. Merchant ships provided an indispensable means of communication for entrepreneurs and government officials alike, and were the most important carriers of letters between the different parts of the French Atlantic. The number of French slave voyages to French and Spanish possessions in America soared after the War of the Spanish Succession; in the 1720s, there were seven times more slave voyages than there had been in the 1670s.[9]

The density of shipping and trade within the Caribbean significantly increased from 1700 onwards. In this intra-Caribbean traffic, Curaçao and St. Eustatius, which were under the authority of the Dutch West India Company (WIC), long played a pivotal role. After receiving free port status from the WIC, both islands became important hubs in the growing traffic between the English, French, Spanish and Dutch colonies in the West Indies and the American mainland. Curaçao in particular was a key source of slaves for the Spanish Caribbean islands and the Spanish Main up until the 1730s. The expansion of the intra-Caribbean network of trade and shipping more than offset the decline in Dutch bilateral trade with the English and French colonies in the West Indies, which started in the later seventeenth century.[10]

Spanish Atlantic shipping, meanwhile, lagged far behind. In the late seventeenth and early eighteenth centuries, fewer ships sailed from Spain to the Americas than a hundred years beforehand. Only a few dozen Spanish merchantmen and warships made the Atlantic crossing each year. Sailing patterns throughout the year remained unchanged: one fleet each to Vera Cruz and the Isthmus of Panama, one combined return fleet from Havana to Spain. Until the 1760s, no more than one mail packet a year left Spain for Cartagena. Spanish ships were almost entirely absent in the slave trade; no more than five slave voyages were carried out under the Spanish flag between 1676 and 1700, and none in the first quarter of the eighteenth century. The number of enslaved people arriving under Spanish flag in the Americas dropped from more than 220,000 between 1580 and 1640, via 21,700 between 1641 and 1700, to a mere 300 in the period between 1701 and 1760.[11]

Slaves for the Spanish American colonies were mostly supplied, legally or illegally, by traders from other European nations. In the seventeenth century, Portuguese traders were the major suppliers of African slaves to the mining industries in the Spanish Americas.[12] The sharp decline in the slave trade under Spanish flag after 1640 was to some extent offset by the growth in imports of slaves from British, Dutch, Danish and French colonies in the Americas. After 1700, there was a massive rise in the direct slave trade from Africa to Spanish America conducted by merchants and mariners from other European nations. Under the Treaty of Utrecht of 1713, the British Crown received the exclusive right to provide slaves to the Spanish dominions for thirty years. Spanish America thus became well connected with the rest of the Atlantic thanks to the growing volume and frequency of shipping between the British, Dutch and French colonies and trading posts and the Spanish American ports.[13]

The Atlantic also became more crowded with fishing boats and whaling ships. From the early sixteenth century, a growing number of European fishermen crossed the Atlantic every year in search of cod and other species of fish that swarmed the sea between Cape Cod, Massachusetts and the Grand Bank of Newfoundland. Year after year, myriads of fishing boats from Portugal, France, England and Spain gathered in the northwest Atlantic to bring in a rich harvest of fish for sale on European markets. The number of English vessels sailing to the Newfoundland fishing grounds rose from about 30 in the 1570s to some 250 in 1615, employing 6,000 men. French cod fishing outstripped the English fisheries by the end of the seventeenth century. The French catch was bigger than the English one, and it remained so until the Seven Years' War. In the 1720s, cod from the banks of 'Terreneuf' was said to be 'eagerly consumed in Paris and other important cities in France'.[14]

A new phenomenon in the later seventeenth century was that colonists from New England and Newfoundland settlers, who had initially only practised inshore fishing, also entered the cod fisheries with their own small vessels and on their own account. They subsequently started to export fish to mainland colonies further south, to English plantation colonies in the Caribbean and eventually to Madeira and ports on the Iberian Peninsula.[15] New Englanders thus began to make a transition from inshore fishing and coasting to offshore fishing and ocean shipping. In this way, transatlantic networks of shipping and trade were built both from the New and the Old World.

Whales were abundant in the northwest Atlantic. Native Americans rarely, if ever, hunted for great whales, but they made use of the remains of drift whales stranded on the shores eastwards of Long Island. From the 1650s, New Englanders ventured out into coastal waters to catch whales. When stocks of whales became depleted in the early eighteenth century, they sailed to Newfoundland and the coast of the Carolinas to practise whaling in the open seas. By 1730, Nantucket was the home port for twenty-five ships employed in long-distance whaling.[16] European whaling ships had entered these parts of the Atlantic before. Basque whalers hunted for whales in the straits between Labrador and Newfoundland between c. 1530 and the early seventeenth century, and then moved the centre of their activities to the ocean area to the west of Spitsbergen. Ships from England, Denmark, France, the Dutch Republic and Northern Germany joined the hunt after c. 1610. When catches in the seas near Spitsbergen showed a sharp decline after 1700, Dutch and German whalers started to look for new fishing areas further to the west. In 1719, twenty-nine ships from the Dutch Republic and four from Northern German ports entered the Davis Strait, between Greenland and Baffin Island, to hunt for whales. Disco Bay on the west coast of Greenland yielded particularly rich harvests. The Inuit used to catch whales near these shores, too, as journals and travel accounts of European whalers attest. In the decades that followed, the annual number of Dutch and German whalers sailing to the Davis Straits ran into the dozens. As a sideline of whaling, some barter trade with the Inuit developed as well.[17] Thus, the expansion of whaling led to a multiplication of contacts across the Atlantic.

Growing shipping and trade in the Atlantic also involved a vast increase in the transport of people. Sailing ships carried huge numbers of people across the ocean. More than 104,000 Africans were transported as slaves on ships under European flags between 1671 and 1680, slightly more than 10,000 per year. In the 1720s, the number of enslaved people transported per year had risen to 47,000. Most of the slaves in this period were brought to the Caribbean and Brazil; the others were mainly carried to the Spanish Main and to mainland North America.[18]

The numbers of voluntary and involuntary migrants who crossed the Atlantic from Europe in this period – as colonists, merchants, soldiers, indentured servants or convicts – are only very approximately known. For the Spanish Atlantic, historians conjecture that migration movement slowed down after about 1650. Whereas some 450,000 emigrants left Spain for America before

1650, only some 250,000–300,000 people migrated to the New World between c. 1650 and 1800.[19] Estimates put the total number of Englishmen, Scots and Irishmen migrating to the Americas between c. 1600 and 1780 at about 650,000. The vast majority of them left in the period between c. 1630 and 1700, mainly to the West Indies.[20] Emigration from France to French Canada in the seventeenth and first half of the eighteenth centuries amounted to about 70,000 people, two-thirds of whom returned to the Old World after a number of years. The French colonies in the West Indies, especially Martinique, Guadeloupe and Saint-Domingue, began to attract a growing number of immigrants from France from the early eighteenth century onwards.[21] Migration to Dutch colonies in the Atlantic was small. Recent estimates put the total number of migrants leaving the Netherlands for the Dutch Guianas, the Dutch West Indies and Dutch trading posts in West Africa in the seventeenth and eighteenth centuries at 15,000, and to North America at 10,000. Another few thousand people went to the Dutch settlement at the Cape of Good Hope.[22]

How and to what extent did this accelerating process of globalization promote the growth of maritime knowledge? This is the core issue in the first chapter of this part, which examines the impact of imperial, religious and commercial 'machines' and self-organizing networks on the growth of infrastructures of knowledge and the circulation of knowledge in the Atlantic world. It investigates the interplay and impact of globalizing forces 'from above' and 'from below' on the development of maritime knowledge.

The second chapter of this part deals with the reverse relationship: having analysed the influence of globalizing forces on the growth of maritime knowledge in the Atlantic world from the 1660s onwards, I examine the impact of developments in maritime knowledge on the advance of globalization. The spread of cartographic tools such as the *Brandende Veen* must have helped to strengthen connections across the ocean, but how and to what extent did the growth of such knowledge in general contribute to globalization in the period between 1660 and 1730? Did it really matter?

The conclusion of this part addresses questions about capabilities and limitations. Which changes in technology, instruments and resources facilitated the development of maritime knowledge in this period? In what respects and why did the growth of maritime knowledge reach its limits? The conclusion ends with a comparative discussion of the relationship between globalizing forces and the growth of maritime knowledge between 1660 and 1730.

1

Globalizing forces and the growth of maritime knowledge

Machines and the making of infrastructure

As Arndt Brendecke and others have demonstrated, Spain was the first European state to build an 'imperial machine'. The principal institutions were already in place before the middle of the sixteenth century. From an early stage, the organization of the transatlantic trade was concentrated in Seville. The Casa de la Contratación, which supervised all commerce and navigation to the Indies, was established there in 1503. The merchant guild of Seville, which came to dominate trade to the New World, was founded in 1543. Annual sailings between Spain and Spanish America were arranged in a system of armed convoys, which became fully developed in the 1560s. A fleet for Vera Cruz would leave in April or May and another one for the Isthmus of Panama in August; after meeting in Havana in the following autumn, the combined fleet would return to Seville. No foreigners were allowed to participate in the transatlantic trade and shipping unless they had explicit permission from the Spanish crown. A Council of the Indies, which was to administer and advise on all matters concerning the Indies (including government, trade, defence and the administration of justice), was established in Madrid in 1523. Ultimate control of the whole system rested with the king and the royal court.[1]

This growing bureaucratic structure was accompanied by an extensive system of communication and information between the metropole and the world overseas. In addition, a number of positions were created that specifically concerned the collection and transmission of maritime knowledge. Specialists in navigation, cosmography, geography, map-making, instrument-making and historiography were appointed at the Casa, the council and the court. These officials were charged with tasks such as teaching and examining pilots, compiling rutters, making maps, coordinating astronomical observations and writing the natural and general histories of the Indies. Ever more detailed instructions were drawn up to regulate their activities.² King Philip II also founded a Royal Mathematics Academy in Madrid in 1583, which aimed to give young men instruction in a wide range of professions based on mathematics, and he took the initiative to collect seeds and plants from the New World at royal botanical gardens in Spain. For the medical care of seamen, the king instructed that every squadron of galleys should carry one physician and three or four barber surgeons. Appointments of physicians and surgeons in the armed forces were partly made by military commanders themselves, partly by *protomédicos* nominated by the Crown who were empowered to examine applicants for the posts. In addition, special temporary hospitals for sailors of the fleet were created in the 1580s and 1590s.³

During Philip II's reign, moreover, the Crown sent a scientific expedition to the Americas for the first time. This mission, conducted under Francisco Hernández in the 1570s, was quite general in nature. Hernández was instructed to gather all sorts of herbs, trees and medicinal plants and to find out everything about their uses, properties and manner of cultivation.⁴ In 1582, the astronomer and mathematician Jaime Juan was sent to Mexico and the Philippines to determine latitudes and longitudes of important places in the Spanish overseas empire.⁵ King Philip III announced in 1598 that anyone who came up with a practical and reliable solution to the problem of determining longitude at sea could claim to a reward, consisting of a sum of 6,000 ducats plus a life annuity of 2,000 ducats and an additional 1,000 ducats for expenses.⁶ The cosmographer Andrés García de Céspedes proposed that an observatory be built at the monastery/royal palace of El Escorial, but the project was not carried out.⁷

In practice, the Crown and interest groups in Seville had less control over trade and shipping in the Spanish empire than the regulations introduced in the early sixteenth century intended. The monopoly system was always punctuated with all sorts of loopholes, which were eagerly exploited by Iberian and foreign merchants. Merchants outside the inner circle of Seville, especially the Portuguese, managed to build their own networks on both sides of the Atlantic. The resulting trade in goods, tax farming and lending to the government benefited both their own families and the Crown.⁸ And when it came to the collection and circulation of natural knowledge, the state apparatus was not as dominant as the older historiography suggests. Historians have only recently realized the importance of the contributions of religious orders and initiatives by 'enterprising settlers and merchants' in overseas colonies.⁹

Beyond the state apparatus, religious orders such as the Dominicans, Franciscans and Jesuits created a large number of monasteries, colleges and hospitals, which also became a vital part of the knowledge infrastructure of the Spanish empire. The colleges which these organizations operated in Mexico, Guadalajara, Quito, Lima, Cuzco and other places in Spanish America in the sixteenth and seventeenth centuries were not only vital educational institutions for Creole elites, but also functioned as centres of inquiry into natural history and other scholarly subjects. Hospitals and religious orders often included pharmacies with rich assortments of medicines, which drew both on indigenous and European traditions of knowledge.[10] Religious organizations also supported the knowledge infrastructure of the state. The rise of universities in Spanish America in the sixteenth and seventeenth centuries was a result of joint efforts on the part of religious organizations and vice-royal administrations. In the metropole, in 1625 the Royal Mathematics Academy merged into the Colegio Imperial de San Isidro, which was staffed by Jesuit teachers.[11] Thus, the imperial machine built by the Spanish state in many ways operated in sync with religious machines.

Although Spain had a head start in building an imperial system of government and a corresponding infrastructure of knowledge, however, it did not retain its lead in the later seventeenth century. Why did this reversal occur? The root of the change lay both in the gradual loss of power of the Habsburg monarchy, which had become evident by 1650, and the way in which the state-sponsored infrastructure of knowledge functioned in practice from the late sixteenth century onwards.

Important contributions to the advancement of knowledge in the Spanish Atlantic rarely became available in print, or at best appeared only in incomplete versions. This was even the case during the reign of the great patron of science, King Philip II. Many treatises by state-sponsored teachers of mathematics in the late sixteenth and early seventeenth centuries were never published. The immense survey by Hernández on the flora of New Spain, completed in the 1570s, only appeared in a truncated version many decades later. The results of Juan's astronomical voyage were almost completely lost.[12] Similar expeditions were not undertaken until the eighteenth century. Spain's underperformance in the circulation of knowledge was partly due to the Crown's deliberate policy of secrecy in areas such as geography, cartography and navigation technology. Secrecy was not constantly maintained, however. Whereas enforcement was relatively strict under the reigns of Philip II (1555–98) and Philip IV (1621–65), secrecy was relaxed during the reign of Philip III (1598–1621). Another relevant factor was that of financial constraints. The shortage of money became an increasing problem for the Spanish government after 1590. The temporary hospitals established by the Crown repeatedly struggled with lack of funds. The crux of the matter was thus that for many years, state political and financial support for the circulation of knowledge was not consistently forthcoming.[13]

The first signs of change can be detected at the end of the seventeenth century. In order to combat the chronic shortage of skilled seafarers (and to provide employment for poor orphans), the Council of the Indies took the initiative to establish the Real Colegio Seminario de San Telmo in Seville. This institute, which opened its doors in 1681, admitted orphans between the ages of eight and fourteen for a basic education in reading, writing, arithmetic and Christian religion, followed by training in seamanship, gunnery and the art of navigation, which would prepare them for a career in the navy or on merchant ships sailing to the Indies. Courses in the latter subjects were taught by the state-appointed specialists at the Casa de la Contratación. While the Colegio enjoyed the patronage of the king, the funding was provided by levying a tax on merchant shipping to the Indies. The management of the school was entrusted to the association of seamen in Seville that had been founded in the sixteenth century by the shipowners, masters and mates in the Indies trade.[14]

San Telmo remained the only institute in Spain specifically devoted to the teaching of navigation until the establishment of the Bourbon regime. One of the early initiatives of the Bourbon government was the foundation in 1717 of a naval academy in Cádiz, which became the new seat of the Casa and the principal base of the Spanish Navy. An observatory was attached to this academy, too. Unlike San Telmo, the Real Academia de Guardias Marinas was intended as an educational institute for the nobility, and its purpose was to train noblemen as naval officers. The teaching staff was, as at San Telmo, initially recruited from the Casa.[15]

Together with the naval and military academies subsequently founded in El Ferrol, Madrid and Barcelona, the institute in Cádiz grew to be one of the leading centres of scientific and technical education in the Spanish Atlantic. In eighteenth-century Spain, it was the armed forces, not the universities, that 'became the main cultivators of modern science'.[16] Significantly, when King Philip V sought Spanish experts to accompany the expedition sent by the Académie Royale des Sciences in Paris to the west coast of Spanish America in 1735, he selected two officers who had been trained at the naval academy in Cádiz: Jorge Juan and Antonio de Ulloa.[17]

The reason why Philip V added Spanish officers to the ten-man French team was partly pragmatic: he wished to prevent the Frenchmen from committing espionage or engaging in illegal trade. Besides trying to protect the interests of the empire, however, the arrangement also had a scholarly purpose. After all, the main goal of the expedition was to help resolve the debate between Cartesians and Newtonians on the shape of the earth by taking measurements of the length of a degree of latitude near the equator.[18] Juan and Ulloa would cooperate with the French scientists, in making observations and calculations, performing measurements and drawing maps. The very fact that the authorities in Madrid allowed Frenchmen to do scientific fieldwork in Spanish overseas territory marked a momentous change in the imperial government's policy on the acquisition and transmission of knowledge. The Bourbon government viewed scientific missions as a significant instrument in its long-term strategy to revitalize Spain's economic and political power and boost national prestige.[19] Tellingly, Juan and Ulloa's detailed account of the expedition in Peru appeared in print only a few years after the team members had finally returned to Europe.[20]

Under French influence, Spanish naval authorities eventually embarked on far-reaching reforms in the shipbuilding industry as well. After 1714, the newly installed Bourbon regime centralized the administration of the Spanish Navy and reorganized the naval yards across the empire. While the building of warships in the Peninsula was largely concentrated in El Ferrol and Santander, Havana became the main production centre in the Americas. The 1730s and the three decades after the Seven Years' War were the Cuban yard's heyday. Over the whole eighteenth century, the output of the colonial shipyard far exceeded the production of the two principal yards in the metropole, especially in the largest category of vessels.[21]

By 1730, the integration of an infrastructure of knowledge with an imperial system of government was more advanced in France than in Spain. Jacob Soll, James McClellan and François Regourd have paid particular attention to the development of an 'imperial machine' in Bourbon France, and their analysis shows both similarities and interesting differences with Brendecke's picture of Habsburg Spain.

The creation of a large centralized apparatus to promote the colonial, national and dynastic interests of the French state and the Bourbon monarchy was mainly the brainchild of Louis XIV's principal minister in the 1660s and 1670s, Jean-Baptiste Colbert.[22] Before Colbert, French colonial expansion had been a haphazard, piecemeal affair. Colonies arose in various places around the Atlantic under the aegis of private investors or chartered companies, without much coordination from state agencies in Paris. Colbert succeeded in forging this patchwork of settlements into a somewhat more coherent whole. He imposed a greater degree of royal control on overseas colonies, made a determined effort to improve the protection of imperial communication lines by expanding the navy, and took firm steps to extend and regulate the flow of information and knowledge between the overseas world and the metropole.[23] Henceforth, a single state agency, the Marine, would in theory serve as the supreme coordinating body for the entire French empire in the Atlantic.[24] Like King Philip II, Colbert built a highly centralized and sophisticated system for collecting and processing information, which in some respects was more limited than the Spanish one and in other respects more comprehensive. The system was more limited than Philip's in the sense that Colbert's efforts were largely driven by a national, rather than by a global or Atlantic-wide, vision. The prime purpose of the system was to strengthen the French state and enhance the power of the king. The New World hardly interested Colbert at all.[25] On the other hand, the French minister built a more comprehensive system in the sense that he gathered data on an extremely wide range of topics, ranging from fiscal, economic and political information to legal, historical, natural and religious knowledge, and he tried to tie the scholarly community closely to his project through patronage networks and institutional facilities, such as the newly founded academies.[26] The imperial machine thus became a more elaborate affair in France than in Spain.

At the very time when the colonial apparatus was first put together, the institutional infrastructure of knowledge in France expanded as well. New state-sponsored centres of science were established in Paris in the 1660s. As well as the Jardin du Roi, which had been created between 1626 and 1635 as a garden for the study of medicinal plants, the Académie Royale des Sciences was founded in 1664 and the Observatoire Royal in 1667. The Académie was entrusted with the supervision and implementation of research on a wide variety of subjects, while the Observatoire was charged with carrying out regular observations of the heavens and collecting and systematizing astronomical data from all parts of the world.[27]

Although Colbert's primary aim was to get the administration of colonies in good order, rather than to gather information about peoples and local conditions in the Americas, even during his lifetime, the state agencies and scientific institutions in Paris and the colonies overseas nevertheless started to communicate about issues other than purely bureaucratic matters. These connections grew further after the great organizer himself disappeared from the scene in 1683.[28] Stimulated by the metropolitan bureaucracy, royal administrators in the colonies in the West Indies, Guiana and Canada began to experiment with novelties from Eurasia such as wheat, vineyards and silkworms. Correspondents overseas sent specimens of plants and animals and data from astronomical observations to Paris.[29] Members of the Académie stressed the usefulness of their work for the ambitions of the French state, especially in the field of astronomy. A degree of cooperation between the Académie and the navy slowly took shape. Together with naval hydrographers, the *académiciens* Jean Picard and Philippe de la Hire completed a marine atlas, the *Neptune François*, which was printed by the Imprimerie royale in Paris in 1693 and contained twenty-nine maps of the coast of Continental Europe, from Norway to Gibraltar. The navy began systematically to collect records of mariners' observations and experiences, too. An ordinance of 1681 obliged all shipmasters in France to deposit their ship's journal at the naval registry. From about 1700 onwards, maps were also added to the collection.[30] In 1720, a Dépôt des cartes et plans de la Marine was established under the supervision of a naval officer, charged with examining and preserving 'des plans, cartes, journaux des voyages, rapports et autres memoires envoyés par les officiers commandants des vaisseaux à leur retour de la mer'.[31]

Expeditions under the aegis of the state, the Académie and the Observatoire fanned out across the Atlantic to gather all sorts of astronomical, geographical and botanical data. In the early 1670s, astronomer Jean Richer first made a voyage to Acadia (Canada) to test Christiaan Huygens's newly invented chronometer, and then travelled to Guiana, where he observed a variety of astronomical phenomena, such as the moment of the equinoxes and the parallax and the movements of the Sun, the Moon, Venus and Mars.[32] Richer's voyages also yielded a host of data on the latitudes and longitudes of various locations around the Atlantic, which were vital to the academy's project to map France and the rest of the world.[33] Astronomers expected that such observations, combined with the exact delineation of the meridian of Paris, would correct 'dangerous errors' in maps and charts and would thus help to bring greater perfection to 'geography and navigation'.[34] In 1681, the Académie Royale des Sciences sponsored a voyage to Gorée near the coast of Senegal and the islands of Guadeloupe and Martinique in the Caribbean. The main purpose of the voyage was to improve the mapping of the earth by determining the latitude and longitude of a number of fixed points in the Atlantic.[35] The botanist Charles Plumier collected numerous items and made many drawings for the benefit of the Jardin du Roi during three state-sponsored voyages to the West Indies between 1689 and 1697. The *mathématicien du roi* Louis Feuillée expanded the stock of data on astronomy, geography and natural history during a series of voyages made on the order of the king to the West Indies, Peru and Chile between 1703 and 1711.[36]

The competence of navigators became a concern of the French state as well. As part of his grand project to endow France with a powerful navy, Colbert created royal chairs in navigation in Le Hâvre (1660) and Nantes (1672), supplied money to Quebec to hire a professor of mathematics and navigation (1671) and founded training colleges for naval officers in Brest, Rochefort and Toulon (1682). In addition, compulsory exams were introduced for naval officers and for navigating personnel in the merchant navy. From 1681 onwards, masters and mates in ocean shipping and coastal navigation were required to take an exam conducted by a state-appointed professor of navigation.[37]

A 'regulatory regime' for medical care in the navy (as Michael Osborne has called it) was established in the 1680s, too. The main elements of this framework were laid down in a general ordinance published in 1689. The state hospitals that had been established in the ports of Brest, Toulon and Rochefort from the 1660s were put under the supervision of a commissary, who in turn reported to the intendant at the top of the local administrative hierarchy. A chief physician, a surgeon major and an apothecary were charged with overseeing the care of the sick and wounded in the hospitals, and checking the medical equipment and supplies of navy ships before departure.[38] The chief physician and surgeon major were also assigned the task of examining the surgeons and apothecaries who would present themselves for service on His Majesty's ships or in the port hospitals.[39] Anatomical instruction would also form part of a physician's job. These naval hospitals would later become the nucleus of an extensive system of medical and surgical training. The ordinance of 1689 further stipulated that naval surgeons had to keep a journal aboard ship, in which they should record all information about diseases, injuries and deaths and about the medicines and other remedies they applied. A hospital ship would be added to each naval squadron of ten ships or more.[40] In addition, the French imperial machine included hospitals in Canada and the Caribbean and a few *médécins du roi* in Canada, Louisiana and a number of West Indian islands (Figure 2).[41]

Finally, the French state also started to establish an infrastructure of knowledge on ship construction. In the eighteenth century, French naval vessels were almost exclusively built in dockyards managed by the government,[42] and the master shipwrights who designed the king's ships were nearly all employees of the state. From Colbert's time onwards, the French government persistently promoted research into a mathematical approach to ship design, especially at the Académie Royale in Paris and at the hydrography schools that had been founded in the major naval ports. Paul Hoste, a professor at the hydrography school in Toulon, composed 'the first synthetic works on the subject, linking ship theory with practical shipbuilding'.[43]

Figure 2 Portrait of Michel Sarrazin (1659–1734), *médecin du roi* and botanist in Canada, by Pierre Mignard. Wikimedia Commons.

The terms 'colonial machine' and 'imperial machines' might conjure up a vision of a more perfect and well-functioning entity than the one that actually existed, however.⁴⁴ The regulation of 1689 on training in hospitals largely remained a dead letter until the 1720s.⁴⁵ In the heyday of the French Atlantic Empire, centralization, control and coherence were in reality never as extensive as Colbert and his successors at the Marine had envisaged. Even in its own dockyards, the French state faced serious difficulties in transforming shipbuilding practices. French shipwrights continued to use iron spikes for fastening their ships, for example, even though Colbert and his successors tried to discourage this custom, as it reduced the life span of vessels.⁴⁶ Moreover, as Kenneth Banks has argued, 'the challenges posed by transatlantic communications impinged on, modified, and increasingly undermined the French state's control over its colonies during the first half of the eighteenth century.'⁴⁷ In practice, it proved to be hard and expensive to ensure regular sailings of royal officials and dispatches from France to the colonies across the Atlantic, and besides, within the empire overseas, the Crown always had to rely on the cooperation of local settlers to disseminate or collect information. The state needed the collaboration of merchants and other private individuals, too, both for realizing its aims in the accumulation of knowledge and for maintaining communications in the empire. Trading companies assisted with the early scientific missions. The expedition to Gorée and the Caribbean in the 1680s, for instance, was crucially dependent on transport facilities provided by the Compagnie du Sénégal.[48] A biannual prize for studies useful to navigation and overseas voyages was funded by a bequest made by parliamentary counsellor Rouillé de Meslay in 1714, with the Académie Royale acting as a jury.[49]

The scientific expertise required to realize the grand designs of the state and state-sponsored institutions was partly supplied by religious organizations. As in the case of Spain, the imperial and religious machines were intertwined. Both Charles Plumier and Louis Feuillée belonged to the order of the Minim friars. Father Le Maire of the Missions Étrangères sent maps and botanical data on Louisiana to a fellow priest in Paris, Jean Bobé, who happened to be a director of the Compagnie des Indes.[50] Jesuits assumed a key role in the development of nautical education. The authors of the best-known textbooks on the art of navigation and naval architecture published in France in the seventeenth century, Georges Fournier and Paul Hoste, were members of the Society of Jesus. Jesuits filled many teaching positions at the training colleges for naval officers established by Colbert. Lessons on navigation were offered *inside* some Jesuit colleges, too, both for boarders and for external pupils.[51] Jesuits provided navigational instruction in Quebec from the beginning of the eighteenth century.[52] For a long time, patient care in the naval hospitals in Brest, Toulon and Rochefort was largely in the hands of religious orders as well.[53]

Nevertheless, religious organizations were not subservient to the interests of the state. Members of religious orders stationed overseas also pursued their own inquiries in astronomy, botany and other disciplines, without informing the state of their work, and they communicated their findings not only to the Académie, the Jardin or the Observatoire but also to other institutions and interested parties in Europe.[54] A vast amount of material gathered by friar Plumier never even reached the desks of state officials. After Plumier's death in 1704, manuscripts with drawings of fish from the Caribbean remained in the library of the Minims in Paris, and were rarely consulted until the end of the eighteenth century.[55]

The size and output of the newly founded institutions of knowledge in the French 'colonial machine' should not be exaggerated, either. For instance, the staff of the Dépôt des cartes et plans de la Marine, founded in 1720, was initially quite small: it merely consisted of two assistants, Jacques-Nicolas Bellin and Philippe Buache.[56] For many years, the Dépôt concentrated on copying, preserving and analysing ships' journals, plans and maps, rather than on producing new charts or aids for seamen. A set of sailing instructions running to some 650 pages for all the coasts and islands in the Atlantic Ocean from 48 degrees north to 35 degrees south, completed by Bellin in 1731 on the basis of 'les memoires et les journaux qui sont deposés au Dépôt des plans de la Marine', remained in manuscript form only. The first new chart made at the Dépôt (representing the Mediterranean) was not published until 1737.[57]

The imperial machine thus only gradually managed to have some impact on the affairs of the French Atlantic, and it never came close to achieving complete control. Yet, by the 1730s it was a more elaborate and effective apparatus than at the end of Colbert's administration, and it was more comprehensive than the system developed by the first Atlantic imperial power, Habsburg Spain.

The imperial machine in Britain emerged later than that in Spain, and it developed more gradually than in France. While permanent English settlements in the Caribbean and on the North American continent were established by chartered companies or private proprietors with royal approval from the early seventeenth century onwards, it was not until the 1670s that the administration of the colonies became more centralized in a newly formed committee of the Privy Council, the Lords of Trade and Plantations. In 1696, this body was succeeded by another, separate committee appointed by the Crown, the Board of Trade and Plantations. The board set out to strengthen London's control of the government of the colonies. Together with other newly created institutions, such as vice-admiralty courts overseas, it strove for more effective enforcement of the statutes concerning shipping and trade in England and its possessions overseas introduced from the 1650s, known as the Navigation Acts, with the express purpose of increasing the wealth of the metropole. The Navigation Acts stipulated that goods to and from the English colonies overseas should only be carried in English-owned ships, largely manned by English crews, and that a large number of goods from countries in Europe could likewise only be imported into England in English ships, or in ships from the producing country, or of the place of first shipment.[58] Although the administration of the English colonies did not become as centralized and homogenized as that of the French or Spanish empires, and British trade and shipping did not entirely match 'the Spanish-style monopoly of the transatlantic trade' (as John Elliott called it), the scope of imperial power definitely increased in the last decades of the seventeenth century.

As in France, institutional infrastructures of knowledge in England significantly expanded in the last decades of the seventeenth century. A Royal Observatory was founded in Greenwich in 1675, for the 'finding out of the longitude of places for perfecting navigation and astronomy'. An Astronomer Royal was appointed to direct the institute and to organize a systematic programme of observations. A Royal Mathematical School, funded by the Crown, to train young men in 'the Art of Navigation and the whole science of Arithmetique' was established at Christ's Hospital, London, in 1673. In the first forty years of its existence, the governing committee of the school repeatedly asked fellows of the Royal Society for advice about how the instruction could be brought up to state-of-the-art scientific standards.[59] Furthermore, England was the first European state to introduce qualifying examinations for officers of the navy. Although potential officers continued to start their careers under the patronage of senior officers, from 1677, the naval authorities had at their disposal a formal instrument to monitor the quality of future personnel. Candidates for the rank of lieutenant were only admitted after serving for a certain time at sea and after passing a seamanship examination before a panel of captains. Exams abroad were conducted by panels appointed by local commanders-in-chief, while those at home were conducted by the Navy Board.[60] Schoolmasters charged with the teaching of arithmetic and navigation appeared on navy ships in *c.* 1700.[61] The institutional structure of knowledge was further extended with the foundation of the Royal Naval Academy in Portsmouth in 1730. The curriculum of this academy for the education of 'young gentlemen for Your Majesty's service at sea' included, among other subjects, mathematics and navigation.[62]

In addition, the navy slowly developed an infrastructure of knowledge for medical care. Regulations and facilities were introduced for the certification and dissemination of medical knowledge, and physicians were appointed in the home ports and squadrons of the main fleet of the English Navy in 1691. From 1709 onwards, naval surgeons were obliged to follow a qualifying course in medicine.[63] The supervision of surgeons' apprentices and the examination of surgeons remained the prerogative of the Surgeons' Company until the end of the eighteenth century. From the 1660s onwards, hospital ships often formed part of English fleets, facilitating the isolation of 'infectious cases ... from ships' companies'. However, purpose-built hospitals to care for seafarers in the navy were not established in port cities in England until after 1740. In the West Indies, a hospital for mariners founded on Jamaica in 1740 had the capacity for just sixty patients. Besides, it was soon abandoned due to its location in a singularly unhealthy part of the island.[64] The navy mainly relied on a system of temporarily contracting for beds in civilian hospitals and private lodgings.

The Royal Society of London granted a charter by King Charles II in 1662, and the British Parliament also became active in the promotion of maritime knowledge. From the outset, the Royal Society showed a keen interest in collecting as many observations about the sea as possible, believing that as a result, 'rules [might] be framed' that might prove to be 'of inestimable use to seamen'. For this purpose, the society drew up a list of 'directions for observations to be made by masters of ships, pilots, and other fit persons in their sea-voyages', which it published in the *Philosophical Transactions* in 1667, and distributed to the seafaring community via the Master of Trinity House. The directions ranged from observing 'the declinations and variations of the compass or needle from the meridian exactly, in as many places as they can, and in the same places, every several voyage', carrying 'dipping needles with them', and marking carefully the flowings and ebbings of the sea, in as many places as may be', to 'sounding the deepest seas without a line, by the help of an instrument', 'keeping a register of all changes of wind and weather at all hours by night and by day' and fetching up 'water from any depth of the sea'. Pictures of newly invented sounding instruments were included as well.[65] Data collected by seamen could be combined with information gathered by fellows of the Royal Society themselves. Edmond Halley embarked on two voyages to the Northern and Southern Atlantic on the specially built naval vessel *Paramore* between 1698 and 1700, to collect data on the variation of the compass.[66] Parliament, too, became concerned with the development of maritime knowledge from 1714 onwards, when it introduced a prize of £20,000 for the best solution to the problem of determining longitude at sea. A special commission was appointed to judge all proposals submitted by inventors to qualify for the reward. This commission, which actually held its first meeting in 1737, became known as the Board of Longitude in the 1760s.[67]

In contrast to France, however, the imperial machine in Britain only concerned itself to a limited extent with developing an infrastructure of knowledge on ship construction. Certainly, the position of surveyor of the navy, which from the 1670s was held by master shipwrights from the royal dockyards, became 'established as that of the navy's principal warship designer', and naval authorities requested shipwrights from 1716 to present solid models of the vessels they planned to build. All ships were classified in six rates and the dimensions of each class were firmly fixed.[68] Know-how about ship construction largely remained a tacit affair, however, which was almost exclusively the preserve of the shipwrights themselves. For a long time, most warship construction was contracted out to private shipyards. Much of the great shipbuilding programme during the Nine Years' War was carried out at private yards rather than at the naval dockyards in Deptford, Woolwich, Chatham or Portsmouth.[69] Master shipwrights in Britain continued to receive their training in the setting of local apprenticeships rather than through a uniform, nationwide schooling system. Admittedly, a compilation of texts with instructions for shipbuilding, based on seventeenth-century writings, was published in 1739, but it seems to have had no 'real relevance to practical shipbuilding in Britain after about 1715'. New books on ship design were still few and far between.[70]

Regular, close cooperation between scientific institutions, state agencies and seafaring men was rarer in Britain at this time than in France. A scientific, state-supported expedition such as Halley's aboard the *Paramore* was still an exceptional event. Other scientific voyages made by fellows of the Royal Society, or undertaken under its aegis, were wholly financed from private sources. Mark Catesby received 'the assistance and encouragement ... from several noble persons and gentlemen' to carry out his planned expedition to study the birds and fish of Carolina, Florida and the Bahamas in the 1720s.[71] A secretary of the society complained in 1694 that the English were still doing less than their principal competitors to promote the collection of knowledge about different parts of the globe, and were also doing less than they might achieve on the basis of their own 'capacity, industry, and judgment in these matters'. ''Tis to be lamented', he wrote, 'that the English Nation have not sent along with their navigators some skilful painters, naturalists, and mechanists, under publick stipends and encouragements, as the Dutch and French have done, and still practice daily, much to their honour and advantage.'[72] The directors of the Hudson's Bay Company, chartered in 1670, did not share 'any of their knowledge with British natural philosophers' during the first century of the company's existence at all.[73]

In contrast to France and Spain, religious organizations in Britain played only a minor role in creating a durable infrastructure of maritime knowledge. Puritans and Dissenters took the lead in the colonization of New England and Pennsylvania, but they did not build and maintain a network of knowledge institutions on a par with that of the Jesuits, Franciscans or Dominicans. Among the chartered trading companies established before 1660, the EIC was the only one to take significant initiatives in establishing an institutional infrastructure of knowledge. In 1614–15, the EIC funded a hydrographer's post and a lectureship in the art of navigation, both held by Edward Wright.[74] As the first surgeon general of the company, appointed in 1612, John Woodall drew up regulations for the EIC's medical personnel, oversaw the examination of the company's surgeons and the provision of surgeons' chests, and attended to sick or injured sailors in a small dockside hospital used by the company near London.[75]

Within the expanding British Atlantic, the relative weight of chartered companies diminished from the late seventeenth century onwards. While the total shipping tonnage in the English Atlantic massively increased from the 1660s onwards, London colonial exports rapidly expanded and the African slave trade grew substantially, after the Glorious Revolution the Royal African Company was forced to relinquish its monopoly on the slave trade and saw its share quickly decline. A large part of English Atlantic commerce and shipping was no longer subject to any privileges for particular groups of entrepreneurs.[76] English captains and traders in the Atlantic world, meanwhile, did not only operate within the borders of English empire, as the framers of the Navigation laws had intended, and for a long-time foreign masters and merchants enjoyed easy access to English ports in the Caribbean and the American mainland. Mercantilism did not yet work perfectly; the English Atlantic system was not watertight. Inter-imperial trade between the English, Dutch, French and Spanish colonies in the West Indies and the Americas continued to flourish until after the War of the Spanish Succession. It was not until about 1730 that the leaks were largely closed.[77]

In the Dutch case, imperial and religious machines played only a marginal role. The Dutch Atlantic, especially from about 1680 onwards, was in effect more a commercial than a colonial affair. To a much greater extent than in the French, Spanish or British cases, the institutional infrastructure of knowledge that came into being in the Dutch Atlantic in the late sixteenth and seventeenth centuries relied on the initiative of local or provincial governments and on contributions from trading companies.

By the 1680s, the Dutch colonial empire in the Atlantic had shrunk to a few strips of land in the Guianas, some small islands in the Caribbean and a number of outposts on the west coast of Africa and the Cape of Good Hope. A centralized colonial administration did not exist. There were only a number of separate administrations of different chartered companies: WIC, the VOC and the Society of Suriname. Yet another colonial administration, the Society of Berbice, was added in 1720. The VOC and WIC were endowed with a range of delegated sovereign powers, such as the power to make war and the power to conclude treaties. In contrast to France, Spain or England, the United Provinces did not have a state-sponsored scientific society, a central observatory, a central hydrographical department or central agencies for supervising nautical education, examining pilots or coordinating the collection of botanical data.

Nevertheless, the Dutch Republic *did* see the emergence of a variety of institutions, regulations and facilities for the creation, certification and dissemination of maritime knowledge. Local or provincial governments founded and maintained universities and illustrious schools, observatories, botanical gardens and municipal professorships or lectureships, which functioned as more or less stable hubs of knowledge on mathematics, astronomy, navigation, botany, surgery and other areas of inquiry. Such institutions were fairly widely spread across the territory of the Republic, but their density was highest in the bigger cities in the seaward parts of the country, such as Amsterdam, Leiden and Utrecht.[78] From the first half of the seventeenth century onwards, surgeons' guilds in port cities such as Enkhuizen and Amsterdam introduced a special examination for ships' surgeons, which required a shorter preparation period than normal exams for master surgeons.[79] In 1680, the municipal government of Amsterdam added a specific provision concerning the quality of surgeons in the merchant marine. All surgeons who intended to sail on merchantmen were henceforth required to sit an exam in the presence of board members of the surgeons' guild. This requirement was later extended to surgeons on whaling ships as well. Moreover, surgeons were obliged to attend public lectures by municipal professors on surgery, anatomy and botany.[80]

As for medical care on warships, from the 1590s onward, Admiralties in the Dutch Republic appointed physicians and surgeons to examine applicants for the position of naval surgeon, although control of the actual training remained in the hands of urban surgeons' guilds.[81] From the Second Anglo-Dutch War (1664–7) onwards, Dutch war fleets carried a doctor general and surgeon general as medical supervisors on board. As for the care of sick and injured seamen on land, the Dutch Admiralties, like the English Navy, relied on a system of contracting for beds in private lodgings and civilian hospitals, such as the *gasthuis* in Middelburg or St. Pieter's hospital in Amsterdam.[82]

Regarding navigation and seamanship, several Admiralties introduced statutory examinations for naval officers and mates at the end of the seventeenth century.[83] Like King Philip III of Spain, Dutch government authorities introduced rewards for solving the problem of determining longitude at sea. On 1 April 1600, the States General of the United Provinces offered a sum of 5,000 guilders plus a life annuity of 1,000 pounds for anyone who could present an adequate solution to the problem of 'the East and West'. A year later, the States of Holland, the second most important government body in the Dutch Republic, likewise promised a reward for the solution of the problem. The reward could be earned in stages: an applicant would receive 150 pounds if he submitted an explanation of his method and was prepared to have it tested at sea, and a sum of 3,000 pounds plus an annuity of 1,000 pounds if 6 to 8 skippers attested that method was completely reliable.[84]

Chartered trading companies in the Dutch Republic played a much more formative role in the development of knowledge infrastructures than in Spain, France or England. In this respect, the VOC and WIC assumed functions that were similar to those of state agencies in other seafaring countries in Europe. In the 1610s, the Amsterdam Chamber of the VOC created a map-making agency and a repository of charts, supervised by a chief hydrographer, and in 1619 it created a position of examiner of pilots (later known as the examiner of masters and pilots). The Zeeland Chamber made similar arrangements four decades later. Arent Roggeveen was its first examiner of pilots, and as a private entrepreneur he also supplied maps for East Indiamen. A VOC depot of charts and map-making agency were established in Batavia in the 1620s. Navigators were required to hand in their charts and ships' journals after arrival in the Dutch Republic or in Asia.[85] The WIC likewise founded a map-making agency and a depot of charts in Amsterdam in 1621, and a hydrographic office in Brazil in 1630. An examiner of pilots was appointed in Amsterdam in the 1660s and in Zeeland in 1680.[86]

By introducing statutory examinations for ships' surgeons, the VOC was ahead of the Admiralties by several decades. The Amsterdam and Zeeland Chambers of the VOC appointed their own staff for the supervision of medical care on board and ashore in the early seventeenth century. A company's physician and a company's surgeon were charged with the task of examining all candidates for the position of first surgeon and surgeon's mate on board (in the presence of directors responsible for personnel). In addition, they supervised the company's pharmacy, inspected the ships' surgeons' medical chests, and examined company employees who suffered disabilities or had fallen ill. Similar arrangements were later introduced in the WIC, too.[87] Both the WIC and VOC showed an early interest in the collection of botanical knowledge. During the short-lived rule of the WIC in Brazil in the 1630s and 1640s, Governor Johan Maurits van Nassau established a hospital, pharmacy and garden with native plants in the newly founded capital, Mauritsstad. When the VOC founded a refreshment station at the Cape of Good Hope in 1652, it quickly proceeded to lay out a botanical garden, where a company's gardener started to experiment with plants from different parts of the world.[88]

Furthermore, it was trading companies, not state agencies, that sponsored long-range scholarly ventures in the Atlantic. In Brazil in 1638, Governor Johan Maurits van Nassau added two young physicians to his staff, Willem Piso and Georg Marcgraf, who were given every opportunity to gather information on local medicines and medical practices, travel inland to collect specimens of local flora and fauna, and carry out systematic observations of the southern skies at an observatory built in the governor's palace. The results of their on-site research on the natural history and medical peculiarities of Brazil were collected in the massive *Historia naturalis Brasiliae*, published in Leiden in 1648 at the expense of Johan Maurits himself, and in another huge book by Piso published ten years later.[89]

Under the aegis of the VOC, several voyages of exploration and experimentation were undertaken in the South Atlantic region in the 1680s and 1690s. Commander Simon van der Stel of the Cape Colony organized expeditions into the African interior to gather information about natural resources and local peoples and to collect data for mapping the area.[90] In 1685-6 and 1690-2, repeated trials were held with a new version of Huygens's marine chronometer on East Indiamen sailing to the Cape. However, the results of these experiments were no more satisfactory than those of the trials conducted under the auspices of the French king some twenty years beforehand.[91] Another series of trials on ships sailing to the Cape took place in the early 1690s with a newly invented device to distil drinking water from seawater. This time, the directors of the VOC reached a more favourable conclusion than in the case of Huygens's chronometer: they judged the trials to be so successful that they decided to equip all outgoing vessels with a copy of the distillation machine. The inventor, Christiaan Nentwigh from Amsterdam, was appointed to supervise the installation of the 'water works' and instruct the personnel hired to operate the machines. Distillation machines remained in use on VOC ships until 1707.[92]

Ship construction in the Dutch Republic took place both at private yards and at dockyards under the management of the Admiralties and the VOC. The private yards built ships for the Dutch mercantile marine, the whaling industry, the fisheries and inland navigation and for customers from abroad, as well as for the Dutch Navy until at least the 1660s. All the ocean-going ships of the VOC were built at the company's own shipyards and most of the naval vessels at Admiralty yards. VOC ships were built according to a standard set of guidelines concerning their overall dimensions. These shipbuilding charters, which existed from the very beginning of the VOC, were laid down by the company's directors and underwent revisions from time to time. Master shipwrights had to declare under oath that they would not deviate from the charters, but they still enjoyed some latitude in decisions about construction details. Standard sets of guidelines for ships' dimensions and armament were introduced in the navy in 1636, too. Overviews of the practice of ship construction in the Netherlands appeared in the late seventeenth century, compiled by a director of the VOC in Amsterdam, Nicolaes Witsen, and by a master shipwright in Rotterdam, Cornelis van Yk. However, neither the VOC nor the Admiralties were yet concerned with building institutions for the creation, certification and transmission of knowledge on ship construction.[93]

Self-organization and social networks

The publication of the *Brandende Veen* in 1675, as I remarked earlier, was an indicator of the growing importance of self-organization as an ingredient in the growth of maritime knowledge in the Atlantic world. The activities of imperial, commercial and religious machines alone can offer only a partial explanation of what happened from the 1670s onwards. We also need to consider the effects of self-organization, which could operate both inside and outside imperial, religious and commercial machines.

To begin with, self-organization was partly facilitated by the very growth of these centralizing, machine-like forces, which spread across a large part of the globe. On the one hand, the rise of imperial, religious and commercial machines meant that increasing numbers of people, who served these big organizations, spent part of their lives in far-flung parts of the world while they simultaneously had access to an extended network of transport and communication. In this way, machines supplied the material infrastructure in which self-organization could thrive. On the other hand, none of the machines that came into existence in the sixteenth or seventeenth centuries were in practice entirely controlled from above. Central governance had its limits. State officials, members of religious orders or employees of trading companies did not always merely follow the instructions of the organization to which they belonged, but they also took their own initiatives and found a variety of ways to pursue their own ends and interests. Within every machine, personnel in the field could independently enter into communication with correspondents in the metropole or other regions of the world, who might not form part of that particular machine at all. Individual members of machines were thus able to act as free agents. And free agency was a feature of the collection and circulation of knowledge, too. In the Hudson's Bay

Company, as Ted Binnema has noted, 'most (perhaps all) of the communication' between servants of the company and scholars in Britain before 1768 took place 'when HBC employees *circumvented* [my italics] the company's London-based Governor and Committee'.[94]

As imperial, religious and commercial machines expanded across the Atlantic, more and more Europeans overseas came into contact with local informants. European traders and seamen visiting the west coast of Africa were impressed by the skills of Africans in building and handling canoes. In their view, shallow dugout canoes, driven by boatmen stroking their paddles in rhythmic succession, were more effective at dealing with surf and manoeuvring in coastal waters than European-style rowing boats. Europeans were quite happy to make use of the services of canoe-men when they were trading on the coast between Senegambia and the Bight of Biafra.[95]

Plantations, trading posts, pharmacies, hospitals and botanical gardens served as 'biocontact zones' where Europeans could exchange knowledge with Amerindians and Africans about the natural world.[96] From the very beginning of European expansion overseas, physicians, missionaries, administrators, colonists and other groups of migrants to the New World and Africa showed themselves to be curious about what Amerindians and Africans knew about the medicinal properties of plants. Could Europeans learn from indigenous and black healers about how to stay alive and how to cure diseases?[97] Communication between these different networks of knowledge was admittedly often hampered by language barriers, practices of secrecy or incommensurability in world views.[98] Moreover, even while borrowing knowledge from Amerindians and Africans, Europeans were rarely prepared to give full credit to the expertise of local informants, and Amerindian and African sources were seldom mentioned by name.[99] Nevertheless, accounts on the Americas, the West Indies and West Africa abound with examples of Europeans borrowing knowledge from local informants. By putting such information in print or by moving to other parts of the world, Europeans helped to bring that knowledge into much wider circulation.

The most famous case of local knowledge on the curative properties of plants being borrowed by Europeans is doubtless that of Peruvian bark, also known as 'Jesuit bark' or quinine. Amerindian healers had long known that the bark of some species of the cinchona tree, which grew in the northern Andes, could protect people against malaria. Jesuit missionaries had brought this knowledge to Europe by the mid-seventeenth century and it had become 'part of common doctors' knowledge by the 1680s'.[100] But Jesuit bark is by no means the only example of how knowledge could be obtained in 'biocontact zones' and then circulate more widely through the mediation of personnel of imperial, religious or commercial machines. Amerindians in Guiana, for instance, taught Spaniards about the power of a root called *contrayerva* as an antidote against poison; this knowledge later travelled to other sites in the Caribbean and the American mainland.[101] Portuguese Jesuits and Dutch doctors in the service of the WIC in Brazil learned from Indians how to prepare the root of the *ipecacuanha* plant as a remedy for diarrhoea and dysentery.[102] European colonists on Jamaica in the late seventeenth and eighteenth centuries had much confidence in the healing powers of African slave doctors. At WIC trading posts on the west coast of Africa in the early eighteenth century, company servants showed an interest in local drugs and healing methods, too. A few of them, especially those who lived with African women, took African medicines in case of fever.[103]

Willem Bosman, a high-ranking local officer of the WIC who wrote the first comprehensive survey of the culture, society, politics and natural environment of the West African coast to be published in Europe, gave a detailed description of local eating patterns and the cures and rites that were commonly practised by native healers. He noted, for instance, the ubiquity of fish in the local diet and the abundance of papayas and bananas. 'Not without surprise', as he frankly admitted, had he seen with his own eyes that local herbs were a very effective means to heal 'serious and dangerous wounds'.[104] After first appearing in Dutch in 1704, Bosman's work rapidly found an eager audience all over Europe. English, French and German and Italian translations were published in quick succession, and further extended editions in Dutch appeared in 1709, 1718 and 1737.[105] Although Bosman took care to add a dedication to the directors of the WIC, the composition of the book was his own initiative.[106]

Outward networking also took place in religious machines. The Society of Jesus was not the centralized monolith that it appears to be in much of the traditional historiography.[107] Horizontal connections between individual Jesuits and correspondents outside the society were not uncommon. Jesuit missionaries in the French Atlantic communicated both with state officials and with members of their own order in various places in Europe. A Jesuit Honorary Member of the Académie Royale, Thomas Gouye, served as go-between between the missionaries and the institutions of knowledge in Paris up until the mid-1720s. It was thanks to Gouye that a report on the observation of a comet in Cayenne made by a Jesuit missionary in French Guiana in 1723 reached the scholars at the Observatoire.[108]

Self-organization in the Atlantic world was not necessarily tied to the structures of large imperial, religious or commercial machines, however. It could also work as a force beyond established organizational structures. In the Dutch Atlantic, for example, trading companies in fact accounted for only a minor part of the total volume of shipping and trade. At its height in the 1640s, the WIC fitted out a mere 20 per cent of all ships for Atlantic voyages from the Dutch Republic, and this percentage declined after 1700. The bulk of the slave trade was in the hands of private merchants.[109] Decentralized 'bottom-up' networks of seamen developed from an early date. Seamen could easily exchange knowledge both within and beyond centralized organizations; after all, they were a highly mobile lot. Seafarers could change ship regardless of the home port of the vessel and irrespective of their own geographical origin. Dutchmen could sail on Iberian ships and Englishmen could muster on Dutch ones.[110]

The very mobility of seamen explains why knowledge gained by experience, for example, on how to preserve the health of people on board, could be shared quite widely in the seafaring world regardless of the specific imperial, religious or commercial context. Contrary to traditional historical views, seamen did not need to wait for the trials by James Lind in the mid-eighteenth century to become aware of the uses of fresh vegetables and fruits, especially lemons and oranges, to prevent and cure scurvy. Spaniards and Portuguese knew about this from experience as early as the sixteenth century, and their knowledge quickly found its way to the Dutch. In his widely read travel account, published in 1596, the Dutchman Jan Huygen van Linschoten, who sailed on Portuguese ships in the Indian Ocean and the Atlantic in the 1580s, described how the Portuguese managed to reduce scurvy by using St. Helena and other spots in the Atlantic as regular refreshing stations. Following the Iberian example, the Dutch often sought to stock citrus fruits on major expeditions to Africa, Asia and America.[111]

Knowledge that travelled among seamen could be combined with knowledge cultivated in other groups and given wider circulation by means of print. Roggeveen's *Brandende Veen* shows how these mechanisms worked in practice. The *Brandende Veen* was the product of cooperation between a theoretically skilled draughtsman, a group of commercial bookmakers and a multitude of experienced 'shipmasters and pilots'. Around the same time, Robert Boyle based his *Observations and Experiments about the Saltness of the Sea* partly on 'authentick informations from sea captains, pilots, planters, and other travellers to remote parts', which he could access thanks to his long-standing membership of the board of supervisors of the EIC and of the royal council in London that governed the English colonies in America.[112]

Knowledge on whales and whale-fishing thus came to be shared between seamen and other groups as well. The *Bloeijende opkomst der aloude en hedendaagsche Groenlandsche visschery* by the seasoned Dutch whaling commander Cornelis Zorgdrager is a case in point. Zorgdrager's book was first published in Amsterdam in 1720. A second, enlarged edition appeared in The Hague in 1727, a German translation in Leipzig in 1723.[113] The *Bloeijende opkomst* was a sort of compendium on whales and whaling in the Atlantic, consisting of several layers. First of all, it contained detailed descriptions of the art of whaling itself, and of the various areas in the North Atlantic where the trade was practised: namely, Spitsbergen, Jan Mayen Island, the Greenland Sea and the Davis Strait. This part was based on notes made over the years by Zorgdrager himself, which were originally only intended for his own use and for circulation among fellow whalers. Zorgdrager's manuscript was then reworked by a professional translator and text editor, Abraham Moubach. Zorgdrager had written 'in the way of a seaman', Moubach explained; the text needed to be improved with a 'cultured' pen, in order to make his work not only useful for his fellow practitioners but also for all 'lovers of interesting writings'.[114] To the first and second editions of the book, Moubach and the publishers added digressions on the history of the 'discovery' of the Arctic and the whaling industry, the biology of whales, the polar climate and astronomical observations in the Arctic region, and a brief description of the cod fisheries near Newfoundland. Finally, the *Bloeijende opkomst* included data on ships, commanders and catches in the Dutch and German whaling fisheries and maps and illustrations 'drawn after life', which had been supplied by 'prominent and interested' merchants active in the whaling industry.[115] Moubach and the publishers thus brought together knowledge from scholars, merchants and practitioners in a single book.

Commander Zorgdrager's manuscript with scholarly and commercial data doubtless benefited from a successful marketing strategy. The first edition of the book rapidly sold out, and a German translation followed quickly. Its existence was also noted in scholarly circles. Leading zoologists in the later eighteenth and early nineteenth centuries, such as Petrus Camper and Georges Cuvier, were familiar with Zorgdrager's work in its Dutch or German versions, but they did not treat it as an important contribution to the body of knowledge in their field.[116] The *Encyclopédie méthodique* quoted the book in its volume on mammals, Petrus van Musschenbroek referred to it in a passage on icebergs.[117]

Scholars formed decentralized, 'bottom-up' networks, too, which after 1660 became more closely knit than before. The period from the 1660s to the 1720s is often viewed as the heyday of the Republic of Letters – that is, the collectivity of those who enjoyed peer recognition as scholars. Publications in transactions of learned societies and critical periodicals surged from the last decades of the seventeenth century, and correspondence between scholars multiplied many times over. The ideal of the Republic of Letters, which originated from before 1660, ultimately came close to being realized.[118] The growth of printing, improvements in postal services and an expansion in overseas travel allowed a greater density of communications between scholars than ever before.[119] Together with imperial administrations, trading companies, missionary organizations and state-sponsored scientific societies – as discussed earlier – this informal 'confederation of weak social associations' between scholars is said to have been a vital force in expanding the scale of scientific practices beyond the local level.[120]

Institutions in newly created infrastructures of knowledge could facilitate the growth of correspondence networks among scholars. A web of contacts developed between members of the Royal Society and the Académie Royale. Hans Sloane, who became secretary of the Royal Society in 1693 (and would hold the presidency from 1727 to 1741) kept up a busy correspondence for over fifteen years with Etienne François Geoffroy, who was elected fellow of the Royal Society in 1698 and became an associate of the Académie Royale a year later.[121] He also corresponded with other high-ranking figures of the academy in Paris, such as Jean-Paul Bignon, Jacques Cassini and Anthoine Jussieu.[122] At the same time, Sloane and his collaborator, apothecary James Petiver, who became a member of the Royal Society in 1695, also developed a network of contacts in the Netherlands. The Dutch correspondents of Sloane and Petiver included professors at universities and illustrious schools such as Pieter Hotton, Herman Boerhaave and Frederik Ruysch, as well as scholars and collectors who were not affiliated to an institution of higher learning, such as Antonie van Leeuwenhoek, Levinus Vincent and Albertus Seba. Most of them would eventually become fellows of the Royal Society.[123] For their part, scholars and collectors in the Netherlands maintained multiple correspondences both in France and England. Christiaan Huygens (himself a *pensionnaire* of the Académie Royale) corresponded for decades with leading lights in England *and* in France.[124]

From the late seventeenth century onwards, correspondents overseas were also increasingly incorporated into these European-based scholarly networks. Doctors, engineers, gardeners and other personnel in French colonies overseas sent a host of specimens of plants and animals and all sorts of observations and descriptions of natural or astronomical phenomena to the great scientific centres in Paris – the royal garden, the Observatoire and the Académie Royale. Some of these local observers were even formally recognized as correspondents of the Académie.

Regarding the British Atlantic, Raymond Stearns has documented in detail how, soon after its foundation, the Royal Society began to promote the practice of science in the Americas in all sorts of ways: by encouraging colonials to send reports and materials to London, by publishing their findings in the *Philosophical Transactions*, by providing them with books, instruments or money and, most visibly, by admitting a number of them as fellows of the Royal Society itself. Between 1663 and 1783, more than fifty colonials were elected fellows of the society.[125]

Scholars in the Netherlands began to call on 'field workers' in Dutch settlements overseas to provide themselves (and correspondents in England) with natural curiosities from the Americas, Africa and Asia. In 1706, Frederik Ruysch, an anatomist and professor of botany at the Athenaeum Illustre in Amsterdam, promised to send Hans Sloane a specimen of the *pipa* toad from America, if he could spare one.[126] Dutch collectors in Haarlem and Rotterdam offered Sloane and Petiver butterflies and other insects from Suriname.[127]

One is struck by the near absence of scholars from Spain or the Spanish empire in these networks of the Republic of Letters in the late seventeenth and early eighteenth centuries. Henry Oldenburg had just four correspondents in Spain between 1653 and 1677, as compared to twenty-four in the Netherlands, twenty-five in Italy and sixty-five in France.[128] Sloane and Petiver corresponded with only one scholar in Spain, the apothecary Joan Salvador i Riera in Barcelona.[129] Christiaan Huygens did not have a single Spanish correspondent nor did Antoni van Leeuwenhoek, whereas they exchanged many letters with scholars in London, Paris and Florence.[130] Few people in Spanish colonies overseas corresponded with members of the Republic of Letters in Europe, either. By and large, scholars from Spain and the Spanish empire were only marginally involved in the correspondence networks of the Republic of Letters between the 1660s and the 1730s.[131]

The relative absence of scholars from Spanish dominions overseas in Atlantic correspondence networks did not imply that news or material objects from these regions were impossible to acquire. Kathleen Murphy has shown that the granting of the *asiento* to the British Crown in 1713, and the subsequent foundation of trading posts of the South Sea Company in ports such as Portobello, Cartagena, Vera Cruz and Havana, made it much easier for collectors in Britain to obtain natural specimens from Spanish territories. From then onwards, the shipmasters and surgeons of British slavers were legally allowed to set foot on

Spanish American soil. Some of them, such as William Houston, grasped the opportunity to gather all sorts of plants, herbs, trees and other *naturalia* for the benefit of scholars in Britain, such as James Petiver.¹³² Petiver's relations with the shipmasters and surgeons of the South Sea Company also illustrate another dimension of networking in the Atlantic. To some extent, networks of scholars became connected with networks of other social groups. Among the 104 known individuals in Petiver's network of correspondents and collectors between 1690 and 1718 were twenty-five ship surgeons, ten shipmasters and eighteen colonial medical practitioners; in addition, it included 'eight clergymen, seven planters or farmers, six colonial officials, five travelling naturalists or gardeners, and four merchants'.¹³³ Kathleen Murphy has stressed that the 'secret to [his] success as a collector lay in his tenacious use of the routes of British commerce and those who traveled them' and, in the Atlantic in particular, 'on the routes of the slave trade'. In this way, Petiver obtained specimens from the coasts of West Africa as well as from places in British or Spanish America where slavers sold their cargo.¹³⁴

The flow of knowledge between different networks was not a self-sustaining process, however; it had to be nourished constantly. Generally speaking, the more the circulation of knowledge worked to the benefit of the different parties involved, the more likely the connections between networks were to remain in operation. As we have seen, the masters of the 'imperial machine' in France and the leading figures of the Royal Society in England had something resembling a quid pro quo in mind from the start. The basic idea was that connections between networks of scholars and seamen would benefit both sides. Seamen would supply scholars with data, scholars would discover patterns that would be of use to seamen and other groups of practitioners (for instance, in the form of maps, or methods for finding longitude) and at the same time help the advancement of knowledge. This quid pro quo mechanism operated at a concrete, individual level, too. Petiver, for instance, tried to keep travelling and overseas collectors committed to his network by sending them copies of his own publications and acknowledging their contributions in print.¹³⁵ Slaves and Amerindians were sometimes paid in money or in kind for collecting rare plants or animals, or sharing their knowledge on local flora. And in exceptional cases, the reward could be much higher. In 1729, the legislature of Virginia granted the slave James Papaw his freedom 'in exchange for his secret remedy for "inveterate venereal distempers"'. In 1749, a slave named Caesar received his freedom and an annual pension of £100 from the legislature of South Carolina for revealing his antidotes to poisons, nicknamed 'Caesar's cure'.¹³⁶

2

Growing maritime knowledge and globalization

How and to what extent did the growth of maritime knowledge contribute to globalization in the Atlantic world from the 1660s onwards? Having analysed the impact of globalizing forces on the growth of maritime knowledge in Chapter 1, I will now examine the reverse relationship. Between 1660 and 1730, knowledge relating the Atlantic Ocean changed in many ways, although the extent of these changes varied by field or subject. These changes in maritime knowledge are the subject of this chapter. The survey begins with ships, navigation and chart-making, then moves to an overview of the study of marine life, and concludes with a discussion of ideas and practices relating to the health of people on board.

Designing ships, navigating the ocean and probing the depths

Before the 1730s, the increased speed of ships was not yet a major factor in improving communications in the Atlantic world. Klas Rönnbäck's recent survey of the estimated speed of slave trading ships during crossings of the Atlantic revealed that irrespective of the nationality of the ship, average ship speeds on all routes from Africa to the Caribbean and North America increased in the course of the eighteenth century, but mainly after 1750.[1] Ships did not really begin to sail faster until the later decades of the eighteenth century.

Still, there were a few changes in ship design between 1660 and 1730 that helped to improve the manoeuvrability of ships, to some extent, and to enhance the average speed of shipping. Ships slowly became better able to steer (and keep) a given course. Improvements were made to rigging and the steering gear in particular. The adoption of jibs and headsails from the late seventeenth century and the replacement of the whip staff by the steering wheel in the early decades of the eighteenth century made it possible for ships to manoeuvre more effectively in contrary winds. Ian Steele has pointed out that these changes were 'most significant on the crossings from England to Newfoundland, New York, and Pennsylvania, although they [also] would improve the time on the northern tobacco routes via the Azores or the direct WSW route'.[2] The time required for crossing the Atlantic thus gradually diminished.

Map-making, navigation and marine science saw more substantial changes. Let us return to the *Brandende Veen*, the first printed full-scale atlas of the Atlantic. Roggeveen's pioneering work was swiftly imitated by other publishers in the Netherlands and elsewhere after 1680. In 1683 and 1684, Johannes van Keulen, a newcomer to Amsterdam's publishing and bookselling market, published a new sea atlas called parts IV and V of De *Nieuwe Groote Lichtende Zee-Fakkel*, which – like the *Brandende Veen* – covered both the American and African sides of the Atlantic, but consisted of entirely new charts and texts. A French edition of these volumes of the *Zee-Fakkel* appeared in the mid-1680s and went through six reprints up until 1736. A Spanish edition was completed in 1695. An English edition was advertised, too, but was never actually published, probably because the English market was already served by a domestic producer.[3] John Sellers of London began to publish the first series of English 'pilot books' for European, Atlantic and East Indian navigation in the 1670s. While Sellers made use of Dutch plates as templates for many of his charts, his sailing directions and charts for navigation to the Americas and West Indies and sailing directions for the East Indies were original pieces of work.[4] France, by contrast, could offer nothing similar as of yet. The *Neptune François* of 1693 only covered French waters. Hydrographic surveys of the waters around Cape Breton, which lay at the entrance to the Gulf of Saint Lawrence in French Canada, started about 1720, but had not yet produced usable charts for seamen.[5]

The quality of the *Zee-Fakkel* exceeded that of the *Brandende Veen* from the very start. Significantly, when Jacobus Robijn took over the publication of the *Brandende Veen* from Pieter Goos in the 1680s, he copied parts of his atlas from the *Zee-Fakkel*.[6] In addition, the contents of the Dutch and French editions of the *Zee-Fakkel*, especially the volumes on the Atlantic, were substantially enriched over the years. After 1700, Van Keulen added a number of new charts, including Mercator charts, improved several old ones and added many topographical and hydrographical details. In the early decades of the eighteenth century, the Van Keulen firm could provide to order large-scale, up-to-date manuscript charts of every sea area covered by the *Zee-Fakkel*, and even of areas – such as the west coast of North America – for which the atlas did not include any printed chart at all.⁷ The very proliferation of the supply of charts and atlases as such suggests that demand for these aids in the shipping industry was growing as well.

Another product of the growth of maritime knowledge which may have promoted globalization in the Atlantic was that of thematic maps. The first thematic map of the Atlantic Ocean was a by-product of the Royal Society's early interest in marine science. During the 1660s, 1670s and early 1680s, fellows of the society conducted a lively debate about issues such as the temperature, salinity and depth of the sea, and how to explain the tides and the motions of the sea and the winds.⁸ New data that could help to reveal general patterns or test sweeping theories on the sea were eagerly welcomed. In his *Treatise Concerning the Motion of the Seas and Winds* (1677), Isaac Vossius declared that he would refuse to admit any motion of the seas and winds 'which I could not if it were necessary confirm by infinite Testimonies and Experiments of sea men'.⁹ The 'Directions' for 'masters of ships, pilots, and other fit persons in their sea-voyages', published by the society in 1667 and distributed to seafarers via Trinity House, aimed to provide exactly those materials. They included instructions for marking 'the flowings and ebbings of the sea, in as many places as may be' 'sounding the deepest seas without a line, by the help of an instrument', 'keeping a register of all changes of wind and weather at all hours by night and by day' and drawing 'water from any depth of the sea'. In 1663, early versions of these directions and copies of the necessary instruments (designed by Robert Hooke) had already been handed to Captain Robert Holmes and John Winthrop, a Royal Society Fellow in Connecticut, for use on voyages to the Straits of Gibraltar, West Africa and New England.¹⁰

Although the Royal Society's interest in the sea waned after 1680,¹¹ the discussions and inquiries conducted in the previous decades led to some concrete cartographical results. In 1686, Edmond Halley published a map of the Atlantic and Indian oceans and the western part of the Pacific, which for the first time showed rows of strokes (and sometimes arrowheads) as symbols to indicate the direction and force of winds. It was, in effect, a worldwide thematic map of winds. In the first decades of the eighteenth century, the wind patterns depicted by Halley were repeatedly reproduced on English and Dutch charts.¹² Another regional thematic chart made by Halley, showing the tides in the English Channel, came out in 1702.¹³

The best-known thematic maps designed by Halley are his charts of magnetic variation, which was also a subject of interest in the early days of the Royal Society. The directions for seamen published by the Royal Society also included instructions for registering 'the declinations and variations of the compass or needle from the meridian exactly, in as many places as they can, and in the same places, every several voyage'. A 'Magnetics committee' of fellows made yearly measurements of declinations and conducted experiments with lodestones. Theories were floated to explain the workings of Earth's magnetism.[14] In his maps, Halley combined observations of magnetic declination that had been recorded over the years in ships' journals with data that he himself had collected at many locations in the Northern and Southern Atlantic during two voyages on the *Paramore*.[15] The combined evidence on magnetic declination formed the basis for a new thematic map, an isogonic chart. The chart of the Atlantic designed by Halley in 1701 was the first to show curve lines connecting points of equal value of magnetic declination, now known as isogonic lines.[16] Indeed, these lines of equal declination were known as 'Halleyan lines' until the nineteenth century.[17] Magnetic charts became more common among seamen once they were included in the range of a London-based commercial publisher, Mount & Page, which 'by 1715 was the publisher of virtually every English nautical book on the market'.[18]

A glowing testimony of the perceived value of magnetic charts for navigation can be found in Antonio de Ulloa's account of his voyage to South America in 1735. *Cartas de variaciones* by 'el Docto Manuel Halley' and other Englishmen and Frenchmen who had followed in his footsteps were useful for implementing the *Sisthema de la Longitud* developed by the Spanish and Portuguese in the sixteenth and seventeenth centuries, namely determining longitude with the aid of magnetic declination. By comparing the variation of the compass observed at a point of known latitude at sea with data on magnetic declination in the Atlantic Ocean shown by isogonic lines in a grid of latitude and longitude in a magnetic chart, a navigator could deduce the longitude of the place where his ship was sailing. Ulloa was aware, though, that observers at sea did not always obtain identical results.[19]

New instruments made their appearance as well. Seamen who sailed the oceans had long been familiar with observation aids such as magnetic compasses, sounding lines, bearing compasses, telescopes, logs and lines and hourglasses, and altitude-measuring instruments like cross-staffs and back-staffs (Davis's quadrants). Much of the data from mariners that were used in the revision of charts or in the making of new sorts of maps, such as those by Halley, had been gathered with the help of these very implements. Other information, such as data on the force of winds, was based on visual perceptions unaided by the use of instruments at all. Experienced seafarers could estimate the strength of the wind by looking at the sails of the ship and the waves of the sea. However, measuring temperatures or the salinity of seawater, air pressure or depths beyond the reach of sounding lines was a different matter entirely. Before the middle of the seventeenth century, equipment to observe these phenomena at sea was still lacking.

The ambitious programmes in map-making, navigation and marine science pursued by the newly established learned societies in England and France from the 1660s thus presupposed innovations and improvements in instrument-making. Instruments were in fact a core interest of the early Royal Society and the Académie Royale. Fellows and academicians frequently discussed the designs and uses of new instruments, and some of them, such as Huygens and Hooke, came up with ideas for new instruments themselves or even acquired the skills of instrument-makers. Christiaan Huygens was an accomplished lens-grinder. Along with his brother Constantijn, he grinded and polished more than forty telescopic object glasses in the 1680s.[20] During the last twenty-five years of his life, he was almost constantly engaged in designing, improving and testing marine chronometers, which would make it possible to compare local time on board with the time at a standard meridian, kept by a chronometer, and thus to determine differences in time and thereby longitude. In this way, Huygens believed, the problem of finding longitude at sea could be solved and the accuracy of maps of improved immeasurably. Trials with Huygens's timekeepers were held on English and French vessels as well as on ships of the VOC.[21] Robert Hooke designed a variety of new instruments in the 1660s and 1670s, including a marine barometer, a water thermometer, a sounding device and a water sampler. He closely collaborated with London-based instrument-makers, such as Henry Hunt.[22] Some of the instruments designed by Hooke and others were described in the 'directions for observations and experiments' by seamen issued by the Royal Society in 1667. The guide explained that these devices could be obtained 'from Mr. Richard Shortgrave, operator to the R[oyal] Society, to be found at Gresham College'.[23]

However, not all of Hooke's ideas for new instruments became known, or aroused interest, outside the circle of the Royal Society. Many of his devices remained neglected in the society's rooms at Gresham College.[24] Nor did Hooke's plans to organize a network of observers, who, with the help of thermometers and barometers, would build a large set of data on weather phenomena at various locations come to fruition. From the 1720s, a renewed effort for coordinated weather observations under the aegis of the Royal Society met with a bigger response – with data coming in from places as distant as Bengal and Massachusetts – but the usefulness of the results remained in doubt. Observers and their instruments were not always reliable and consistent. In some places, the continuity of the project as such was put at risk by the sheer lack of instruments. In Boston, for example, there were no barometers or thermometers before 1727.[25]

Moreover, none of the instruments for use at sea designed by Hooke, Huygens or any other scholarly inventor proved to work satisfactorily in practice, and they were not adopted by seamen. The usual set of instruments employed by seafarers in the Atlantic between 1660 and 1730 hardly changed. One of the few new instruments that *did* find acceptance, at least among Dutch mariners between *c.* 1660 and the 1770s, was a new kind of cross-staff equipped with a glass mirror, called the *spiegelboog* (mirror-staff). It was designed in 1660 by a master of naval equipment from Zeeland, Joos van Breen, and was tested in the presence of, among others, Arent Roggeveen. The advantage that the *spiegelboog* had over comparable altitude-measuring instruments was that it allowed the observer to take a back sight of a weak sun in a cloudy sky and to take backsight readings of stars. The *spiegelboog* was the first nautical instrument to rely on the principle of reflection.[26] It preceded instruments designed by Robert Hooke (1666) and Isaac Newton (1699), which used single and double reflection, respectively, and which were equipped with a telescope. Neither of these devices was tried at sea and neither was used by seamen.[27]

It was not until 1730 that a new double reflection instrument appeared, which was widely adopted by seafarers after some time. This instrument, now commonly known as the octant, had two mirrors, a telescope and a scale graduated on an arc that was one-eighth of a circle. The octant was almost simultaneously invented by a glazier in Philadelphia, Thomas Godfrey, and by a mathematician and astronomer in London, John Hadley, who also happened to be vice-president of the Royal Society.[28] By this time, different social networks in the Atlantic had become more interconnected. Godfrey's patron in Philadelphia was James Logan, a land speculator, fur trader and self-educated scientist, who entered into correspondence with Hans Sloane, Peter Collinson and other scholars in Europe. When Godfrey's invention had been perfected in November 1730 and tested on voyages to the West Indies, Logan sent a report to the Royal Society in May 1732 – just a few months after the society had received a report on a similar device from John Hadley. Further information was supplied by both Logan and Godfrey in 1733 and 1734. Accounts of Hadley's and Godfrey's innovations were published in the transactions of the Royal Society, albeit a few years apart.[29] Ideas hailing from different social and geographical backgrounds thus came together at the same site – the meeting rooms of the society in London – and in the same medium, the *Philosophical Transactions*.

The fact that Hadley's and Godfrey's ideas for new instruments arrived almost simultaneously at the same centre of knowledge does not mean that they had equal chances of diffusion. When it came to access to markets and decision-makers, a craftsman from the American colonies was clearly at a disadvantage compared to a reputed scholar from the metropole. Not only did the report on Hadley's invention appear much more quickly in the *Philosophical Transactions* than the account on Godfrey's[30] but Hadley's device was also promptly tested on a naval vessel and received a patent as early as 1734. No such support was given to Godfrey. Hadley's octant was on sale in eight instrument-makers' workshops in London by 1738.[31] On his voyage to Spanish America in 1735, Antonio de Ulloa used a copy of the instrument, bought by Godin in London, which he found to be 'of great utility'. A translation of the report in the *Philosophical Transactions* was included in his travel account.[32]

Like Huygens, Halley and Hadley also engaged in the age-old quest to solve the problem of determining longitude at sea. These scholars' proposals exemplify the principal directions in which the solution to the problem was sought in the late seventeenth and early eighteenth centuries. Huygens was convinced that the answer could be found by devising an accurate marine chronometer. Hadley's new altitude-measuring instrument was seen as a useful aid in solving the longitude problem along the astronomical route, for example, by calculating lunar distances.[33] Halley suggested that his map of magnetic declination might be helpful not just in correcting courses but also in estimating longitude at sea. The variation of the compass could serve as a good indicator of longitude in those places in the Atlantic, such as in the area near the Cape of Good Hope, where the isogonic lines ran more or less in a north–south direction and were in close proximity to each other.[34] However, none of these methods proved to be feasible on-board ship as of yet. The rewards promised by state agencies in Spain, the Dutch Republic and Britain and the essay prize from the Rouillé fund established in France attracted a host of proposals from inventors from all over Europe, but an adequate solution to the longitude problem remained elusive.

In practice, seamen found their way across the ocean with the help of knowledge from a variety of sources, something that is illustrated by the routes actually followed in transatlantic crossings. Most of the routes between Western Europe and the America remained almost unchanged throughout the seventeenth and eighteenth centuries. Ships sailing from Spain to the West Indies and the American Mainland, or from England, France and the Netherlands to colonies in the Caribbean, Guiana or the Gulf, or from Northwest Europe to Newfoundland, New England or Canada, continued to follow more or less the same trajectories over the years. The same observation applies to homeward journeys.³⁵ More variation can be found in routes between England and Virginia. The 'tobacco routes' became more diverse in the later seventeenth and early eighteenth centuries. In the early phase of English expansion, ships bound for the middle North American colonies from London and other southern ports normally followed the Spanish route up to the Caribbean before branching off to the north. The usual route ran via Madeira to Barbados or the Leeward Islands and then curved north via the Bahamas to the Chesapeake. Later on, northerly variants were added to the repertoire as well. One of these northerly routes ran from Madeira via Bermuda to Virginia, another went via the Azores, and yet another almost straight south-west from England, well to the north of the Azores. Ships leaving from northern ports in Britain, such as Glasgow, Whitehaven or Liverpool, began to follow an even more northerly route, leading along the north coast of Ireland. In general, the more northerly the route, the more time could be saved on the crossing to America.³⁶

At this time, the choice of routes and decisions about steering courses and handling sails along the way were based on a body of knowledge on the patterns of winds, currents and other marine phenomena in the Atlantic that had been accumulated by seamen from various countries over the years, which circulated orally or in printed and manuscript travel accounts and sailing directions. William Bullock's *Virginia Impartially Examined* in 1649, for example, discussed different routes to the Chesapeake.³⁷ The VOC's printed sailing directions spelled out how ships could safely and without delay cross the equator in the Atlantic, taking account of all the information about local winds and currents that masters and mates had collected over the years.³⁸ The most comprehensive survey could be found in William Dampier's *A Discourse of Trade-Winds, Breezes, Storms, Seasons of the Year, Tides and Currents of the Torrid Zone throughout the World*, which appeared in 1700. Dampier described these phenomena at the lower latitudes all around the world, both on the basis of his own experiences during his voyages as a Caribbean buccaneer and global explorer and on the basis of 'relations' from 'friends'. Letters from a Captain John Covant and a Commissioner Henry Greenhill of the Royal Navy at Portsmouth were included *verbatim* in his book.³⁹ Dampier's descriptions 'remained authorities for English navigation throughout the following century'.⁴⁰ His work soon circulated in Dutch and French translations too.⁴¹ Ulloa's account of his outward voyage to Spanish America in the 1730s, which was circulated in print from the late 1740s, added further information on wind patterns in the sea area between Cartagena and Portobello.⁴²

Observing living creatures in and above the water

Mapping the world, navigating the ocean and studying features of the seas were subjects of interest for scholars as well as for seamen, whalers, fishermen and other practitioners of knowledge between 1660 and 1730. Members of the Republic of Letters, however, were much less concerned with the living creatures that swam in the depths, floated on the surface or flew in the air above the waters. Unlike seamen, whalers or fishermen, scholars were not very keen to collect knowledge on fish, mammals or birds.

A scholarly literature about fish did exist, but most of the species that were described could be found in the Mediterranean or in the rivers and coastal waters of Northwest Europe, not in the Atlantic near America or Africa.[43] Scholars who studied fish in the Atlantic had different interests from fishermen. In the *Historia naturalis Brasiliae* (1648), Georg Marcgraf described and portrayed several species of fish in South America, but dealt solely with their morphology, nomenclature and taxonomy.[44] The *Historia Piscium* by Francis Willughby and John Ray, which appeared under the auspices of the Royal Society in 1686, built on earlier studies such as Marcgraf's but contained descriptions and pictures of many more species of fish. Its main preoccupations were nevertheless the same: morphology, nomenclature and taxonomy.[45] Charles Plumier's work on the Caribbean in *c.* 1700 and Hans Sloane's section on fish in his book on the West Indian islands likewise focused on forms and classifications – and occasionally, on medicinal properties – rather than on function, motion or reproduction.[46] Scholarly studies on fish did not reach a broad audience. Most of the 480 copies printed of the lavishly illustrated book by Willughby and Ray remained unsold.[47]

Scholars were hardly more interested in seabirds than in fish. Again, among the few exceptions were the naturalists Willughby and Ray, who joined the Royal Society in 1660 and 1667, respectively. Willughby and Ray shared not just a curiosity about fish, but also a passion for birdwatching. During a joint trip on the European continent in the mid-1660s to visit fellow naturalists, gather observations and collect illustrations and naturalia, they took notes on all sorts of birds that they observed en route.[48] They studied seabirds on a tour of the west coast of England and the Isle of Man in 1662. Four years after Willughby's death in 1672, Ray published the results of their collaborative work as *Ornithologia libri tres*. An enlarged English edition appeared in 1678 under the title *Ornithology ... in Three Books. Wherein All the Birds Hitherto Known, Being Reduced into a Method Suitable to Their Natures*. As in other books by Willughby and Ray, the emphasis in the *Ornithology* was on taxonomy and careful descriptions, based on personal observations and information from fellow members of the Republic of Letters.[49]

Willughby's and Ray's *Ornithology* became an authoritative text on the subject,[50] but it did not directly stimulate new studies on birdlife, nor was it circulated among seamen, whalers or fishermen. Hans Sloane included some information on birds in his natural history of the West Indian islands, published in 1725, but he showed only a dim awareness of what seamen knew about birds' behaviour.[51] When pelicans 'were seen at sea', ran a rare note, 'it is a sign of being near land'.[52] Following Sloane and Willughby's and Ray's works, Mark Catesby later substantially expanded the store of knowledge on birds in Carolina, Florida and the Bahamas. He even happened to have a copy of the *Ornithology* to hand when, on his outward voyage in 1722, 40 miles from the coast of Florida, crew members managed to catch a turnstone or sea dotterel: 'By comparing this with the description of that in *Will. Ornithog*, which I had then on board, I found this to be the same kind with that he described,' the naturalist noted with satisfaction.[53] However, turning the vast amount of material collected during his stay in America into a fully fledged book proved to be a costly and lengthy undertaking. The first volume of *The Natural History of Carolina, Florida and the Bahama Islands*, with dozens of magnificent drawings of birds, was published in 1731; the second one, with equally beautiful illustrations of fish, did not appear until 1743.[54]

Yet, knowledge about fish and birds in the Atlantic definitely increased among people who sailed the ocean. For fishermen, studying morphology or giving proper names was less relevant than knowing how fish behaved, where and when they could be found and how they could be caught. Fishermen accumulated knowledge about places where fish could be caught by 'recording ocean depths, fare after fare, year after year'.[55] Experience taught them things about which scholars knew nothing. From the 1650s, for example, fishermen in Massachusetts were acutely alert to the possibility that stocks of mackerel in the nearby part of the Atlantic could be depleted by over-intensive fishing. They were very much aware of the risk of overfishing.[56] Whalers, too, gathered precious information about the behaviour and habitat of whales. Zorgdrager's *Bloeijende opkomst* related how, time and again, whalers moved to different areas, because whale populations in traditional hunting grounds diminished and whales retreated from the coast of North Atlantic islands into the open seas. Whalers followed 'the fleeing fishes'.[57]

Sailors and travellers were mesmerized by the beauty and vigour of dolphins – and also tempted by the taste of their flesh. They were in awe of the antics of flying fish and horrified by sharks, which were wont to prowl in a ship's wake.[58] François de Meyer, who travelled as a passenger on a French ship headed for Martinique in 1698, peppered the account of his voyage with drawings and descriptions of various sorts of fish caught en route: dorado, porpoises, Atlantic bonitos, pilot fish, flying fish and so forth. De Meyer was not a skilled draughtsman, but he took care to note down details about measurements, behaviour and taste. His travel account was in fact a brief memorandum on fish.[59]

People sailing the ocean were also keen collectors of lore about birds.[60] Seabirds could help seamen, fishermen and whalers to find their position at sea (and in particular, how far they were from the nearest land) and could also occasionally serve as food. Writing on remedies for scurvy on whalers, the surgeon Johannes Verbrugge remarked upon the 'abundance of good birds' that provided 'good food of good taste'.[61] Friedrich Martens, who mustered as a surgeon on a Hamburg whaling ship sailing to Spitsbergen in 1671, described and depicted eleven kinds of birds sighted en route or in the hunting grounds in the north, and carefully noted details such as size, feet, legs, tail, colour of the head, eyes and body, patterns of behaviour and the quality of the bird's flesh. Little auks, for example, were supposed to be second-best after sandpipers, because they were fleshy and had a lot of fat. 'Boil and roast them,' Martens advised.[62]

Zorgdrager's book devoted a few pages – probably based on a French source – to four species of birds that could be found on the Grand Bank of Newfoundland.[63] These four species were known in Dutch as *levervreeters, waterhoenders, kruissers* and *pygmeen*. *Levervreeters* ('liver-eaters') were said to circle 'greedily' around fishing boats with their eyes on discarded livers; their very greediness sometimes made these birds easy prey for fishermen. *Waterhoenders* (moorhens) lived on small fish and liver, too, but were less greedy than *levervreeters*. *Kruissers* ('cruisers') were called such because they cruised steadily back and forth, though not close to fishing boats; they lived on small fish such as herring and sardines. *Kruissers* could be spotted about a hundred miles from the coast. *Pygmeen* ('pygmies') were 'a strange kind of bird, specked black and white. They could not fly, because they had only two short wings.' They supposedly 'dived to the bottom of the sea to find their food'. *Pygmeen* could sometimes be spotted about a hundred miles from the coast. They would carry their young on their back to the Grand Bank. A young bird was not bigger than a chicken, but an adult could become as large as a goose. Fishermen used these birds 'as food', the description concluded, although they were 'distasteful' and 'reeked of cod-liver oil'.[64] Zorgdrager's *pygmeen* were probably Great Auks, which became extinct in the middle of the nineteenth century.

Keeping the humans on board alive

Human life on board was not a lively subject of discussion in scholarly circles, either. Sickness and death in the Atlantic ranked lower on the list of subjects worthy of interest in the Republic of Letters than, say, magnetism, longitude or instruments, even though mortality in the slave trade or on naval expeditions to the Caribbean was much higher than on merchant ships in general. The average mortality among slaves who embarked on European ships in Africa hovered around 20 per cent between 1670 and 1720, and reached a peak of over 30 per cent on French slave ships between 1690 and 1700, before declining slightly from the 1720s onwards.[65] The high rates of sickness and death among enslaved people during the transatlantic crossing can be explained by a combination of crowded conditions and inadequate food on board, and of disease in the regions of embarkation in Africa. Smallpox, dysentery and scurvy were the greatest killers.[66]

Crew mortality in the slave trade was relatively high, too, although partly for different reasons than in the case of slaves. The annual death rate among Europeans in WIC forts on the Gold Coast amounted to more than 20 per cent in the 1720s and 1730s.[67] Many seamen and soldiers died on the coast of Africa because they were exposed to a host of diseases to which they had no immunity, such as malaria and yellow fever. Dysentery, smallpox and Guinea-worm disease also claimed many victims. Willem Bosman observed that Africans living on the coast were not as vulnerable to the 'insalubrious conditions' as Europeans, but that they were more prone than Europeans to suffering from smallpox and worm infection.[68] During long trips across the Atlantic, crews could be afflicted by scurvy, too. Scurvy was a scourge on slave ships and warships as well as on the whalers and ships carrying passengers and goods between Europe and the Americas.[69]

In the Caribbean, British and French naval expeditions from the late seventeenth century were repeatedly crippled by rampant fever among soldiers and seamen. Crews and armies in the West Indies could be decimated in a matter of weeks. Malaria had been endemic in the area since the early sixteenth century, and yellow fever became entrenched as a major killer in the 1690s. The yellow fever virus, as it is now known, thrived on the spread of sugar plantations and the growth of shipping in the Caribbean. Ships carried the virus from one port to the next, offering crew members as hosts along the way. In the French West Indies, yellow fever became known as the *mal des matelots*.[70] Morbidity and mortality from these fevers was much lower, though, among populations that had already lived in the area for some time and had thus built up resistance to attacks, such as planters, slaves, Creole militiamen or seasoned troops from Spain.[71] Antonio de Ulloa reported that whenever a fleet stayed for some time in the port of Portobello, between one-third and one-half of the crew members perished. Portobello was known as the 'grave of Spaniards', but it could equally be called 'the grave of all nations'. The basic cause of the high mortality, according to Ulloa, was that Europeans, unlike Creoles, were simply not accustomed to the local climate.[72]

At the end of the seventeenth century, the health of seamen eventually *did* become a topic of discussion in a new genre of writings, namely manuals written by surgeons or physicians destined for use by ships' surgeons. As the introduction of special examinations for sea surgeons in the first half of the century suggests, the body of knowledge that sea surgeons were expected to possess came to be distinguished, in some respects, from the body of knowledge associated with surgeons who practised in cities or villages. While all surgeons were required to learn the same theoretical notions about the human body and master the same set of basic techniques (such as bloodletting), sea surgeons were supposed to be both *less* and *more* knowledgeable than their colleagues ashore. On the one hand, sea surgeons were not expected to be able to perform the same range of operations as surgeons on land.[73] On the other hand, sea surgeons were required to be familiar with many subjects that were considered ashore to belong to the privileged domain of physicians, notably the treatment of diseases. After all, medical care at sea was almost exclusively provided by surgeons; a physician on board was a rare species indeed. Moreover, health problems faced in northern waters or tropical regions could differ from those encountered closer to home.

The rise of this new class of writings on medical care was closely related to the growth of an institutional infrastructure of knowledge in navies and trading companies. The authors of the first Dutch manuals for sea surgeons published in the 1660s and 1670s, the surgeon Johannes Verbrugge and the physician Cornelis van de Voorde, were serving at the time as examiners of surgeons at the Zeeland Chamber of the VOC. Verbrugge's *Heel-konstige examen* was composed in the form of a series of questions and answers. Part of the book specifically dealt with 'particular diseases' occurring on voyages 'in foreign countries', such as in the whaling trade and the trade with Africa, the West Indies and the Guianas. Verbrugge's manual went through ten reprints up until 1768.[74] Van de Voorde's book, which originally appeared as a general work about surgery, was transformed step by step into a manual that was especially useful for sea surgeons, after the author became a public lecturer in anatomy in Middelburg and examiner of surgeons at the local Chamber of the VOC. In 1668, a description of the surgeon's chest on East and West Indiamen was added (by Verbrugge), and a long treatise by the author himself on sixteen frequent diseases on ocean voyages, framed in a question-and-answer format, was added in 1679. An extended and revised version of the latter treatise appeared as a separate book, *Nieuw chirurgijns zee-compas*, in 1719.[75] In 1696, one of the supervising physicians appointed in the English Navy during the Nine Year's War, William Cockburn, published the first book specifically devoted to the 'nature, causes, symptoms, and cure of the distempers that are incident to seafaring people'. Cockburn's *Account* was for the most part based on personal observations of diseases, treatments and their outcomes made during his voyages at sea since he had entered the navy, interspersed with comments and critical remarks on other medical writers. Preceding these stories of 'sicknesses' (carefully noted in a journal) was a survey of the victualling of seamen, the circumstances of their work on board and their general way of living 'as to their temperance of debauches', in order to 'see and deduce as naturally, as is possible, those infirmities, that most especially follow thereupon'.[76]

Cockburn's treatise, reprinted in 1710 and 1736, was followed by manuals for sea surgeons published by Thomas Aubrey and John Atkins in 1729 and 1734, which likewise contained a large number of case histories recorded during their authors' travels offshore. Nothing was as instructive as 'being acquainted with practice, and the management and seasonable change of applications that have been tried and warranted', Atkins declared. Aubrey put in long service as a doctor on the coast of Guinea, and Atkins worked for many years as a surgeon on Royal Navy ships on voyages to Guinea, Brazil and the West Indies. Based on their experience in Africa, both writers also specifically discussed the nature and cure of diseases affecting slaves, and measures that should be taken to keep slaves in good health.[77]

Cockburn's account is also a revealing example of growing differences of opinion and practice in medical matters, even though this dissension did not lead to a radical change in conventional wisdom. John McNeill observed that European doctors, faced with a surge of fever in the West Indies, mostly preferred to stick to traditional interpretations based on concepts handed down from writers in antiquity, such as Galen or Hippocrates. The basic cause of diseases such as malaria or yellow fever was, in their view, a disruption of the balance between the humours, due to a person's constitution, behaviour and physical environment. The common remedy was to restore the patient's balance by measures such as bleeding, purging, blistering or applying medicines.[78]

Cockburn noted, however, that there were great differences of opinion about the quantity of blood to be drawn off. 'The advices of our great Masters ... in this affair [were] imperfect and useless,' he judged. It was 'evident' that there were 'as many opinions about this ... as there [were] physicians'.[79] As for fever in the West Indies, 'some medical professionals with long experience wondered whether Caribbean diseases were indeed the same as those familiar in Europe and discussed in hallowed texts,' McNeill remarked, but the majority of physicians preferred to stick to time-honoured views.[80] By the end of the seventeenth century, experience had taught that the risk of the outbreak of fever in the Caribbean was greater in some months of the year than in others. Nevertheless, naval authorities in England or France did not take warnings about 'insalubrious months' into account when planning expeditions to the West.[81]

Ideas about the causes of scurvy proliferated in the later seventeenth century, too. In the wake of the growing practice of iatrochemistry, some medical authors sought to explain the disease in terms of 'acid' or 'alkaline' conditions of the blood instead of disrupted humoral balances.[82] Cockburn and others were not at all impressed by these theories about 'chymical principles'. Diseases had many more causes than acids and alkalis alone, the fleet's physician insisted, and he thought 'the impudence, as well as ignorance, of the common chymists [to be] incorrigible'.[83]

The repertoire of drugs, potions and techniques used to treat diseases on board did not remain entirely static. A few items were added to the traditional stock. Guaiac from the Caribbean islands was widely adopted as a remedy to treat syphilis. Verbrugge and Van de Voorde recommended its use in their manuals for surgeons.[84] WIC ships regularly carried supplies of guaiac to Europe.[85] The use of oranges, lemons, limes and their juices to combat scurvy became quite common on European ships in the Atlantic in the sixteenth and seventeenth centuries. Regulations for WIC slavers from 1685, for instance, stipulated that masters should take care to procure a good quantity of lime juice before departing from the coast of Africa, in order to preserve the health of slaves during the transatlantic crossing. In 1732, the directors claimed that 'experience had taught' that lime juice was an 'infallible' remedy against scurvy.[86] Europeans sometimes adopted practices that were common among African slaves, such as using smoke to keep mosquitoes away, even if the connection between mosquitoes and fever was still unknown. And for all the growing divergence in views between medical writers, by the end of the seventeenth century, there was a broad consensus on the uses of one remedy in particular: cinchona, otherwise known as 'Indian bark' or 'Jesuits' powder'. European doctors were agreed that this medicine was a potent curative for malaria, as healers in Peru had known for many years; and even they did not use it as frequently or effectively as they might have done, because it was not in abundant supply, and knowledge about its proper application was not always on hand, although its efficacy was widely acknowledged.[87] Another new departure in the health care of seamen in the late seventeenth century was the use of mechanical devices to improve living conditions on-board ship. In the VOC directors' view, the distillation machine introduced on Dutch East Indiamen in the 1690s was at least a partial solution to the problem of increasing morbidity and mortality on board. Statistics on mortality on outward-bound ships in the years 1691–4 collected by the director of the Amsterdam Chamber of the VOC, Caspar van Collen, showed that mortality on the voyage to the Cape on ships *with* a 'water work' was considerably lower than on ships *without* such a device: 9 1/7 per cent as opposed to 13 ¼ per cent. With a distillation machine on board, crews on East Indiamen would no longer face the risk of lacking fresh drinking water. Van Collen's data, combined with optimistic estimates of the quantity of firewood needed to fuel the machines, supplied the directors with a convincing argument to adopt the 'water works' on VOC ships.[88] Distillation machines were viewed as a partial solution, however – not as the only one. At the same time, the directors also adopted other measures to reduce disease and mortality on board, such as issuing revised lists of victuals and medicines and new instructions for the commanders regarding frequent exercise for the crew and regular cleaning of the ship. Moreover, all surgeons were obliged to keep a journal about disease and deaths under way, which had to be handed in after arrival in the Cape, Batavia or Ceylon.[89]

The machines were not in operation for long, however. The main reason for their disappearance was not that the beneficial effect of the machines on the health of seamen proved to be spurious, but rather that many VOC commanders wanted to have a liberal supply of drinking water stored on board, and the quantity of firewood needed to fuel the distillation machines required much more extra storage space than the company directors had originally envisaged. 'Water works' on VOC ships were therefore abandoned after 1707.[90]

Conclusion

Knowledge relating to the Atlantic Ocean thus underwent significant changes between the 1660s and 1730, but the extent of these changes varied by subject or field. Map-making, navigation technology and the study of patterns of winds and currents saw more remarkable advances than ship design, medical care for humans on board or knowledge about the living creatures that swam in the depths, floated on the surface or flew in the air. To understand these variations, we should take a closer look at the techniques, instruments and resources that facilitated the development of maritime knowledge, as well as at the factors and circumstances that limited its growth. Capabilities and limitations are discussed in the first half of this conclusion. The second half summarizes the main changes in the relationship between globalization and the growth of maritime knowledge between *c.* 1660 and 1730.

Capabilities and limitations

On the one hand, techniques, instruments and resources to collect, classify and interpret data and to reproduce and transmit information showed some significant advances in several respects. One of the ways in which capabilities for the development of maritime knowledge were enhanced consisted of improvements to the means of organization and measure of control. Scientific expeditions were undertaken to obtain and record data on the natural world in a systematic manner; they were supplied with specific instructions, provided with special equipment and staffed with select personnel (such as draughtsmen or astronomical observers), who sometimes received special training for this purpose. The voyages of Richer, Halley and Plumier in the last decades of the seventeenth century are excellent cases in point. Controlled experiments or trials were undertaken to assess the performance and effects of new inventions under realistic conditions at sea, such as Huygens's marine chronometer and Nentwigh's distillation machine. Slight improvements were made to instruments for astronomical observation at sea. Some navigation instruments were equipped with glass mirrors, which allowed the use of reflection to make observations of celestial bodies more precise.

In addition, new techniques were developed to order, interpret and present data and to preserve raw materials for inquiry. Statistics began to be applied to evaluate the outcome of trials in a more accurate way. Van Collen's analysis of mortality on-board VOC ships in the 1690s is an early example of this practice. At the same time, observational data on the physical properties of the environment were summarized and visualized by means of new types of symbols in charts, such as isolines and strokes. Halley pioneered this graphic technique by depicting isogones and rows of strokes, showing equal magnetic declination and the direction and force of prevailing winds, respectively, on his maps of the Atlantic and Indian oceans. Little by little, techniques for preserving organic materials improved from the end of the seventeenth century onwards. Injection techniques for the preparation of the dead bodies of humans and animals, pioneered by Lodewijk de Bils in the 1650s and elaborated at Leiden University thereafter, were more widely practised after 1700, reaching a peak of sophistication in the hands of Frederik Ruysch and Albertus Seba in Amsterdam.[1] In this manner, Ruysch and Seba managed to preserve priceless specimens of *pipa* toads from Suriname.

The growth in resources was an important aid to the development of maritime knowledge as well. These resources included financial expenditure and the provision of material facilities, as well as the recruitment of expert personnel. Between 1660 and 1730, state agencies, scientific societies, urban governments, trading companies and religious organizations in the British, French, Spanish and Dutch Atlantic created and maintained numerous observatories, schools, examiner boards, lectureships, botanical gardens and depositories of maps, charts, journals and travel accounts. The expansion of these institutional infrastructures facilitated the collection, processing and preservation of data as well as the certification and transmission of knowledge.

On the other hand, the development of knowledge encountered a number of obstacles. Lack of financial resources was a recurrent problem. In England after the 1680s, for example, the Royal Society no longer had sufficient funds to continue its ambitious marine research programme, as losses on the unsold copies of the *Historia Piscium* had seriously depleted its financial resources.[2] Private funding was crucial for the publication of standard works on natural history, such as Ray and Willughby's *Ornithology* and Catesby's *Natural History*. Willughby's widow paid for the illustrations in the *Ornithology* and Catesby had his *Natural History* 'printed at the expense of the author'.[3] In France, the lack of skilled personnel impeded the efforts of the imperial machine to produce maps, charts and atlases. The Dépôt des cartes et plans de la Marine did not start to turn out its own maps until fifteen years after its foundation.[4] Spain was perennially plagued by a shortage of money and of skilled maritime personnel until the advent of the Bourbon regime.

Instruments and techniques for the collection of data and the preservation of natural specimens suffered from limitations, too. Despite some improvements in navigational implements, instruments designed for making observations at sea often lacked accuracy and reliability. Notably, data on the depth of the ocean or on the pressure and temperature of the air could not be read very exactly, and scales of measurement varied wildly.[5] As for fauna and flora in and around the sea, the accumulation of knowledge was heavily dependent on the availability of verbal reports or visual representations. For a long time, gathering shells, bones, plants or insects in cabinets of *naturalia* was a much easier task than conserving specimens of dead fish, birds or mammals, or keeping plants or animals alive during long-distance transport overland or overseas.[6] Scholars could learn about *levervreeters* or *pipa* toads from a distance, but not study these species hands-on. In this period, the study of animals and plants concentrated on morphology and taxonomy rather than on physiology.[7] The development of knowledge on the natural history of the Atlantic was thus constrained by the capacity of existing techniques, even though some of these techniques, such as the art of drawing and engraving as practised in Amsterdam and Paris, had reached a very high standard.[8]

Finally, the development of knowledge was also hampered by lack of communication between different social networks and by limitations in institutional infrastructures. In practice, connections between networks did not always function as smoothly as contemporary scholars or policymakers envisaged. Probably only a small minority of English seamen and travellers really ever cooperated with the Royal Society.[9] While Robert Boyle benefited from the input of some 'sea captains, pilots, planters and other travellers to remote parts' for data on the saltiness of the sea, he also admitted that he often considered the 'informations' from these sources to be too unreliable to accept.[10] Scholars scarcely took notice of the rich body of knowledge on fish or seabirds accumulated by seamen, whalers and fishermen. The directors of the Hudson's Bay Company did not share knowledge with the scholarly world at all.

Prior to 1730, the infrastructures of knowledge in ship construction or medical care at sea were more patchy than those in the fields of map-making and navigation technology. Beyond the French Atlantic, navies and trading companies were not yet very active in building institutions, drawing up regulations and providing facilities for the production and distribution of knowledge about the construction of ships. Colbert's example was not followed in other countries until many decades later. Beyond the French Atlantic, moreover, purpose-built hospitals for seamen or special schools for sea surgeons did not exist. Although the appointment of supervising physicians and surgeons in navies and trading companies from the late seventeenth century did indeed lead to an increase in writings about medical problems at sea, publications about this subject remained much less common than cartographic works books on navigation, and they did not travel across imperial or linguistic borders. Unlike Roggeveen's *Brandende Veen*, Verbrugge's or Van der Voorde's books were not circulated in English, French or Spanish translations, nor was Cockburn's manual consulted on the European continent as of yet.

Changes

Globalization accelerated in the Atlantic world between 1660 and 1730. Contact, interaction and exchange between different parts of the Atlantic region became more frequent, leading to increasing interdependence. As argued in Chapter 1, the forces from above and from below which drove this accelerating process of globalization contributed to the growth of knowledge by establishing more or less durable infrastructures of knowledge and by facilitating and stimulating growing flows of data, information and ideas. Globalizing forces comprised a range of imperial, commercial and religious 'machines', as well as a variety of self-organizing networks that arose and operated both inside and outside these different machines.

Habsburg Spain was the first to build a wide-ranging imperial machine that also contained an infrastructure of knowledge – that is, a set of institutions, regulations and facilities for the creation, certification and dissemination of knowledge. Bourbon France created a more complicated and coordinated system, which in the scholarly debate has become the model for a 'colonial' or 'imperial' machine as such. Both the Spanish and the French imperial machines were intertwined with similar systems developed by long-range religious organizations, such as the Society of Jesus, which, however, were not subordinate to particular states and which also pursued global aims of their own. In the Dutch and British Atlantic, imperial machines, albeit less elaborate than in Spain or

France, were active to varying degrees in forming infrastructures of knowledge, too, whereas religious organizations played only a minor role. Commercial machines, built by trading companies such as the VOC and the EIC, meanwhile served in a way as functional equivalents for imperial or religious machines. The VOC's map-making agency, chart depot and embedded examiners of masters, pilots and surgeons formed no less an effective infrastructure of knowledge than the institutions erected by Colbert or the king of Spain.

Imperial, religious and commercial machines also boosted the circulation of knowledge, both within these machines themselves (e.g. from naval officers to a map-making agency or scientific academy, and vice versa) and in societies in the Atlantic world at large, and even beyond (e.g. from seamen to owners of libraries, botanical gardens or cabinets of curiosities). The circulation of knowledge further increased thanks to another powerful force of globalization: self-organization. Self-organized, decentralized networks were created from below by actors inside or outside 'machines', who communicated across the borders between states, empires and organizations. Such networks flourished not only among scholars in the expanding Republic of Letters, which had neither formal admission rules nor any formal hierarchy, but also in networks of seamen, fishermen and whalers and between people from different social backgrounds: Amerindians, African mariners, merchants and slaves and European seamen, traders and colonists from Europe. Networking was not all-inclusive or boundless, however. Notably, scholars from Spain and Spanish America were less integrated in the correspondence networks of the Republic of Letters in the late seventeenth and early eighteenth centuries than people from other parts of the Atlantic world.

Conversely, how and to what extent did the growth of knowledge contribute to globalization? The analysis in Chapter 2 suggests at least two ways in which this reverse effect may have occurred, even though the connections cannot be demonstrated as conclusively as one would wish. First of all, infrastructures of knowledge established by imperial, commercial and religious machines, such as repositories of charts, lectureships in hydrography and supervisory positions for examiners of pilots and sea surgeons, facilitated the growth of the output of charts, books, instructions and other aids for the benefit of seafarers who ventured into the Atlantic. Atlases, thematic maps, manuals on medical care at sea, the VOC's sailing directions – all of these devices helped people to cross the ocean with more precision and a somewhat greater chance of survival than before, and thus eased interactions between different parts of the Atlantic world. Second, both these infrastructures created from above and the self-organized networks emerging from below facilitated an increased circulation of knowledge within and between different social groups. This circulation of knowledge did not just take place through print, but also orally, in writing or through the exchange of objects. In this way, knowledge about the powers of *contrayerva* and *ipecacuanha*, about patterns of winds and currents or about the behaviour of birds in the Northern Seas could travel from one social network to another across linguistic or imperial borders.

Despite this, knowledge in some fields or subjects changed more than in others. Although the capabilities for the development of maritime knowledge by and large grew, they did not do so in every area in equal measure, and their growth was subject to various limitations, as the final section of this chapter argued. The lack of financial means, imperfections in techniques and instruments, lacunae in institutional infrastructures and gaps in communication between social networks all formed restrictions, which could differ by field or subject. Part II will examine the extent to which this relationship between capabilities and limitations in the growth of maritime knowledge changed after 1730, and how this change was related to the process of globalization in that period.

Part II

Maritime knowledge and globalization in the Atlantic world, c. 1730–1800

Introduction

Globalization between c. 1730 and 1800

Harrison's timekeeper may be the best-known example of a solution to one of the key problems faced by humans at sea, but it was not a unique advance in maritime knowledge in the later eighteenth century. All sorts of mechanical solutions to improve the health of travellers, for example, appeared on the market too. Wind-making devices or 'ventilators' were probably the most promoted items in this class of hardware. From the 1740s onwards, inventors from Britain, Sweden and France presented ventilators as an excellent means to reduce sickness on board by replacing 'contaminated' air below decks with 'fresh air'. Ventilators came in various shapes and sizes. Stephen Hales and Mårten Triewald proposed to install a set of bellows operated by hand. Samuel Sutton and Alexander Brodie advocated the use of pipes, in which the draught was driven by heat. Jean Théophile Desaguliers and Henri-Louis Duhamel du Monceau described machines that used vanes to bring about the circulation of air in closed spaces. All these wind-making machines seemed to offer a more effective answer to the problem of dispelling 'foul' air than the traditional expedients of using suspended sails or linen sleeves as cooling systems.[1]

Timekeepers and ventilators are conspicuous examples of technological advances after 1730 to improve the accuracy of navigation and enhance the chances of survival of those on board. Beside eye-catching techniques and instruments such as these, however, there were many other changes in knowledge related to the ocean. Moreover, the most visible novelties were not necessarily the advances that contributed most to the growth of globalization. Incremental, barely perceptible changes may have been at least as important for the shaping of globalization as radical, highly publicized innovations that were said to represent significant breakthroughs. The question of how and to what extent changes in maritime knowledge after 1730 had an impact on globalization will form a major focus of this part of the book.

In the process of globalization, Atlantic trade in terms of volume after 1730 continued to far outstrip trade between Europe and Asia. The long-term growth rate of the former was twice that of the latter. As for value, Jan de Vries has estimated that in the 1770s, the share of imports from the Western Hemisphere as a total of European imports was probably at least three times that of the Asian trade. In Britain, 38 per cent of the total value of imports came from the Atlantic, as compared to 16 per cent from Asia. In France, the proportion was 42 per cent compared to 5 per cent. In the Dutch Republic, the value of commodity imports from the West Indies quadrupled after 1730, and caught up with the total value of imports from Asia via the VOC by 1780.[2]

However, increasing imports in Europe reflected only part of the growing extension and intensity of interconnections in the Atlantic world. Many of the imports from the Western Hemisphere consisted of commodities such as sugar, tobacco or coffee, which were mostly produced under conditions of slavery. A massive expansion of the slave trade between Africa and the Americas lay at the root of the growth of colonial imports in Europe. The number of slave voyages across the Atlantic rose from about 1,800 per decade before 1750 to more than 2,900 in the 1760s, and after a slight decrease to about 2,500 per decade in the 1770s and 1780s, before peaking again at nearly 2,900 in the 1790s. The slave trade under British and Dutch flag reached an all-time high in the 1760s, with 1,484 and 204 voyages respectively, while the slave trade under French flag culminated with almost 800 voyages in the 1780s. With the increase in the number of voyages came an enormous growth in the number of enslaved people carried across the ocean. The totals in the 1780s were almost 60 per cent higher than in the 1720s: 868,000 as opposed to 548,000.[3]

There was likewise a vigorous expansion in shipping and trade between Europe, the west coast of Africa and the Caribbean. Like the number of transatlantic slave voyages, the number of ships leaving England for West Africa peaked in the 1760s and again in the 1790s. The total tonnage of English ships sailing to West Africa at the end of the eighteenth century was nearly twice as high as forty years previously.[4] A growing number of vessels were involved in the transport of manufactures and food from the British Isles to the West Indies. In fact, in the late 1760s, the tonnage of British ships sailing to Jamaica engaged in this general trade was much larger than that employed in the slave trade.[5] The density of shipping and trade between ports in the western part of the Atlantic increased as well. The number of ships leaving the Dutch colony of Suriname for destinations other than the Dutch Republic doubled from about thirty a year in the 1720s to about sixty in the early 1750s, and culminated in more than 100 in the late 1780s. Most of these ships headed for ports in the British colonies in North America.[6]

Boston, New York, Philadelphia and Charleston meanwhile developed into major hubs of shipping and trade. By 1740, for example, the total number of vessels entering these ports from the British Isles, Southern Europe, the British West Indies and other ports in North America was four times higher than in the 1670s. By the end of the 1730s, more than 350 sailings a year were recorded from ports in North America to the Caribbean.[7] The number of merchant ships departing from Salem, New England, in the 1750s amounted to some 200 a year, compared to fewer than 120 annually during the first decades of the eighteenth century. Salem vessels used for deep-sea fishing during the summer headed for Pennsylvania, the Chesapeake or the West Indies in the winter, where they traded fish, timber and farm products for meat or molasses, rum and salt.[8]

For New England in the mid-eighteenth century, the north-to-south route became a more important artery of shipping and commerce than the traditional route to Southern Europe. The Southern American colonies and the West Indian islands developed into the biggest market for dried cod and other exports from New England.[9] This shift in market orientation partly had to do with expanding demand from New England rum distilleries for molasses, which could not be imported from Southern Europe, and partly with increasing diversification in the quality of dried cod. While the quantity of cod produced by the New England fishing industry nearly tripled between about 1715 and 1765, its quality no longer remained as uniformly high as before. As the curing of the cod increasingly became a two-stage process – wet-salting offshore, followed by air-drying on land – a greater part of the produce was branded by fish merchants as 'refuse', which could not be sold in Europe. The slave population in the Southern Colonies and the West Indies became the principal market for this low-grade cod.[10] The English and French cod fisheries near Newfoundland, Cape Breton Island and Labrador also grew tremendously after the War of the Spanish Succession. Total exports of codfish from North America to European and Caribbean markets probably became four times larger in the course of the eighteenth century.[11] However, the relative shares in the fisheries changed after the Seven Years' War. While the British output first the overtook the French one, the centre of gravity of the British cod fisheries shifted to the other side of the Atlantic. From the 1790s, the industry was no longer dominated by migratory fishermen from South Devon, but by British settlers on Newfoundland.[12]

In the meantime, there was also further expansion in shipping and trade from the British American colonies to the Iberian Peninsula and to the Spanish colonies in America, despite the frequent wars between Britain and Bourbon Spain.[13] Ships from New England, New York, Pennsylvania and South Carolina fetched logwood from Central America, carried foodstuffs and flour to Havana and Santo Domingo and took fish, lumber, wheat, flour and rice to Spain in exchange for gold and silver. Regular connections with the French West Indian islands were established as well. As in the case of the British West Indies, the development of this trade was closely linked to the massive growth of slavery and the huge increase in the slave population.[14]

Whaling in the Atlantic vastly increased after 1730. Whaling ships from New England ventured ever farther into the ocean and stayed ever longer from home. While journeys to Newfoundland, which began in about 1730, lasted up to three months, voyages to the Davis Strait, the Azores and the West Indies, which became common after 1760, took four to five months, and journeys to the west coast of Africa or to Brazil, the Río de la Plata and Patagonia, which started in the 1770s, lasted more than half a year. In 1791, the first American whaler, the ship *Rebecca*, rounded Cape Horn to hunt in the Pacific.[15] On the eve of the Revolution, some 360 whaling ships were sailing from ports in the American colonies each year. The largest centre of American whaling, Nantucket, was at that time producing ten times more whale oil than in the early 1730s. Next to dried cod, whale products were New England's most valuable exports. Nantucket oil lit the streets of London.[16] Whalers from Europe, on the other hand, sailed in greater numbers to East Greenland and the Davis Strait. Between 1730 and 1800, several dozen ships from Europe visited the area each year in search of whales and seals and to conduct barter trade. Up until the 1770s, most of these European whalers came from the Dutch Republic and Hamburg. After that, Britain and Denmark supplied the bulk of the European whaling fleets in the northwest Atlantic.[17]

Given the growth of transatlantic shipping and trade and the expansion of colonial settlements and plantation economies in the Americas and West Indies, it is unsurprising that the Atlantic became a more central theatre of war in clashes between the European powers after 1730 than during previous conflicts.[18] Fighting in the Caribbean or North America was no longer a sideshow to the battles fought on the European continent and in the surrounding waters. During the War of Jenkins' Ear and the War of the Austrian Succession, and even more so during the Seven Years' War, the American War of Independence and the Revolutionary Wars after 1793, the warring European parties repeatedly sent sizeable squadrons and substantial expeditionary forces across the Atlantic. Operations in the West became an integral part of the war effort. Transatlantic voyages by warships belonging to neutral powers became common as well. From around 1740, for example, the Dutch sent a few men-of-war to Curaçao and Suriname each year to escort merchant ships.[19] Major European powers' increasing interest in the world overseas was also manifest in the more frequent organization of voyages of exploration with both scientific and political objectives. Between 1760 and 1808, the Spanish government sponsored no fewer than fifty-seven expeditions to its colonies in the Americas and Asia. During these expeditions, of which Alejandro Malaspina's to the Pacific in 1789–94 is perhaps the most famous, travellers collected data on natural history, conducted astronomical observations, carried out geographical explorations and produced all sorts of maps and charts. The British and French imperial machines launched a series of similar long-range ventures, including, for instance, James Cook's, Louis-Antoine de Bougainville's and Jean-François La Pérouse's voyages across the Pacific. The French were often in the lead, with the British following closely behind.[20]

With the increase in shipping, commerce and warfare in the Atlantic from 1730 came growth in movements of people. The eighteenth century initially saw a huge rise in the transatlantic slave trade, as discussed earlier. Additionally, there was large growth in the numbers of other groups of people crossing the ocean. Although emigration from Europe to Spanish America and to the British, French and Dutch colonies on the American mainland and in the West Indies after 1700 was lower than before,[21] the numbers of seamen, soldiers and passengers embarking on merchantmen, whalers, fishing boats and warships crossing the Atlantic Ocean vastly increased. The number of men employed by the whaling fleet of New England, for example, had grown to 5,000 by 1770. Another 10,000 men annually sailed on boats in the cod fisheries.[22] The number of seamen and soldiers crossing the Atlantic en route to Asia on Dutch East Indiamen rose from 71,700 between 1721 and 1730 to 85,500 between 1761 and 1770. English and French East Indiamen sailing to Asia in the 1780s had almost four times as many people on board as in the 1720s.[23] The flows of people across the Atlantic also showed some striking changes in origin and destination. Some 100,000 Germans and Scandinavians made the crossing to the British American colonies, many of them as indentured servants. Within the Americas, New England, Pennsylvania, Maryland, Virginia and other mainland colonies after 1730 attracted many more European immigrants than plantation colonies in the Caribbean.[24]

The Atlantic world thus became increasingly integrated, especially but not exclusively in the economic sphere. Globalization grew apace. 'The density of economic exchanges deepened and thickened to the point where each "national" development contributed to the enrichment of all,' Nicholas Canny and Philip Morgan have claimed.[25] In what ways and to what extent did changes in knowledge have an impact on the advance of globalization after 1730? This is the question with which we start Part II of this book. We begin by analysing the effects of developments in maritime knowledge on the advance of globalization. Chapter 3 shows that ships could sail faster, and the chances for survival on board were better than before, thanks to changes in knowledge on ship construction, navigation, chart-making and the maritime environment, as well as improvements in knowledge on medical care at sea. Chapter 4 argues that imperial, commercial and religious machines and self-organization as globalizing forces, on the other hand, had a greater impact on the growth of maritime knowledge in the Atlantic world than ever before. The chapter analyses how this came about and how it affected different fields of maritime knowledge, such as shipbuilding, navigation technology and medical care on board. Finally, the conclusion to this part argues that there was a substantial increase in capabilities for the development of maritime knowledge between 1730 and 1800 in terms of techniques, instruments and resources, but that some limitations nevertheless continued to exist.

3

The maritime knowledge supporting globalization

After 1730, advances in maritime knowledge had a much greater impact on globalization in the Atlantic orbit than before. Knowledge *did* make a difference to globalization, with changes in knowledge on ship construction, navigation, chart-making and the maritime environment playing a key part in this breakthrough.

Historians have long noted improvements in the productivity of shipping in Atlantic in the eighteenth century. Productivity gains have been estimated using a variety of indicators, such as freight rates, ton/man ratios and the duration of voyages. The extant data suggest that freight rates on routes between London, the West Indies and British colonies on the American mainland generally declined between the 1670s and the outbreak of the Revolution, although there were distinct differences by route and commodity. Freight rates in the tobacco trade from the Chesapeake and the rice trade from Carolina, for example, dropped much more than freight rates in the sugar trade from Barbados and Jamaica.[1]

Why this decline occurred is still a matter of debate. Lower freight rates – in Russell Menard's neat summary of the discussion – could be the result of 'safer seas', 'smoother markets', 'better ships' or 'better navigators', or a combination of these factors.[2] Douglass North, James Shepherd and Gary Walton have ascribed the phenomenon primarily to increased safety at sea and improved organization of colonial markets. In their view, the drop in freight rates in the Atlantic trades was in no small part a consequence of the decline in piracy after 1730, which led to a fall in insurance rates and a reduction in the armaments of merchantmen and hence a decrease in the size of crews. The number of tons served per man in the Atlantic trades increased by 50–70 per cent in the course of the eighteenth century. Improvements in the convoy system after about 1750 meant that British and colonial merchantmen could sail more lightly armed in wartime, too. Further savings were facilitated by a reduction in turnaround times for ships in colonial ports in America and the West Indies; as arrival times were better attuned to the availability of goods, there was improved information about local markets, and cargo was loaded more rapidly and efficiently.[3] Robin Craig has suggested that from the late eighteenth century, shipmasters may also have become more adept at handling their tasks in port thanks to the diffusion of printed guides such as *The Universal Directory or Complete Pocket-Assistant for Merchants, Masters of Ships, Mates etc.* or *The Ship-Masters' Assistant and Owners' Manual*. The spread of knowledge about market operations thus helped to advance productivity in shipping.[4]

Still, it was hard to reduce the number of days spent in colonial ports as long as merchants continued to rely on the time-consuming consignment system of marketing goods (especially tobacco), instead of using the time-saving direct-buying system. The former system was preferred by London merchants, the latter was practised by Scottish traders and their colonial agents. When the centre of the tobacco trade moved from London to Scotland, however, the system of marketing changed as well, and the time spent in colonial ports decreased.[5] As far as the slave trade was concerned, turnaround times on the African coast even *increased* rather than decreased as a result of the growing demand for slaves.[6]

Faster ships

In addition to these organizational and institutional changes, advances in knowledge probably contributed to a rise in productivity in shipping, too. Despite Shepherd and Walton's claims to the contrary,[7] 'better ships' and 'better navigators' may have been important factors in making voyages faster and cheaper. It was not just the reduction in port time or improvements in the convoy system that led to a decline in the duration of voyages but also an increase in the speed of ships at sea. Klas Rönnbäck's survey of the estimated speed of slave trading ships during voyages across the Atlantic suggests that average ship speeds on all routes from Africa to the Caribbean and North America increased from the 1750s onwards. In the 1800s, the speed of British, French, Dutch, Portuguese and American ships crossing the Atlantic was about 30 per cent faster than fifty years beforehand. *Pace* Shepherd and Walton, ship speed was *not* constant.[8]

How could this have happened? 'Better ships' is part of the answer. However, ships did not become better because ship construction changed as a result of advances in science. Theoretical inquiries into the physical behaviour of ships were still in their infancy, and attempts to apply scientific insights were largely confined to a few continental navies.[9] More important were the changes to sail plans and rigging that were introduced in the course of the eighteenth century. The sail area was broken up into smaller units; the number of sails gradually multiplied and rigging was adapted accordingly. It became increasingly common to equip merchant ships with two masts instead of three – and not just small ones. In Britain, even ships of 140–150 tons were usually two-masted by the 1760s. These gradual improvements not only saved labour but also allowed ships to sail closer to the wind, which may have saved time.[10]

Another technological change that helped to increase sailing speed was the adoption of copper sheathing in the last quarter of the eighteenth century. Earlier attempts at protecting underwater hulls by the adoption of lead sheathing had been frustrated by the problem of the corrosion of iron fastenings.[11] The issue of corrosion was finally solved by adopting alloy bolts as a substitution for iron nails.[12] Sheathing hulls with copper had the advantage of protecting vessels from damage by shipworms and prevented the accumulation of seaweed and other marine fouling, which slowed them down. It also reduced the need for frequent docking. Peter Solar and Klas Rönnbäck have shown that coppered ships sailed 16 per cent faster than ships without copper sheathing. Copper sheathing was a key factor in the increase of speed of British ships from the late 1770s. Within a few years, nearly 75 per cent of British slave ships had coppered hulls. By the end of the eighteenth century, 90 per cent of British slave ships sailing to Africa, 50 per cent of vessels sailing to the West Indies and South America and more than 90 per cent of East Indiamen were equipped with copper sheathing.[13] All of the vessels of the British navy were coppered from 1780 onwards, which was an asset in the wars against France and Spain.[14]

Another part of the answer to the question of why ships sailed faster, which has received much less attention until now, may have been 'better navigators'. Rönnbäck mentioned 'increasing navigational skills' as a possible relevant factor in the increase of ships' speed, but did not elaborate upon this.[15] Interestingly, his figures showed that ships' speed increased not just in British but in *all* Atlantic slave shipping (even though other nations lagged behind the British in the introduction of coppered hulls), and that the increase started well before copper sheathing was adopted on British slavers on a massive scale. I would suggest two ways in which improvements in navigation may have affected the speed of ships at sea.

First of all, it is significant that most of the ships sailing between London and the American colonies in the eighteenth century 'remained in the same trade for several years'. The same vessels plied the same routes for years on end.[16] A regular connection between particular ships and particular routes meant that navigators had more opportunity to gain experience, and thus more knowledge, of the natural conditions (winds, currents, depths, etc.) in specific parts of the Atlantic, which could then usefully be applied in improving navigation. The more frequently navigators crossed the same maritime area, the more familiar they became with its specific circumstances and the better able they were to take account of those circumstances while navigating their ship, and thereby to realize safer and faster voyages. If masters could indeed command the same ship for several voyages in succession, as Ralph Davis suggests,[17] this implies that they were placed in a unique position to learn by doing. A sample of seventy voyages by the Dutch Middelburgsche Commercie Compagnie in the period 1750-97 shows that captains often sailed to the same area several times, either as captains or in some junior capacity.[18]

Second, evidence suggests that masters and mates in the Atlantic trades in the second half of the eighteenth century also adopted new navigation techniques and instruments. Dutch navigators in Atlantic trade after 1760 increasingly employed the so-called Douwes method for finding latitude. This new technique, devised in the 1740s by the Amsterdam-based teacher of navigation, Cornelis Douwes, rested on the idea of taking double altitudes of the sun – one in the forenoon and one in the afternoon – combined with the position calculated by dead reckoning. Thus, seamen were no longer dependent on visibility conditions at noon. They could enhance the frequency of checks on their estimated position and thereby reduce uncertainty about their exact location at sea.[19]

Using double altitudes for finding latitude was in itself not a new discovery. The singular merit of Douwes's contribution was that he had devised a double-altitude method that could be applied at sea relatively easily, and moreover supplied a set of tables that greatly facilitated its use. The eminent Spanish expert on navigation technology, José de Mendoza y Ríos, remarked in the 1790s that Douwes's method was the only one widely adopted by navigators.[20] An explanation of this method, which had been circulated among Dutch seamen in manuscript form since the late 1740s, first appeared in print in the transactions of a Dutch learned society in 1754; the accompanying tables were published in 1761.[21] Even before this happened, an English version of Douwes's 'solar tables' and instructions for their use was published by Richard Harrison in London, though without mentioning Douwes's name. An analysis of this treatise was presented at a meeting of the Royal Society in November 1760.[22] After an English naval officer had sent a copy of Douwes's tables from Amsterdam to London, the Board of Longitude in 1768 awarded the Dutch mathematician a reward of fifty pounds 'for his trouble in correcting, improving and illustrating' his 'solar tables'.[23] Thanks to Astronomer Royal Nevil Maskelyne, an extended version of Douwes's tables for the double altitude was included in the *Tables Requisite* (which accompanied the *Nautical Almanac*) from the early 1770s onwards. José de Mendoza y Ríos propagated Douwes's method in Spain. In the United States, Douwes's method for finding latitude gained wider currency thanks to Nathaniel Bowditch's new edition of J. Hamilton Moore's manual *The Practical Navigator*, published in 1799. It was only in France that his contribution to navigation technology was barely noticed by astronomers and seamen.[24]

About 1750, English navigators also began to substitute the octant for the back-staff and cross-staff as the instrument of choice for measuring altitudes. The master of the Royal Mathematical School at Christ's Hospital recommended Hadley's instrument explicitly in his new navigation manual of 1754, stating that it 'far surpasse[d] all others for the taking of altitudes and zenith distances of celestial objects at Sea, not only for the accuracy with which it shews the altitude, but also the readiness and ease with which they are taken'.[25] Seafarers in the American colonies increasingly adopted the new instrument after 1750.[26] In the second half of the eighteenth century, navigators in the merchant navy of the Dutch Republic had an almost equal preference for octants and back-staffs; in fact, quite a few masters and mates in the Atlantic trades possessed an octant.[27] Octants were employed a few times on French naval vessels in the 1730s, but they did not begin to be disseminated more widely until the 1750s onwards. It is not known, however, in which branches of shipping the instrument was used.[28] The same holds for Spain; it is certain that Antonio de Ulloa used an octant, bought by Godin in London, during his voyage across the Atlantic, and that he and his fellow officer Jorge Juan did their best after their return to make the merits of the instrument more widely known in their homeland, but the influence of their published work on Spanish seafaring practice has yet to be established.[29]

New methods for finding longitude at sea were much slower to have an impact on Atlantic shipping than new techniques and instruments for the measurement of latitude. By the end of the 1760s, the problem of determining longitude at sea had at last been solved in such a way that the proposed methods actually worked. It had long been known, in theory, that longitude at sea could be determined by measuring the difference in time on-board ship and on a prime meridian. This could be done by using a marine chronometer to keep standard time, or by observing lunar distances (i.e. the angle between the moon and a fixed star) on board and using pre-calculated data on the same phenomenon for a prime meridian as a reference point. Astronomers and instrument-makers struggled for many years, however, before they succeeded in transforming these theoretical solutions into methods that could be used at sea. Britain and France led the way in making longitude by chronometer and longitude by lunar distances a feasible option. The Board of Longitude awarded huge sums to the inventor of the first reliable timekeeper, John Harrison, and also paid considerable amounts of money to astronomers who helped to perfect the method of lunar distances, and instrument-makers who designed improved chronometers.[30] French chronometer-makers had matched Harrison's achievement by the late 1760s.

But these new methods could only be put into practice if seafarers both had access to the required aids and instruments and possessed the necessary skills to use them. These requirements were met more quickly for the lunar distances method than for the chronometer method. Implements for the determination of longitude by lunar distances – specifically almanacs, sextants and/or reflecting circles – were available at an earlier date, in larger numbers, and at a lower price than the key tool needed for finding longitude by chronometer, namely an accurate timekeeper. All of these conditions were fulfilled by the 1780s. Additionally, the skills needed for using the lunar distances method started to spread among seamen in the last decades of the eighteenth century onwards via manuals, tracts and instruction in nautical schools. Cook, La Pérouse, Malaspina and other commanders of long-range expeditions sponsored by European states successfully applied the method on their exploratory voyages across the globe.[31]

The rank and file of navigators slowly followed. A survey of ships' logs from the Royal Navy and the EIC revealed that most British ships did not use lunar distances before the 1790s, and that EIC navigators were slightly ahead of naval officers in adopting the new method. Lunar distances were only adopted early on voyages of exploration.[32] Ships' journals from the Netherlands show that the method was sometimes used at sea on Dutch Navy and VOC vessels in the late 1780s and 1790s, but not yet on merchantmen in the Atlantic trades.[33] Jane Wess has conjectured that the 'Golden Age' of the lunar distances method did not begin until the nineteenth century.[34]

With the exception of EIC ships, it remained rather unusual to have a chronometer on board, even in Britain and France until after the Napoleonic Wars. Timekeepers were first carried on British East Indiamen in the 1770s and 1780s, although they were not always used. A column for longitude by chronometer was added to the standard logs of the company in the 1790s. Their introduction to the Royal Navy went much more slowly. A British naval captain complained in 1812 about the Admiralty's inability to provide all ships with chronometers, and the navy sometimes borrowed timekeepers from the EIC.[35] In 1815, the French navy had no more than forty-three timekeepers at its disposal. A decade later, there were only eighteen chronometers in the entire French mercantile marine.[36] Regarding the Netherlands and Spain, there is no indication that chronometers were used on other ships than naval vessels before the beginning of the nineteenth century.[37] One may safely conclude that the method of finding longitude by chronometer can only have had a marginal impact on the speed of shipping in the Atlantic before 1800.

The growth of knowledge about magnetic declination probably had more effect. Before the spread of accurate and practical methods for finding longitude, seafarers could only partially and approximately check whether the position estimated by dead reckoning was actually the correct one. Apart from the determination of latitude by astronomical observations, information could be gathered by soundings, by sightings of birds or plants or by the identification of landmarks and coastal profiles. Magnetic declination was sometimes thought to provide clues about the position of the ship as well.[38] Although the declination of the compass needle from the true north at any given place had been known to change over time ('secular variation') since the 1630s,[39] the belief among scholars and seafarers that observations of the compass variation on board combined with the determination of latitude could help one to get a sort of 'fix' of the position at sea did not disappear altogether. Indeed, the appearance of Halley's chart of magnetic declination in the Atlantic in 1701, discussed in chapter 2, gave this idea a new lease of life. As Halley himself suggested, his map with isogonic lines could be helpful in estimating longitude at sea. Observations of variation of the compass on board could serve as a good indicator of longitude at those places in the Atlantic, such as in the region near the Cape of Good Hope, where the isogonic lines ran more or less in a north–south direction and came close to each other.[40]

Halley's original chart was based on a limited amount of data. During his voyage with the *Paramore*, he recorded 170 observations of the variation of the compass.[41] Cartographic displays of data on magnetic declination became more useful for checking a ship's position at sea, when not only observations for any given place were kept up to date (taking account of secular variation) but the size of the underlying data set also massively increased. Scholars and seafarers from various countries contributed to this effort in the eighteenth century,[42] but Britain accounted for the lion's share. In 1744 and 1756, the firm of Mount & Page, which had published Halley's first magnetic chart, produced updated editions of his world map with the help of two fellows of the Royal Society,

William Mountaine and James Dodson. The new editions were compiled from navy logbooks as well as those from the EIC, the Royal African Company and the Hudson's Bay Company. The 1756 chart was sold in a Dutch and French edition, too, and appeared in an adapted version in a French sea atlas compiled by Jean-Nicholas Bellin in the 1760s. A new version of Halley's magnetic chart of the Atlantic was published in 1760. Other variation charts were published by Samuel Dunn in 1775 and John Churchman in 1794.[43] In the Dutch Republic, a copy of Halley's magnetic chart of the world was included in Louis Renard's *Atlas van zeevaart en koophandel der gehele waereldt* of 1745. New charts with isogonic lines appeared a few years later.[44] In Spain, mariners could find a small copy of the magnetic chart of the Atlantic (dating from 1744) in the *Compendio de navegación* by Jorge Juan, published in 1757 (Figure 3).[45]

Whether seamen actually used magnetic charts at sea, and if so, whether they did so with the purpose of finding longitude, remains a moot point. Ulloa and Juan's account of their voyage to America in the 1730s illustrates that this sometimes *did* occur. In his manual of 1757, Juan advised using the magnetic chart only if the variation of the compass could not be determined by observation, taking care to allow for secular variation since 1744.[46] H. L. Hitchins and W. E. May suggested that 'ship-masters who had previously supplied themselves with azimuth compasses so that they could observe the variation and thus correct their courses, now economized by buying variation charts to tell them what variation to allow', but they did not offer evidence to support this.[47] What we do know is that navigators on Dutch ships making direct voyages across the Atlantic after 1750 seldom observed the variation of the compass, whereas navigators on ships engaged in the triangular trade between the Netherlands, Africa and the Americas after 1750 frequently *did* record observations of the variation of the compass.[48] This may mean that navigators on the direct route to America made use of magnetic charts as a source of data on variation (as Hitchins and May suspected), whereas navigators in the triangular trade either had no magnetic charts on board or used magnetic charts as an aid to check their estimated longitude (combining data on latitude with observations of the actual variation of the compass).

A comparison with sailing directions for Dutch East Indiamen shows that the latter interpretation is not too far-fetched. The new edition of the sailing directions produced by the directors of the VOC in 1768 explicitly advised masters and mates, on the recommendation of the examiners of pilots, to take account of the variation of the compass as an indicator of longitude when nearing the equator.[49] Pybo Steenstra, an examiner at the Amsterdam Chamber, extolled

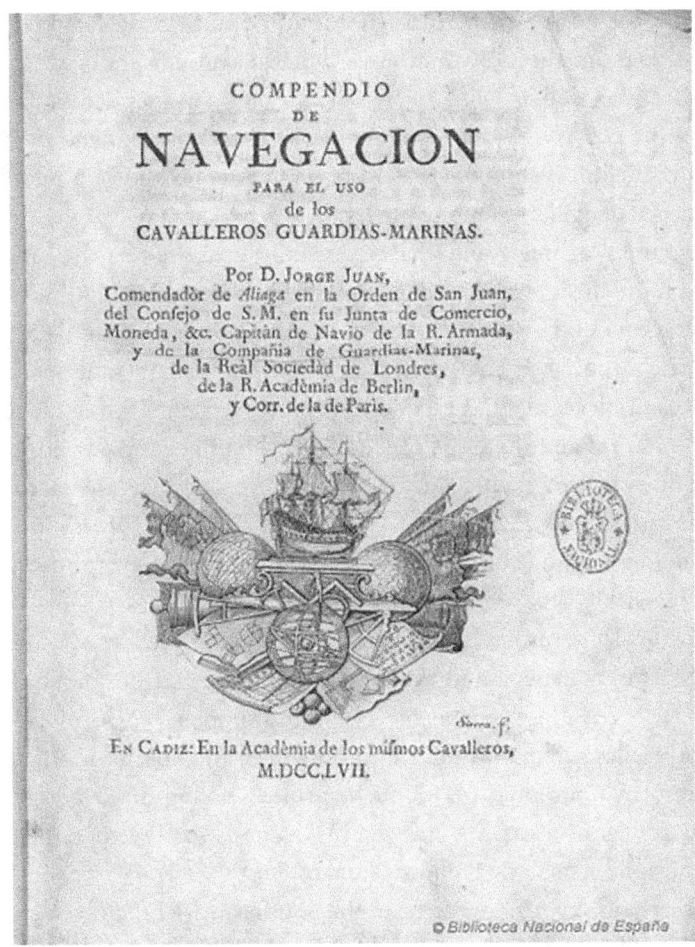

Figure 3 Title page of Jorge Juan, *Compendio de navegación* (Cádiz: 1757). Wikimedia Commons.

the value of the data from Mountaine and Dodson in particular.[50] Ships' journals from Dutch East Indiamen reveal that from the 1770s onwards, navigators did indeed use magnetic declination as an indicator of longitude, as the sailing directions suggested.[51]

Apart from magnetic charts, the supply of all sorts of maps, charts and atlases of the Atlantic vastly increased and their reliability was greatly improved. France, not the Dutch Republic, now led the way in cartographic production. The Dépôt, founded in 1720, finally started to publish charts at the end of the 1730s, and it stepped up production in the early years of the Seven Years' War.[52] These changes in France had ramifications far beyond the Hexagone itself. French charts and pilot books, for example, increasingly found their way to seafarers from the Netherlands. From the 1750s onwards, Dutch naval officers began to consult French charts, as well as Dutch materials, on their voyages across the Atlantic and along the coasts of France and Spain. Logbooks made mention of the use of charts by Bellin, Fleurieu and Verdun de la Crenne and of a pilot book by D'Après de Mannevillette, among others.[53]

The accuracy of maps and charts generally improved as the longitude of more and more locations around the Atlantic was determined by astronomical observations under the auspices of the Académie Royale, the Royal Observatory in Greenwich, the Observatorio Real in Cádiz or other institutions. Once the coordinates of places such as Quebec, Louisbourg, Saint-Domingue, Cayenne, Cádiz, the Azores and the Cape of Good Hope had been fixed with precision, the reliability of cartographic aids related to these data increased accordingly.[54] In the *Atlas maritimo de España* of 1789, for example, Vicente Tofiño was able to indicate the longitude of the Azores with reference to four prime meridians: Paris, Greenwich, Cádiz and Tenerife.[55]

Some knowledge on currents, winds and tides, which was also of prime importance for the speed and safety of shipping, could be found in printed media as well. The most general surveys were Dampier's *A Discourse of Trade-Winds* and Halley's map of winds in the Northern and Southern Atlantic. More specific information could be found in printed sailing directions relating to particular routes or areas, such as the instructions for the route between the Netherlands and Asia issued to navigators of the VOC. Travel accounts, such as Ulloa's description of his voyage from the Southern Atlantic to Cape Breton in July 1745, sometimes contained a wealth of observations on wind patterns, too.[56]

Benjamin Franklin was one of the pioneers of making ocean currents visible in print. In 1768, living in London while holding the position of postmaster in America, Franklin suggested to the post office in the metropole that it might be useful for seafarers seeking fast passage across the Atlantic (such as captains of packet boats) to have a chart depicting 'the Dimentions Course and Swiftness' of the current along the American coast, which seamen commonly called 'the Gulph Stream'. Franklin had a mariner from Nantucket mark the Gulf Stream on an existing chart, which was then forwarded to London and printed by Mount & Page. Revised versions of the chart were published by Franklin himself in 1782 and 1786, the latter in the second volume of *Transactions of the American Philosophical Society*. Another chart of Atlantic currents made by an English physician, Charles Blagden, appeared in the *Philosophical Transactions* of the Royal Society in 1781.[57] What Franklin began was continued on a much greater scale by a former seaman, EIC surveyor and fellow of the Royal Society, James Rennell. Scanning large numbers of ships' journals and other sources, Rennell brought together a huge amount of data on every ocean in the world. Although his magnum opus on currents in the Atlantic Ocean was not published until 1832, some of his ideas and findings were circulated in Britain (and beyond) long before that date.[58] A Dutch translation of Rennell' s observations on a current to the west of the Scilly Islands, first published in 1793, appeared in Amsterdam a year later. Added to Rennell's text were translations of selected parts of Blagden's article of 1781 and summaries of observations on the Gulf Stream published in an American magazine.[59]

However, much of the knowledge on currents, winds and tides accumulated by seafarers in the course of time was circulated orally or in writing, rather than in printed form. In 1769, a Dutch naval captain noted in his ship's journal that all seamen knew that in the month of July currents on the west coast of Africa near the Canary Islands ran strongly to the east.[60] William Dampier, himself every inch a seaman, offered a glimpse of this underlying network of knowledge in the opening of his chapter on currents:

> 'Tis generally observed by Seamen, that in all Places where Trade-winds blow, the Current is influenced by them, and moves the same way with the Winds; but 'tis not with a like swiftness in all Places; neither is it always so discernable by us in the wide Ocean, as it is near to some Coast; and yet it is not so discernable neither, very near any Coast, except at Capes and Promontories, that shoot far forth out into the Sea; and about Islands also the Effects of them are felt more or less, as they lye in the way of the Trade-Winds.'[61]

Improving the chances of survival: Mortality and health care

Ships were not just sailing faster; the odds of surviving a voyage in the Atlantic improved, too. In the transatlantic slave trade, mortality declined markedly in the latter half of the eighteenth century. By the 1790s, slaves were more likely to survive the ordeal of the crossing of the Atlantic than fifty years beforehand. The average mortality of slaves during the passage from Africa to the Americas declined from 15.4 per cent in the 1730s to 12.7 per cent in the 1760s, and dropped further to 5.4 per cent in the 1790s.[62] On British slave ships, the mean crude death rate of slaves per month fell from 61 per 1,000 in the 1720s to 32 in the 1790s, and on French slavers from 59 in the 1720s to 32 in the 1770s, before rising again in the 1780s.[63] Crew mortality rates on British and French slave ships, which were generally lower than those of slaves, also showed a slight decline in the late eighteenth century, except for a brief rise on French slavers after 1780.[64]

Mortality on naval vessels likewise diminished. In British and French squadrons sent to the West Indies during the Seven Years' War, 'normal' mortality meant that on a ten-month trip, 9–10 per cent of those on board died, most of them from disease. The death rate on British ships was usually higher than on French or Spanish ones.[65] But a change was evident by the turn of the century; the British naval physician, Gilbert Blane, observed that there was 'in … [1804] a great decrease of sickness and mortality *on the European stations*'. Compared to 1801, the number of sick seamen had been halved.[66] In August 1805, after two years at sea in the Mediterranean and the Atlantic Ocean, Admiral Horatio Nelson reported that all crews in his squadron were 'in the most perfect health'.[67] The Dutch Navy showed a similar pattern. Death rates on Dutch ships carrying troops from the Netherlands to the West Indies, the Cape Colony and the East Indies in 1802–3 fell to remarkably low levels: only 3 to 4 *per thousand* of all those who embarked died from disease en route, as compared with on average 4 *per cent* on Dutch East Indiamen in the early 1790s.[68]

Nevertheless, slaves and crews on slave ships and sailors and soldiers on naval vessels had a greater chance of dying during a transatlantic voyage than passengers and crew members on many other ships that crossed the Atlantic. Convicts or free emigrants from Europe were much more likely to reach the American shore alive. The mean crude death rate per month of convicts carried on British ships to the colonies in North America dropped from 56.5 per 1,000 between 1719 and 1736 to a mere 12.5 between 1768 and 1775. Among German emigrants to Philadelphia between 1727 and 1805, the rate amounted to no more than fifteen.[69] Mortality on voyages of English merchantmen in European and Atlantic trades and in the whale fisheries in the early 1770s was less than 1 per cent.[70]

Sometimes, naval forces faced calamities that led to losses far in excess of the 'standard' level of mortality. Each of the great naval wars between Britain, France and Spain in the eighteenth century saw major health disasters in the West Indies. During the expedition under the command of Admiral Vernon and General Wentworth to capture Cartagena and Santiago de Cuba at the beginning of the War of Jenkins' Ear, an estimated 22,000 of the 29,000 soldiers and sailors perished between 1740 and 1742; 21,000 of them presumably died from yellow fever.[71] The conquest of Havana by British army and navy forces in the summer of 1762 came at a high cost in human lives. After the Spanish surrender on 14

August, some 4,700 British soldiers and 3,000 British sailors died in the two months that followed.⁷² The British also suffered tremendous losses during the war with France in the West Indies in the 1790s. Eighty thousand men perished between 1793 and 1796, mostly from disease. The French met a similar fate when they tried to reconquer Saint-Domingue after 1802, when the invasion force was almost entirely destroyed by yellow fever.⁷³

Mortality in the Atlantic after 1730, thus, did not show a uniform pattern. There were differences between slaves and crews of slave ships, between categories of emigrants, between blacks and whites, between settlers, soldiers and sailors and between crews from different European nations. Contemporaries were not unaware of such variations. In 1791, the physician Robert Jackson observed that newly recruited British troops in the West Indies suffered more from 'dangerous diseases' than French or Spanish soldiers.⁷⁴ Doctors, surgeons and other contemporary observers also noted that slaves rarely fell victim to malaria or yellow fever, but were more prone than whites to suffer from diseases such yaws, leprosy or elephantiasis.⁷⁵ Nevertheless, mortality *did* decline in particular groups or shipping branches. How could this happen? And why did this fail to occur in other cases? And how and to what extent were such variations related to advances in knowledge?

Robert Haines and Ralph Shlomowitz have suggested that an advance in knowledge may have made a difference, at least in the case of British slave ships. In their view, the decline in mortality on British slavers in the eighteenth century can 'largely' be ascribed to a more 'sophisticated understanding of disease', which allowed more effective preventive measures to be taken on board. Even before the adoption of Dolben's Act in 1788, which aimed to reduce crowding on slave ships and to stimulate captains and surgeons to make every effort to curtail mortality, 'health and hygiene measures were routinely applied'. Haines and Shlomowitz insisted that maritime surgeons knew the importance of such basic practices as keeping a clean ship, improving ventilation below decks, using purified water and isolating the sick, and they did their best to get these more widely accepted. In their opinion, the advance of knowledge owed much less to insights derived from traditional medical learning than to improved understanding gained from accumulated experience. It was mainly an outcome of observations and systematic experiments undertaken in practical situations at sea, which were communicated between surgeons employed in the slave trade and other settings with 'crowded populations', such as prisons, convict ships, naval vessels and government emigrant ships.⁷⁶ Regarding the British navy, Patricia Crimmin has argued that advances in medical science were a less important factor in the reduction of sick rates and mortality than advances in 'hygiene, improved diet, and the more regular provision of clean, warm clothing'.[77] F. N. Groustra and J. R. Bruijn have explained the decline in mortality in the Dutch Navy in c. 1800 with reference to improvements in medical organization and the introduction of more effective measures for the prevention of disease, including checks on the medical condition of sailors before departure.[78]

Even though traditional medicine saw only modest changes, knowledge of on-board medical care in the Atlantic world *did* advance in many ways. What was new in the second half of the eighteenth century was that medical knowledge increasingly flowed across national and imperial borders. The Atlantic world became a single space for the exchange of knowledge on best medical practices at sea. Know-how travelled between the British, French, Dutch and Spanish Atlantics via medical writings, personal contacts and observations on site. The number of books on the causes, prevention and cure of diseases on board soared, cross references multiplied and translations proliferated.

Most of the authors of these texts were medical men themselves, as one would expect. Stephen Hales, a Cambridge-educated clergyman, and Sébastien-François Bigot vicomte de Morogues, an officer in the French navy, were exceptions in this respect. With regard to education, career or position, the medical men were a diverse group. Some of them were trained physicians who had no first-hand experience of medical care at sea. They worked in private practice, such as John Huxham and Vicente de Lardizabal; they pursued careers in the army and noble households, such as John Pringle; or they held government-appointed positions in cities or on the on-shore supervisory boards of the navy or state hospital service, such as Salomon de Monchy, Henri-Louis Duhamel du Monceau or Antoine Poissonnier-Desperrières. Other writers, such as David Henri Gallandat, Lodewijk Rouppe, James Lind, James Trotter and Pedro Maria Gonzalez, served as surgeons on slave ships or naval vessels for several years before taking a university degree in medicine and moving into private practice, a post in a public hospital or some other medical institute ashore. After a career at sea, naval surgeon Abraham Titsingh assumed a leading post in his craft guild in his hometown of Amsterdam. Other authors, such as Elliott Arthy, William Northcote and Gilbert Blane, remained active as on-board naval surgeons or physicians. All in all, the number of writers with naval connections was much larger than that of those with first-hand experience of life on slave ships or other sorts of merchantmen.

The surge in publications on medical care at sea from the 1740s onwards in fact had more to do with warfare than with the slave trade. In contrast to the emerging medical literature on colonies in the Americas and West Indies, which devoted ample attention to the diseases suffered by slaves,[79] writings that dealt specifically with the treatment of slaves on board were exceedingly rare. Gallandat's guide to how to prevent and cure illness among slaves during the trading season on the African coast and the transport across the Atlantic was quite exceptional.[80] De Monchy discussed diseases on voyages to the West Indies, and De Lardizabal was concerned with the medical problems that could be encountered on voyages of the Basque company trading with Caracas, but they ignored slaves.[81] Most writings on medical care at sea appearing after 1740 arose out of the crucible of war. Titsingh's publications drew on his experience as a naval surgeon during the War of the Spanish Succession. The War of the Austrian Succession and the Seven Years' War spawned another crop of medical texts in Britain, France and the Dutch Republic, including works by Pringle, Morogues, Duhamel, Lind, Rouppe, Northcote and Poissonnier-Desperrières.[82] Blane's book on diseases of seamen, published in 1785, was an outcome of his observations as physician to Admiral Rodney's fleet during the War of American Independence.[83] Jackson's, Trotter's and Arthy's treatises and manuals arose out of their experiences in the American and Revolutionary Wars. The recurrent message was that even the best warships were useless as fighting machines if their officers and administrators failed to take sufficient care of their men.

While writings on the causes, prevention and cure of diseases on board were thoroughly grounded in observations made by the authors themselves during voyages at sea, personal experience of life on-board ship was not the only source of information and insights. Some authors also borrowed information from colleagues or collected evidence by talking with seasoned seamen or insiders in high places. Titsingh frequently referred to letters and accounts of voyages by fellow surgeons.[84] De Monchy, who never once set foot on deck, 'had not a little conversation with masters of ships, long employed in the West Indies trade, and other persons who have occasionally visited those parts'. He further mentioned the assistance of 'a very judicious Englishmen of [his] acquaintance, who had been four years and a half in the West Indies, on the coast of Guinea, and at Barbados' and of a British Lord of the Admiralty.[85] De Lardizabal in San Sebastian received valuable information from Joseph Alsinet, doctor to the royal family in Aranjuez.[86] In 1776, John Pringle offered a state-of-the-art overview of improvements in preserving the health of seamen, based on Captain Cook's account of his circumnavigation of the world and conversations with a number of Cook's 'experienced friends'.[87]

All of the authors were also avid readers. Besides classic texts on medicine, such as those by Galen, Hippocrates, Boerhaave and Sydenham, they perused transactions of scientific societies, medical journals and general magazines and consulted books and treatises that specifically dealt with medical care at sea, published in a variety of languages.[88] Titsingh frequently referred to Cockburn's *Account*. Duhamel borrowed substantially from works by Morogues, Hales and Lind. De Monchy used Titsingh as well as 'many English writers, especially those of the greatest repute and the most recent', such as Pringle, Huxham and Lind.[89] Rouppe cited studies by Morogues, Duhamel, Lind, Huxham, Pringle and De Monchy. De Lardizabal and Poissonnier-Desperrières approvingly referred to Rouppe, Lind, Huxham and Hales. In the 'Bibliotheca scorbutica' in the third edition of his *Treatise on the Scurvy* in 1772, Lind included a lengthy summary of Rouppe's work as well as a brief reference to Poissonnier-Desperrières's treatise.[90] Blane built on work by Lind and on Pringle's account of 1776 relating to the report by Captain Cook.[91] Gonzalez was familiar with the works by Lind, Duhamel, Morogues, Rouppe and Poissonnier-Desperrières, but he remarked that these were not well known in Spain, because they had been written in foreign languages. De Lardizabal's *Consideraciones* was, in his view, the most complete work in Spanish.[92]

The language barrier hardly hindered the circulation of knowledge in medical writings between Britain, France and the Dutch Republic. Translations increased after 1750, and they often appeared very soon after the publication of the original version. Lind's treatise on scurvy of 1753, for example, appeared in a French translation three years later. His book on the most effective means to preserve the health of seamen (1757) was translated into French in 1758 and into Dutch in 1760. Duhamel's *Moyens de conserver la santé aux équipages des vaisseaux*, published in 1759, was rendered into Dutch one year later. De Monchy's treatise of 1761 on the causes and cures of common diseases in voyages to the West Indies appeared in English in 1762. Rouppe's work on diseases of seamen, originally published in Latin, became available in a Dutch translation in 1765 and an English version in 1772.[93]

What was significant about these publications was not the originality of the insights into the causes of diseases in general; in fact, the recommendations in these writings largely consisted of recycled lore on the imbalance of humours, the influence of bad air and putrefaction. Much more important was, first of all, the very fact that many writings about medical care on board, wherever they were first published, now rapidly became accessible to practitioners in the British, French and Dutch Atlantic alike. Knowledge based on empirical observations thus circulated more widely and faster than before, and thereby increasingly took on the character of an open-access toolkit. Moreover, particularly innovative features of those medical writings included the special attention paid to conditions at sea and the array of practical suggestions concerning prevention and cures that they contained.

'Ships', 'seamen' or 'crews' figured explicitly in many titles. Authors dealt with all sorts of aspects that were in some way specific to life at sea, ranging from the regional origins and social make-up of people on board and living conditions below decks to the composition and quality of victuals, and the impact of sailing and staying in different environments. Lodewijk Rouppe, for instance, emphasized that one should know 'of what kind of men the crew [was] composed'. Were they used 'to live near the sea' and thus accustomed to maritime conditions, or did they come from 'inland countries'? Were they 'young hearty seamen' or 'old worn out men, very inactive, and generally troubled with some bodily disorder'?[94] Differences in susceptibility to diseases between groups were partly explained by variations in 'acclimatization' to tropical circumstances, partly by the physical characteristics of different populations. One current of opinion held that although 'new arrivals' in tropical environments were highly susceptible to diseases, all men were by nature capable of adapting to and surviving in parts of the world other than their original habitat. Another view held that some 'bodies' were less able to survive in particular climates than others, either because of unhealthy habits of eating and drinking (as Jackson argued about English soldiers as compared to French and Spanish ones)[95] or because of fundamentally different physical characteristics (as more and more writers argued about blacks as compared with whites from the late eighteenth century).[96] Careful consideration was also given to questions such as these: What were the effects of crowding and humidity? Which foodstuffs and which preservation methods were good or bad for the health? Which refreshments should be preferred? John Huxham suggested that the 'health of seamen' on long voyages could best be preserved by supplying ships with 'a sufficient quantity of sound, generous cyder'. A 'pint of cyder' per sailor per day would significantly help to prevent scurvy.[97] As for the impact of environmental conditions, authors pondered whether hot or cold climates were good for the health of seamen, and whether they were generally healthier at sea than in a port or roadstead.[98]

Medical texts also contained plenty of practical suggestions for preventing and curing illnesses on board. Along with well-known recipes, such as sprinkling vinegar to purify the air or using Peruvian bark as a remedy for fever,[99] after

1750, many authors – following Lind's experiments and years of experience at sea – urgently recommended that ships be supplied with lemons, oranges, sauerkraut or fresh vegetables as a means to combat scurvy. Various methods were discussed for purifying water or making fresh water from seawater. The use of ventilators was recommended to provide fresh air below decks.[100] French writers such as Duhamel and Poissonnier-Desperrières were concerned to explain what precautions should be taken to prevent cattle and fowl infecting the air between decks. Keeping animals on board appears to have been much more common on French vessels than on British ones. Some French warships carried more than a hundred sheep. One of Duhamel's suggestions was to put chicken coops on the main deck, clean the coops and the deck frequently of dung, and not to carry pigs or other animals 'qui répandent une grande infection'.[101]

Several such suggestions for prevention and cure were followed up in practice. Lemon juice became standard issue on British warships on foreign missions from 1794 onwards, and on naval vessels in home waters a few years later. The Royal Navy considered the supply of 'fresh limes and lemons, or the juice of those fruits' a powerful means both to prevent and to cure scurvy. 'A certain proportion of lemon juice taken daily, as an article of seamen's diet, will prevent the possibility of their being tainted with the scurvy, let the other articles of their diet consist of what they will,' the Sick and Hurt Board argued in 1795. The general issue of lemon juice is said to have almost eliminated scurvy in the Channel Fleet by the end of 1800.[102] The EIC experimented with lemon or lime juice in the 1780s, but it did not prescribe its use on board its ships.[103] The VOC instructed its captains in 1750 to obtain 'a sufficient quantity of lemons for the refreshment of the crews' on the Cape Verde islands and make a note of it in the ship's journal.[104] Lime juice became standard issue on Dutch East Indiamen in the late 1780s. Sauerkraut was likewise added to the diet on VOC ships, and from 1797 it also became a standard item on Dutch naval vessels.[105]

Mechanical devices were adopted, too. Ventilators – probably of Hales's design – made their first appearance on VOC ships as early as 1746 (Figure 4).[106] The Admiralty of Rotterdam supplied ventilators to its ships from the 1760s onwards.[107] In 1755, Stephen Hales reported to the Royal Society that his machines had proved in many cases to be of 'great benefit ... in preserving the health and lives of people' on British men-of-war, as well as on slave ships and transport ships to Nova Scotia. Hales's ventilators were installed on all larger Royal Navy ships the following year.[108] In 1764, the French king ordered that all warships sailing the oceans should be provided with a distillation machine designed by Pierre-Isaac Poissonnier. The Compagnie des Indes followed

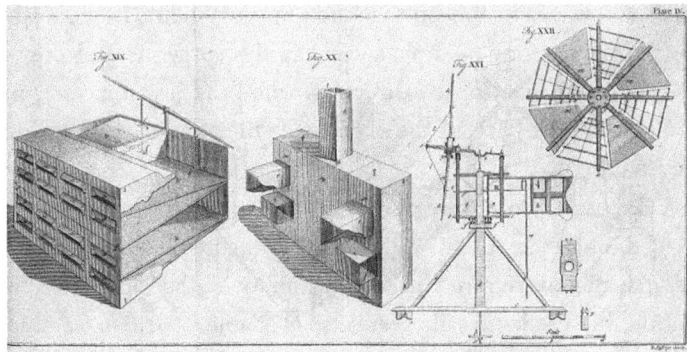

Figure 4 Hales's ventilation apparatus, from Stephen Hales, 'An Account of the Great Benefit of Ventilators', *Philosophical Transactions of the Royal Society* (1755–6). Wikimedia Commons.

the navy's example in 1765, and private slave ships headed for Africa and the Caribbean likewise began to use Poissonnier's device.[109] Another type of distillation machine was, at the suggestion of James Lind, occasionally installed on British navy ships heading out on long-distance voyages across the globe in the late 1760s and 1770s.[110]

And yet, even when people knew, or could have known, about the possible risks to the health of particular groups in particular situations, and even when appropriate measures or devices were available, officials, politicians or entrepreneurs still could choose to adopt a different course. In fact, the knowledge at hand was not always used. At the end of the eighteenth century, governments in Britain and France, for example, still sent thousands of fresh soldiers and seamen to the West Indies at a time of year that patently diminished their chances of survival.[111] Political calculations could overrule insights gained from experience and systematic inquiry.

Cost-benefit calculations could come into play as well. David Gallandat noted in his 1769 guide for slave traders that Dutch slave ships lacked equipment such as bellows or ventilators for producing fresh air below decks, even though these devices were known to be beneficial to the health of slaves. In his view, the reason was not only that Dutch slavers were relatively small but also that shipowners simply refused to make the necessary investment.[112] But the failure of a slave trading company such as the Middelburgsche Commercie Company to install ventilators in their ships, or even to provide instructions about such matters as the screening of enslaved people before departure, the separation of the sick from the healthy or purifying the air below decks by means of wind sails or fumigation, did not mean that such improvements in medical practices on Dutch slavers did not take place. It was the surgeons and crewmembers themselves, rather than company directors, who put these measures into effect; and they did so on the basis of the experience they had gained during voyages across the Atlantic.[113]

In the VOC, ventilators were abolished on homeward-bound ships in 1771 and discarded altogether in 1791. The directors considered the devices rather expensive, that they were rarely used and moreover, that other effective means for ventilation, such as wind sails, were also available.[114] British warships did not always carry ventilators, either, despite the instruction issued by the Admiralty in 1756. John Pringle learned from James Cook that on the voyage of the *Endeavour*, Cook had used wind sails rather than a ventilator, and that 'he had found them at times most serviceable, and particularly between the Tropics'; they were foolproof, took up little space and required no labour to operate.[115] The navy replaced Hales's ventilators with other types in the 1780s.[116]

Copper sheathing of ships' hulls was not universally adopted, either, due to cost-benefit calculations. Although coppering shortened voyage times and thereby helped to reduce death rates among slaves, the innovation did not spread as rapidly on French or Dutch slavers as it did on British ones. Solar and Rönnbäck suggest that the benefits of investing in copper sheathing in the former case were not as obvious as in the latter.[117] The VOC did not send its first copper-sheathed vessel to Asia until 1791, and it did not request that all newly built ships should be protected by copper sheathing until the end of 1792. A major reason why the VOC postponed the adoption of this new technology had been the consideration that it would be costlier to apply in the Dutch context. The shallow approaches to the port of Amsterdam put limitations on the draught of vessels; some experts thought the copper hulls might be damaged by the devices (called 'camels') that were used in some places to lift ships across the shoals. Moreover, experiments with copper sheathing in the Dutch Navy in the previous decade had yielded disappointing results.[118] Besides, even the British merchant marine did not adopt the new solution across the board. Less than half of all ships sailing to North America or the Mediterranean, for example, had coppered hulls by 1790.[119]

Finally, differences in morbidity and mortality were also determined by factors that were not, or barely, perceived by contemporaries. Variations in shipping patterns could significantly increase or diminish the risk of disease or death without people being particularly aware of this. During the Seven Years' War, for example, British men-of-war took longer to cross the Atlantic to the

Caribbean than French ones, because they followed a more southerly route; and the longer duration of the voyage – up to ten days as compared with the French route – resulted in a higher number of deaths.[120] Mortality on British ships carrying convicts or free emigrants to America was lower than on British slave ships, because the former sailed in a temperate climate zone instead of a tropical one.

Deaths of slaves and crew members on slave ships in fact varied markedly depending on the region and port of departure on the African coast. In the Bight of Biafra, mortality on slavers departing from Old Calabar was higher than on those leaving Bonny.[121] Slave mortality on transatlantic crossings by ships belonging to the Middelburgsche Commercie Compagnie in the second half of the eighteenth century was relatively low, because its trade was focused on the Windward Coast and the Gold Coast instead of Senegambia, the Bight of Biafra or the Bight of Benin.[122] The chief reason why overall *crew* mortality on British and French slavers declined in the eighteenth century may have been a shift in the main areas of trade from the more unhealthy regions of Senegambia and the Bight of Benin to the less lethal coast of Angola.[123] This is knowledge in hindsight, however; contemporaries were not aware of the underlying causes.

4
The globalizing forces supporting maritime knowledge

Maritime knowledge supported globalization, and globalization in turn supported the growth of maritime knowledge. Between 1730 and 1800, globalizing forces had a greater impact on the growth of knowledge in the Atlantic world than ever before. This chapter analyses how this came about and how it affected different fields of maritime knowledge, such as navigation technology, shipbuilding and medical care on board. How did the imperial, commercial and religious machines and self-organization contribute to the growth of knowledge infrastructures and the circulation of knowledge?

Imperial and commercial machines and the growth of infrastructure for maritime knowledge

The increasing speed of ships and improving chances of survival were in part related to the growth of institutional infrastructures of knowledge. After 1730, such infrastructures expanded in every domain that was crucial to the productivity of shipping and medical care at sea, even though this growth took place in different ways and to different degrees. Imperial and commercial machines took the lead, separately or in concert, but they were often supplemented by decentralized, self-organized networks. Religious machines, by contrast, lost much of their former importance.

The growth of knowledge infrastructures in the Atlantic world was especially impressive in the field of navigation technology. The period between 1730 and 1800 saw not only striking changes in the organization and content of nautical education, along with innovations in the examination of navigating personnel, but also a remarkable expansion of facilities for the production and distribution of charts and nautical instruments.

In the French and Spanish Atlantic, states strengthened their grip on nautical education by bringing existing institutions under their control or by creating new ones. In France, Jesuit professors at naval training schools were replaced by laymen from the 1760s. The curriculum was standardized with the adoption of a new textbook written by the academician Étienne Bézout, who was appointed examiner of naval cadets in 1764. A further reform in the 1780s subjected teachers to a competitive selection system, and charged examiners with inspecting schools to ensure equal standards of instruction. Meanwhile, new navigational schools for training pilots in the merchant marine arose in many major and minor ports around the country, which were in some cases supported by local governments, councils of commerce or state officials. During the Revolution, the imperial machine extended its control over nautical instruction still further, by creating a number of schools that would train navigators both for the navy and for the mercantile marine.[1]

A similar development took place in Spain. The curriculum of the College of San Telmo in Seville, which trained seamen for the navy as well as the merchant marine, was reformed in the late 1770s after the model of the naval academy in Cádiz. A decade later, the institute was brought under the jurisdiction of the department of the navy.[2] Once the liberalization of trade to the Americas had started in the 1760s, a host of new nautical schools was founded by local authorities or citizens' associations in Barcelona, Gijón, Alicante and other port cities along the north and east coasts of Spain and on the Balearic Islands. Although most of these *escuelas libres* were local initiatives, by the end of the century, the content of the courses showed a degree of convergence along the outlines set out in general instructions drawn up under the auspices of the navy in 1790.[3]

Nautical education in the Netherlands in the eighteenth century largely remained in the hands of private entrepreneurs and local governments, but the role of the state gradually expanded. A number of innovations brought Dutch infrastructure somewhat closer to the British model, which included institutions such as the Royal Mathematical School at Christ's Hospital and the Royal Naval Academy in Portsmouth. In c. 1750, the Admiralties of Amsterdam and Rotterdam joined forces with the VOC and the governments of both port cities to establish colleges for training masters, mates, gunners and naval officers. After the merger of the Admiralties into a centralized navy, a separate institute for the education of naval cadets was created in 1803.[4]

In all major seafaring states, imperial and commercial machines used regulations on exams to stimulate improvements in navigators' skills. Knowledge of specific new methods and instruments was made a prerequisite for appointments or promotions. Candidates for the positions of officer and mate at the EIC had to take an exam set by the Committee on Shipping. This body included teachers of mathematics and navigation from the Royal Mathematical School at Christ's Hospital, the Royal Naval Academy at Portsmouth and private schools. From 1768 onwards, the EIC required that all candidates for officer or mate positions had to prove that they were able to determine longitude by lunar distances.[5] At the VOC, new statutes on examinations issued in 1793 ruled that navigators must demonstrate a command of the method to find latitude by means of double altitudes of the sun and of the lunar distances method to determine longitude; they were also required to be familiar with the use of octants and sextants.[6] Revised rules for navigators' exams in the Spanish Navy in 1790 stipulated that third mates should be familiar with the method of lunar distances for finding longitude and the method of double altitudes of the sun for finding latitude. Merchant seamen were subject to these regulations as well, because the education of masters and mates in the merchant marine was still closely related to the needs of the navy.[7]

The most significant innovation in the content of nautical education was the introduction of the method of lunar distances. Instructors on mathematics and navigation who sat on the EIC's Committee on Shipping had to be able to teach the method themselves. Manuals written by teachers of navigation, including examiners at the EIC, began to devote more attention to lunar distances by the end of the eighteenth century, too.[8] In 1804, the directors of the EIC recommended that all officers who had 'not been instructed in the method of finding of longitude of a ship at sea, by lunar observations' follow instruction from a certain Lawrence Gwynne at Christ's Hospital.[9] In the Dutch Republic, lunar distances were taught at the nautical college in Rotterdam from the 1780s onwards and at the newly founded Kweekschool (training college) in Amsterdam from 1786, which guaranteed that some future navigators of East Indiamen and the merchant marine would become acquainted with the method as well. Furthermore, the subject became a standard part of the curriculum of the new schools for naval masters and mates founded in Amsterdam and Rotterdam in 1795 and the institute for navy cadets established eight years later.[10]

In Spain, the new method for finding longitude was taught to a group of young naval officers on a voyage by the frigate *Rosalía* to the South Atlantic as early as 1774.[11] Shortly afterwards, it became a regular part of the curriculum of the schools of navy cadets, and from the 1790s it was included in the programme of private nautical schools as well. José de Mazarredo, a naval officer who had first applied the method himself on a voyage in 1772, added a long chapter on lunar distances to the much-used textbook by Jorge Juan, which circulated in manuscript form from 1777 and appeared in print in 1790.[12] In France, by contrast, the introduction of lunar distances in nautical education was long hampered by disputes between scientists and naval officers and discussions about how exactly the method should be made fit for practice at sea, and whether training programmes for naval cadets should be opened to candidates other than noblemen's sons.[13]

Imperial machines further transformed the making of charts. In France in 1773, the Dépôt des cartes et plans de la Marine was officially designated as the exclusive producer of cartographic aids for seamen. By the mid-1780s, it had grown into a department with two chief officers and nineteen employees, including six *ingenieurs-dessinateurs* specialized in drawing maps and copying materials relating to geography.[14] But the Dépôt did not operate entirely as a non-profit institution; it had a commercial side as well. Until the nineteenth century, the agency derived part of its income from the sale of charts and prints to customers outside the navy. Catalogues with a full list of the printed materials on offer were issued for that very purpose in the early 1770s.[15] Beside the Dépôt of the navy, in 1762 the Compagnie des Indes established a hydrographic department of its own, which collected and edited charts of the Indian Ocean. This department became a branch of the Dépôt eight years later.[16]

The French approach inspired changes in Spain and Britain, too, although it took a while before institutes on the model of the Dépôt finally came into being. New regulations for the Spanish Navy issued in 1748 stipulated that after returning from a voyage all pilots in the navy and the mercantile marine had to hand in their ships' journals to the *piloto mayor* of the navy, so that discoveries and other useful observations could be incorporated into charts and sailing directions. A draughtsman would assist the *piloto mayor* in this task. In practice, navigators in the merchant navy could not be forced to comply with this rule; they hardly delivered any material at all. Moreover, there were not enough skilled engravers available to produce a sufficient supply of new or improved charts. Thus, for many decades Spanish merchantmen and naval vessels continued to use charts bought from abroad.[17]

Spanish hydrography nevertheless made significant advances in the second half of the eighteenth century. Naval officers trained at the nautical school in Cádiz accurately charted large parts of the west and east coasts of Spanish

America, the Spanish islands in the Caribbean and the west coast of Africa during scientific expeditions in the 1770s, 1780s and 1790s.[18] In the mid-1780s, an expedition led by the director of the school, Vicente Tofiño, charted the entire coast of Spain itself as well as the Canary Islands, the Azores and the coast of North Africa. The results of Tofiño's team were published in the magnificent *Atlas maritimo de España* in 1789.[19] The original materials were stored in a newly created institute, the Depósito. Following up on these advances, a plan was proposed to the minister of the navy in 1792 to found a vast 'museo de Marina', which would house all the facilities needed for training personnel and the equipment of naval vessels, including workshops and stores of books, models, instruments and cartographic aids. Part of this design was realized a few years later, namely the hydrographic office. Starting with a staff of three in 1797, this *dirección hidrográfica* not only functioned as a storehouse but was also responsible for the printing of charts, maps and coastal views.[20]

In contrast to France, for many years, state agencies in Britain remained more or less aloof from the production or distribution of charts, atlases and other sorts of cartographic aids. From the 1740s onwards, the Admiralty did occasionally provide ships and personnel for carrying out hydrographical surveys, for example, by Murdoch Mackenzie in the Scottish isles, James Cook in the Saint Lawrence River and around Newfoundland, Joseph Desbarres in the coastal waters of New England and Nova Scotia and Thomas Hurd around Bermuda. Sometimes it actually subsidized cartographic publications, such as Desbarres's *The Atlantic Neptune*, which set a new standard of accuracy in mapping the eastern seaboard of North America in c. 1780. However, the repeated pleas of naval officers and others for the creation of a state-sponsored hydrographical department after the French example fell on deaf ears. The production and marketing of cartographic aids was largely left in the hands of private publishers, such as Mount & Page, Sayer & Bennett and Aaron Arrowsmith.[21] From the early 1780s onwards, the Hudson's Bay Company also assisted in this spread of knowledge, by finally sharing data from its surveys, native informants and traveller's accounts with cartographers and geographers in Britain. Arrowsmith's map of North America of 1795 was heavily reliant on information supplied by this trading company.[22]

Personal contact between French and British hydrographers and surveyors, meanwhile, became more frequent from the 1750s. Alexander Dalrymple, who became the first official hydrographer of the EIC in 1779, kept up a regular correspondence for many years with his colleagues D'Après de Mannevillette and Fleurieu at the Compagnie des Indes and the Dépôt, respectively. Between

1784 and 1788, a team led by William Roy, fellow of the Royal Society, on the British side and by the Cassinis on the French side carried out a triangulation between Greenwich and Paris, which allowed them to determine the relative positions of the observatories in the two places much more exactly than before.[23] British map-making experts were thus well aware of the state of the art in their field on other side of the Channel. Ironically, it was the outbreak of a new all-out war between Britain and France in the 1790s that finally convinced the naval authorities in Britain of the usefulness of creating a hydrographical office based on the model of the Dépôt. In August 1795, Dalrymple was appointed hydrographer to the Admiralty.[24] The Hydrographic Office collected existing manuscripts and foreign printed sources, but from 1800 it also engraved and printed its own charts. The first chart published by the new department was a plan of an island in Quiberon Bay. The imperial machine in Britain thus finally assumed a greater share in the production of charts. Nevertheless, the Hydrographic Office did not sell its products on the market and it outsourced some of its printing jobs to private firms.[25]

Commercial impulses long remained dominant in chart-making in the Dutch Republic. Apart from the long-established hydrographic office of the VOC, private publishers and booksellers, mainly based in Amsterdam, supplied the bulk of the cartographic aids for seafarers. One new development after 1730 was the growing share in the Dutch market of charts, atlases and pilot books imported from France or copied from French models. The Van Keulen firm in Amsterdam, for example, advertised the sale of a map of Saint-Domingue and Puerto Rico by Frezier (1733), a chart of the east coast of Martinique by 'a French sea captain, who had sailed and lived there for many years' (1758), and a map of North America based on French surveys (1777).[26]

Dutch naval authorities eventually took a leaf out of the French book: they concluded that the production and distribution of cartographic aids in the Netherlands could no longer be left entirely to market forces. In 1787, the Admiralty of Amsterdam established a committee, called the *Commissie tot de lengtebepaling op zee en de verbetering der zeekaarten betreffende* (Committee on the determination of longitude and the improvement of marine charts, or Longitude Committee for short), which, among other things, was charged with making a selection of the best available charts and making all necessary improvements therein for the benefit of seafarers in the navy and the merchant marine.[27]

The Longitude Committee, funded by the Amsterdam Admiralty, initially consisted of two scientists, Jan Hendrik van Swinden and Pieter Nieuwland, and a commercial publisher, Gerard Hulst van Keulen. Van Swinden was professor of philosophy, mathematics, physics and astronomy at the Athenaeum Illustre in Amsterdam, while Nieuwland was his most promising student, who would soon become lecturer in mathematics, astronomy and navigation at the same institute. Van Keulen, director of the Van Keulen firm, also held the post of hydrographer of the Amsterdam Chamber of the VOC and had a keen interest in the sciences and mathematical instruments.[28] In 1789, Jacob Florijn, who simultaneously served as examiner and teacher of navigation at the second most important naval agency in the Dutch Republic, the Admiralty of Rotterdam, joined the Commissie as a member-correspondent. After Nieuwland's premature death in 1794 and the creation of a centralized navy a year later, Florijn was promoted to become a full member. In a few years, the committee undertook a remarkable amount of work, although on a much more modest scale than the Dépôt in France or the hydrographic offices in Spain and Britain. Committee members studied numerous ships' journals, travel accounts, maps and plans of Dutch and foreign provenance in order to produce improved cartographic aids for seamen.[29] Unlike the Dépôt in France, however, the Commissie was not responsible for distributing its own publications. The risk of publishing the charts, books and other printed materials was assumed by Van Keulen, who, for his part, was assured of regular sales both to the Admiralties and to the VOC.[30] Unlike the hydrographic offices in Spain and Britain, moreover, the Dutch committee could not use fresh data collected on state-sponsored scientific expeditions to far-flung parts of the world, as such voyages were not undertaken by Dutch naval vessels before the end of the Napoleonic Wars.

In all seafaring countries in Europe, state agencies also took the lead in promoting the spread of the lunar distances method. The diffusion of this method for finding longitude crucially depended on the intervention of imperial machines. The key element was the regular publication of a nautical almanac that contained tables with the predicted distances between the moon, the sun and some other celestial body that could be observed at particular times at a given meridian. In Britain, a *Nautical Almanac* appeared under the aegis of the Royal Observatory in Greenwich from 1765 onwards. The Astronomer Royal set up a system of computers to calculate the tables and comparers to check the computers' work. The first year to which the almanac's tables referred was 1767.[31] As Guy Boistel has demonstrated, the *British Almanac* was probably an adaptation of the lunar tables computed by the French astronomer Nicolas-Louis de Lacaille, published in 1755. The French, in turn, first borrowed from the work done in Greenwich to complete lunar tables that were added to the *Connoissance des Temps* and then started to produce their own tables, reduced to the meridian of Paris, with the help of a computer based at the Observatoire Royale. After the Revolution, the computation and publication of the tables was assigned to the Bureau des Longitudes.[32] Spain boasted its own nautical almanac from 1791, too, with lunar tables based on the British model, but reduced to the meridian of Cádiz. An Oficina de Calculadores, affiliated with the observatory in Cádiz, was founded for this very purpose. The appearance of the Spanish almanac was accompanied by the publication of other treatises on methods for finding longitude, either as part of the almanac itself or in the form of separate books. José de Mendoza y Ríos included an explanation of new longitude methods in his *Tratado de navegación* of 1787.[33] In the Dutch Republic, the publication of a nautical almanac, and manuals explaining its use and methods for finding longitude in general, became – in addition to the improvement of charts – the principal task of the Longitude Committee. The Dutch almanac, published from 1788, was based on the British one, but recalculated for the meridian of Tenerife. The computation job was assigned to Nieuwland and Florijn. Van Swinden wrote a manual on the lunar distances method and a treatise on the construction and use of octants and sextants, published under the supervision of the committee in 1787 and 1788, respectively.[34]

Why did maritime powers in the Atlantic world by the end of the eighteenth century consider chart-making and the production of nautical almanacs to be affairs of state? Why did state agencies in all of these countries assume a coordinating role in these specific fields of knowledge? This change may be explained by a combination of two factors. First of all, both the general improvement of charts and the production of nautical almanacs required a sustained commitment to the collection and processing of large amounts of data, which no private entrepreneur or large organization outside the state was able, or willing, to provide. Even long-distance trading companies, such as the VOC or the Hudson's Bay Company, only earmarked resources for data collection in the region to which the charter of their own organization applied, or which lay en route to this destination. Second, state intervention in these fields of maritime knowledge was promoted by rivalries between seafaring imperial powers. Given the vital importance of accurate cartographic data and exact positioning methods for the deployment of naval power and the support of territorial claims, no state could afford to remain uninvolved, lest it run the risk of losing military and political competitiveness.

The case was different for nautical instruments. While instrument-making, just like the production of charts or almanacs, demanded a high level of skill, it did not involve a constant process of collecting and processing data. Access to a variety of raw materials, however, was an essential requisite. Copper, brass, glass and wood (especially ebony and mahogany) were the principal materials for making high-quality instruments in the early modern period. If skills and materials were sufficiently present and the size of demand was relatively large, state involvement in the manufacture of nautical instruments remained limited and production was largely left to the market. Governments only intervened when, for want of skills or materials, or because of inadequate demand, private domestic entrepreneurs did not offer instruments of the particular type or quality required by the navy, army or some other public agency, and imports were not considered a sufficient alternative to fill the gap.

In the eighteenth century, the widest range of instruments on offer in the Atlantic world could be found in London, Amsterdam and Paris. In these cities, people could buy almost any mathematical, navigational, optical or philosophical instrument they wanted at any time. The main differences were that exports of instruments from London and Amsterdam were larger than those from Paris, and that exports from London, in contrast with those from Amsterdam, were directed to the Americas as well as to the European continent.

Other regions in the Atlantic world were much more dependent on imports than Britain, the Dutch Republic or France. In North America, most mathematical, navigation, optical and philosophical instruments came from Britain until well into the nineteenth century, except items such as surveying compasses and, after *c.* 1770, electrostatic machines.[35] In the late eighteenth century, Spain depended equally heavily on imports from abroad for its supply of instruments. In the 1750s, the equipment of the newly founded observatory in Cádiz largely came from London.[36] The same applied to the astronomical and navigational instruments used in Malaspina's expedition nearly four decades later. Physical instruments for the expedition were ordered from Paris, but these did not arrive in Cádiz in time to be taken aboard.[37] In addition, Malaspina's ships carried two marine chronometers made by Ferdinand Berthoud, which belonged to the collection of the observatory at Cádiz.[38]

What leading centres of instrument-making such as London, Amsterdam and Paris had in common was not just the ability to attract talent from elsewhere,[39] but also the sheer amount and diversity of skills and knowledge that were formed and transmitted locally. On the one hand, there were many specialists who had mastered crafts such as grinding a lens, graduating a scale, cutting a setscrew or fine-tuning the working of a clock. On the other hand, these cities also had a considerable number of people who had a firm grasp of the physical and mathematical knowledge involved in making the most sophisticated navigational, optical or philosophical instruments. Sometimes these abilities were combined in a single person, such as Jesse Ramsden in London or Ferdinand Berthoud in Paris, but they could also appear more or less separately in different persons, who might join forces if the opportunity arose and circumstances gave them an incentive to do so. In the 1760s in Amsterdam, for example, Carl Bley and Jan van Deijl teamed up to make the first Dutch prototype of an achromatic telescope soon after the news of Dollond's invention had reached the Netherlands.[40] In other cities in the Atlantic world, such a critical mass of people with the range of abilities needed for making top-notch instruments did not yet exist. In colonial Philadelphia, the appearance of an instrument-maker-cum-scientist such as David Rittenhouse was clearly an exceptional phenomenon. It was precisely because of the rarity of his skills that the Assembly of Pennsylvania offered Rittenhouse a position in Philadelphia in 1770, so that he might 'inaugurate the manufacture of optical and mathematical instruments' in the city.

Moreover, instrument-makers in entrepôts of world trade such as London or Amsterdam normally enjoyed the advantage of ready access to all the materials they needed. London instrument-makers, for example, long had easy access to copper mined in Cornwall and Anglesey and brass made in Bristol, Flint and Cheshire. Bottlenecks in supply of copper and brass for instrument-making did not begin to occur until the end of the eighteenth century, when domestic copper production declined and a growing part of the output was bought up by large customers such as the Admiralty and the EIC.[41] In the 1770s, however, the Dutch entrepôt was still so well stocked that instrument-maker John Bird of London preferred to order a long brass bar for a mural quadrant in Oxford from a supplier in the Netherlands than to buy two smaller ones in Cheshire.[42]

Instrument-makers in the British American colonies, by contrast, were faced with a continuous scarcity of copper, brass, ebony and mahogany. In the eighteenth century, copper mining in the British American colonies was only carried out on a minor scale. In the 1790s, the newly established mint of the United States was even plagued by a severe shortage of copper. Brass was not produced on a large scale until domestic zinc mining started in the 1830s. There were imports of metals and woods from Britain before the nineteenth century, but transport from overseas naturally led to higher costs for American producers. Glass fit for optical instruments was not produced in America until after the 1780s.[43] As a consequence of this relative scarcity of resources, American instrument-makers worked more in wood (native hardwoods included) than their counterparts in Britain or on the European continent, and hardly produced any optical instruments and some types of navigation instruments (such as sextants) until well into the nineteenth century.[44]

In response to the growth of demand for instruments, instrument-makers in England and the Dutch Republic introduced a change in the organization of production. Until the middle of the eighteenth century, instruments in London were normally made to order in a workshop at home. Small-scale production was the rule. When demand rapidly expanded from the 1750s onwards, according to Anita McConnell, 'major instrument makers responded ... by specialising either as retail suppliers of a wide range of small or medium sized apparatus, or as precision engineers, concentrating on the production of large apparatus to order, supplemented by retail sales'.[45] While in the former case production usually remained spread over a variety of small workshops, in the latter case production was increasingly concentrated in a large establishment at a single location. Subcontracting could occur in both cases, but in the latter variant the emphasis lay much more on the division of labour within the workshop than on the division of labour between workmen at different sites. The finest example of such scaling up of production was the firm run by Jesse Ramsden. Ramsden created an interlocked set of workshops near St. James's Churchyard in the 1770s and 1780s, where he probably employed forty to fifty workers at the same time. He also developed a dividing engine to graduate his instruments more speedily and accurately.[46]

Subcontracting in instrument-making developed in eighteenth-century Holland too. The Van Musschenbroek firm in Leiden, for example, employed only a few people in its own workshop, but it had specific parts of instruments made by specialists such as glass-blowers, clockmakers, painters and carpenters at other sites in Leiden and elsewhere.[47] It is not unlikely that the biggest producer of navigation instruments in Amsterdam, the Van Keulen firm, made use of subcontracting as well. Between 1731 and 1748 Johannes van Keulen supplied the staggering number of 1,148 cross-staffs to the VOC alone. In addition, the firm also sold cross-staffs to many other clients, as well as back-staffs, compasses and mathematical aids. From 1744 onwards, Van Keulen made octants as well, and from about 1780 the firm added sextants to the range of instruments on offer.[48] Like London, Amsterdam in the late eighteenth century saw a scaling up of production in instrument-making. In *c.* 1780, Van Keulen installed a copy of Ramsden's dividing machine in his workshop. In 1791, Van Keulen obtained a patent for a dividing engine of his own design, which he put to use shortly afterwards. The total number of sextants made under Van Keulen's supervision has been estimated at 500.[49] Also in Amsterdam, in 1781 Jan Marten Kleman founded a 'factory' for making mathematical, optical and physical instruments, which in 1806 had a workforce of thirty people. After the Napoleonic Wars, Kleman landed a contract for supplying sextants to the Dutch Navy.[50]

Subcontracting among instrument-makers also took place in contemporary Paris. However, Anthony Turner has argued that 'guild restrictions in the mid-18th century came to weigh increasingly heavily on the luxury trades of Paris', because corporations 'disputed the rights of one another's members to engage in particular types of manufacture, restricted the size of workshops, and decreed what materials and methods could be use'. These restrictions were especially crippling for instrument-makers, Turner argued, as their 'activities crossed and re-crossed the boundaries of different trades'.[51] Major changes to the organization of production were not carried out until the entire corporate edifice had been swept away by the French Revolution.

In late eighteenth-century Spain, skilled instrument-makers were a much rarer species than in other major seafaring nations. The size of demand for nautical instruments was smaller as well. In contrast with the successful training programme in maritime cartography, efforts to improve domestic capacity in instrument manufacture failed to bear fruit. On the order of the state, in the 1780s and 1790s young Spaniards were apprenticed to instrument-makers in Paris and London to learn the art of making and maintaining chronometers, reflecting circles and similar sophisticated nautical equipment, but none of them eventually practised the trade for more than a few years.[52] The instrument-making trade in Spain was hardly in a better shape after the end of the Napoleonic Wars. Although craftsmen in Barcelona and a few other port cities were able to produce sextants and octants by 1820, the lack of dividing engines and components such as coloured glasses made it hard to deliver reflecting instruments of the highest standard.[53]

Compared with other countries, Spain still showed the highest degree of state involvement in the instrument-making trade. In France, state agencies such as the navy and Académie des Sciences were supportive in the development of the first marine chronometers, but they did not directly intervene in the production of nautical instruments.[54] In Britain, demand from government agencies such as the Board of Longitude, the Greenwich Observatory and the Board of Ordnance provided a powerful incentive for improvements to the accuracy of instruments,[55] but it was not crucial for the growth of the instrument-making industry as such. The commercial output of marine chronometers, sextants and other reflecting instruments expanded on a massive scale from the 1770s onwards.[56] In the Netherlands, the production of precision nautical instruments did not depend on encouragement from the government, either. In 1806, the Amsterdam-based clockmaker Friedrich Knebel managed to construct the first Dutch timekeeper without any help, or incentive, from a state agency. A few dozen more chronometers left his workshop in the following decades.[57]

Among the major seafaring powers in the Atlantic world, nowhere did the interaction between different parts of the knowledge infrastructure in navigation technology and marine cartography become more intense than in France, faithfully reflecting the extremely sophisticated structure of its imperial machine. It was only in France that this interaction was given a regular, institutionalized basis after the mid-eighteenth century. Although this development originally started as a private initiative by a group of naval officers, it soon received state backing. An informal society of officers, which regularly convened in Brest from 1749 onwards, received recognition from the minister of the navy as an 'Académie de Marine' three years later. After an interruption due to the Seven Years' War, the institution was reorganized as the Académie royale de marine in 1769, which continued to exist until the general dissolution of academies ordered by the revolutionary regime in 1793.[58] This Académie was a learned society, dedicated to the exchange and advancement of maritime knowledge, and included almost every prominent expert in France active in the fields of navigation and cartography. Among its seventy odd members were staff members of the Dépôt of the Navy (such as Jacques-Nicolas Bellin) and its counterpart at the Compagnie des Indes in Lorient (led by Jean-Baptiste d'Après de Mannevillette), professors at the state-controlled navigation schools in Brest, Toulon and Rochefort (such as Pierre Bouguer), members of the Académie des Sciences (such as Henri-Louis Duhamel du Monceau and Joseph-Jérôme de Lalande) and naval officers knowledgeable about science (such as Jean-Charles de Borda and Charles-Pierre Claret de Fleurieu). Like its unofficial predecessor, the Académie continued to hold frequent meetings. Between 1769 and 1793, it convened on average thirty-two times a year.[59] The *académiciens* studied ships' journals, advised on new charts and books on navigation, evaluated new techniques and instruments (notably, for the determination of longitude at sea) and prepared a 'dictionnaire de marine'.[60] The Académie de Marine, in short, served as a mechanism that short-circuited and accelerated the circulation of nautical knowledge in France.

Compared with navigation technology, the growth of knowledge infrastructures in ship construction after 1730 was far less spectacular.

Nevertheless, shipbuilding increasingly became an object of concern among imperial machines. State agencies, especially in France and Spain, actively engaged in stimulating improvements in ship construction by creating new institutions for the accumulation and exchange of knowledge. France's early lead in this area was related to two particular factors. First of all, in the eighteenth century, French navy ships were almost exclusively built in government dockyards, and the master shipwrights who designed the king's vessels were nearly all state employees. Second, ever since Colbert's time, the French government had persistently promoted research into a mathematical approach to ship design, especially at the Académie des Sciences in Paris and at hydrography schools in a number of port cities. A series of conferences on ship construction was staged by Colbert at Versailles in the 1680s, and tests with hull models were made in Brest and Toulon. Professors at hydrography schools and *académiciens* such as Pierre Bouguer, Jean and Daniel Bernouilli, Leonhard Euler and Jean le Rond d'Alembert wrote profound theoretical studies on subjects such as calculating the displacement and stability of a ship, determining water resistance or understanding the movements of rolling and pitching. In the 1770s, *académiciens* conducted trials with ship models to test hydrodynamic theories. One of the highlights in the development of this mathematical approach to ship design came in the 1730s, when the notion of the 'metacentre' as a crucial element in determining the stability of a ship was first suggested.[61]

French naval administrators considered these theoretical contributions to be 'useful' knowledge for shipbuilders. From the 1740s, they encouraged improvements in ship construction by creating institutes for formal schooling, by assembling shipwrights together at royal dockyards in a newly established corps of naval engineers, introducing formal examinations as a requirement for promotion, and sponsoring the publication of textbooks and treatises that would make allegedly 'useful' theoretical insights easily accessible to ship constructors. A model text of this kind was the manual published in 1752 by the first director of the École des Ingénieurs-Constructeurs de la Marine, Henri-Louis Duhamel du Monceau, *Éléments de l'architecture navale*, which combined new ship construction theory, presented in a simplified fashion, with rules and principles based on best practice.[62]

For a brief period in the 1750s, when Jorge Juan headed naval shipbuilding in Spain, Spanish shipyards adopted some construction practices from England. Juan himself had been well acquainted with *construcción a la inglesa* since his espionage mission to Britain in 1749. During his tenure as supervisor of Spanish naval construction, dozens of shipwrights were recruited from the British Isles to Spain and Cuba.⁶³ For most of the time, however, France remained the leading model for shipbuilding in Spain. Following the French example, in the 1770s the Spanish authorities created a corps of naval engineers, founded an academy for the training of schooling of naval constructors and introduced formal rules for promotion.⁶⁴ Juan's own textbook on naval architecture, published in 1771, drew heavily on theoretical insights from France, too. French naval architects and scientists reciprocated by widely using and citing its French translation in their own classes and publications.⁶⁵

Historians have shown that the actual impact of this mathematical approach to ship design was nevertheless more modest than bureaucrats and scientists at the time believed. The idea that state support for scientific research was key to the French pre-eminence in building faster warships is largely based on the polemics of the Society for the Improvement of Naval Architecture in Britain, which was very active in the early years of the Revolutionary Wars.⁶⁶ In practice, French warships designed in the 1770s in accordance with the latest theoretical insights about stability proved to be too frail to be of much use at sea.⁶⁷ And in reality, it was the shipwrights, not the scientists, who made the difference in France. Shipbuilders in French naval yards professionalized over the course of the eighteenth century, both as a consequence of deliberate government policies aimed at enhancing the status of shipwrights and as an outcome of their own efforts. The knowledge that shipwrights in France employed was in fact based less on mathematical theory than on precepts derived from observations and experience accumulated over the years.⁶⁸ The introduction in c. 1740 of a new type of cruising warship, the frigate, which would become a conspicuous feature of all major navies in the later eighteenth century, was not a product of the science-oriented approach to ship design propagated from above, but the result of a flash of inspiration experienced by a practising ship constructor.⁶⁹ Besides, the quality of Spanish warships in the eighteenth century, especially those built in Havana, actually owed much to the superb properties of Cuban timber.⁷⁰

Shipbuilders and naval administrators outside France and Spain were not unaware of the developments in ship construction in the Bourbon-ruled states, if only because so many French and Spanish warships after 1740 were captured by the British. Although a large number of these prizes were incorporated into the British fleet, it almost never happened that the designs of particular foreign warships were copied exactly. Nicholas Rodger has pointed out that this would in fact have been hard to achieve, because the British had different practices of timbering and rigging and also had different requirements for the use of their vessels. Unlike the French ships, British warships 'were built to stand the strain of prolonged sea-time at all seasons, they were stored for long cruises, and they were built to fight. They were also built to last.'[71] These requirements would not easily have been satisfied by simply adopting French designs.

Neither in Britain nor in the Netherlands did the knowledge infrastructure for ship construction change substantially before 1800. Admittedly, the British surveyor of the navy *did* manage to put his stamp on the design of warships, notably during the tenure of Thomas Slade between 1755 and 1771. Slade's designs set the standard until the first decades of the nineteenth century.[72] At the same time, however, naval authorities for the building of ships continued to be heavily dependent on contracts with private yards, as the royal dockyards did not have enough labour and materials to expand their capacity rapidly in wartime. Shipyards themselves remained key sites for the accumulation and circulation of knowledge on ship construction.

A few changes in the construction process nevertheless occurred. The use of measured multi-view plans in ship design became standard practice in warship-building in Britain by the eighteenth century. 'In the mould lofts and drawing offices of the dockyards', Rodger has explained, British shipwrights at the time 'in most respects [received] as sophisticated' a training as their colleagues in France.[73] Moreover, like the French before them, some constructors in Britain tentatively made use of hull models in ship design. In the 1730s, shipwrights at the naval yard in Deptford determined, with the help of models, 'the new manner of building [of ships] from that shape which moved through the water with most ease'.[74]

The 'architectural tradition' in shipbuilding, in David McGee's words, was also adopted at the dockyards of the Rotterdam and Amsterdam Admiralties in the 1720s and 1730s, as well as those of the VOC from the 1740s onwards. Warships and East Indiamen were built to standardized dimensions in accordance with measured plans, drawn up before the keel was laid.[75] Pieter van Zwyndregt Pauluszoon, master shipwright at the Rotterdam dockyard in the 1750s, conducted a number of tests with models to improve the hull lines of his ship designs.[76]

The emerging mathematical approach to ship design also spawned the first attempts at theorizing about stowage. In these theories, stowage was conceived in a broad sense, namely as the art of placing and arranging everything on board – from the cargo and ballast to the masts and sails – as solidly and favourably as possible, in order to prevent damage and preserve the sailing qualities of the ship.[77] The Liverpool dock master (and former seaman) William Hutchinson remarked in 1777 that this subject urgently needed 'the labour of some of our greatest mathematicians, to account from fix'd principles, and give reasons, why ships, or the same ship, may be ... differently effected by stowage, so as to instruct seamen in this most important point of duty, because, success, as well as safety, may greatly depend on it'.[78] But the French mathematician Charles Bossut observed in 1761 that there was as yet no known rule for stowage at all. Everything was done the same way as it had been done a century before. It was all a matter of experience and tentative proceedings.[79] Tellingly, commanders of ships chartered by the VOC in the 1780s were reluctant to assume responsibility for the stowing of cargo for the return voyage from Batavia, because they were not acquainted with the weights and volumes of Asian products. Stowing should be done by somebody 'who had handled such matters more on several occasions', they argued.[80] In contrast to what the famous image of the stowage of the Liverpool slave ship *Brookes* around 1790 might suggest, stowage plans or 'stacking plans' were not a common phenomenon on slave ships, either. There is no evidence that prior to the voyage, captains of slave ships routinely drew up a plan 'through precise mathematical calculations' for the allotment of space to slaves.[81] The calculations for the 'stowage' plan of the *Brookes* were in fact made by a committee of abolitionists.[82]

Medical provision at sea clearly benefited from the expansion in knowledge infrastructures after 1730. It was no coincidence that quite a few of the authors of medical writings discussed earlier – such as Lind, Blane, Titsingh, Gonzalez or Poissonnier-Desperrières – were employed in a medical function by the navy, or held a position in some other institute concerned with the care of people at sea. All major maritime powers in the Atlantic world after 1730 saw a substantial expansion in hospitals, training facilities and regulations concerning the competence of medical personnel. This growth in infrastructure made it possible to collect, process, certify and transmit knowledge on the causes, prevention and cure of diseases on board more systematically and continuously than ever before. Imperial and commercial machines were important driving forces in this process.

The most complex knowledge infrastructure was developed under the aegis of the imperial machine in France. As a follow-up to the creation of naval hospitals and the introduction of a comprehensive 'regulatory regime' in the general ordinance of 1689, schools of medicine and surgery, linked to hospitals, were established in Rochefort, Toulon and Brest between 1722 and 1731. *Médecins de la marine* and *chirurgiens de la marine* were appointed to supervise medical care in the hospitals, serve as medical experts at sea and in the colonies and give instruction in the medical and surgical schools. The Rochefort School had no fewer than 30 surgeons and about 100 junior surgeons during the Seven Years' War. Additional regulations were introduced in the post-war era. The curricula at the three schools were standardized, and specific rules were laid down for the frequency and contents of the exams for surgeons. By the later eighteenth century, there was definitely something like a 'corps' of medical officers in the French navy. The build-up of the imperial medical hierarchy after the Seven Years' War culminated with the creation of supervisory functions for the whole fleet and the colonies, the *inspecteur* and *directeur general de la médecine de la marine et des colonies* (in 1764) and an *inspecteur des hôpitaux de la marine et des colonies* (in 1775).[83] Both functions were informally linked to other institutions of the French 'colonial machine'. Pierre-Isaac Poissonnier and his brother Antoine, who held these supervisory positions until the Revolution, were also very active members of the Société Royale de Médecine, which at the end of the eighteenth century became the foremost centre of the circulation of medical knowledge in the French Atlantic.[84]

The elaborate structure of the medical organization in France did not guarantee, however, that medical care on French men-of-war actually functioned better than on vessels belonging to other countries. In his bestselling manual of 1767, Antoine Poissonnier-Desperrières voiced the opinion that most naval surgeons in France were not very well qualified for the job and received promotion too easily. He rated leading British naval surgeons higher than French ones, although he also thought that France did not lack excellent surgeons ashore, notably in Paris. In his view, the exam and promotion system to improve the quality of the medical staff in the navy was urgent need of reform.[85]

Bourbon Spain followed the French example at a distance. The centre of change was the port of Cádiz. In 1718, the surgeon general of the navy, Juan de Lacomba, took over the directorate of the largest hospital in the city, the Real Hospital, from the religious order that had managed the institution since the 1670s, the Orden de San Juan de Dios. From 1728, the new director organized an in-house training programme for the staff, including compulsory attendance at anatomical lessons delivered in a newly founded anatomical theatre. Next, in 1748 the navy established a school in the hospital, dedicated to educating surgeons for the fleet. The courses at the Real colegio de cirugía, which were concluded with a formal exam, aimed to give surgeons both an extensive training in practical skills and a thorough grounding in theory. A grant programme, which enabled students from Cádiz to complete their training in London, Paris or Leiden, was introduced, too.[86] The *colegio* in Cádiz became the model for similar schools for army surgeons in Barcelona and civilian surgeons in Madrid. The state-controlled infrastructure in Cádiz itself was further extended in 1756 with the foundation of a hospital in the local naval yard, which added another 250 beds to the over 1,000 beds provided by the Real Hospital.[87] No wonder that the overview of naval medicine published in 1805 was written by a professor at the *colegio* in Cádiz, Pedro Maria Gonzalez.[88]

Britain showed a somewhat different pattern. If British naval surgeons by the 1760s were truly as skilful as Poissonnier-Desperrières believed, this was not due to a high degree of state intervention in their training or in testing of their competence. State-sponsored schools for the education of naval surgeons like those in France did not exist in Britain, and the examination of naval surgeons remained the privilege of the Surgeons' Company until the end of the eighteenth century. Warrants for surgeons to practise on naval vessels were issued by the Navy Board. It was not until 1796 that the Sick and Hurt Board finally managed to take over these tasks. At the same time, this state agency was transformed from a mainly administrative body into a department dominated by medical experts.[89] On the other hand, sea surgeons meanwhile managed to improve their professional knowledge on their own. Even before the middle of the eighteenth century, it was not unusual for surgeons in the Royal Navy to take a medical degree at the University of Edinburgh, Glasgow or Aberdeen before being examined by the Surgeons' Company. James Lind did exactly that before entering the navy as a surgeon's mate in 1739.[90] More and more students enrolled in independent schools of surgery after an Act of Parliament of 1745 lifted the ban on private dissection.[91] By the end of the century, 'an increasing number of prospective medical practitioners' benefited from 'the growing opportunities for formal medical instruction' offered not just by universities but also in teaching hospitals in London, Edinburgh, Dublin and Glasgow, in medical colleges and in private lectures.[92]

The most significant initiative on the part of the British state to improve medical care for seamen was the establishment of naval hospitals. Faced with growing numbers of sick and wounded after the renewed outbreak of war in 1739, the Admiralty finally decided to replace the old system of temporarily contracting for beds in civilian hospitals and private lodgings by accommodating seamen in permanent naval hospitals supervised by the Sick and Hurt Board. A huge hospital in Portsmouth, known as 'Haslar', was built between 1746 and 1761; another one opened in Plymouth at the end of the Seven Years' War. Haslar could accommodate 1,800 patients, Plymouth almost 1,000.[93] Although these state-run hospitals, unlike those in France, did not house a school of medicine and surgery, they did have a permanent staff of physicians, surgeons and apothecaries, who had ample opportunity to make observations and compile statistics about diseases, injuries and treatments. The work of James Lind, senior physician at Haslar between 1758 and 1783, shows that the creation of this new hub substantially aided the accumulation of knowledge, in addition to the collection, registration and dissemination of data by surgeons and physicians serving on vessels at sea, culminating in surveys by Gilbert Blane or Thomas Trotter.[94] Moreover, some ships in fleets or squadrons were assigned by the Navy Board to serve as hospital ships.[95]

In the Netherlands, the education and examination of sea surgeons long continued to be a decentralized, local affair. Surgeons commonly received their training with masters under the supervision of the local surgeons' guild. In some places, they were also obliged to attend public lecturers on anatomy delivered by a professor or lecturer paid by the urban government. In 1749, the Admiralty of Amsterdam arranged that during the winter months, its medical staff would henceforth offer a regular course on surgical practice for naval surgeons and other surgeons who intended to enter the navy's service.[96] The urban government of Amsterdam strictly upheld the rule that surgeons who intended to sail on a whaler or a merchant ship had to sit an exam in the presence of board members from the surgeons' guild, in accordance with regulations issued by the local authorities, and Rotterdam's government introduced a similar instruction in 1735.[97] Surgeons who wished to enlist on a naval vessel or an East Indiaman were, as usual, required to prove their competence before examiners appointed by an Admiralty or a Chamber of the VOC.

Meanwhile, the body of certified knowledge showed some measure of convergence due to the sheer size of Amsterdam as a pool of employment for seafaring surgeons. The best-known manuals for sea surgeons in the middle of the eighteenth century were written by authors from Amsterdam, Abraham Titsingh and Joannes Daniel Schlichting. As the examiner of surgeons at the Admiralty of Amsterdam, Titsingh was in a unique position to bring together a wealth of data and observations on medical care at sea, based on his own experience and on reports by other surgeons.[98] In 1734, the Amsterdam-based physician and surgeon Joannes Daniel Schlichting published a revised version of a textbook originally composed by Johannes Verbrugge in the 1670s to prepare candidates for an exam as a sea or army surgeon, which he enriched with plentiful notes on anatomy and surgical and medical practice. Schlichting's book was praised by the Amsterdam surgeons' guild as 'the most useful manual for young surgeons' and reached its tenth edition in 1768.[99]

Central state agencies became more directly involved in medical care at the end of the eighteenth century. Like the British navy, when caring for seamen ashore, the Dutch Navy made a transition from a contract system to a system of state-run hospitals. The immediate cause was likewise the outbreak of a major war, followed by a wave of epidemic disease in the fleet. The first naval hospitals opened in Enkhuizen and Hellevoetsluis during the Fourth Anglo-Dutch War (1780–4). During the next war with Britain, which started in 1795, the medical staff in these hospitals was enlarged and the provisional establishment in Hellevoetsluis was relocated to a permanent building in Rotterdam, which could accommodate some 700–800 patients. Both institutions developed into training grounds for naval surgeons and centres of accumulation of medical knowledge.[100] A single board of examiners was established for all naval surgeons and the entire medical staff of the navy was, as in France, eventually placed under the supervision of one director, a 'Doctor-Generaal'.[101]

Self-organized networks and the circulation of maritime knowledge

Self-organization contributed to the increasing circulation of maritime knowledge, too. Self-organized networks functioned as channels of knowledge about navigation, ships, medical care and the maritime environment. As before, cross-Atlantic networks of maritime knowledge after 1730 expanded and operated both inside and outside the imperial, religious and commercial machines. In this period, the exchange of knowledge across imperial borders and between different social networks became *more*, not *less*, common than before.

The period after 1730 saw the continued growth of the 'scholarly Atlantic': a Republic of Letters on an intercontinental scale. The principles of the Republic of Letters likewise underlay scholarly networks of knowledge in the North Atlantic in the eighteenth century. Although relations between 'colonials' in the Americas and 'metropolitans' in Britain and Continental Europe may initially have been unequal,[102] such connections could nevertheless be beneficial for both. For colonials, being a valued supplier of specimens and information in regular correspondence with established scholars in Britain or Continental Europe served as a mark of distinction and provided admission to a wider scholarly world. For metropolitans, engaging in correspondence with colonials not only provided a useful source of 'raw materials' for their own work but also enhanced their status among fellow members of the scholarly world: the more clients and admirers, the higher they rose.[103]

These correspondence networks cut across different imperial spaces. In the eighteenth century, exchanges across political or cultural borders in the Atlantic world were not as difficult as some historians have claimed.[104] Relationships developed not just between actors based in Britain, the continent and the British American colonies but also between American colonials or European continentals and people living in South America, notably in Dutch Guiana. By the end of the 1740s, networks of knowledge between correspondents in the Dutch Republic and the British American colonies were, judging by the frequency of contact, almost as highly developed as those between American colonists and learned men in England.

By the end of the eighteenth century, self-organizing networks of knowledge began to assume more specialized, institutionalized forms. Aside from general associations such as the Royal Society and local 'literary and philosophical societies', there arose new, discipline-focused organizations. The prime example was the Linnean Society, founded in London 1788 and granted a charter in 1802, which devoted itself exclusively to the 'cultivation of the science of natural history in all its branches'. Although most of its 300-odd members were British, the society also had some eighty members from abroad, based in France, Germany, Spain, Italy, the Netherlands and other countries on the European continent. A doctor from Philadelphia, Benjamin Smith Barton, also featured on the first membership list.[105]

Networks of knowledge could also emerge more or less spontaneously from encounters between people from different social networks. Benjamin Franklin's pioneering chart of the Gulf Stream, for example, was a result of his role as a go-between between different groups in the British Atlantic that were not normally in contact with each other. Franklin wrote that he got the information for his chart from 'a very intelligent mariner of the island of Nantucket', Captain Timothy Folger, who in his turn had learned from local whalers that 'the whales are generally found near the edges of the Gulph Stream, as strong current so called which comes out of the Gulph of Florida, passing northeasterly along the coast of America, and the[n] turning off most easterly running at the rate of 4, 3 ½, 3 and 2 ½ miles an hour'.[106] Franklin subsequently used his contact with officials and tradesmen in London to bring the knowledge on the current gathered by seamen into wider circulation, by making the Gulf Stream visible in a printed chart.

A similar cross-cutting network aided the circulation of knowledge about another marine phenomenon relevant to the improvement of shipping: the effects of pouring oil on water. In an essay published in the *Philosophical Transactions* in 1774, Franklin reported how, during a voyage with the British fleet headed for an assault on Louisbourg (Cape Breton) in 1757, he had observed that the wakes of two ships were smoother than the others. When asking the captain for the reason, he was told that the phenomenon must have been caused by the greasy water emptied into the sea by the ships' cooks. Later remembering that he had once come across a remark in Pliny's *Natural History* that 'everybody is aware that … all sea water is made smooth by oil', Franklin resolved, during his stay in England in the 1760s and 1770s, to find out more about the effects of stilling waves with oil by carrying out a number of experiments in London and elsewhere. Furthermore, he acquired some first- and second-hand accounts on the smoothing effects of oil observed by seamen or fishermen, including a letter written by an official from the VOC. From these data, Franklin concluded that oil could under certain conditions be usefully employed to diminish the ripples created by wind, still the waves and enhance the safety of ships and crews.[107]

The next phase of the story took place in the Dutch Republic. One of Franklin's experiments in London was witnessed by three acquaintances with a Dutch background, namely Count Willem Bentinck, one of the most powerful noblemen in Holland and a member of the governing board of Leiden University, his son John Bentinck, a captain in the British navy, and Jean Allamand, professor of mathematics and philosophy in Leiden. After returning to the Netherlands, Allamand repeated Franklin's experiments in a canal in Leiden in the presence of a number of friends: a retired naval captain, a natural philosopher and a merchant and cloth manufacturer, Frans van Lelyveld.[108] Van Lelyveld then gave the debate a further twist by inquiring among friends, acquaintances and other interested persons scattered all over the maritime provinces of the Dutch Republic whether they knew anything about the practice of smoothing waves with the use of oil or a similar substance. In 1775, he published a 200-page treatise containing all of their replies and reports, plus translations of a selection of writings on the topic by 'the very famous English philosopher Benj. Franklin'. A French translation appeared a few years later.[109] The most important finding from this exercise was that the practice of smoothing waves with oil turned out to be common knowledge among various groups of seamen and fishermen in Holland and in many other parts of the world, although groups in different localities were often unaware of its practice in other places. Knowledge on this subject *did* exist, but it was localized until Franklin, Allamand and Van Lelyveld brought it into wider circulation.

Self-organized networks of scholars, seamen and administrators within Britain and the Netherlands also began to concern themselves with issues of ship construction and nautical education. In Britain in *c.* 1760, the Society for the Encouragements of Arts, Manufacture and Commerce ran a series of trials with towed ship models in water tanks, attended by a number of officers of the Royal Navy. In 1791, naval administrators, shipyard owners, fellows of the Royal Society and other self-declared experts in the theory of ship design founded the Society for the Improvement of Naval Architecture, which aimed to reform work practices in dockyards. Some 1,700 experiments with hull models were conducted under the aegis of the society in the following years; the data from these trials, however, were not published in full until 1834.[110]

A learned society in the Dutch Republic likewise concerned itself with matters of ship construction. In 1777–8, the Zeeuwsch Genootschap der Wetenschappen, the governing board of which included several VOC directors, organized a prize competition on the question of which ships would be 'the most suitable, useful and most profitable' for the VOC. Answers to the question had to consider draught and manoeuvrability as well as safety, health and carrying capacity. The jury consisted of three skippers, a physician and two rear admirals from the Admiralty of Zeeland. The prizes for the best essays, which argued for a new type of ship, the three-decker, were awarded to a surgeon and a master shipwright.[111]

Furthermore, the period between 1730 and 1800 also saw the rise of a new kind of local association of seamen that would become a crucially important carrier in the circulation of knowledge about the maritime environment: namely, the shipmasters' society. Shipmasters' societies originally emerged in the eighteenth century as separate insurance associations for masters (and sometimes mates). While some of these associations were actually offshoots of general seamen's associations or developed out of long-established organizations such as fraternities or skippers' guilds, others were entirely new foundations. In 1738 and 1756, for example, a number of masters who had just seceded from the old Sea Box founded the Shipmasters' Society and the Friendly Society of

Shipmasters in Bo'ness, Scotland. In Amsterdam, a new shipmasters' society, called the 'Blaauwe Vlag', was founded in 1795.[112]

'Marine societies' of shipmasters multiplied rapidly in North American ports after 1740, including Boston, Salem, Marblehead, Newburyport, Newport, Portland, New York and Philadelphia.[113] The purpose of these societies was to relieve 'indigent and distressed shipmasters, their widows and orphans' and 'to make navigation safer'. Their membership was composed of active or past masters of merchantmen, wherever they sailed.[114] An exception was the Salem East India Marine Society, founded in 1799, which only admitted masters or supercargoes from Salem who had navigated the seas beyond Cape Horn of the Cape of Good Hope.[115] The marine societies of Newburyport and Salem described their aim of promoting the safety of navigation in more specific terms, such as to 'gain knowledge of the various ports and unknown seas, winds, currents, courses and distances' or 'communicating their observations, inwards and outwards, of the variation of the needle, soundings, courses and distances, and all other remarkable things about it, in writing, to be lodged with the Society'.[116] In practice, early efforts at the improvement of navigation concentrated on the organization of pilotage and the building and maintenance of lighthouses, beacons and buoys near port entrances. The Salem marine society petitioned the US Congress time and again about the matter in the 1790s.[117] The East India Marine Society distinguished itself by formulating two more ambitious objectives. The society aimed to collect facts and observations for the benefit of 'the improvement and security of navigation', by issuing 'blank journals' to its members in which 'all things worthy of notice' during a voyage could be recorded, which upon their return would be deposited with the society. Additionally, 'natural and artificial curiosities' gathered on voyages beyond Cape Horn and the Cape of Good Hope would be placed in a museum to be established in the society's meeting hall. The circulation of knowledge was thus an important goal of this association from the very beginning.[118]

Although common sailors did not yet develop permanent, formal organizations on a par with shipmasters' societies, as we have seen, they *did* have networks of an informal, 'bottom-up' nature. Through these informal, self-organized networks, they could exchange knowledge within and beyond centralized organizations such as navies and trading companies. And by accumulating and circulating knowledge in this way, they also had an impact on medical care on board. Rebecca Earle has shown, for example, that the diet on British navy ships in the eighteenth century was determined by ideas held not only by the Victualling Board (charged with the supervision of naval provisioning since 1683) and medical authorities but also by the views of officers and crews themselves about what constituted 'nutritious food'. What was the rate of exchange between butter and sweetened rice? How much sugar or cocoa was equivalent to one pound of butter? Decisions on such matters were not merely a top-down affair. Common seamen in the Royal Navy also had a say on the kind and quantity of food that was supplied on board. In practice, the food regime on naval vessels was based on 'constant micro-negotiations, in which ordinary sailors maintained a tense but ongoing dialogue with representatives of the state'.[119]

Other groups of seamen in the Atlantic world exchanged information in self-organized networks, too. Jeffrey Bolster has shown that many enslaved Africans sailed the Atlantic waters as seafarers themselves. Slaves in the British West Indies and the North American colonies were routinely employed as fishermen or boatmen on coastal and inter-island sea trips, but they also worked as sailors on long-distance voyages on a regular basis. Slave mariners travelled as crew members on British or American ships across the ocean between Jamaica, Charleston, the Chesapeake and London. Maritime slavery became an important phenomenon in slave colonies in the later eighteenth and early nineteenth centuries. On the Bahama Islands or Nevis in the West Indies, more than 10 per cent of all slaves were employed in some maritime activity by the 1830s.[120]

Like Franklin's network of correspondents and informants, this extensive web of connections between maritime slaves served as a convenient channel for the exchange of knowledge and skills. Some enslaved mariners brought the skills that they had acquired as boatmen on the west coast of Africa to the other side of the Atlantic. African maritime traditions also left an imprint on the practice of boat-building in the Caribbean and the coastal areas of North America. According to Bolster, small craft commonly used in the Americas, such as pettiaugers and canoes, can be seen as a kind of fusion between African, Amerindian and European techniques.[121] Africans, Afro-Americans, Amerindians and Europeans also became involved in self-organized networks that exchanged of knowledge on medical care across the Atlantic. White doctors and surgeons in European settlements overseas slowly became more familiar with African, Afro-American and Amerindian medical cultures. Although, according to Richard Sheridan, 'very few' European medical men in the British sugar colonies in the West Indies 'conformed to [the] ideal' of trying 'to learn the folk wisdom of the blacks, study their herbal remedies, and search out indigenous plants that have medicinal value', contact between African and European medical cultures nevertheless became more frequent.[122] Even if whites were seldom prepared to credit individual blacks or Amerindians as sources of knowledge about plants, herbs, drugs or medical practice,[123] they *did* show interest in borrowing information.[124]

The premier site of contact was that of private slave hospitals on plantations, which – in British American colonies at least – became more common after the middle of the eighteenth century. In slave hospitals, encounters between white doctors and black assistants and attendants became more or less a matter of routine. While white doctors acted as supervisors and gave instructions for treatment, male and female black personnel took care of the patients. In doing so, they also used practices and herbal remedies that formed part of the medical culture transmitted from Africa and adapted in the American colonies.[125] Europeans also became acquainted with African medical practices through contact with practitioners in Africa itself. The surgeon David Henri Gallandat from Flushing, who had sailed on a Dutch slave ship himself, claimed that he had personally observed native African practitioners curing dysentery and diarrhoea with guajava roots, simarouba and other *simplicia* that could be found on the coast of Guinea.[126]

French doctors, surgeons and missionaries in Canada, Guiana and Louisiana learned remedies for snake bites, leprosy and dysentery from Native Americans. They also noted details about 'slave medicines' to counter poisons and about the uses of plants to cure diseases in native African practice.[127] For their part, Africans in Spanish America may have borrowed practices from other medical cultures, including Amerindian ones, on sites such as hospitals and pharmacies and Spanish households, 'where Indians and Africans laboured side by side'.[128]

Finally, after 1730 self-organized networks expanded into distant regions in the North-West Atlantic, which likewise contributed to the growth of the circulation of knowledge. As European missionaries, seamen and traders came to Greenland and the Davis Strait in greater numbers and for longer periods of time, Europeans and Inuit met each other more often and exchanges of knowledge occurred more frequently than before. One new, eager actor in the missionary field was the Moravian Society for the Furtherance of the Gospel among the Heathen, commonly called the 'Moravians' or 'Herrnhutters'. The Moravian movement was an outgrowth of the pietist strand in Lutheranism that assumed a distinct organizational identity in the 1720s, although in contrast to religious machines, it was not established or chartered by a higher sovereign authority. Headquartered in Herrnhut, Saxony, the movement soon began to develop missionary activities in the Atlantic world. Moravian volunteers, mostly recruited from Germany, established a far-flung network of mission stations in the orbit of the Danish, Dutch and British empires. Starting in the Danish West Indies and Greenland in the early 1730s, the Moravians expanded their activities to Suriname and the Cape of Good Hope a few years later, and further extended their network in the British West Indies, Newfoundland and Labrador in the mid-eighteenth century.[129]

As the number of mission stations increased, so did communication across the Atlantic, and not just about religious and organizational matters. Self-sufficiency in food production was a key part of Moravian ideology. Thus, the newly created networks also began to carry all sorts of information about flora and fauna across the Atlantic. Herrnhutters brought plants and animals from Europe to missions overseas, learned about indigenous botanical traditions and spread knowledge about natural history from places in the Americas to botanical gardens and collections in Europe.[130] A vast amount of knowledge about Greenland's nature and the society and languages of the Inuit collected at mission stations over the years was published in the multi-volume *Historie von Grönland* by the Moravian David Cranz in Leipzig in the late 1760s, which was soon translated into English and Dutch.[131]

In East Greenland and the Davis Strait, a lively barter trade sprung up between European whalers and Inuit. Axes, timber, coloured textiles, tobacco, firearms and metal utensils were exchanged for furs, skins and salmon. A small number of European traders settled permanently in Greenland with the permission of the Danish king. A few Inuit are known to have travelled to Europe on board Danish, Dutch and German ships.[132] In the later eighteenth century, relations between Europeans and Inuit were increasingly based on mutual trust. Conflicts were rare, and if they occurred they were peacefully resolved.[133]

Whalers were impressed by the Inuit's intimate knowledge of the maritime environment. 'Males are very experienced in the knowledge of movements of the ice, the winds and the weather', a Dutch seaman observed in 1777, adding: 'this holds to that extent that one can safely rely on their predictions (Figure 5).'[134] The light, fast-moving boats made from wooden or whalebone frames covered with sealskins, which Greenlanders used for transport or for hunting whales and seals, also aroused the interest of Europeans. The large ones, called 'umiaks' or 'women's boats', which could carry fourteen persons or more, were sometimes hired by European whalers as a substitute for whale-boats, along with Inuit crews. The small ones, called 'kayaks', which carried one or two persons, were much sought after as a kind of souvenir.[135] Inuit were masters in making sealskin water

Figure 5 An Inuit and his canoe, pictured in Cornelis Gijsbertsz. Zorgdrager, *Bloeijende opkomst der aloude en hedendaagsche Groenlandsche visschery* (The Hague 1727²). Het Scheepvaartmuseum, Amsterdam.

proof. They used this technique, one that was 'peculiar to themselves', not only to produce superior coverings for their boats but also, as Europeans did not fail to note, to make clothing that provided human beings with perfect protection in all conditions. 'The jackets and trousers made of skin by the Esquimaux', William Scoresby remarked, 'are in great request among the whale-fishers for preserving from oil and wet.'[136]

Conclusion

Capabilities and limitations

How and to what extent did the balance between capabilities and limitations for the development of maritime knowledge change between 1730 and 1800? I would argue that capabilities showed a striking advance. The techniques, instruments and resources to collect, classify and interpret data and to reproduce and transmit information improved in many respects, a point that is perfectly illustrated by the long-range voyages launched from Britain, France and Spain in the later eighteenth century. These scientific expeditions were remarkable not only for their scale, frequency and geographical range but also for the sheer amount and sophistication of the techniques, instruments and other facilities at the disposal of their commanders. James Cook, for example, carried a copy of Harrison's marine chronometer number 4 made by Larcum Kendall. Louis-Antoine de Bougainville had a new distillation machine designed by Pierre-Isaac Poissonnier on board.[1] The Spanish empire in the late eighteenth century truly functioned as a productive 'image-making machine'. The dozens of Spanish scientific expeditions sent overseas after 1760 yielded thousands of illustrations, objects and written reports and accounts, 'so that imperial nature could be collected, classified, transported, and seen both locally and across distances'. Alejandro Malaspina employed no fewer than nine specialized artists on his voyages, in addition to the naval officers who drew maps and charts.[2] The increase in capabilities was thus striking indeed.

First of all, techniques for systematically gathering and assessing evidence underwent further refinement. Stephen Hales and Sébastien-François Morogues, for example, substantiated arguments about the pollution of air and the benefits of using ventilators by making calculations on human exhalation in closed spaces and the quantities of air displaced by the newly invented types of bellows.[3] In 1747, James Lind analysed the effectiveness of various suggested cures for scurvy by comparing six pairs of similar patients. In addition to their normal diet, each received something different to eat or drink. The result of the test was,

Lind concluded, that those who had taken oranges and lemons recovered faster than the others.[4] Following Lind's approach, in 1783 the surgeon Thomas Trotter conducted an experiment on a slave ship to study the effectiveness of different fruits as anti-scorbutics. During this experiment, he divided nine slaves into three groups. The first group received limes three times a day, the second one was given green guavas and the third ripe guavas. While the slaves in the first and second groups recovered, those in the third group hardly got better. Trotter used the outcome of the trial to make the point that 'ripe fruits, that [had] lost their acidity' had less therapeutic value than fresh ones.[5]

From the mid-eighteenth century onwards, the statistical approaches pioneered by VOC director Van Collen in the 1690s were also applied more frequently. In the 1750s, James Lind collected data about temperatures in different places in the Atlantic World between Jamaica and 80 degrees north by sending 'the same thermometer abroad with careful persons'.[6] As *inspecteur* and *directeur general de la medicine de la marine et des colonies* in France between 1764 and 1791, Pierre-Isaac Poissonnier compiled (with the aid of standard printed forms) detailed statistics on diseased persons in the French navy to determine systematically which crews fell sick and which did not.[7] As the physician to the fleet during the American War of Independence, Gilbert Blane put together summary tables of morbidity and mortality in different navy hospitals across the Atlantic Ocean between 1780 and 1783.[8]

Furthermore, instrument historians have shown that measurement devices in the later eighteenth century became more accurate, more varied and more plentiful than before. Advances were not only made in the production of sextants, octants, telescopes and chronometers but also in the manufacture of balances, barometers, thermometers, hygrometers, electrometers and other sorts of mathematical, optical and philosophical instruments. Advances in instrument-making were supported by the design of new tools to make better and more accurate instruments, such as dividing engines for making graduations, pyrometers to measure degrees of expansion or contraction, and vitrometers to measure the dispersive power of different pieces of glass.[9]

Descriptions and assessments of improvements in instrument-making were circulated by means of journals, periodicals and books. Instruments and instrument-makers featured regularly in the *Philosophical Transactions*.[10] General journals, as the Dutch *Vaderlandse Letter-oefeningen*, also published accounts on newly designed instruments, such as electrometers.[11] In 1778, Van Swinden wrote an extensive report on all sorts of thermometers as an aid to assess and compare data obtained with different instruments.[12]

Controlled tests to assess the performance of new inventions under realistic conditions at sea became much more common. Systematic trials of new cures for diseases, for example, were conducted under the auspices of the Sick and Hurt Board of the Royal Navy.[13] The ventilators made by Hales and Sutton were tried out on British naval ships in *c.* 1750. Experiments with Poissonnier's distillation machine were held on French naval vessels and on Dutch VOC ships sailing from Batavia to the Netherlands in the 1760s and 1770s.[14] Several innovations in ship construction at the VOC were adopted after a step-wise process of decision making, which took account of expert opinions and actual experiences at sea, as well as of variations in shipbuilding practices and environmental conditions in different regions of the Netherlands. A new design for *retourschepen*, for example, which featured three closed decks instead of a main deck with a waist between the forecastle and the campaign, was first accepted by the board of directors as an potential solution in 1780 after a series of experiments, during which the impact of this innovation on the stability of the ship in shallow waters, safety on the high seas, the health of crews and the amount of space for storing commodities were carefully scrutinized. It was made compulsory for all company yards in 1793, when the directors concluded that the new design had proven superior over the old.[15] Copper sheathing became standard practice for all newly built VOC *retourschepen* in 1794, after 'test runs' at sea by ships from selected company yards and the assessment of evidence from other organizations (such as the EIC) had shown the advantages of the new technique.[16]

The merits of this cautious, balanced empirical approach[17] stand out clearly when compared with the high cost of rash decision making in the Royal Navy during the War of the American Revolution. The coppering of the entire British fleet was rushed through during the war in a 'centralizing drive' by the Controller of the Navy, Charles Middleton, with the strong backing of the First Lord of the Admiralty, the Earl of Sandwich. Unlike in the VOC, there was no extensive consultation and experimentation. From about 1782, however, it emerged that the technique that Middleton had chosen to solve the problem of corrosion, namely to apply 'lacquered brown paper' as a seal between the copper and the hull, failed to work after a while, and could even jeopardize the ship by exposing the iron parts to decay. As result, the entire fleet had to be docked 'at a considerable cost' to replace all iron nails in the ships.[18]

Communication across the Atlantic became ever better organized after 1730, and information could flow faster and more regularly. One of the reasons for this improvement in capability was the sheer growth of shipping and trade. Often, the merchantmen that crossed the Atlantic did not merely carry letters and packages by the order of the shipowners or merchants who organized the shipment of the cargo, but also on request for third parties within or beyond the seafaring world. The naturalist Johan Frederik Gronovius in Leiden and his scholarly correspondents on the other side of the Atlantic, for example, repeatedly referred in their letters to the merchants whom they saw as a safe pair of hands to carry their letters and parcels across the sea. In the 1730s, Lewis Johnston in New York asked Gronovius to leave packages in the care of 'mr. Bernard van der Grift', a merchant on Keizersgracht in Amsterdam. At the time, Gronovius himself relied for his safe correspondence on Hudig and Papin in Rotterdam and on Messrs. Van der Velde and Messrs. Van Zadelhoff in Amsterdam.[19]

Mail services sponsored by imperial machines helped to improve communications still further. It was the British who first achieved a regular transfer of letters and packages across the Atlantic by the inauguration of packet boat services between England and the West Indies from 1744, and between England and North America from 1755. The express purpose of these services, which were initially introduced for military reasons, was to guarantee a monthly correspondence between the colonies and the metropole.[20] After the Seven Years' War, the Spanish state also established a regular mail service connecting the different parts of the empire, which replaced the system of packet boats operated by merchants from Cádiz. Each month from 1764 onwards, a vessel left La Coruña for Havana, and from there sailed to other ports in the Americas to deliver and collect letters, packages and freight. A bimonthly service to Buenos Aires was soon established too. Moreover, all Spanish ships crossing the Atlantic, private ones included, were obliged to carry an official mailbox that had to be delivered to the authorities in the port of destination.[21] In the French empire, 'the exchange of information' in the later eighteenth century was more intense than before, but still suffered somewhat under 'temporal dislocations', as McClellan and Regourd put it. Letters and packages could take a long time to reach their destinations and the exact time of arrival was not always easy to predict.[22]

Despite the overall growth in capabilities, the development of knowledge encountered several limitations. Communication across the Atlantic continued to suffer from a variety of shortcomings. Shipping and trade were sometimes disrupted by the vagaries of the weather or the impact of military events. In times of war, correspondents from different countries tried to maintain friendly relations as usual, even if the armed forces of their sovereigns were causing all sorts of trouble. During the War of the Austrian Succession, for example, John Bartram in Pennsylvania complained to Gronovius that 'it was very discouraging to think that all [his] labour and charges' might fall into the hands of French or

Spanish privateers, who would take 'no further care of them than to heave them overboard into the sea. If [he] could know that they fell into the hands of men of learning and curiosity [he] would be more easy about them.' Cadwallader Colden in New York found a practical solution. On the outside of his package addressed to Gronovius, he added a polite request in French, asking privateers to send the content 'to the gentlemen of the Royal Garden in Paris'.[23]

Within the Spanish imperial machine, information flows were also hampered by obstacles of a more structural nature. The mass of data gathered by seamen, naturalists and artists and stored at institutions in the metropole, such as the Council of the Indies, the observatory, the Royal Botanical Garden or the Royal Natural History Cabinet, was much larger than the amount of data that was actually processed and made accessible to a wider audience. Circulation stalled due to a lack of technical or financial resources or to sheer political obstruction. The intendant-general of the navy, Luis María de Salazar remarked in 1809 that the pilot-major did not have enough skilled engravers at his disposal to produce new and corrected charts that took account of all the observations recorded by the navigators of naval vessels. This was one of the reasons why foreign charts 'full of errors' continued to be used in the navy and the mercantile marine.[24] Due to court intrigue, hardly any of the enormous quantity of data gathered during the Malaspina expedition in the 1790s found its way into print before the end of the nineteenth century. The only publication that was allowed to appear relatively quickly was a memorial on astronomical observations in different parts of the world, which was considered to be politically harmless.[25]

Moreover, not every field of maritime knowledge advanced at the same rate after 1730. Failures and lags occurred as well. The Sick and Hurt Board of the Royal Navy failed to initiate research into the causes of diseases, even after 1750, when it was dominated by doctors who believed 'in the efficacy of the scientific method'. Time constraints and other pressing matters prevented the agency from doing more to support the development of knowledge on medical care at sea.[26] Advances in marine science and the study of weather patterns in the later eighteenth century fell short of contemporaries' expectations. Whereas machines and self-organized networks in this period brought together much more data about oceanographic and meteorological phenomena than before, and theorizing developed greatly, none of these efforts eventually resulted in a corresponding increase in what people at the time considered to be useful knowledge.

The study of marine science in the Atlantic world did undergo a great revival in the second half of the eighteenth century. All sorts of topics that had initially featured prominently on the research agenda of the Royal Society, but had since more or less faded into the background (Luigi Marsigli's studies on the Mediterranean being the great exception[27]), reappeared in the public eye after 1750. Scholars again began to look for data and search for patterns in marine phenomena, such as the salinity and density of sea water, the surface and subsurface temperatures of the sea, the action of the tides, the depth of the ocean and the direction and velocity of currents.[28] To measure these variables, scholars and instrument-makers came up with a variety of new instruments, such as sounders, gauges and thermometers, which were sometimes actually employed at sea.[29] Franklin's and Blagden's Gulf Stream charts from the 1780s, for example, were partly based on measurements of the temperature of the sea made with the aid of thermometers.

The study of the tides occupied great numbers of people from different backgrounds on both sides of the Atlantic.[30] *Académiciens* in France, building on seminal work by Newton, made significant advances in the development of a theory of the tides.[31] The Paris Academy took repeated initiatives to collect systematic observations on tidal periods in French ports with the help of royal professors of hydrography and naval commanders. By the 1770s, huge masses of data had been stored in the library of the Dépôt des cartes et plans de la Marine.[32]

Meteorological data were also collected in large quantities after 1770. The immediate cause of this was the assumption that the weather and climate somehow had an influence on the incidence of disease. Medical societies were at the forefront of this meteorological campaign. In France, the Société Royale de Médecine, founded in 1776, was the driving force behind a huge project to make regular, standardized measurements of air pressure, temperature, winds, humidity, the amount of rain and similar variables in numerous locations across the French Atlantic, the Indian Ocean and East Asia. This functioned as part of the French imperial machine.[33] A more modest project of a similar nature in the Netherlands was mounted by the Natuur- en Geneeskundige Correspondentie Sociëteit, established in 1779, which involved physicians and apothecaries as well as tax collectors, military officers and Protestant ministers from all over the Dutch Republic. In contrast to the Société Royale, this association – in the words of one of its founders – was not created on 'orders from on high', but organized 'on a voluntary basis'. Like its French counterpart, this Dutch society was committed to collecting both meteorological and medical data, such as figures on mortality (with information on the causes of death).[34]

Yet, in the early nineteenth century, seamen still relied on time-honoured methods, based on experience, to get specific local information on tides rather than on predictions derived from tidal theory. Tide tables in almanacs, rules of thumb in books on seamanship and, of course, the assistance of local pilots remained their most valuable aids when sailing in or out of ports.[35] Meteorology fared no better. While the 1770s and 1780s saw an unprecedented outburst of books and treatises on meteorology, the results were largely disregarded. Jan Hendrik van Swinden, a key figure in the Correspondentie Sociëteit, complained in 1800 in a letter to Louis Cotte, a staunch pillar of the Société Royale, that so many efforts had borne so little fruit. It was 'a shame that people [were] currently of the opinion that the usefulness and perhaps even the spirit of this beautiful science were less appropriate at this time'.[36]

The lack of impact of these growing activities in marine science and meteorology was not due to a lack of development in instruments. In fact, measurement devices in the later eighteenth century became more accurate, more varied and more plentiful than before, as we have seen. The reason for the limited impact should rather be sought in shortcomings in the sphere of theories and concepts. Developing a theory of the tides was one thing, predicting a tide in a specific place and time quite another. While theorizing in this field in England and France had attained a high degree of sophistication by 1800, it still proved impossible to generate the kind of accurate predictions of the time and depth of tides that seamen needed to sail safely in or out of a particular port or waterway.[37] In meteorology, the rate of accumulation of data far outpaced scholars' capacity to make sense of them. Vast numbers of observations were gathered, but the conceptual tools to 'convert these ... into usable results for analysis' were hardly developed.[38] Researchers were overwhelmed by the wealth of material.

Marine biology, meanwhile, which at the time was subject to more modest expectations than the study of the waters and the weather, edged forth at a slower, quieter pace – but it advanced nevertheless. In the middle of the eighteenth century, the natural history of fish, in the words of the French nineteenth-century biologist Georges Cuvier, began to turn into 'a truly scientific form'.[39] The Dutch Republic lay at the heart of this transformation. Albertus Seba in Amsterdam and Johannes and Laurens Gronovius in Leiden built huge collections of fish from different parts of the world. Peter Artedi, the leading ichthyologist in the 1730s, left his native Sweden to work and study in the Netherlands. After his untimely death in an Amsterdam canal in 1735, his magnum opus *Ichthyologia* was published in Leiden by his junior compatriot Linnaeus, who had just travelled to the Netherlands, too, to obtain a degree.[40] Hundreds of pictures of fish and other marine animals living in the seas of the East Indies were published in subsequent editions of Louis Renard's *Poissons, écrevisses et crabs* in Amsterdam in 1719,

1754 and 1782.[41] Seba's and Gronovius's collections and Artedi's work formed the foundations of a series of path-breaking general surveys on ichthyology published in Leiden and Amsterdam the 1750s and 1760s, including the *Museum ichtyologicum*, the *Zoophylacium Gronovianum* and the *Locupletissimi rerum naturalium Thesauri accurata descriptio*.[42]

Seamen, whalers and fishermen continued to make observations about living creatures that swam in the depths, floated on the surface or flew in the air above the sea. Scholars likewise became more interested in marine life. A burgomaster from Hamburg, Johann Anderson, compiled an extensive account of Iceland, Greenland and the Davis Strait region, published in 1746, which was translated into Danish, French and Dutch. Even though Anderson never visited the area himself, his *Nachrichten* gave a more comprehensive overview of the Northern Atlantic than classic works such as Martens's or Zorgdrager's. Anderson's book not only described the physical characteristics of the islands and the culture, religion, government and economic activities of their inhabitants but also gave an overview of a wide range of topics from natural history, including whales, fish and bird life.[43] In addition to scrutinizing books and periodicals such as the *Philosophical Transactions* (his main source of information on whales near the coast of New England),[44] the burgomaster also appears to have seized every opportunity to socialize with skippers, whalers and traders returning from the North Atlantic and question them about what they had seen, heard or experienced.[45] Seamen provided him with a specimen of a narwhal and a live specimen of a fulmar from the Davis Strait, whose behaviour and features he observed at his home and described at length in his book.[46] In bringing together the material for his magnum opus, Anderson was driven both by commercial and scholarly interests. The *Nachrichten 'zum wahren Nutzen der Wissenschaften und der Handlung'* contain estimates of the volumes of oil produced by different species of whales and also present a system for classifying whale species.

Anderson's account of the living fulmar is rather exceptional. Scholars were more concerned with devising rules for the 'proper preparation of skins and stuffed specimens' than offering advice on how specimens of animals could be kept alive while being carried overseas.[47] A typical example was a publication by Johannes Gronovius in the *Philosophical Transactions* of 1742, which described a new method for preparing specimens of fish by drying their skins.[48] In contrast with methods to transport seeds and plants, techniques for carrying live specimens of animals across long distances overseas largely remained to be developed.

Conclusion to Part II

Changes

Between 1730 and 1800, the web of connections in the Atlantic world became much broader and deeper. More and more links were established between different parts of the Atlantic, including outlying regions such as the Davis Strait and Río de la Plata, and existing relations grew increasingly dense. Imports of colonial products from the Western Hemisphere in Europe surged, while the slave trade between Africa and the Americas was vastly expanded, shipping and trade between Europe and Africa increased, and more and more ships sailed between British colonies in North America and the Spanish, French and Dutch West Indies. Cod fishing near Newfoundland and deep-sea whaling in the northwest Atlantic, the Davis Strait and the Southern Atlantic intensified, too. The Western Atlantic turned into a more or less permanent area of operations for European men-of-war and became a frequent scene of warfare after 1740. The numbers of people who were voluntarily or forcibly transported across the ocean also grew significantly. This expansion in shipping movements, commercial activities and military operations was in many ways connected to the expansion of slavery and the slave trade and the growing demand for colonial products and raw materials from the Americas, although other factors, such as the increased demand for whale products, made a contribution as well.

After 1730, the advance of globalization in the Atlantic world was supported by developments in maritime knowledge to a greater extent than in the previous period. Ships could make faster voyages thanks to advances in knowledge about ship design, navigation, chart-making and the maritime environment, among other things. Some of these advances in maritime knowledge, particularly new aids and instruments for navigation such as octants, sextants, reflecting circles and nautical almanacs and new techniques for determining a ship's position at sea, such as the lunar distances method and double-altitudes method, were firmly grounded in theories and concepts from astronomy, physics and mathematics. In turn, the spread of innovations in navigational technology among seamen helped to improve the accuracy of maps and charts. In addition to these theory-informed improvements, many advances in knowledge stemmed from the continuous accumulation of observations and experiences gathered over the years by myriad seafarers, shipwrights, instrument-makers and other groups of skilled workers. This 'crowdsourcing' of data lay at the base of a growing body of knowledge on patterns of winds, currents, tides and magnetic declination, and also contributed to the introduction of gradual adaptations in ship design. These data and insights were explicated and disseminated in print to a greater extent than in the past.

People's chances of survival when crossing the Atlantic also improved thanks to advances in practical knowledge about the prevention and cure of diseases such as scurvy or malaria, which was increasingly shared across national and imperial borders. The key to these improvements in medical care lay in the gradual accumulation of experiences and empirical observations, not a breakthrough in medical science. Additionally, the improvements were also to some extent supported by the adoption of mechanical devices such as ventilators and distillation machines.

Globalizing forces, in turn, had a significant impact on the advancement of knowledge. Whereas long-range religious organizations such as the Society of Jesus lost their prominence as engines for the acquisition and dissemination of knowledge, other machines remained vital factors in the development of institutions, regulations and facilities for the creation, certification and dissemination of knowledge. The extent of these machines' involvement admittedly differed according to the domain of knowledge and maritime power. Imperial machines in the French, Spanish, British and Dutch Atlantics were especially active in the building and maintenance of infrastructures of knowledge in navigation technology and medical care at sea. They became involved in nautical education and the examination of navigators, as well as the production and distribution of maps, charts and nautical almanacs, the establishment of naval hospitals and the supervision of the quality of sea surgeons. In Britain and the Dutch Republic, similar functions were to some extent fulfilled by commercial machines such as the VOC. Ship construction became an object of concern for imperial machines, particularly in France and Spain, while instrument-making was largely left to private entrepreneurs in all cases. The expansion of infrastructures in turn contributed to the increased circulation of knowledge. Many of the aids for navigation and medical writings that circulated in print in the latter half of the eighteenth century, for example, were produced by experts associated with the very institutions that were created and maintained by imperial or commercial machines, such as observatories, map-making agencies and hospitals.

Self-organized networks, meanwhile, spread ever more widely across the Atlantic. The period after 1730 not only saw a further expansion of the 'scholarly Atlantic' that cut across different organizations and different imperial spaces but also witnessed an increasing density in relations between people from different regions and different social networks. This growing network from below allowed communication between such diverse groups as tradesmen in Philadelphia, fishermen in Holland, seafarers in Nantucket and Moravian missionaries and Inuit in Greenland. Self-organization as a globalizing force thus facilitated the exchange of all sorts of observations concerning the maritime environment, such as patterns of winds and currents or the behaviour of whales, fishes and birds, and of practical experience in coping with disease and extreme conditions at sea.

Finally, the development of maritime knowledge was aided by substantial improvements in techniques, instruments and resources to gather, classify and interpret data and to reproduce and transmit information. Evidence was collected more systematically, measurement devices became more precise, more diverse and more abundant, new inventions were tested more rigorously, mail services were better organized. Nevertheless, advances were not infrequently obstructed by time constraints or financial resources, or hampered by the vagaries of war or political resistance, notably in the case of Spain. Variations between domains of knowledge continued to exist as well. The study of tides and winds and weather patterns made less progress than map-making or navigation technology.

In the first half of the nineteenth century, the differences in speed between globalization and the advance of maritime knowledge and the balance between capabilities and limitations in knowledge development in the Atlantic world would change significantly, and these changes form the subject of the third part of this book.

Part III

The reshaping of the Atlantic world and the collectivization of maritime knowledge, *c.* 1800–60

Introduction

Globalization between c. 1800 and 1860

In early April 1832, HMS *Beagle*, under the command of Captain Robert Fitzroy and on her second voyage to the South Atlantic, passed Cape Frio on the coast of Brazil. At the time, the *Beagle* was serving as an exploration vessel for the Hydrographic Office of the Royal Navy, and among its passengers was the young naturalist Charles Darwin. In his account of the voyage, Fitzroy devoted six pages to what had happened at Cape Frio just two years beforehand: namely, the sinking of HMS *Thetis*. Fitzroy thought that perhaps no shipwreck in recent years had 'excited so much astonishment, or caused so much trouble and discussion, as the loss of that fine frigate the *Thetis*'. 'Had any seaman been asked, on what frequented shore there was least probability of a wreck, I almost think he would have answered on that of Cape Frio.' How was it possible that the *Thetis* had nevertheless perished? After reconstructing the vessel's last movements, chiefly from information from 'old friends and shipmates', Fitzroy concluded that the disaster must have been caused by a previously unknown strong current near Cape Frio, which carried her much closer to the shore than the officers had assumed, based on the position calculated by dead reckoning. One of the lessons of the fate of the *Thetis*, and the subsequent inquiry, was that the existence of an 'unsuspected danger' in this part of the ocean had been revealed.[1]

Fitzroy's account offers a glimpse of some significant changes in the Atlantic world in the first decades of the nineteenth century. British ships now were frequent visitors to the coasts of South America. Shipwrecks became a subject of thorough investigation, revealing shortcomings in knowledge that needed to be resolved before globalization in the Atlantic world could safely proceed. Institutions such as hydrographic offices built up an ever more accurate and comprehensive picture of the ocean, and navies and naval officers were dedicated collaborators in this task.

But the claim that an 'Atlantic world' still existed after 1800 is not self-evident. Some historians have argued that the Atlantic world actually began to dissolve from the late eighteenth century onwards. 'Forces of divergence and globalization began to bring to an end the patterns of coherence and congruity that make it possible to speak of an Atlantic World in the first place,' Thomas Benjamin has claimed.[2] Nicholas Canny and Philip Morgan are also of the opinion that 'the region's original integrity was breaking apart', as differences within the region increased and the Atlantic itself became part of a 'single global market'. Emma Rothschild has argued that the 'multiple connections' that made up 'a distinct Atlantic world' in the eighteenth century had disintegrated by the 1830s.[3]

'Dissolution' is in some ways an apt description of what happened to the Atlantic world after 1800. Long-established links were loosened or even cut entirely. The French and Spanish colonial empires in the Americas for the most part succumbed to conquest or revolutions in the early nineteenth century. French Guiana, a few islands in the Lesser Antilles and Cuba were all that remained. A British Atlantic empire of sorts continued to exist after the loss of the North American colonies in the 1780s, but the centre of gravity of British imperial expansion increasingly moved to Asia, especially to India.[4] Dutch imperial connections with Asia were also strengthened, while the presence of the Dutch in the South Atlantic, with the loss of the Cape and most of the colonies on the Wild Coast, was significantly diminished.

The transatlantic slave trade, which had long formed a linchpin of the Atlantic commercial system, went into prolonged decline. As a result of the abolition of the slave trade by the British Empire and the prohibition of the import of slaves in the United States in 1807, the number of slave voyages decreased, except for a brief upsurge in the 1820s due to increased imports in the French colonies and Brazil. The abolition of slavery in the British colonies in 1833 and in other regions of the Western Hemisphere in the mid-nineteenth century undermined the trade still further. Some 1,400 slave voyages were undertaken in the 1830s, compared to more than 2,700 between 1800 and 1810. In the 1850s, the number of voyages dropped to about 200. The numbers of enslaved people leaving Africa fell from nearly 775,000 in the first decade of the nineteenth century to fewer than 500,000 in the 1830s, and fewer than 100,000 in the 1850s.[5] The slave trade's share of all trade between Africa and the Atlantic world dropped from two-thirds in the 1820s to less than 2 per cent in the 1860s.[6]

Some trading companies that had been present in the Atlantic for many years vanished from the scene at the end of the eighteenth century. The WIC and the VOC were liquidated in the 1790s. The Compagnie des Indes was suppressed during the French Revolution. British commercial machines continued to be active in the Atlantic orbit for some time after 1800, however, notably the

Hudson's Bay Company and the EIC. The fleet of the EIC reached its maximum size during the first decade of the nineteenth century. At that time, the company was sending some fifty ships to Asia a year, compared to twenty-five in the 1760s.[7] The role of the EIC as a shipping company only slowly diminished after the Napoleonic Wars, and came to an end when the EIC lost its monopoly on trade with India and China.

While long-range religious societies continued to exist, none of them could match the global reach, intricate organization and machine-like mode of operation once exhibited by the Society of Jesus. This also applied to the restored Society of Jesus, which in 1814 succeeded the old organization dissolved by Pope Clement XIV in 1773. The new Jesuits focused more on education in Europe than on missionary activities in the rest of the world. The Missions Étrangères, which likewise came back to life after the Napoleonic Era, mostly focused its missionary activities in the nineteenth century on East Asia.[8] New Protestant missionary organizations founded around 1800, such as the London Missionary Society and the Church Missionary Society, concentrated their efforts for a long time on the Cape, Asia and the Pacific rather than on West Africa or the Americas.[9] Religious machines thus largely lost their importance as a globalizing force in the Atlantic world.

Yet, even if the slave trade substantially declined and even if many 'machines' retreated into the background, shifted their energies to other parts of the world or disappeared entirely, the maritime network in the Atlantic world as such did not contract. The patterns of shipping and trade changed, but the web of connections across the ocean did not fall apart. The intensity of interconnectedness, the extensity of networks and the velocity of flows of ships, people and goods in the Atlantic did not diminish. While some spheres showed unmistakable decline, there was indisputable growth in other areas and branches of activity, and self-organization became an increasingly important globalizing force in the Atlantic orbit.

After the abolition of the slave trade to the Americas, the trade between Africa and other parts of the Atlantic world did not collapse, but rather changed in nature. It more than doubled in value and quintupled in volume between the 1820s and the 1860s, with most of the growth taking place in West Africa. Exports of slaves were replaced by exports of commodities. Africans exported growing volumes of agricultural products to Europe – especially to Britain – and bought increasing quantities of manufactured goods in return. By far the most important export commodity was palm oil, which was mostly produced in the region east of the river Volta and west of the Cameroons. The expansion of palm oil production involved the growing local use of slave labour. Palm oil made up an estimated three quarters of all African exports to the Atlantic by value in the 1860s. By then, its total value was almost as great as that of the slave trade at its peak in the 1780s.[10]

Exports of raw cotton from the United States to Britain virtually exploded after 1790 in response to the fast-growing demand from the British cotton industry, powered by the breakthrough innovations of the Industrial Revolution. Exports multiplied by a factor of ninety-three in the 1790s, and increased sevenfold between 1800 and 1820. Between 1820 and 1860, total exports of cotton from the United States multiplied by almost ten times. Raw cotton made up more than half of all US exports on the eve of the Civil War. The expansion was largely realized by means of slave labour.[11] While up until the 1820s, the greatest part of cotton exports originated from South Carolina and Georgia, exports from southern states to the west grew massively thereafter. Alabama, Mississippi, Louisiana and Arkansas accounted for more than half of cotton production by 1860, and more and more ships headed for the Gulf of Mexico. Mobile and New Orleans rivalled Savannah and Charleston as American cotton-exporting ports. On the British side, Liverpool overtook London as the main port of importation in around 1800.[12]

From the 1810s onwards, the Southern Cone of the Americas increasingly became part of the network of Atlantic trade and shipping, too. After the end of Spanish rule, the newly independent states opened their ports to trade with all nations. Foreign, non-Spanish merchants settled in South American cities. Shipping traffic with European countries and the United States expanded, and Britain became the largest trading partner. Chile and the River Plate provinces exported increasing amounts of primary products, such as copper, hides, tallow and wool to the UK, in exchange for growing imports of manufactures, in particular printed cottons. Like West Africa, countries in the Southern Cone long benefited from a favourable movement in terms of trade, largely thanks to a prolonged decline in the prices of industrial products.[13] Buenos Aires saw its shipping traffic rapidly expand in the second quarter of the nineteenth century. The vast majority of vessels sailing to Río de la Plata were British. Liverpool, again, was the chief centre of this burgeoning trade. Some commodities also found their way from Argentina to other destinations in the Americas. Hides and wool were exported to the United States and salted meat was transported to Cuba and Brazil.[14]

Moreover, the South Atlantic became crowded with ships on their way to the Pacific or the Indian Ocean. The growing density of shipping in southern waters initially had to do with the massive expansion of American whaling after the War of 1812. In no time, the United States became the dominant nation in the global whaling industry. While the number of American whalers in 1815 amounted to less than a quarter of the number of British ships, the roles were completely reversed three decades later. In the 1840s, the Americans sent some 675 whaling ships to sea each year, compared to the British sending a mere 34. The Americans accounted for an estimated 60 per cent of all whaling activities in the world by the 1830s, and even enlarged their share to 70 per cent in the 1840s and 1850s.[15] While only a handful of American ports were involved in the whaling industry in the 1800s, there were thirty-eight in the early 1840s, almost all of them in New England and New York. New Bedford, near Boston, overtook Nantucket as home of the largest whaling fleet in the 1820s.[16]

Along with the growth in size of the whaling industry came a shift in hunting grounds. The Arctic, the Indian Ocean and especially the Pacific became key destinations for whaling voyages, in addition to the North Atlantic. American whalers entered the Western Arctic through the Bering Street in the 1840s, and also started hunting in Hudson's Bay and near Baffin Island, where they cooperated with the Inuit. At about the same time, increasing numbers of whaling ships sailed into the Indian Ocean to hunting grounds between Madagascar and the Persian Gulf. The bulk of the fleet headed for the Pacific, however. The percentage of New Bedford whaling voyages destined for the Pacific Ocean rose from 45 per cent in 1816–25 to more than 58 per cent in 1846–55.[17] To reach the rich hunting grounds off the coast of Chile, in the central Pacific and near the coasts of Alaska and Japan, hundreds of American whalers passed through the South Atlantic on their way to Cape Horn each year. For a while, South Georgia became a favourite spot for seal hunters to cull fur seals, whose pelts could be sold at a good profit in China.[18]

Together with the rising demand for fertilizers in farming, especially in Britain, the expansion of the whaling industry was also a major trigger of the growth of the Peruvian guano trade. In the early 1840s, reports on field experiments with guano in the British agricultural press extolled the virtues of this bird excrement as a natural fertilizer, which helped set off a rush for guano in many places in the world. The American whaling industry in the Pacific, meanwhile, had boosted the trade of the newly independent state of Peru, which happened to own the largest deposits of guano in the world. Much of the global trade in guano soon concentrated on the coastal regions of Peru and the nearby bird islands. Exports of guano from Peru to Britain, Continental Europe and the United States soared in the late 1840s and 1850s.[19] Like the whalers, the British, Dutch or American merchantmen that came to fetch the guano on the Peruvian coast sailed in droves through the South Atlantic to reach the Pacific around the Horn.

News about the discovery of gold in California in 1848 gave another boost to the growth of shipping traffic in the South Atlantic. Gold-diggers, traders, shopkeepers, builders and all sorts of other adventurers flocked to the Sacramento Valley along the overland routes in North America and across the Isthmus of Panama, as well as around Cape Horn and across the Pacific Ocean.[20]

The South Atlantic also became a busy thoroughfare for ships sailing to and from Asia and Australia around the Cape of Good Hope. American trade with Asia swelled during the 1790s and 1800s, thanks to the US's neutral position during the lengthy wars between European powers. The larger American vessels took the route around the Cape of Good Hope, the smaller ones sailed around Cape Horn. Of the nearly 600 merchant ships arriving in Dutch Batavia between 1796 and 1807, two-thirds were American-owned. Almost all of the thirty-eight ships that made it from the Atlantic to Spanish Manila between 1796 and 1815 came from the United States as well. Dozens of US vessels arrived in Canton each year in the first decade of the nineteenth century. After the end of the Napoleonic Wars, American trade with the East Indies continued at a modest level.[21] The number of ships leaving Britain for Asia meanwhile quintupled between 1814 and the late 1830s. The expansion was entirely due to the growth in non-Company shipping, which benefited from the EIC's loss of the monopoly on trade with India and China in 1833. While the number of vessels hired by the EIC slowly fell, the number of non-Company ships – which were smaller than the EIC ships – massively increased.[22] Moreover, Australia became a much-frequented destination for shiploads of convicts from England and Ireland. The transportation of prisoners to new colonies in Australia, which started in 1787, accelerated after the end of the wars with France. The number of convict ships sent to New South Wales and Van Diemen's Land in 1816–20 was five times higher than in 1811–15. An all-time peak was reached in the early 1830s, with 133 convict vessels arriving in Australia.[23]

Dutch maritime links with Asia recovered fitfully after the slump during the Napoleonic Wars. Although shipping to the Dutch East Indies after 1815 grew faster than sailings to the Americas, the West Indies or destinations in Europe, it did not really take off until the 1830s. Key factors were the foundation of the Nederlandsche Handel-Maatschappij (NHM) in 1824 and the introduction of a system of forced labour in the Dutch East Indies, which obliged farmers to supply export products such as sugar and coffee to the government for a price that was fixed by the colonial authorities. Unlike the VOC, the NHM was not a shipping organization and did not govern territories, conclude treaties or conduct war. It was in essence a trading company. The NHM had a monopoly over the purchasing and transport of the colonial export goods and their sale in the Netherlands. For transportation, the NHM only chartered ships sailing under the Dutch flag, and preferably built in the Netherlands.[24] Once the new company and the new labour system were in place, the East Indies trade became the most powerful source of the growth of the Dutch shipping industry. It was the East Indies trade that drove the expansion of the Dutch merchant fleet from about 1,100 vessels in 1824 to 1,800 in 1850 and 2,400 in 1858, with capacity nearly trebling in size; the Netherlands – after Britain, the United States, France and Sweden/Norway – thereby became one of the largest maritime carriers in the world once more. In the early 1850s, some 140 merchantmen sailed from the Netherlands to the Dutch East Indies each year. Most of these ships took the direct route to Java around the Cape of Good Hope, some called at ports in Australia in between and a few of them arrived in the Indies via Cape Horn, California or China.[25] Some ships sailing to the Dutch East Indies were chartered by the government to transport troops for the colonial army. Troop transports peaked in the period 1815–30 and again after 1850, with an average of nineteen and twelve ships per year, respectively, carrying soldiers to the East.[26]

Until the end of the 1850s, almost all ships crossing the Atlantic were sailing vessels. The large-scale shift from sail to steam in the major maritime nations did not take place until after 1860. Steamships *did* make their appearance on the ocean from the late 1830s, but they were almost exclusively employed for carrying mail, first-class passengers and high-value goods. A network of intercontinental steamship routes was created between 1837 and 1857, successively connecting Britain, the Iberian Peninsula, Boston, the West Indies, India, Chile, Peru, Brazil, Río de la Plata, West Africa, Canada and South Africa. A steamship line based in the United States operated on the New York-Liverpool route between 1845 and 1858. The first steamship companies that catered for the mass transport of passengers to America were founded in the 1850s, with home bases in British, Belgian and German ports.[27]

Migration from Europe to the Americas gathered momentum after the Napoleonic Wars. The numbers of Europeans arriving in the United States rose from less than 10,000 a year in the first decade of the nineteenth century to some 30,000 to 40,000 annually in the immediate post-war period, and surged to 200,000 to 300,000 per year in the late 1840s. After a dip in the 1850s, immigration again reached high levels in the 1860s. Englishmen, Irishmen and Germans formed the bulk of these migrant flows to North America.[28] Migration to the newly independent states in Central and South America was more limited as of yet. Argentina, for example, recorded merely 20,000 entries and 8,500 departures of migrants in 1857–60.[29]

The period between 1800 and 1860 thus saw a reshaping rather than a disintegration of the Atlantic world. Existing connections across the ocean remained partly intact, while new extensive networks of shipping and commerce came into being, especially in the South Atlantic. Vast amounts of goods and large numbers of people regularly crossed the ocean. The Atlantic world in 1860 was by no means less interconnected than sixty years before. Moreover, the routes and the velocity of communication were to a great extent still dependent on the manoeuvrability and speed of sailing ships. In this respect, the Atlantic world did not undergo a profound transformation until after 1860, when the large-scale transition from sail to steam in the major seafaring nations, the laying of transoceanic telegraph cables and the opening of the Suez Canal radically transformed the fundamentals of Atlantic transport and communication.

In some ways, the changes in shipping and trade taking place after 1800 were a consequence of government policies. The decision by newly independent states in South America to open their ports to non-Spanish ships and merchants is a striking case in point, but there are other examples as well. The upsurge in exports of guano from Peru in the 1840s, for instance, was made possible by a deal struck between European merchants and the Peruvian government to exploit this natural resource in a large-scale, commercial manner.[30] The repeal of the Navigation Acts by the British Parliament in 1849 enabled foreigners (such as Dutch merchantmen) to get a share in the carrying trade between Britain and its colonies in Asia and Australia.[31] The policy of the state-sponsored NHM from the 1820s to give preferential treatment to Dutch goods and Dutch vessels in colonial trade and shipping gave a mighty boost to the expansion of the Dutch shipping industry. And state subsidies were a crucial factor in the early growth of intercontinental steamship lines based in Britain, the United States and France.[32]

Yet, government policies were neither a necessary nor a sufficient condition for expansion. After all, between the 1810s and early 1840s the heavily subsidized British whaling industry lost out to whalers from the United States, which, apart from the statutory obligation to buy their ships from domestic builders or owners, operated in 'an economic environment largely free of government restrictions or subsidies'.[33] On the other hand, state policies could create opportunities, but they did not determine whether these opportunities would be exploited or not. It was the myriad interactions between individuals and groups from many different places, operating without any form of direct, centralized control, such as merchants, brokers and shipowners from Liverpool or New York, marine insurers from London and sea captains from New Bedford or Veendam, that made the reshaping of the Atlantic world possible.[34] Time and again, self-organization was a key factor in this process.

During the long peace after 1815, the Atlantic was much less frequented by warships than before. The Royal Navy, which at the end of the Napoleonic Wars 'possessed half of all the world's warships',[35] shrank dramatically in the following years. The number of ships in commission dropped from more than 700 in 1814 to a mere 120 four years later. The number of people on board fell from 140,000 to 20,000, while the number of commissioned officers fell from 2,448 to fewer than 600.[36] The chief task of the navy remained to ensure the safety of the seas, but the nature of its activity changed. Warships were dispatched to patrol the west coast of Africa to suppress the slave trade, to guard the shipping route to India (relying on a string of bases established in the South Atlantic and Indian Ocean), to explore unknown passages in the north and the south and to survey and chart the seas and coastlines throughout the world.[37] These new tasks kept at least some of the numerous commissioned officers employed. One of them was Robert Fitzroy on the *Beagle*. Of the thousands of officers for whom the navy had no employment at all, some joined the coastguard or the merchant marine guard, while others moved abroad.[38]

Globalization in the Atlantic world thus continued to advance after 1800, although the spatial patterns of shipping and trade changed and the driving forces were in several ways different from before. In Part III of this book, the central questions are how and to what extent did developments in maritime knowledge influence globalization, and how and to what extent did globalizing forces stimulate the growth of maritime knowledge? As in Part II, we start by investigating the effect of changes in maritime knowledge on globalization, ranging from map-making, navigation technology and ship construction to medical care and technology for harvesting resources from the sea (Chapter 5). Chapter 6 then examines how and to what degree globalizing forces affected the expansion of maritime knowledge. What impact did globalizing forces have on the development of knowledge infrastructures and the circulation of knowledge? In the conclusion, we discuss the changing balance between capabilities and limitations in the development of maritime knowledge between 1800 and 1860.

5

Maritime knowledge and globalization
Advances and lags

Globalization in the Atlantic world after 1800 was strongly supported by the growth of maritime knowledge. The speed of shipping increased, chances of survival on board improved and harvests from the sea became more abundant. In all of these ways, advances in knowledge facilitated an increase in contact, interaction and exchange, which resulted in greater interdependence between different parts of the Atlantic world. But knowledge was not always sufficient. The following sections will show that globalization in the period between 1800 and 1860 also could outpace the growth of maritime knowledge, with side effects that could leave contemporaries at a loss for explanations and solutions.

Increasing speed, lagging safety

Long before the large-scale transition from sail to steam began, there was a striking increase in the speed of shipping in the Atlantic and an impressive fall in the duration of voyages. For the slave trade, Klas Rönnbäck has shown that the estimated speed of slave ships crossing the Atlantic Ocean on most routes continued to rise during the early decades of the nineteenth century. For the Asia trade, the duration of voyages by English East Indiamen to Asia diminished by a quarter to a third between the 1770s and the 1820s.[1] In the period 1842–69, Dutch ships carrying troops to the East Indies completed their voyages in (on average) slightly more than 108 days, as compared to 128 days in the late 1820s.[2] At the end of the 1860s, voyages by Dutch merchantmen from the English Channel to Strait Sunda in Indonesia took about ten to thirteen days less than in the early 1850s – a decrease of about 10 per cent.[3]

The duration of voyages between Britain and Chile around Cape Horn fell by almost 50 per cent between the 1810s and the 1850s.[4] Crossing times between European ports and New York declined equally dramatically after the Napoleonic Wars. The average duration of all voyages from Liverpool to New York fell from 49.4 days in 1816 to about 42 days in 1826. Scheduled packet ships, which made their appearance from 1818 onwards, made even faster runs across the ocean, even though cargo space took priority over potential speed. By the middle of the nineteenth century, westbound voyages, which faced more adverse winds than eastbound ones, took less time than three decades before. Westbound sailing packets from Liverpool in 1848–57 took on average only 34.6 days to reach New York, as compared to 37.9 days in the period 1818–32. The average duration of packet crossings from London to New York in the same period fell from 37.7 to 35.1 days, and from Le Hâvre to New York from 40 days to 36.7. This all happened in the age of sail. When steam liners were introduced from about 1840, the Atlantic crossing time fell further to a mere twelve days in the late 1860s.[5]

Faster ships and shorter voyages did not necessarily go hand in hand with greater safety. The shipwrecks tell a different story. D. F. H. Grocott investigated more than 900 shipwrecks of large sailing ships during the Revolutionary and Napoleonic Wars between 1793 and 1815, which cannot be ascribed to military actions. He found that weather conditions were probably the primary cause of 46 per cent of these shipwrecks, and errors in navigation accounted for some 31 per cent. The rest of the shipwrecks were caused by leaks, fires and other mishaps.[6] Contemporaries also showed a keen interest in the frequency and background of such fatal accidents. In the mid-1830s, the British Parliament became increasingly worried about the growth of 'shipwrecks ... during the last ten years'. *Lloyd's List* showed that the number of merchantmen wrecked or missing between 1833 and 1835 was more than 40 per cent higher than in the period from 1816 to 1818, and the amount of property lost at sea had risen to the same extent. The number of human lives lost per year had shot up by 13 per cent.[7] The increase in the incidence of shipwrecks was the very reason why the House of Commons set up a series of inquiries in the 1830s and 1840s. A 'select committee appointed to inquire the causes of shipwrecks' in 1836 was followed by a 'select committee on shipwrecks of timber ships' in 1839, and another 'select committee on shipwrecks' that reported in 1843. All in all, these parliamentary committees produced over 1,600 pages of interviews and analyses about what had gone wrong with the safety of British merchant shipping.

The committee of 1836 was specifically asked to ascertain 'whether such improvements might not be made in the construction, equipment and navigation of merchant vessels' in order to reduce the loss of life and property at sea. In all these respects, the committee's report indeed identified major defects in the British merchant navy, which contrasted unfavourably with the performance of the American mercantile marine. Apparently, the growth of knowledge in the British shipping industry had not yet caught up with the increased pace of globalization after the Napoleonic Wars. It took another twenty to thirty years before the gap had largely been closed.

The committee called the construction of British ships 'defective'. One of the shipowners interviewed by the committee even claimed that 'not one ship is built sufficiently strong in Britain'.[8] While from the late eighteenth century, the shipping industry successfully increased the speed of sailing vessels by adopting copper sheathing, ship design in most respects hardly changed.[9] The 'most important innovations' in the Royal Navy, according to Nicholas Rodger, 'were in building practice rather than design'. Various measures were introduced to strengthen the structure of ships. In vessels docked for repairs, the ship's frame was stiffened by bolting down diagonal riders over existing timbers. Repair jobs could thus be completed much more quickly than before. For new warships, a system of diagonal braces devised by Surveyor of the Navy Robert Seppings was universally adopted after 1813.[10] But in the merchant marine, these improvements were embraced to a much lesser extent than in the navy. Shipowners appear to have reasoned that the costs of these improvements would not outweigh the benefits and might even reduce the competitiveness of the British merchantmen (Figure 6).[11]

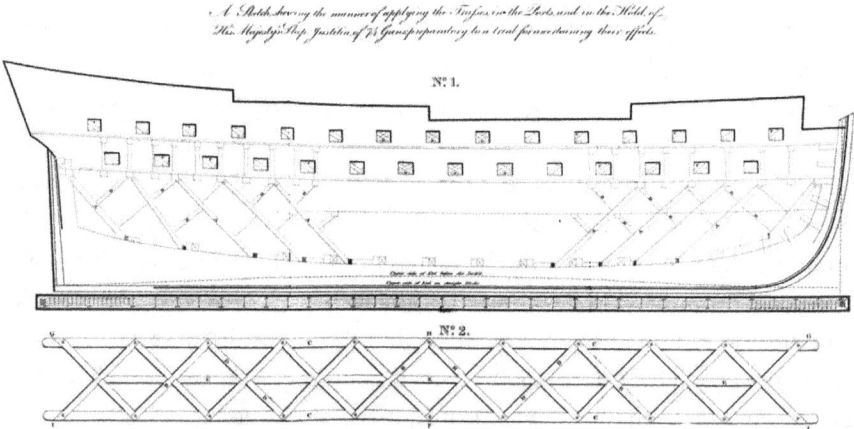

Figure 6 Diagonal braces for ships, from Robert Seppings, 'On the Great Strength Given to Ships of War by the Application of Diagonal Braces', *Philosophical Transactions of the Royal Society* (1818). Royal Society London, Public domain.

Major transformations only began with the large-scale introduction of iron in ship construction after 1830. Ships were strengthened with iron frames, equipped with iron masts and even provided with all-iron hulls. All-iron sailing vessels became more common in ocean shipping from the 1840s onwards. The increased use of iron not only made ships better able to withstand extreme conditions at sea, and thus safer, but also ensured that they became more durable, cheaper to construct and less expensive to repair. It further allowed shipbuilders to build bigger ships, which could sail faster as well.[12] Iron began to replace hemp in wires and cables in standing rigging. Iron-strapped blocks, geared winches and capstans, screw- and lever-operated rod rigging and turnbuckles increasingly came into use. Ironwork was introduced in masts and spars. Sails were increasingly fashioned of cotton instead of hemp or flax.[13] The faster passages of sailing packets between Europe and the United States, especially in the late 1840s, were partly due to an increase in the size of ships, which went hand in hand with a greater sail area in proportion to the hull.[14]

A further increase in the speed of ships was made possible from the 1840s by the adoption of wave-line bows. The American merchant navy introduced this improvement before the British, even though the concept of the wave line was originally devised by a shipbuilder and scientist from Scotland, John Scott Russell. Russell reasoned that a vessel would meet least resistance when moving through the water if its hull was designed in a wave-line fashion, with the bow shaped in a hollow, concave form.[15] The first sailing ships with wave-line forms were built in shipyards in the United States from the mid-1840s onwards. The hollow wave line became a distinct characteristic of clipper ships built in New York and Boston for the rapid transoceanic transport of passengers and high-value goods, such as tea. Clipper-builders in Britain did not adopt the wave line in hull design until a few years later, and they abandoned it after 1860. French and Dutch shipyards continued to build wave-lined clippers for some time.[16] These changes in design in merchantmen spread to the American whaling fleet, too. For a long time, most whalers were in fact adapted merchant ships.[17]

Another major shortcoming afflicting the British merchant marine was highlighted by the parliamentary committee installed in 1839, which was concerned with the rising number of shipwrecks of timber-laden vessels sailing between Canada and the UK. 'The primary cause of all the mischief', this committee claimed, 'was the improper over-stowage of the ships, by carrying heavy loads of timber upon deck, and thus, whether with or without ballast in their holds, rendering them top-heavy, and liable to upset, or to be thrown upon their beam-ends, by the first heavy sea which strikes them.' As a result,

Parliament imposed legal restrictions on carrying deck-loads that remained in force until 1862, albeit without leading to a decrease in the loss of ships.[18]

Early attempts at theorizing about stowage in France and Britain in the late eighteenth century had not resulted in any widely accepted principles or reliable general guidelines. In the 1830s and 1840s, British and American writers on nautical practice complained about the 'long and shameful neglect' of the subject of stowage, and remarked that 'fixed rules' for the process of stowing continued to be 'great desideratum'. Among the many works published for the benefit of shipmasters, there was not a single one 'calculating the probable quantity of any merchandize their ships would stow or carry'. It would be an 'inestimable boon', one author added, if statistics were to be recorded that would enable masters 'to arrive at more just conclusions as to what their vessels [would] carry than forming vague conjunctures, as [was] now frequently the case'.[19]

In practice, knowledge about stowage *did* gradually grow. Midshipmen of the US Navy John McLeod Murphy and William Jeffers, who published a book on nautical practice, stowage and navigation in 1849, observed that stowage had become 'not only a distinct department by itself, but subsequently indeed, a separate profession', 'exclusively' based on shore, which was often practised by people who had 'never been at sea'.[20] Still, much of the lore on this subject had been accumulated by mariners themselves, by means of a process of learning by doing. After all, even if a shipmaster entrusted the supervision of the stowage to a first mate or to a stevedore on shore, he was still – as the representative of the shipowner – fully responsible for any damage due to the insufficient or improper storing of cargoes.[21] Both Murphy and Jeffers and the British authors who published the first general surveys on stowage in the mid-nineteenth century consulted masters, mates and naval captains as informants. Robert White Stevens, who published a manual on stowage for the benefit of 'young sea officers' in 1858, for example, quoted 'Mr. Brady (Master in the US Navy)' and 'Capt. Sedgwick (East India Company's Service)' as his sources.[22] Stevens offered a vast array of facts, figures and descriptions of practices related to the stowage of all sorts of commodities, ranging from 'Acids' and 'Ale' to 'Vitriol' and 'Wool', and made distinctions by type of ship (sail or steam, naval or merchant marine), type of trade (coasting, colonial or foreign) and even by the density of seawater in different seas of the world, in proportion to the quantity of salt. *Stevens on Stowage*, as his work became commonly known, became the bestselling book on the subject in the last decades of the nineteenth century (Figure 7).[23]

Yet another bottleneck appeared in the supply and use of charts and sailing directions. Although Britain was by far the largest producer of charts and pilot

Description	Specific Gravity	℔	Description	Specific Gravity	℔
River Water ...	1,000	62½	North Atlantic ...	1,028	64¼
Sea of Azof ..	1,008	63	South Atlantic ...	1,029	64₁₆⁵
Black Sea	1,014	63¾	Arctic Sea	1,026	64⅛
Baltic Sea	1,015	63₁₀⁷	Mediterranean ...	1,030	64⅜
White Sea	1,019	63¹¹⁄₁₆	Caspian Sea	1,036	64¹¹⁄₁₆
Yellow Sea	1,023	63¹⁵⁄₁₆	Dead Sea	1,211	75¹¹⁄₁₆

Figure 7 Stevens on the density of seawater in different seas of the world, in proportion to the quantity of salt, and its implications for the draft of ships, from Robert White Stevens, *On the Stowage of Ships and Their Cargoes* (London 1850). Koninklijke Bibliotheek, The Hague.

books in the world at the end of the Napoleonic Wars,[24] G. S. Ritchie has observed that 'the few existing charts were completely inadequate for safe navigation'. Of the more than 1,000 charts examined by a special committee of the Admiralty in 1807, only 200 were deemed to be of sufficient quality to be utilized by the Royal Navy. Half of these were Admiralty charts, the rest had been produced by private publishers.[25] The output of new, high-quality charts by the Hydrographic Office and the sale of Admiralty charts to merchant navies did not begin to accelerate until the 1820s. The proportion of charts of North America, the West Indies and South America almost doubled between 1821 and 1829.[26]

Shipping was not always quick to take advantage of better cartographic data, however, as the example of shipping in the South Atlantic shows. Before the early nineteenth century, few seamen outside the Iberian Peninsula were familiar with the sea routes to Argentina and the west coast of South America. Because of the restrictions on foreign shipping with the American colonies imposed by the Spanish imperial government, it was difficult for navigators from other European countries to accumulate knowledge on, for example, the best way to access the Río de la Plata or the safest route around Cape Horn. For a long time, local knowledge gathered over the years by Spanish seafarers largely remained inaccessible to strangers.[27] Things only changed after British naval vessels began to frequent the area from 1807 onwards. Captain Peter Heywood of the Royal Navy thus compiled a set of 'instructions and observations for navigating the Río de la Plata, or River Plate', which in 1819 found their way into the sailing directions for South America, West Africa and the Cape of Good Hope, published by J. W. Norrie as well as into the second edition of James Horsburgh's sailing directions for the East India trade. Horsburgh's *The India directory*, including Heywood's instructions, was reprinted many times and even appeared in a Dutch translation in 1841. And yet, the incidence of navigational errors, delays and accidents on this route from Europe and the United States to the Southern Cone long remained relatively high. More than a hundred British vessels were shipwrecked en route between the UK and the southern tip of America between 1816 and 1859, many of them on the banks of the Río de la Plata.[28]

From the end of the 1840s, cartography turned into a powerful tool to exploit knowledge with regard to winds, currents and other marine phenomena to enhance the safety of ships, as well as to reduce the duration of voyages. The key innovation was a thematic map. The originator of this improvement was the then superintendent of the US Naval Observatory in Washington, Matthew Fontaine Maury. Maury managed to produce charts depicting winds, currents and related atmospheric phenomena in oceans all around the world, based on a systematic analysis of much more data from ships' logs than Halley had ever been able to gather and process (Figure 8).

Initially, Maury extracted information from existing ships' journals reaching back as far as 1796, but he soon designed a new, 'abstract' logbook, in which seamen could record data on latitude, longitude, current direction and velocity, wind direction and force, variation observed, barometer readings, soundings, ocean temperatures by depth and observations of other phenomena.[29] 'Abstract' logbooks were first issued to American mariners. Following an international meteorological conference held at the initiative of Maury in Brussels in 1853, they were introduced in other seafaring nations as well. The final report of the conference included both a model for naval vessels and a template for merchant ships.[30] The intention was that at the end of a voyage, the logbooks would be handed in at Maury's observatory or at a counterpart in another country involved in the project, such as the Koninklijk Nederlands Meteorologisch Instituut (KNMI) in the Netherlands, headed by Christopher Buys Ballot. The data would then be analysed and organized into information that could be visualized in charts or incorporated into sailing directions.

Based on the data recorded in ships' logs, between 1847 and 1860 Maury produced several types of wind and current charts of the Atlantic, Indian and Pacific Oceans. Series A, called the 'track charts', showed the tracks covered by naval vessels and merchant ships (with names and dates); series B charts depicted trade winds and regions known for calm winds; series C consisted of pilot charts showing the point of the compass from which the wind blew in all parts of the ocean in every month of the year; series D contained charts with data on the temperature of the surface water; series E presented storm and rain data in every 5° square in the ocean; and series F provided information about the

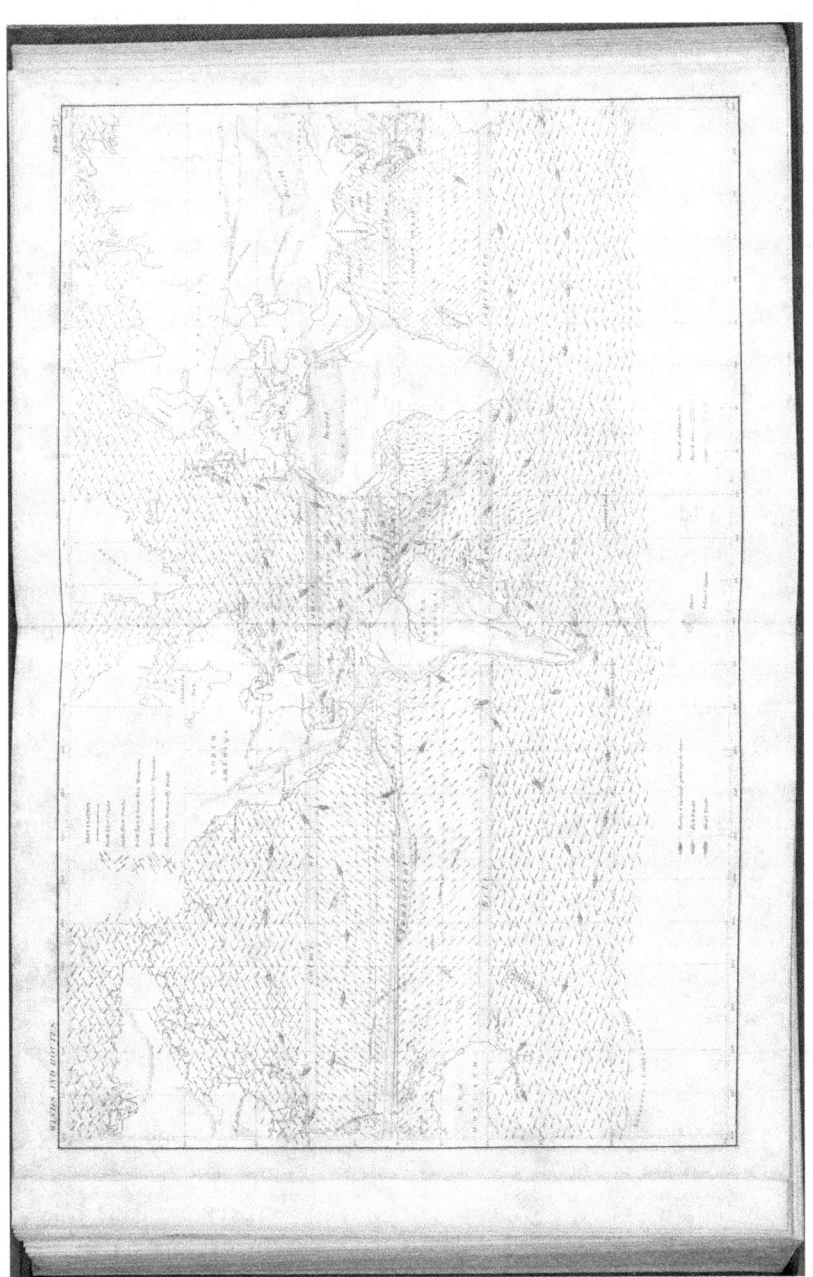

Figure 8 Map showing the patterns of winds across the globe and optimal routes for sailing ships, from Matthew Fontaine Maury, *Explanations and Sailing Directions to Accompany the Wind and Current Charts* (Philadelphia, 8th edn. 1858). Het Scheepvaartmuseum, Amsterdam.

occurrence of whales.[31] An elaborate set of symbols, such as small brushes for winds, arrows for currents, simple numerals for temperatures and colour codes to indicate different times of the year, was utilized to make the data as easily readable and interpretable as possible.

The track charts in particular earned Maury the nickname 'pathfinder of the seas'.[32] These new charts did not only allow seamen to see at a glance the conditions that their 'predecessors may have encountered in the same region and at the same time of the year' (as the author put it in 1848)[33] but also served as a convenient means to plot the fastest courses in particular parts of the ocean at different times of the year. Moreover, Maury added a companion volume, which presented an extensive discussion of the underlying data on the wind and current charts, and offered reasoned advice about the fastest passages ships might take from one port to another. These *Explanations and Sailing Directions*, first published in 1850, went through eight editions in a few years' time. Due to the continuous input of new data from logbooks supplied by seafarers from all over the world, the book became ever larger.[34] Hydrographers and marine scientists outside the United States made a few additions or improvements of their own to Maury's models. In 1858, for example, the British hydrographer Alexander Findlay published a new wind and currents chart of the North Atlantic with a 'very simple and intelligible' system of symbols. In 1859, the Dutch meteorological institute produced new monthly sailing directions for the passage from the Channel to Java, largely based on data from the abstract logs of Dutch merchant ships.[35]

Within a few years, the international cooperation project started by Maury was engaging huge numbers of seamen. In the 1858 edition of his *Explanations*, Maury reported that almost all the maritime 'States of Christendom' – from Britain, the United States, France, Sweden/Norway and the Netherlands to Spain, Portugal, Belgium, Chilé and Peru – had begun to take part. Abstract logs on the Brussels model were kept at thousands of ships and ever more logbooks had become available for the updating of wind and currents charts and sailing directions. Since the publication of the previous edition, no fewer than 180 journals of ships that had rounded Cape Horn had reached Maury's office, as well as data from almost 600 Dutch and American ships sailing between the Channel and the equator.[36] Dutch merchant captains had been particularly keen to join the cooperation project.[37] Aside from the Americans, in the late 1850s and early 1860s the Dutch were the greatest suppliers of data. 'The seamen of Holland are very accomplished – none more so,' Maury remarked; 'They are patient observers, and they return admirably kept abstract logs.'[38]

By 1860, more than 210,000 sheets of the wind and currents charts had been distributed and more than 20,000 copies of the *Explanations* had been sold.[39] The diffusion of these materials was boosted by a kind of circular flow model of information set up by Maury and his collaborators in other countries: in exchange for delivering abstract logs to the scientists, seamen would receive copies of the charts and companion guides for free.[40] Although 'the demands for the fruits of our labour [thus was] continually on the increase', Maury observed,[41] it is a fair guess that only a minority of all mariners in the major seafaring nations nevertheless had access to these aids for navigation.

For ships that *did* use these aids, the benefits could be great. Maury calculated in 1858 that voyages from the East Coast of the United States to Rio de Janeiro had been reduced from 41 to 34 days (17 per cent), to California from 180 to 128 days (some 25 per cent), and to Australia from 127 to 95 days (also 25 per cent). The reduction in the duration of voyages of Dutch ships from the Channel to Strait Sunda by some 10 per cent was ascribed to the use of the charts and sailing directions based on Maury's model as well.[42] If 'the saving already effected by the Dutch, English, and American publications amount[ed] to the general average of 10 percent, upon all voyages', Maury reasoned, this would mean that 8,000 ships of 500 tons each would annually save 36 days – and a fair amount of money.[43] The growth of knowledge about winds and currents could thus reduce the costs of globalization.

The storm and rain charts which Maury completed in the mid-1850s could give seamen a rough idea of where, and at what times, to expect rain, calm, fog, thunder and lightning or a storm, and from what direction this would come. The purpose of these charts, he modestly stated, was to show 'the exceptions to what may generally be considered the prevailing conditions of the weather at sea'.[44] Although Maury did not claim so, the storm and rain charts might thereby help to identify risks at particular times and in particular places at sea, and thereby indirectly make a contribution to enhancing the safety of shipping. Predicting storms at sea was not yet possible. The best Maury, Buys Ballot and their fellow collaborators hoped for at the time was to establish a system of meteorological stations on both sides of the Atlantic, which, together with the use of the telegraph, would allow the transmission of warnings about actual storms over great distances. Storm warning services in the Netherlands and Britain came into operation in 1860 and 1861.[45]

Like storms, tides could play havoc with ships. All parties involved in maritime affairs – from mariners, shipowners and naval authorities to merchants, insurers and underwriters – were fully aware of the risks.[46] Tide tables giving predictions of tides for particular places remained as vital as ever for the safety of seafaring. What was different was that tables for use on board became more accurate and covered many more places on the globe. This advance largely took place in the second quarter of the nineteenth century. The *British Almanac*, published by the Society for the Diffusion of Useful Knowledge from 1828, brought a real improvement in the accuracy of tide tables compared to those in existing almanacs. Whereas the new almanac sold more than 40,000 copies in a month at the beginning of 1830, traditional almanacs rapidly lost market share or ceased to appear altogether.[47] A further improvement occurred when the Hydrographic Office of the British Admiralty started to publish its own tide tables from 1833. The *Admiralty Tide Tables* gave accurate predictions of tides for all major ports in the UK as well as for numerous ports abroad. By 1850, the tables of the Hydrographic Office contained data for more than 100 ports in the British Isles. Although local and national tide tables continued to appear, the Admiralty tables had become the most authoritative and widely-used publication in the field.[48]

Navigation technology saw further improvements, too, but it took a while before these affected the speed and safety of shipping. One of the major advances was the growth in the supply of chronometers for the determination of longitude at sea. Some 100 timekeepers had been carried on EIC ships between 1800 and 1833. Half of these were owned by the Company; the rest belonged to the officers themselves.[49] While the British Admiralty around 1810 was not yet able to provide every vessel with a chronometer if so requested,[50] fifteen years later it possessed so many timekeepers that it could supply an extra timepiece to every captain or master who already owned a chronometer. By the mid-1820s, more than forty marine chronometers were issued to naval vessels a year. In the late 1850s, more than 600 chronometers were in use at sea, or about three per ship.[51]

A similar development on a smaller scale took place in the French, American and Dutch navies. At the end of the Napoleonic Wars, the French navy possessed no more than forty timekeepers. Twenty years later, the number had risen to 143, and in the late 1850s to almost 370. French naval vessels were supplied with chronometers on a regular basis from the 1840s onwards.[52] In the US Navy, timekeepers only came into more widespread use from the 1820s. More than 100 new chronometers were purchased in the 1830s. By 1846, the total number of timepieces owned by the American navy had risen to 200.[53] In the Dutch Navy, the number of marine chronometers increased from 5 in 1802 to 85 in 1835. At least 243 were bought up until 1860.[54]

Timekeepers did not change navigation technology overnight, however; many navigators in the merchant marine either adopted the alternative method of finding longitude by lunar distances with the aid of sextants, octants and nautical almanacs, or were unwilling or unable to employ any of the new methods. This was one of the additional causes of shipwrecks identified by the Committee of the British Parliament in 1836. 'Cases of loss have ... in numerous instances arisen from want of proper charts, chronometers, and other instruments,' the committee observed. 'Many commanders [could] not for want of funds purchase these things, and they [were] tempted to say that they [had] them when they [had] not. Many captains [went] without chronometers' or were incapable of using them if they had them on board.[55] Only East Indiamen appear to have been well provided with chronometers from the early nineteenth century onwards.[56] In the French merchant navy, timekeepers slowly spread from 1840 onwards, but their use did not become common until after 1870.[57]

While the alternative method for the determination of longitude, namely by lunar distances, saw only small adjustments after 1800, major changes occurred in other branches of celestial navigation at sea. From the 1820s, new solutions were introduced in England and the Netherlands for the problem of determining latitude by double altitudes, which were less time-consuming and needed less additional data than the Douwes's method. Unlike the latter, these new techniques no longer depended on the input of the estimated position by dead reckoning. Some of them made use of simultaneous observations of fixed stars instead of the sun, thus dispensing with the need to measure time elapsed between observations. The solution that became most popular among Dutch seafarers was devised by a shipmaster in the mercantile marine, Abraham Hazewinkel.[58]

An even greater advance in celestial navigation was the rise of position-line navigation. In December 1837, an American merchant captain, Thomas Sumner, sailing from Charleston, South Carolina, to Greenock, Scotland, was struck by the insight that a single altitude of the sun, taken at any time, together with the chronometer time, could be used to calculate the position of a ship. The underlying idea was that the observed altitude of a celestial body was the same anywhere on a circle on Earth, with the point on the earth's surface directly below it as its centre. This was called 'a parallel of equal altitude'. When this parallel was plotted on a Mercator chart, a straight 'line of position' could be found. The ship's position on this line could be fixed by crossing it with other position lines, or by using data on the azimuth of the celestial body that was observed and the longitude by chronometer. After explanations of the method by Sumner himself and by a British naval officer, Harry Raper, had appeared in print in 1843 and 1844, the new position-finding technique was widely adopted by navigators in the American and British navies and merchant marines within a few years' time. French and Dutch seafarers followed after 1860.[59] The great advantage of the method, which soon became known as 'Sumner's method', was that it allowed navigators to get a more frequent reading of the position of a ship. Moreover, it was fairly easy to use.

In order to find their way across the ocean, seamen also needed a reliable steering compass, of course. A steering compass had to show the direction of the true north, taking into account that the indication of the compass needle had to be corrected for errors. One of the causes of errors was magnetic declination, which varied from place to place on Earth and changed over time. In the eighteenth century, the pattern of magnetic variation had become better known and made visible in world maps showing isogonic lines, such as those produced by Mountaine & Dodson. Charts of 'the variation of the magnetic needle' continued to be produced by private firms or individuals after the Napoleonic Wars.[60] What was new from the second quarter of the nineteenth century onwards was the growing involvement of the British Admiralty and the higher degree of accuracy and increasingly up-to-date nature of the charts. The Admiralty became engaged in a campaign led by some of the most prominent scientists in Britain, known as the 'Magnetic Crusade', which aimed to gather a huge amount of data on terrestrial magnetism at sea- and land-based observatories all over the world. It supported expeditions to polar regions and maintained observatories in Toronto, St. Helena and the Cape of Good Hope, among other places. The Hydrographic Office of the Admiralty finally published its own 'charts of the curves of equal magnetic variation', the first appearing in 1858. Besides their high degree of accuracy, the Admiralty's magnetic charts were also eminently useful for navigators, because they provided information about the rate of change of variation and were updated at regular intervals.[61]

But the quality of compasses, too, revealed a gap between the pace of globalization and the growth of maritime knowledge. Many steering compasses proved unreliable. In 1820, the professor of the Royal Military Academy, Peter Barlow, described most of the Royal Navy's compasses as 'mere lumber'. 'I am aware that many nautical men set very little value on the compass', Barlow remarked, 'but this I consider to arise from the constant defects it is found to exhibit.' In 1837, the hydrographer of the navy, Francis Beaufort, stated that 'many instances of HM Ships [had] been endangered and their service delayed through the badness of their steering compasses'. Asked for advice by the Select Committee on Shipwrecks of the British Parliament in 1843, the Lords Commissioners of the Admiralty also ascribed the loss of ships in the merchant marine, among other things, to 'bad compasses'.[62] It took a special committee of the Admiralty a number of years and a long series of trials to develop a new, improved type of compass, called the Admiralty Standard Compass. This new compass showed several distinct features, such as four needles arranged with their ends at 15° and 45° from the ends of the diameter, a card of mica covered with paper, and an iridium pivot turning in a sapphire cup. The Admiralty Standard Compass was introduced in the Royal Navy in the 1840s and was later adopted in the British merchant marine and several navies and mercantile marines abroad, too.[63]

The increasing use of iron in ship construction, meanwhile, turned the ship itself into a magnet, and this became another source of compass distortion. The effect of iron on the compass needle came to be known as 'deviation'. British naval officers began to describe and investigate the phenomenon in the 1810s and 1820s. It took some time, however, before scholars and officers had identified the different components of the disturbances and had uncovered their causes. A system for correction of the compass was developed by the Astronomer Royal George Biddell Airy in the late 1830s, building on the work of the French mathematician Siméon Poisson, and formulated in a set of practical rules published in 1842. Airy's rules described how the deviation of a ship could be determined, where the compasses should be placed on board and how the various components of deviation could be compensated for with an arrangement of permanent magnets and soft iron. This system was adopted by the navy soon thereafter. It was also later applied on iron ships in the British merchant navy, as well as in foreign navies and mercantile marines. The *Practical Rules for Ascertaining the Deviations of the Compass which Are Caused by the Ship's Iron* ran to eleven editions until the end of the nineteenth century.[64]

Improving the chances of survival: Mortality and health care

In 1830, the former physician to the fleet, Gilbert Blane, published a treatise on 'the progressive improvement of the health of the Royal Navy at the end of the eighteenth and beginning of the nineteenth century'. Following on from his studies on disease on His Majesty's warships during the War of American Independence, Blane argued that medical records showed that the health of seamen in the British fleet had significantly improved in recent decades. The proportion of seamen sent to hospitals in all parts of the world to the total number of seamen enlisted in the navy had declined from 1:3.3 in 1782 to

1:10.75 in 1813. 'Thus it appeared that only a third part of the sickness prevailed in 1813 that did in 1782,' he claimed. Admittedly, the proportion had slightly increased to 1:8.8 in 1819 and 1:8.9 in 1829, but that change could be ascribed to 'a great prevalence of the yellow fever'. But the old scourges of the navy had largely been eliminated in 'the last fifty years', according to Blane. 'The scurvy had been extirpated; and the means of contracting fevers have so far been attained, that can never prove a serious evil under such vigilant, zealous, and intelligent commanders and medical officers as now belong to the naval service.'[65]

These statistics were not without problems, as Blane himself acknowledged. One of the problems identified in the medical journal *The Lancet* a few years later was that the number of seamen sent to hospitals was in fact only a small proportion of all sick crew members, because, as conditions on board improved after 1800, fewer sick people were being sent ashore. Yet, this very fact can also be taken to indicate that a real change for the better was taking place in the Royal Navy's medical care in the early nineteenth century.[66]

More detailed formation on morbidity and mortality on naval ships in the middle decades of the century is contained in the *Statistical Reports on the Health of the Navy* from 1840 onwards. These reports provided an annual overview of the state of health of the navy per geographical region ('station' or 'command'), including tables showing the number of cases of different diseases and injuries, the number of people sent to hospital, invalided or who had died, as well as the ratios of the cases and numbers per mean strength of the naval personnel employed at a particular station. The tables were compiled from data drawn from the journals of medical officers sent to the navy's Medical Service in London. Like Blane's figures, the data in the *Statistical Reports* suffer from several imperfections, such as incomplete returns or errors in classification, and they must therefore be used with caution.[67] The reports for the years 1830-6 reveal that the proportion of seamen on the ships of the South American and Mediterranean and Peninsular commands sent to hospitals ashore each year amounted to no more than 1:90 and 1:25, respectively. For the West Indian and North American station, which covered the notoriously unhealthy West Indies, the figure was 1:10.

Death rates on Atlantic voyages by naval vessels remained at more or less the same level in the mid-nineteenth century. The average annual death rate on the squadrons of the South American, Mediterranean and Peninsula and West Indian and North American stations in the years 1830-6 was 8.9, 11.1 and 19.6 per 1,000 men, respectively. In 1856-8, the average death rate per year on ships of the Home Fleet and the Mediterranean stations amounted to about 10.0

per 1,000 men, as compared to 24.0 per 1,000 on vessels of the West Indian squadron.⁶⁸ Scurvy was no longer mentioned as a cause of death. The 'most prolific source of sickness and death' in the navy, as in the army, was respiratory disease, followed by diseases classified as 'alvine fluxes', such as diarrhoea, dysentery and cholera. 'Fevers' were sometimes and in some places still a severe problem, too. Venereal disease was on the increase.⁶⁹ A sustained decline in mortality began in the 1860s. Whereas the annual ratio of deaths per 1,000 men in the navy as a whole had been 20.4 in 1834, it had declined to 11.3 by 1865 and 8.8 in 1875.⁷⁰ This decrease in mortality more or less coincided with the decline in death rates among British soldiers in the colonies after the middle of the nineteenth century.⁷¹

Chances of survival on transatlantic voyages did not only improve aboard Royal Navy vessels. Data from other branches of British shipping show a similar tendency. They concern mortality among various groups of migrant populations who sailed as passengers from Europe to North America, South Africa or Australia after the Napoleonic Wars. The measure used is the crude death rate per 1,000 per month; that is, the number of deaths on voyage divided by the average population at risk, taking account of the average length of the voyage. Only completed voyages have been counted; deaths by shipwreck have been left out.⁷² Among British and Irish convicts transported to Australia, the crude death rate dropped from 11.3 between 1788 and 1814 to 2.4 in the period 1815–68. While the death rate among free emigrants sailing from British ports to Australia between 1838 and 1853 on average amounted to 7.4, it decreased to 3.4 in the period between 1854 and 1892. For migrants on voyages to South Africa between 1847 and 1864, the comparable figure was 4.8. Crude death rates among emigrants on voyages between British, Continental and Scandinavian ports and New York between 1836 and 1853 amounted to 10.0 per 1,000 men per month, and thus exceeded those on voyages from Britain to Australia. They were nevertheless lower than those recorded among free German emigrants sailing from Europe to Philadelphia in the period 1727–1805 (15.0 per 1,000 per month).⁷³

For crew members of merchant ships, information on death and disease is more scarce than for passengers.⁷⁴ Pioneering work was done in the early 1860s by James O. McWilliam, a Medical Inspector for Her Majesty's Customs.⁷⁵ Williams collected data from the records of the registrar general of Shipping of Seamen of the Board of Trade, colonial custom collectors and British consuls for the years 1852–61. He found that among the (on average) 170,723 seamen sailing in the British merchant navy each year, the number of deaths at sea or in hospitals ashore amounted to 3,588 per year, or 20.66 per 1,000. Of these lethal cases, 7.94 per 1,000 were due to drowning, 4.29 to fevers, 1.29 to cholera, 1.02 to dysentery, 0.21 to scurvy and 4.23 to other diseases and casualties, while 1.64 per 1,000 were ascribed to 'causes not ascertained'.[76] The average death rate in the British mercantile marine in these years was thus much higher than the average annual death rate on naval ships in the Home Fleet and at the Mediterranean station in 1856-8, but lower than that on the vessels of the West Indian command, even though – as McWilliam remarked – 'during the past ten years, there has been a greater than ordinary amount of bad yellow fever among the merchantmen of all nations trading to the West Indies and to the coast of Brazil'.[77]

The decline of mortality on voyages in the Atlantic was not a purely British phenomenon. Statistics on the death rate among troops transported on government-chartered merchantmen from the Netherlands to the East Indies, for example, showed a similar downward trend to that among convicts and free emigrants from Britain to Australia. While in the period 1826–30 7.5 per 1,000 soldiers did not survive the sea voyage, the death rate dropped to 5.0 in the 1830s, 3.3 between 1842 and 1856 and 2.8 between 1857 and 1872.[78]

The major branch of shipping where mortality long remained at a relatively high level was the slave trade. After the Napoleonic Wars, shipments of enslaved people continued for decades, mainly under Spanish and Portuguese or Brazilian flags. On Spanish slave ships, the percentage of people forcibly embarked in Africa who died during the crossing of the Atlantic amounted to 15.3 per cent in 1801–20 and 15.7 per cent between 1821 and 1864, while the death rate on Portuguese and Brazilian slavers throughout this period hovered between 8 per cent and 9 per cent.[79] The crude death rate on Portuguese or Brazilian slavers sailing between Africa and Brazil between 1817 and 1843 has been calculated at 61 per 1,000 per month, vastly exceeding the mortality among convicts, soldiers and free emigrants sailing from Europe to America, Asia or Australia. The chances of survival on slave voyages were clearly much worse than on non-slave voyages.[80]

The decline in disease and deaths that occurred on naval vessels and in large parts of merchant shipping after 1800 was not merely due to an increase in shipping speeds and the shortening of voyages. The fact that seamen and passengers were at risk for shorter periods will of course have contributed to the observed decrease in morbidity and mortality. Peter Solar and Luc Hens have suggested that the incidence of scurvy on voyages to Asia may have been reduced by faster sailing, thanks to the copper sheathing of East Indiamen. Ships may thus have reached their destination before vitamin C deficiency became a serious problem.[81] On the other hand, the available statistics on the British merchant navy also reveal a decrease in crude death rates *per month*, which means a decrease in mortality irrespective of the duration of voyages.

There is ample evidence that the decline in morbidity and mortality that evidently took place was also related to advances in knowledge. None of these advances resulted from some seismic shift in medical science. 'Miasmatic', and 'contagionist' theories on the causation of disease existed alongside one another (and sometimes even in one and the same person), with one side emphasizing the effects of 'noxious airs' (and thus the need for clean environments) and the other the role of human contact (and thus the need for quarantine to prevent the spread of 'fevers' and cholera), although the environmental position gained ground in the 1840s. New ideas, for example about the relationship between nutrition and health, did not lead to fundamental changes, but were simply added to the current body of theories.[82]

The crucial advances in knowledge instead took place in unspectacular, but quite effectual improvements in preventive practices on board and ashore. Rigorous measures were taken to maintain hygiene and to keep the spaces below decks dry and airy. 'Dryness, cleanliness, and ventilation' – this was essentially what the medical regime on naval vessels and many passenger ships was about.[83] Washing bodies and clothes, the regular scrubbing of decks, tables and cooking equipment, daily fumigation between decks, constant ventilation – such practices were meticulously observed to reduce the risks of sickness and death. Several new devices for better ventilation were adopted, too. The quality of water and food on board gradually improved. Commanders and surgeons were instructed to ensure that standards of hygiene were strictly maintained. 'Empirical experimentation' by surgeons on the coast of West Africa led to the regular use of chinchona (or 'Peruvian') bark as a prophylaxis against malaria from the middle of the nineteenth century onwards. Additionally, the incidence of disease and deaths and the performance of medical officers themselves were more closely monitored by the gathering of data from surgeons' journals, reports and questionnaires, the results of which were widely publicized after 1840.[84]

Moreover, successive British and American passenger acts from the early nineteenth century onwards introduced ever more elaborate regulations about the density of passengers allowed on-board merchant ships, including specific prescriptions about the amount of space in square feet required per passenger and the quantities of food, water and medical equipment that should be carried on an oceanic voyage. Enforcement of the British acts became increasingly effective from the end of the 1830s. Regulations to reduce overcrowding and enforce standards of hygiene and medical care issued by the body that supervised emigration to Australia from 1840 were even stricter than those for passenger ships at large.[85] Passenger selection procedures helped to lower the incidence of disease and deaths as well. Passengers on emigrant ships bound for Australia were screened by a surgeon prior to departure. As 'an excess of children', in particular under four years of age, could increase the risk of high mortality, the number of very young children per family allowed to embark was limited from the 1840s. Infant mortality on voyages from British and Irish ports to New York between 1838 and 1853, where no such selection existed, was much higher than on voyages to Australia in the same period.[86] Between 1815 and 1860, mortality declined most sharply in branches of seafaring where governments actively intervened to preserve the health of passengers or crews by making and enforcing strict rules about the medical regime to be followed on the way, and/or by imposing tight regulations concerning the selection and accommodation of those on board. Naval vessels and government-chartered ships transporting convicts and emigrants to Australia were less haunted by death than merchantmen in other sectors of the shipping industry.

Just as in the period between 1730 and 1800, knowledge about best medical practices in seafaring after 1815 was circulated widely across national and imperial boundaries.[87] In 1844, for example, the Dutch physician J. B. Dompeling adapted a recent French manual on naval medicine by Charles-Polydore Forget for the use of seafarers from the Netherlands. The list of references added at the back included not only Dutch and foreign authorities from the eighteenth century (such as Rouppe, De Monchy, Lind, Pringle, Trotter and Duhamel de Monceau) but also translations of more recent German, French and English treatises on yellow fever and a book by a British doctor, James Johnston, on the influence of tropical climates on Europeans.[88] A surgeon from the US Navy, G. R. B. Horner, who in 1854 published a manual on seamen's diseases and injuries based on twenty-eight years of experience in the American naval service, showed that he was familiar with practices on-board French and British vessels as well. He had observed with his own eyes the accommodation of the sick on 'English ships of war'.[89] French naval officers, who visited British and American men-of-war after the Napoleonic Wars, were struck by the multitude of arrangements that had been introduced to improve the health of seamen.[90] A professor at the *École de médécine navale* in Brest Jean-Baptiste Fonssagrives recommended in his *Traité de hygiene navale* of 1856 that the French, like the British, should adopt the use of 'jus de citron (*lime-juice* des Anglais)' as a prophylactic against scurvy. Lime juice could be cheaply prepared in French colonies and it would be a 'inappréciable resource pour les navigations lointaines'.[91] British and Americans, in turn, would later make frequent reference to Fonssagrives's work, once he had emerged as the foremost international 'authority of medicine under steam'.[92]

Nevertheless, the knowledge that was available was not always applied, or only applied with long delays. Scurvy resurfaced as a recurrent problem on convict ships to Australia from the 1830s, despite the well-known findings about the benefits of lemon or lime juice from the trials conducted by James Lind and others.[93] It took more than fifty years after the mandatory introduction of lime juice in the Royal Navy before its use was prescribed for the vessels of the French navy.[94] Within Britain, disparities between the navy and the mercantile marine continued to exist. When the National Association for the Promotion of Social Science in 1862 asked some experts for advice about the health of seamen in the British merchant navy, it received the reply that 'the men of the [British] Merchant Service [were] liable to more sicknesses and greater mortality than men employed in the Royal Navy', and that one of the remedies 'to counteract the evils existing in the merchant service' was 'an approximation to the regulations of the navy, as far as practicable'.[95]

Growing harvests from the sea: Fishing, sealing and whaling

During much of the nineteenth century, people in the Atlantic caught more fish, slayed more seals and killed more whales than ever before. They carried loads of guano from bird islands. As the harvests of marine resources increased, however, concern about the impact on the natural environment grew, too.

The cod fisheries long continued to produce better yields. British catches in the Newfoundland fishing industry tripled in the nineteenth century. Moreover, after 1840, Britain saw the rise of a domestic mass market for fresh white fish caught from ports along the North Sea.[96] The mackerel fishery in New England, which had only been of minor importance in the late eighteenth century, expanded on a huge scale in the late 1810s. Landings of mackerel exploded from at most 8 million pounds in 1816 to more than 116 million pounds by 1825 and remained, with fluctuations, at a very high level until the 1880s. The fishing of menhaden, valued for its oil and use as bait and fertilizer, developed into a major industry in the Gulf of Maine from the late 1850s. Halibut and haddock were caught in increasing quantities as well.[97]

This massive growth in output occurred before steam power had entered the fishing industry and before fisheries science had significantly advanced. But small adaptations in techniques *did* matter. The shift from hand-lining from schooners to lining from small dories in the cod fisheries, the introduction of seines in cod fishing and menhaden fisheries, the adoption of jigs instead of baited hooks in mackerel fishing, and the extension of trawling in herring fishing and halibut fishing (and the use of ice to preserve the catch) – all these changes helped to make it possible that by the 1860s, harvests from the North Atlantic were much larger than sixty years previously.[98] In addition to changes in technology, shifts in geographical area could also help to keep up or increase production. Atlantic Canada saw a northward expansion of the cod fisheries along the coast of Labrador in the nineteenth century, in response to declining catches in inshore cod fishing in Newfoundland. Many fishermen also began to hunt seals to supplement their income.[99]

Seal hunting developed into a major activity in the Atlantic after the peace of 1815. Innu and Inuit in Labrador and Beothuks on Newfoundland had long hunted harp seals to harvest their meat, skins and oil for food, clothing, cover, heating and lighting, but it was the English settlers wintering on the northeast coast of the island who turned the hunt into a commercial undertaking. Using small sailing boats, they began to actively pursue seals on the southward flowing pack ice instead of passively waiting for a chance to net a handful of animals. Exports of seal products to Europe slowly grew from the 1790s, then increased by leaps and bounds between 1815 and 1845, and subsequently hovered at a high level for three decades more. Spring seal hunting. It provided seasonal employment that allowed a large number of cod fishermen in Newfoundland to remain on the island all the year round.[100] Hundreds of thousands of sealskins were shipped to Britain each year to be processed into 'hats, boots, gloves, cases, trunks, harness, carriage upholstery' and all sorts of accessories for the army, the navy and the factories. Seal oil was used to lubricate machines, to keep lights burning in homes and to fuel lamps in the increasing numbers of lighthouses that were newly constructed along the coasts of the British Isles. Seal oil was viewed as a suitable alternative for sperm-whale oil or vegetable oil. The demand for seal oil only declined in the second half of the nineteenth century when more and more households and lighthouses switched to gas and petroleum and electrical lighting became more common.[101] In the South Atlantic from the late eighteenth century, seal hunters from England and the United States descended upon South Georgia and smaller islands in the region. Seals were killed en masse on the beaches where they bred. The seal hunt first peaked between 1786 and 1802 and then intensified again between 1814 and the mid-1820s. Fur seals were especially sought after because of their pelts, which could be sold at a profit in China.[102]

Whaling saw vast growth after the Napoleonic Wars, too. The real value of output in the American whaling industry increased by a factor of twelve between 1815 and 1860, which more than offset the collapse of British whaling in the North Atlantic in the late 1830s. Whalers caught both sperm-whales and baleen whales. Sperm oil was used for lighting and for lubricating high-speed machines, while the oil of baleen whales was employed as a lubricant for heavy machinery and illuminant for homes, and their bones were valued as materials for making garments and utensils such as corsets and umbrellas.[103] The growth in output was partly facilitated by changes in technical knowledge. Some of these changes occurred in the design of the ships. After 1850, more vessels were purpose-built for the whaling industry, most of them barks. Barks were three-masted ships, which not only had the advantage that they could briskly manoeuvre among the drift ice in the Arctic but also allowed the easy handling of whaling boats at the stern and could effortlessly be operated by a small number of men when most of the crew were busy with the hunt.[104] However, most of the technical advances in whaling occurred in the machinery and equipment on deck and in implements used for hunting. New types of windlasses, winches, pumps and steering gear were adopted between 1820 and the mid-1840s. From the late 1840s, whalers also began to employ new types of harpoons and harpoon-launchers, enhancing the productivity of the industry.[105]

Sealers and whalers, for their part, served as trailblazers for the guano trade in the middle of the nineteenth century. A captain of a sealing ship from New York wrote in 1832 about the large amounts of bird manure he had seen on Ichabo Island near the coast of Namibia, while his crew was busily slaying fur seals. A decade later, American whalers helped a Liverpool merchant to relocate these abundant deposits of guano and within a few years, other vessels had arrived to carry away all the manure from islands in the region. This rich harvest, in turn, sparked new expeditions to other locations, which led to increasing supplies, falling prices and growing demand for guano, which was eventually largely satisfied by Peru.[106]

Contemporaries did not fail to comment on the expected impact of this increased exploitation of marine resources on the natural environment. From around 1850, fishermen in New England, Atlantic Canada and Northern Europe became increasingly worried about the depletion of stocks of fish. Cod became scarce on the inshore fishing grounds of Newfoundland. The landings of mackerel, menhaden and halibut along the northwest coast of America sharply dropped in the 1880s and 1890s. Observers sometimes ascribed overfishing to the use of new techniques and implements such as seines or longlines.[107] By the end of the century, there were also growing worries about the over-exploitation of seals on Newfoundland. Seal hunting on South Georgia ceased for more than forty years after the 1820s, because the population of fur seals had almost entirely vanished.[108] Some twentieth-century historians and environmentalists have claimed that the American whaling industry had a similar impact on whaling populations, in the North Atlantic, the Arctic and the Southern Hemisphere, too.[109]

Although intensified harvesting in reality may have affected the natural environment less than some observers suspected,[110] there surely were relationships between the availability of marine resources, changes in technologies and shifts in fishing and hunting grounds. When the catch of marine resources in particular areas of the ocean became more difficult or costly, fishermen, sealers and whalers tended to respond by adapting their techniques and implements, or by moving to other fishing or hunting grounds that promised a more abundant harvest. Thus, the perceived impact on the natural environment could be an impetus both for changes in knowledge and for an increase in contact, interaction and exchange between different parts of the Atlantic world.

6

Globalizing forces and the collectivization of maritime knowledge

In what ways and to what extent did globalizing forces promote the growth of maritime knowledge after 1800? This is the central question that we shall consider in this chapter. The following sections will show that the growth of maritime knowledge in the first decades of the nineteenth century, as before 1800, was supported by a combination of globalizing forces 'from above' and 'from below'. State-sponsored machines and self-organized networks of scholars, seamen and other groups engaged in maritime activities in the Atlantic played an instrumental role in shaping and sustaining infrastructures and the circulation of knowledge. To a greater extent than before, however, the period after the Napoleonic Wars saw a mixture of cooperation and rivalry between different countries around the Atlantic in the making of maritime knowledge, both at the level of institutions and at the level of groups and individuals. Producing knowledge related to the ocean increasingly became a collective undertaking, even if relations within the collectivity were often strained.

Imperial machines, infrastructure and the circulation of maritime knowledge

After 1800, the growth of knowledge relating to the ocean was driven more than ever before by the rivalry and cooperation between the imperial machines of Atlantic seafaring nations. New institutions were added to the set of organizations established in the seventeenth and eighteenth centuries, and existing institutions sometimes assumed new tasks. Long-distance trading companies played a less important role than in the past, and religious machines largely vanished from the scene as a globalizing force in the Atlantic world. Among the imperial machines, Britain led the way in the expansion of institutional infrastructures of knowledge in many respects, with France and the United States following in its wake, and Spain and the Netherlands bringing up the rear.

Hydrographic offices and agencies concerned with the determination of longitude now became core elements of these imperial machines. When the Hydrographic Office was founded by the British Admiralty in 1795, it initially had a rather limited remit. The duty of the hydrographer was to care for 'such plans and charts ... deposited in this office belonging to the public' and to select and compile 'all such information as may appear to be requisite for improving the navigation, and for the guidance and direction of the Commanders of Your Majesty's ships'. He had neither the authority nor the means to commission or execute any surveys himself. Apart from the hydrographer himself, the office staff consisted only of a single engraver and a single draughtsman.[1]

Despite these limitations, within a few decades, the hydrographers managed to turn their department into a highly productive centre of the accumulation and dissemination of knowledge. The first incumbent, Alexander Dalrymple, put his previous experience as hydrographer of the EIC to good use by providing the Admiralty with copies of hundreds of charts, views and plans from the EIC's collection.[2] By supplying ships with 'Remark Books' to keep a record of observations relating to ports, coasts, anchorages and suchlike, the Hydrographic Office received a growing flow of information from naval officers that could be incorporated into sailing directions.[3] Under Dalrymple's successors, the office also received many reports from naval officers commissioned by the Admiralty, especially after 1815, to conduct surveys in home waters as well as far-away places such as the Gulf of Saint Lawrence or the west coast of Africa. A corps of naval surveyors was established by the Admiralty in 1817.[4] The corpus of charts kept at the Hydrographic Office was further expanded by exchanges of information with similar departments in other countries, notably in Denmark and Spain, which served as a kind of model for the office in Britain. Contact with France and Denmark provided the office with up-to-date charts of the Mediterranean and the west coast of Greenland, among other things.[5] In 1828, the office received a copy of all publications by its French counterpart, the Dépôt général de la Marine.[6] The liaison with the *dirección hidrográfica* in Spain yielded a rich harvest of charts and plans of South America, Cuba and Puerto Rico. After the appointment of Francis Beaufort as head of the Hydrographic Office in 1829, his Spanish colleague Martín Fernández de Navarrete sent him seventy-two charts and publications from the *dirección*, many of which were a product of the Malaspina expedition thirty years previously. The Spanish hydrographers received copies of a recent work by the British office in return.[7]

The staff of the department increased to eight in the middle of the 1820s and seventeen in the early 1850s.[8] The total number of charts in print rose from 575 in 1821, via 986 in 1829 and 1,116 in 1839, to 1,980 in 1855, while the number of new charts published per year soared from 19 in 1830 to 130 in 1855.[9] In 1819, the Admiralty also authorized the office to sell Admiralty charts to the public for 'the general use of navigation as well as to meet part of the expenses of the Hydrographical Department'. Of the 55,720 charts printed in 1848, for example, 22,819 were sold to the general public. Admiralty charts gradually edged out charts produced by private publishers. By the 1850s, the number of remaining independent chart publishers had declined to three.[10] The EIC, meanwhile, left the position of hydrographer vacant after the death of James Horsburgh in 1834, although it continued to publish its own charts for a while.[11]

The responsibilities of the Hydrographic Office over time extended to other domains of maritime knowledge, too. In 1808, Hydrographer Thomas Hurd managed to get the supervision of all surveying instruments in the navy transferred from the Navy Board to his own department. The following year, he further received the commission of supplying timekeepers to naval vessels, which created an additional source of funding, although he had to relinquish this task to the Astronomer Royal twelve years later. From 1810 to 1817, Hurd also served as secretary of the Board of Longitude.[12] An assistant from the Royal Navy, Joseph Dessiou, was added to the department's staff in 1828, specifically charged with the task of compiling sailing directions. The latter had been issued by the office almost from the very beginning, but a new feature was that the directions were now produced in a uniform format and used all the latest data recorded in the 'Remark Books' of naval officers. Like the Admiralty charts, they could be bought by the general public. A *West India Directory* 'for navigating the Caribbean Sea and the Gulf of Mexico ... compiled from documents in the Hydrographical Office' was published in this manner in 1829.[13]

With the appointment of Francis Beaufort as hydrographer in 1829, the department became a major hub in a growing network of cooperation with other institutions and organizations within and beyond the Royal Navy. The hydrographer was put in charge of the budget of the Scientific Branch of the Admiralty, established in 1831, which comprised the Hydrographic Office, the astronomical observatories in Greenwich and the Cape of Good Hope, and the offices dealing with the *Nautical Almanac* and marine timekeepers. Beaufort became 'the link between the scientific elite and the British government'.[14] He was not only, like Dalrymple, a fellow of the Royal Society but also a fellow of the Astronomical Society, a member of the Geological Society and the British

Association for the Advancement of Science (BAAS) and a founding member of the Royal Geographical Society. While he had serious disagreements with Astronomer Royal George Biddell Airy about the maintenance of chronometers, he developed a highly fruitful working relationship with William Whewell, professor of mineralogy and moral philosophy and master of Trinity College, Cambridge, in particular concerning the emerging field of 'tidology'.[15]

To begin with, Beaufort allowed his assistants, Dessiou and Daniel Ross, to devote part of their time at the office to the calculation of tide tables under the supervision of Whewell.[16] In the mid-1830s he succeeded, thanks to his influence in the Admiralty, in realizing two large-scale operations of simultaneous tide observations, yielding massive amounts of data which were stored and processed at the Hydrographic Office and then subjected to a theoretical analysis by Whewell; the first one took place at some 400 Coast Guard stations in Great Britain and Ireland and the second one, in 1835, at 650 stations on both sides of the Atlantic and a number of points along the Pacific and Indian Oceans, involving participants from Great Britain and Ireland as well as from France, Spain, the United States, the Netherlands, Portugal, Sweden, Norway and Denmark. Whewell, for his part, obtained additional data on far-away places through private correspondence with missionary societies and also managed to get substantial funding for this tidal research programme from the BAAS. The most innovative result of this vast cooperative effort in 'tidology', which provided a template for the 'Magnetic Crusade' a few years later, was the creation by Whewell of a map of cotidal lines showing the progress of the tide wave along the shores of the British Isles and the countries around the North Sea. Whewell also ventured to produce an 'isomap' with tidal lines of the world oceans.[17] From then onwards, the Admiralty used the isomap 'as an imperial tool' to 'keep [its] vessels safe'.[18]

The publication of a new monthly magazine, *The Nautical Magazine*, from 1832 onwards owed much to the support of the Hydrographic Office as well. The *Nautical Magazine* aimed to advance hydrography by 'the diffusion of useful information' to 'all classes of readers', especially 'particulars of all maritime discoveries, whether islands, harbours, rocks, or shoals', 'reviews of interesting voyages' by Britons and foreigners, 'critical notices of all publications directly appertaining to navigation; especially of new charts, plans, and sailing directions' and news about improvements in nautical instruments. The 'safety of seamen' was its prime concern.[19] Beaufort himself also gathered a stellar team of scientific experts as contributors to the first edition of the *Manual of Scientific Enquiry* in 1849, including Airy on astronomy, Whewell on tides and Edward Sabine on terrestrial magnetism. This manual, published by authority of the Admiralty, aimed to give a state-of-the-art overview of all branches of science 'for the use of Her Majesty's Navy'.[20] It was also Beaufort who in 1842 suggested to the Admiralty that a new office be created for the superintendence of the testing, storing and installation of the improved compasses of the navy, as well as for the determination of instrument errors and for the instruction of naval officers in compass matters. This office came to be known as the Compass Department.[21] In these ways, the Hydrographic Office played a leading role in promoting the circulation of knowledge relevant to navigation both inside and outside the navy, which went far beyond the making and selling of charts and sailing directions.

In fact, after 1830 the Hydrographic Office replaced the Board of Longitude as a key institution in the British imperial machine. Yet this did not appear to be the situation immediately after the end of the Napoleonic Wars. Thanks to the president of the Royal Society, Joseph Banks, at first the status of the board was bolstered, rather than diminished. Following a new Longitude Act prepared by Banks's political allies and adopted by Parliament in 1818, the board was reshaped as a body with an increased number of fellows of the Royal Society, supported by a larger salaried staff, furnished with a more substantial budget (paid for by the navy) and charged with a new set of tasks. The reformed Board would be responsible not only for administering rewards for improvements in navigation but also for rewarding discoveries relating to a northern passage between the Atlantic and Pacific Oceans and the approach to the North Pole. Two expeditions to find a Northwest Passage were launched by the Admiralty that very year, and several more followed in the next few decades. The driving force behind these efforts was the second secretary to the Admiralty, John Barrow, who persuaded his superiors that voyages of exploration in the Arctic were both opportune and urgent, as many officers and vessels in the Royal Navy were idle after the end of the war, and expeditions with the same purpose were being mounted in Russia as well. Barrow insisted that Britain should grasp and keep the momentum. The Hudson's Bay Company assisted these ventures of the Royal Navy with material resources and information and also mounted new explorations of its own.[22] Additionally, the Board of Longitude was charged with overseeing the regulation of the Admiralty's chronometers and supervising a new observatory established at the Cape of Good Hope in 1820. In its structure and tasks after 1818, the Board of Longitude thus resembled its French counterpart, the Bureau des Longitudes, with which it began to cooperate more closely.[23]

The board was dissolved in 1828, however, and its tasks were distributed among various officials and institutions, including the Hydrographic Office and the observatories, which were from 1831 subsumed under the newly created Scientific Branch of the navy. Hydrographer Beaufort then became deeply involved in the organization of voyages of exploration in the Arctic in the 1830s and 1840s, including the famous expedition commanded by John Franklin in 1845 and the numerous expeditions sent out later to discover its fate.[24]

Although the main purpose of these voyages of exploration was the search for northern passages between the Atlantic and the Pacific, they added to knowledge about natural history in the Arctic region as well. Military men now became as knowledgeable about birds as whalers, in all senses of the word. In 1818, Captain Edward Sabine, as astronomer on the first Arctic expedition under the command of John Ross, made perceptive observations about birdlife in the Davis Strait and Baffin Bay. He discovered a new species, now known as 'Sabine's gull', of which he sent a specimen to his brother in London, who presented it at a meeting of the Linnean Society. A memoir of Sabine's observations 'on the ornithology in that part of the world' made during the voyage appeared in the transactions of the society the following year. John Barrow, son of the second secretary of the Admiralty, later managed to obtain a large set of specimens of birds collected by naval officers on Arctic exploration voyages between 1848 and 1855, which he donated to the University Museum in Oxford.[25] On the other hand, naval officers, like whalers and Inuit, also became connoisseurs of the qualities of different birds as food. In 1851, Captain H. W. Austin declared that the Brent grouse and various sorts of ducks and divers were 'excellent eating', but in 'flavour and delicacy' the ptarmigan and the willow grouse were second to none. 'These may be used in pie, stewed, boiled, on roast, at pleasure, and are easily shot.'[26]

In its final phase, the Board of Longitude briefly concerned itself with meteorology, especially with meteorological instruments. In 1823, a 'thermometer carefully adjusted' was sent to the observatories in Greenwich, Oxford and Cambridge. In the following year, on the orders of the board, Commissioner John Herschel made a comparative survey of meteorological instruments in the principal observatories on the continent.[27] After the dissolution of the board, Herschel continued to pursue his meteorological inquiries with financial support from the BAAS, while in 1840 Astronomer Royal Airy founded a Magnetic and Meteorological Department at the observatory in Greenwich.[28] The Hydrographic Office became deeply involved in meteorology during Beaufort's tenure. The wind force scale named after him was adopted by the Royal Navy in 1838. The department supplied barometers to all naval vessels from 1843, and a few years later all surveying ships were required to make meteorological observations as desired by the BAAS.²⁹ A government agency specifically dedicated to marine meteorology was not founded until after the international conference held in Brussels in 1853, however. A Meteorological Department under the supervision of the Marine Department of the Board of Trade was charged with the task of supplying instruments, instructions and registers to merchant and naval ships and to compile statistical records on the basis of the completed registers of meteorological observations at sea. Its first director was the former commander of the *Beagle*, Robert Fitzroy. The storm warning service, which went operational in 1861, was set up within this department, too. In the light of its key role in the regulation of the British merchant marine, the Board of Trade was seen as a more fitting home for this new agency than the Royal Observatory or the Hydrographic Office.³⁰

The long-standing French counterpart of the Hydrographic Office, the Dépôt des cartes et des plans de la Marine, was initially better staffed and better funded than the fledgling department in Britain. Renamed the Dépôt général de la Marine after the Revolution, its staff increased from 18 in 1800 to 27 in 1839. Its level of education was higher than ever before. By the 1840s, most of the employees were engineers who had graduated from the École polytechnique or had been trained by the long-time leader of the Dépôt, Charles-François Beautemps-Beaupré, himself.³¹ The collection of maps and charts after 1800 grew at a rate of 175 a year, as compared to 53 annually between 1759 and 1791.³² Twelve major voyages of exploration were mounted from France between 1791 and 1840, all of them destined for the Pacific, which yielded a huge catch of data to be processed at the Dépôt. The exchange of information with hydrographic departments in other countries, especially Britain, Spain and Denmark, increased markedly.³³ Yet, although the proportion of all naval officers in France engaged in hydrographic surveys in 1840 was four times as high as in the 1770s, the absolute number of officers involved was on average only half of that working in the service of the Hydrographic Office in Britain: thirty as opposed to sixty each year. Moreover, by 1840 the Dépôt could only spend half as much money per year on surveys as the British office under Beaufort.³⁴ The changing relationship between the Dépôt and the Hydrographic Office also became visible in the shifting direction of mutual influence. Whereas in around 1820, the British office imitated the model of the Dépôt in starting the sale of naval charts to the general public,³⁵ in the 1830s the French agency followed in the footsteps of the Hydrographic Office by assuming a leading role in the research on tides. Beautemps-Beaupré eagerly engaged in the large international cooperative project mounted by Whewell and Beaufort in 1835, by organizing the simultaneous collection of data on tides in sixteen ports in France and the Channel Islands. Moreover, together with a fellow member of the Bureau des Longitudes, François Arago, in 1839 he managed to get responsibility for the observation of tides in the naval port of Brest transferred from the Bureau to the Dépôt. A Service des Marées was added to the Dépôt. It was a hydrographer from the Dépôt who published the first yearbook on tides in France.[36] The checking and rating of chronometers was transferred from the Bureau to the Dépôt in 1847 (Figure 9).[37]

Founded in 1795, the Bureau des Longitudes was a much later creation than the Board of Longitude, but its remit was far broader than that of its British counterpart from the outset. The new body was conceived as a small-scale successor to the Académie Royale des Sciences, which had been closed down during the most radical phase of the Revolution two years previously.[38] Apart from taking over the Académie's responsibility for compiling the *Connoissance*

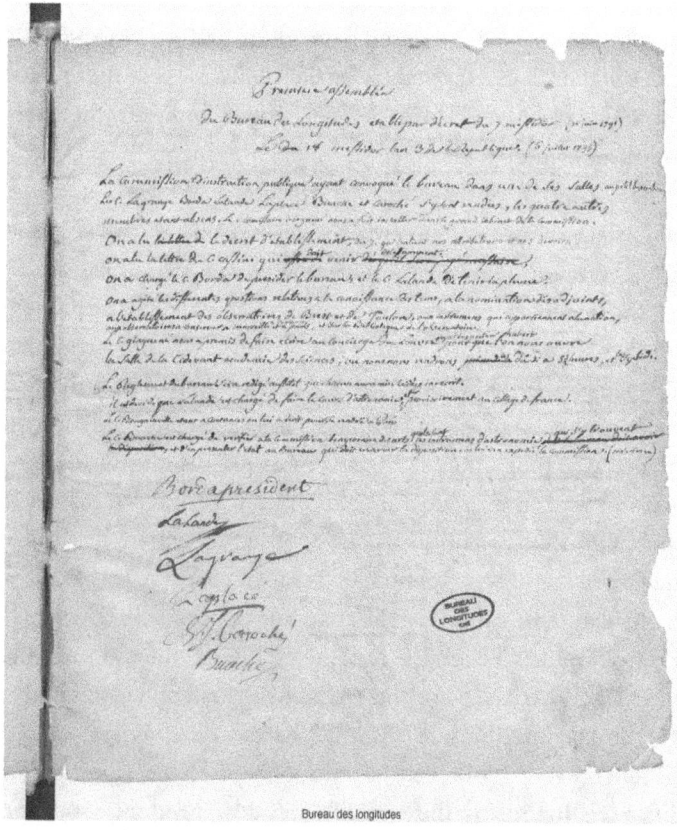

Figure 9 Minutes of the first meeting of the Bureau des Longitudes in Paris, 6 July 1795, from http://bdl.ahp-numerique.fr, Public domain.

des Temps, the Bureau was charged with the tasks of improving astronomical tables and methods for the determination of longitude, publishing astronomical and meteorological observations, supervising the Observatory of Paris, the observatory of the former École Militaire and associated establishments and taking care of 'all the astronomical instruments that belonged to the nation'. Furthermore, the Bureau was required to advise the government about the number of observatories to be maintained or created in the service of the Republic and to maintain correspondence with other observatories at home and abroad. Each year, one of the members of the Bureau had the duty of teaching a course on astronomy. The membership of the new institution consisted of two geometers, four astronomers, two former navigators, a geographer, an astronomical instrument-maker and four adjunct astronomers.[39]

The foundation of the Bureau, the scope of its mission and the composition of its membership cannot be separated from the continuous rivalry between France and Britain, either.[40] In the debate in the Convention nationale prior to its creation, the author of the proposal, Henri Grégoire, insisted that the promotion of astronomy by the state, through its impact on navigation and geography, was key to the mastery of the seas. In his view, British maritime successes since 1760 amply proved the point.[41] After the return of peace in 1815, for the British the Bureau became both a valued partner for cooperation and a formidable competitor. While in the 1820s, the Board of Longitude and the Bureau des Longitudes started to collaborate in pendulum-based research into gravity and in the re-determination of longitude between the observatories of Greenwich and Paris,[42] British scientists such as Herschel and Sabine (appointed as scientific adviser to the Admiralty in 1829) became worried about French advances in research on geomagnetism, which they regarded as 'a British province'.[43] Both Herschel and Sabine became driving forces in the launching of the huge, worldwide campaign for the collection of magnetic data from 1830 to 1845 known as the 'Magnetic Crusade', which was intended to put Britain in the lead once more.[44]

The Bureau des Longitudes, meanwhile, evolved into a leading centre of astronomical and geodetic research in France and a key intermediary between the government and the scientific world, as an organizer of expeditions and voyages of exploration and promoter of the foundation of observatories both at home and abroad. Even after the Paris Observatory had been separated from the Bureau in 1854, the institute continued to play a central role in the promotion of several branches of science, such as geography, geodesy and astronomy, as well as in practical applications in navigation and the design and testing of astronomical instruments.⁴⁵ It was only marginally concerned with meteorology, however. Although the Bureau received packages of wind and current charts from Maury himself in the 1850s, it was not involved in the international collaborative project launched at the Brussels conference in 1853.⁴⁶ The observatory had a meteorological department, but the development of meteorology was hampered by sudden changes in leadership and staff in the 1850s. In fact, the French navy depended for a while on the British storm warning system. Meteorology in France eventually became a shared responsibility on the part of the hydrographic office of the navy and the national observatory. In 1859, the government charged the Dépôt with the implementation of the agreements in Brussels, and the observatory sent its first storm warnings in 1863.⁴⁷

Infrastructures of knowledge in hydrography and navigation technology in the United States arose later than in Britain and France, and they were clearly influenced by European models to some extent. When Lieutenant Louis Goldsborough suggested to the US secretary of the navy in 1830 that a central depot of charts and instruments should be created, which would also take care of the rating and repair of marine chronometers, he explicitly referred to the 'examples and experiences' of the Spanish, French and British navies.⁴⁸ Many of the charts and instruments used at the time by the American navy, including most of its timekeepers, were of European provenance, too.⁴⁹ The navy quickly approved Goldsborough's proposal and allocated the personnel and facilities needed to get the new Washington-based agency operational within a matter of months. An observatory for the purpose of rating timekeepers formed part of the depot from the very start. The difference, compared with the European seafaring countries, was thus that the task of chronometer-rating was not assigned to an existing institute, but that a new body was created in response to the 'technological imperatives' of 'caring for instruments essential for safe navigation'.⁵⁰

Once the depot had been established, the range of its activities rapidly expanded. Apart from taking care of chronometers, the agency became responsible for the purchase, repair, supply and quality control of all other navigational aids of the navy and for the reproduction of charts and the collection of ships' journals. It began to publish charts from 1837 onwards, and the collection of ships' journals became the basis for Maury's wind and current charts, which started to appear from the late 1840s.⁵¹ The scope of observations carried out at the institute soon became much broader than that needed for the rating of timekeepers. This was partly due to the ambitions of the officers in charge, and partly to growing demand from the navy. In August 1838, for example, the secretary of the navy ordered the depot's observatory to make observations of transits of the moon and certain stars and planets in order to determine longitude differences between Washington and places visited by the US Exploring Expedition, which was ready to sail to the Pacific. More than 10,000 transits were observed during the next four years. Moreover, after the return of the exploring expedition in 1842, the depot was endowed with a new, more lavishly equipped observatory, funded by Congress, which unofficially became known as the 'Naval Observatory' or 'the National Observatory' and in 1854 was officially named the 'US Naval Observatory and Hydrographic Office'.[52] Regular magnetic and meteorological observations at the depot were undertaken from the late 1830s, too, which under Maury's leadership became a prominent feature of the institute's research programme after 1850.[53]

In terms of its size and scope of activities, however, the depot was eventually surpassed by an agency of civilian origin, namely the US Coast Survey. The Coast Survey was established in 1807 by Congress with the task of mapping 'the islands and shoals, with the roads or places of anchorage, within twenty leagues of any part of the shores of the US, and also the respective courses and distances between the principal capes and headlands', to examine shoals or banks off the American coast and to carry out hydrographic and oceanographic research on the coastal waters, including the Gulf Stream. The rationale of this decision was both military and economic. It was expected that the United States, by creating its own surveying service, would become less dependent on the supply of charts of its coastline from Britain or France (which at the time still dominated the market) and that it would be better able to prepare its defence in coastal waters. The Coast Survey would also serve the interests of the expanding American shipping industry by making navigation near the shore less time-consuming and safer.[54] The agency duly produced a large number of maps and charts, and its rate of production accelerated in the mid-nineteenth century. By 1858, it had published more than fifty finished and almost eighty preliminary sea and harbour charts, plus 120 preliminary hydrographic sketches. Some 40,000 maps and charts were distributed each year. A contemporary scientific report estimated that in this way, by helping to prevent shipwrecks, the coastal survey saved the shipping industry three million dollars each year. With the aid of a battery of instruments, some of which were specially developed by the agency's instrument department, the Gulf Stream was studied more systematically and at greater depths in the 1840s and 1850s than ever before. Direction, velocity, salinity, temperature, organic life in the deep sea – no aspect was left unexplored by the parties of the Coastal Survey.[55]

Under the leadership of Alexander Dallas Bache, who became superintendent of the institute in 1843 and held this position until his death in 1867, the research programme at the Coast Survey developed far beyond the specific goals laid down in 1807. This extension was made possible by a rather flexible clause in the founding act, which ruled that the president of the United States and the superintendent of the service would decide on the specific natural subjects that should be studied, including 'such other matters that he would deem proper for completing an accurate chart of every part of the coast'.[56] Bache exploited this opportunity to the full. Using European agencies such as the Bureau des Longitudes as his model, he turned the Coast Survey into a centre of knowledge production and dissemination in tidology, meteorology and oceanography, surveying and hydrography, as well as the study of terrestrial magnetism, physics, natural history and astronomy in the service of geodesy. The Coast Survey established hundreds of tidal stations, cooperated with many observatories at colleges and universities across the United States and exchanged information with numerous scientists and scientific organizations abroad. The staff of the agency tripled in size to nearly 800 employees in the early 1850s, and its annual reports mushroomed from 134 pages in 1850 to 464 eight years later.[57] Bache managed to boost the federal budget for his institute to more than half a million dollars a year in the late 1850s. At the time of his death, the Coast Survey had become the most prominent scientific institution in the United States.[58]

Before 1850, neither Spain nor the Netherlands saw growth in their institutions on the scale seen in Britain, France or the United States. The knowledge infrastructure that had been put in place in Spain before the end of the eighteenth century continued to function, although the work of the *dirección hidrográfica* was seriously disrupted by the military and political upheavals between 1808 and 1814 and again in the 1820s. The cooperation between the hydrographic service and the Royal Observatory in Cádiz remained close. Spanish hydrographers began to exchange charts and plans with their British colleagues, too. In the eyes of the Spanish hydrographer Felipe Bauzá (who lived as a refugee in London after 1823), the number and variety of charts made by the *dirección* was in fact in advance of those produced by the British navy. For the British, about 1820, the internal work organization of the Spanish office was a model of its kind.[59] But Spain's early lead was not retained in the following decades. For example, Spain was not represented at the groundbreaking maritime conference in Brussels in 1853, although Spanish seamen became involved in Maury's international project a few years later.[60] A state-sponsored meteorological institute in Spain was not founded until 1887.

The Netherlands showed a more volatile picture. Although the sophisticated infrastructure of knowledge of the VOC disappeared about 1800, together with the collapse of the company itself, new positions and institutions were created under the aegis of the newly centralized Dutch state. However, the distribution of functions between different officials and agencies changed repeatedly until the 1850s.

From 1795, the navy commissioned a mathematician and examiner general to examine, among other assignments, all journals of naval ships to detect whether 'some new discoveries, trials or observations had been made, that could benefit seafaring'. The new official, Jacob Florijn, also became a full member of the Longitude Committee.[61] At Florijn's suggestion, a depot of the Navy was created in 1808, which not only would function as a repository of charts, plans and drawings but also was also charged with the tasks of improving the charts and care of the navy's timekeepers. In his proposal, Florijn explicitly referred to existing arrangements in Britain, France, Denmark, Portugal and Spain.[62]

When the Longitude Committee – after its temporary abolition between 1811 and 1815 during the incorporation of the Netherlands into the French empire – was reinstated in 1815, it was instructed to combine the functions of the old Committee and the mathematician and examiner general of the navy. Aside from the annual publication of the nautical almanac and (once again) the improvement of charts, it now also became responsible for the examination of naval officers. After 1823, the committee was further charged with the task of examining candidates for different ranks of mate in the navy and the merchant marine, and testing the competence of newly appointed state-paid lecturers in mathematics and navigation in the principal seaports. The care of the navy's chronometers was entrusted to the committee between 1824 and 1832, too, after which it was transferred to the state lecturer in mathematics and navigation in Amsterdam, Jacob Swart. Swart also happened to be the director of the principal firm publishing books and cartographic aids in the Netherlands, Hulst van Keulen, and he became a member of the Longitude Committee a few years later.[63] The task of the publication of the nautical almanac, meanwhile, became redundant after the Netherlands switched prime meridians. At the suggestion of the Longitude Committee, the king decreed in 1826 that the meridian of Greenwich would henceforth form the basis for the lunar tables in the Dutch almanac, which meant that it was no longer necessary to recalculate data in the British *Nautical Almanac* to the meridian of Tenerife.[64] The committee's responsibility for ensuring the improvement of charts did not mean that it now served as a hydrographic office. The production of maps, plans and charts was still largely left to private firms, although naval officers *did* carry out a number of surveys of Dutch home waters and waterways in the Dutch East Indies and prepared the results for printing.[65]

More durable changes in the infrastructure of knowledge were introduced in the 1850s. The Longitude Committee was finally abolished in 1850, and a navy hydrographer was appointed in 1855. A separate position of controller and curator of naval instruments was created in 1858. The first holder of this post was the professor of astronomy at Leiden University and director of the university's observatory, Frederik Kaiser.[66] In 1854, professor of mathematics Christopher Buys Ballot from Utrecht University managed to get state funding to transform his small observatory for terrestrial magnetism and meteorology into a full-blown research institute, the KNMI. The institute comprised two departments, one for terrestrial magnetism led by a former fellow student of Buys Ballot, the other for maritime meteorology, headed by the naval officer Marin Henri Jansen. Jansen had met Maury in Washington a few years before, had participated in the Brussels conference and had subsequently invited the famous American to give a series of public lectures in the Netherlands. Jansen's zealous lobbying of the minister of the navy, along with Buys Ballot's well-timed emphasis on the importance of meteorology for the Netherlands as a seafaring nation and colonial empire, had been crucial in obtaining the government's support for the new institute. Although Buys Ballot and Jansen fell out within a year, the KNMI soon proved to be a key player in the realization of Maury's grand international project of systematically collecting massive amounts of data about the oceans.[67]

In all the major seafaring nations, the main task of hydrographic offices and other agencies concerned with the marine environment in the first decades of the nineteenth century was to improve the effectiveness of the armed forces. The more accurately vessels were able to survey and measure seas and waterways, anticipate the behaviour of winds, currents and the weather and navigate the oceans, the better the state would be able to assert its power vis-à-vis other states. At least, this was the initial idea. But the scientists or naval officers in charge frequently happened to steer these state-sponsored institutes in directions that went far beyond their original mandates. In many ways, dominant figures such as Beaufort, Beautemps-Beaupré, Bache, Buys Ballot or Maury managed to shape the agencies under their leadership in accordance with their own ambitions and designs. These founding fathers of maritime science not only were dedicated to promoting the interests and status of their formal principal, the state, but were also keen to boost their personal reputation and build networks of collaboration that crossed national boundaries.

Moreover, governments of seafaring nations broadened their concept of national interest to include the improvement of the safety of navigation of merchant navies, too. In this respect, France and Spain were far ahead of the Netherlands, Britain or the United States for many years. All masters of foreign-going ships and coastal vessels in France were required to take an exam in the theory and practice of navigation. These regulations were in fact a kind of model for shipowners, consuls and other experts in Britain in the 1830s and 1840s.[68] Before 1800, the Spanish state had already introduced compulsory exams for navigators in the merchant marine (under the remit of the navy) and issued an elaborate set of rules concerning navigational schools. While military authorities in the nineteenth century long remained involved in supervising the training of masters and mates in the merchant marine, from about 1850, the Ministry of Commerce, Education and Public Works tightened its grip on nautical education. New guidelines were introduced for the navigation schools' curriculum under the supervision of the state in the major ports of Spain. Private schools, which prepared candidates for the state-supervised exams, were closed down shortly after 1870, because they were attracting such large numbers of students that the labour market was overflowing with certified masters and mates.[69]

After the Napoleonic Wars, the Dutch and British imperial machines acquired facilities for the diffusion and certification of nautical knowledge in the mercantile marine that were similar to those in France and Spain. In the newly formed Kingdom of the Netherlands (which until 1830 comprised both present-day Belgium and the former Dutch Republic), the central government in 1823 introduced an ambitious scheme to improve the knowledge and skills of masters and mates in the mercantile marine. State-paid lecturers in mathematics and navigation, who would offer free instruction to anyone wishing to be trained as a pilot for the navy or the merchant marine, were appointed in the four main port cities of Amsterdam, Rotterdam, Antwerp and Ostend. In addition, the state introduced optional exams on the theory of navigation for mates in the merchant marine. These were similar to the (compulsory) exams for mates in the navy, which were graded from fourth to first mate. Members of the Longitude Committee acted as examiners.[70]

After these state-funded facilities had been abolished in 1856 (for reasons that will be explained shortly), the NHM stepped in with another initiative, which had a far-reaching impact on the merchant marine. In 1858, the directors of the NHM ordered 'in the well-understood interest of shipowners and insurers' that on every ship chartered by the company, two or three mates (depending on the size of the ship) should possess a certificate of examination. This measure probably affected some 40 per cent of all mates in the Dutch mercantile marine. Ten years later, the requirement was extended to include all mates on merchantmen chartered by the NHM. State-supervised, optional examinations of mates were re-established in 1877 and exams were finally made compulsory for all mates on ships over 100 tons in the merchant navy in 1904.[71]

Although the NHM's decision in 1858 was occasioned by the high number of shipwrecks in the previous year, in the Netherlands there was never as much concern about the competency of navigators in the merchant fleet as there was in Britain. In the 1840s, a shipwreck on the route to Asia was actually regarded as a rare event.[72] In Britain, by contrast, the extension of the state's role with regard to the education and qualifications of navigators was an (admittedly belated) response to the alarming rise in the number of shipwrecks observed in the 1830s. The committee on the Causes of Shipwrecks of 1836, chaired by the dedicated social reformer James Silk Buckingham, identified the incompetency of shipmasters as a major cause of the problem. Among the remedies proposed was the creation of a Mercantile Marine Board, which would concern itself, among other tasks, with the examination of officers and the establishment of 'cheap' nautical schools. The committee pleaded for the introduction of statutory examinations for navigators in the British merchant fleet after the example of the Royal Navy, EIC, 'the French, the Dutch, the Danes, the Swedes and even ... the Russians'.[73] In the Royal Navy, all those aspiring to a commissioned rank had had to pass a lieutenant's exam since the late seventeenth century. After the Napoleonic Wars, the Admiralty managed to tighten its grip on the formation of its officer corps by introducing stricter rules for the approval of midshipmen appointed by captains themselves. From 1839, the Admiralty could compel these 'First Class Volunteers' to sit an exam, too, and in 1851 it could actually reject candidates if they failed to pass the test. In the EIC, all candidates for promotions from the rank of fourth mate upwards had to pass an exam as well.[74]

The slow response by the British Parliament to the recommendations of the committee concerning examinations in the merchant navy was due both to reluctance among MPs to extend the legislative role of the state and resistance to government interference by powerful interests in the shipping industry. These interests found a mouthpiece in the General Shipowners' Society, established in 1833. This did not mean that all shipowners were opposed to examinations per se. After 1836, mutual insurance societies of shipowners in Sunderland, South Shields and other places created their own 'marine boards', manned by experienced seamen and a few experts in theory, which offered candidates the opportunity to obtain a certificate of competence for commanding an insured merchant ship by taking an exam in navigation.[75]

The resistance to state regulations could only gradually be overcome. First, the Board of Trade introduced voluntary examinations for masters and mates in the mercantile marine in 1845, which could be taken in most of the major British ports. These exams were usually supervised by Trinity House, which was already experienced in examining pilots. Soon thereafter, the Admiralty stipulated that merchantmen could not be hired as freighter, transport or convict ships unless the masters and mates possessed a certificate of competency. This rule was subsequently extended to Post Office packets. As a result of these measures, the number of certificates issued by examining boards established in the major seaports soared. More than 3,000 certificates were awarded between 1845 and 1850, the majority of them by Trinity House London. Finally, examinations were made compulsory under the Mercantile Marine Act of 1850. From 1 January 1851, 'no foreign-going vessel [would] be permitted to clear out from any Custom-house in the United Kingdom without the masters and mates respectively being in possession of certificates.'[76] The supervision of the system was entrusted to a newly created Marine Department under the Board of Trade, a modest version of the Mercantile Marine Board proposed by the committee of 1836. Local boards would be responsible for conducting the exams.[77]

The 'cheap' nautical schools envisaged by the Committee of 1836 materialized once the compulsory exams had been introduced. Although it took some seventeen years in all before the recommendation of the committee was finally implemented, nautical education was nevertheless the first branch of technical education to become an object of concern for the British state.[78] In 1853, a Department of Science and Art (DSA) was created under the Board of Trade, which set out to promote the teaching of applied sciences by subsidizing local schools. Within a decade, no fewer than seventeen schools in British and Irish ports received funding in this way from the national treasury.[79] Subsequent changes in the central financing system, however, led to a precipitous decline in state-subsidized nautical education in the 1860s. By 1876, only three DSA-supported navigation schools remained.[80]

In the United States, the federal government was more sluggish in taking steps to improve the competency of navigators in the merchant marine than national governments in the Netherlands and Britain. In the early days of the Republic, Congress did not even bother to make regulations concerning the training or quality control of personnel of the US Navy. Although an American navy had formally been established in 1794, it took a long time before standard education for naval officers was put in place. Candidates could either choose to serve some time as a midshipman on a navy vessel, or they could learn the tricks of the trade in the merchant marine. Examinations for lieutenants in the navy were not introduced until 1819 and a naval academy for the training of officers, including a standardized curriculum and a regular schedule of exams, was not created until 1845.[81] Significantly, the foundation of the Annapolis academy took place in the very period when the US Congress also facilitated the expansion of the Coast Survey and the growth of the Naval Observatory. It was not until ten years after the Civil War that the federal government did something to support the improvement of the skills of merchant seamen for the first time. It obliged the US Navy to put ships at the disposal of local nautical schools for the training of navigators in the mercantile marine. Active-duty naval officers became instructors on these school ships. Thus, the reasoning went, the bonds between the navy and the merchant marine would be strengthened for the benefit of national power.[82]

And what about the control on the quality of instruments used at sea? While imperial machines after 1800 made provisions for the care of instruments such as chronometers and devices for astronomical or meteorological observations, especially for the navy, they hardly concerned themselves with the construction of instruments as such, except in an indirect way. The US Coast Survey under Bache, for example, boasted its own instrument shop, but it bought most of the sophisticated instruments for surveying and astronomical observations from European instrument-makers, such as Troughton and Simms in London and Henri Prudence Gambey in Paris.[83] Chronometers, sextants, quadrants and telescopes for the depot were also supplied by European firms in the 1830s.[84] American seamen long continued to procure most of their octants and sextants from England. It was not until about 1860 that American firms managed to increase their share on the home market, thanks, among other things, to investing in dividing engines.[85]

The production of instruments for use at sea in the Atlantic world was largely left to the market. London remained the largest centre of instrument-making, with Paris in second place. Instrument-makers in these cities sold their products both on home and foreign markets. Amsterdam continued to be a production centre in its own right, although its output was now mainly geared to the domestic market. Notably, after the Napoleonic Wars the Netherlands succeeded in building a small domestic industry for producing timekeepers. Of the eighty-five chronometers owned by the Dutch Navy in 1835, seventy-four came from Britain, one from France and nine from the Netherlands itself.[86]

From the 1830s, state institutions in some places *did* offer a facility that made it easier for merchantmen and naval vessels to check their chronometers in harbour. Observatories began to send out time signals by the drop of a time-ball or by signs from towers. The first time-ball was installed at Greenwich in 1833. The Cape of Good Hope and St. Helena followed a few years later, and the Naval Observatory in Washington sent out time signals from 1845 onwards. Systems for time signals in Dutch ports came into operation in the following year.[87]

In ship construction, knowledge infrastructures in Britain and the Netherlands started to change under the impact of the Revolutionary and Napoleonic Wars. Old patterns in the creation, certification and dissemination of knowledge on ship design underwent a profound transformation. Views on ship design that had long been considered authoritative were called into question.[88] The locus of decision making about issues such as the requisite skills of ship-designers, and how a ship design should be judged, shifted among a range of groups and institutions.

The effects of these lengthy wars on the development of knowledge in shipbuilding became visible in several ways. The titanic conflict with France, which broke out in 1793 and continued almost uninterruptedly until 1815, put unprecedented demands on the capacity of the shipbuilding industry in Britain. Many more naval vessels needed to be built, repaired and refitted than ever before. As the royal dockyards were not able to produce sufficient new ships, much more work had to be contracted out to private yards than during any previous war. Of all the warships built between 1803 and 1815, as many as 84 per cent came from private shipyards. Moreover, the contracts involved a far greater number of yards, spread out all over the country, instead of clustering in the neighbourhoods of London and Portsmouth. Dozens of private yards in Devon, Cornwall, Norfolk and North-East England now got contracts for building vessels for the Royal Navy, too, especially for frigates and other small ships.[89] But the dispersal of contract-building meant that the Navy Board ran the risk of losing its grip on the quality of construction. Keeping a check on building in a limited number of trusted private yards not far from the main naval bases was easier than supervising the process in a large number of yards in distant parts of the country.[90] In that sense, the board became more dependent on the knowledge nurtured at the shipyards themselves. On the other hand, the board was still able to exert a certain measure of control over private yards, *ex ante* and *ex post*, by inviting tenders for contracts and by introducing a system of rewards and penalties for the shipyards' performance.[91] The very extension of contract-building also left the board better informed about standards of construction in private yards throughout the country, and more private yards became familiar with the building of warships. The circulation of knowledge thus increased.

Within the navy, control over ship design after 1800 increasingly became a hotly contested field between master shipwrights, naval architects and naval officers. Robert Seppings, surveyor of the navy from 1813 to 1832, was the last man in that office who had risen through the ranks of the royal dockyards from apprentice to shipwright, quarterman, foreman, assistant to Master Shipwright and Master Shipwright at Chatham yard.[92] Far from being a mere 'dockyard matey', as a champion of an opposing party derided him in the 1830s, Seppings was an articulate and innovative thinker, who published in the *Transactions* of the Royal Society and received honours from scholarly organizations both at home and at abroad. In 1818, the Royal Society awarded him the Copley Medal for his papers on improvements in ship construction.[93]

In the eyes of advocates of 'naval architecture', however, the dockyard learning of master shipwrights was 'derived from imperfect experience', which left ship design largely dependent on 'accident and chance'. Ship construction should instead be more based on theory and controlled experimentation, following the supposedly superior example of France. Hulls should be designed according to regular geometrical forms, which had to be subjected to large-scale model trials. These conceptions, which were forcefully promoted by the Society for the Improvement of Naval Architecture from the 1790s onwards, were a source of inspiration for the government-sponsored School of Naval Architecture founded at the Portsmouth dockyard in 1811. The school offered instruction in mathematics, geometry and hydrodynamics to selected dockyard apprentices, separate from the other workmen.[94]

The authority of both naval architects and master shipwrights was in turn contested by naval officers, who claimed that they themselves were best qualified to judge whether a ship was well designed or not. After all, they were the ones who had experience with handling ships at sea. When the Whigs ousted the Tories from power in 1830, naval officers joined forces with the incoming First Lord of the Admiralty to overhaul the management of shipbuilding for the Royal Navy. The Navy Board was abolished, Seppings was dismissed and the School of Naval Architecture was closed in 1832. The locus of decision making on ship design now shifted to a newly appointed surveyor, the naval officer William Symonds, who managed all affairs relating to naval shipbuilding under the supervision of the Admiralty.[95] Despite incessant criticism from graduates of the School of Naval Architecture and from master shipwrights, who persisted in defending Seppings' legacy, naval officers remained in the ascendancy until the late 1840s. It was yet another turnabout in British politics in 1847 that led to the rearrangement of responsibilities in the supervision of ship design, which diminished the dominance of naval officers. Although the post of surveyor continued to be held by a naval officer, the actual design was left to a technical staff consisting of naval architects and master shipwrights. When evaluating designs, the surveyor henceforth had to consult a Council of Science, which included experts from a variety of backgrounds.[96]

In the Netherlands, the knowledge infrastructure relating to ship construction underwent even greater changes than in Britain, as a direct result of the Revolutionary and Napoleonic Wars. Under the new 'Batavian' regime, which came to power in 1795 with the support of the French army, naval shipbuilding was centralized under a constructor general. France became a leading example for Dutch shipwrights. A state-sponsored mission was sent to France in 1797 to visit engineering schools, examine model collections and study construction methods at dockyards along the Atlantic coast. Inspired by the French example, a central collection of models was established at the naval base in Amsterdam. A number of Dutch students received training in naval architecture in France from 1806. Some of these French-trained students rose to become leading shipbuilders in the newly founded Kingdom of the Netherlands after 1815. A school for naval engineering after the French example was founded in Rotterdam in 1822, and an engineering corps of the navy was formed in 1843.[97] Thus, the Netherlands, too, witnessed the rise of formal training in ship construction, the increased use of theory in ship design and the professionalization of naval architects.

However, naval shipbuilding in the Netherlands was never entirely dominated by the French model, except during the annexation by France between 1810 and 1813. Dutch shipwrights introduced adaptations in French-inspired designs and often made use of half models in the design process, which was uncommon in France. After 1815, Dutch naval constructors and naval officers also studied construction methods in situ in Britain. One of the results of these missions was that Seppings' system of diagonal braces, with some modifications, was adopted in the Dutch Navy as well.[98] Dutch textbooks on naval architecture published in 1840 and 1859 frequently referred to British as well as French and Spanish sources.[99] Ironically, while Dutch ship constructors pored over the work of Jorge Juan, the development of the knowledge infrastructure relating to shipbuilding in Spain itself had shifted into reverse gear. The number of constructors declined during the French occupation between 1808 and 1814, and the corps of naval engineers, was abolished thirteen years after the return of independence.[100]

In naval medecine, France in the nineteenth century became the 'undisputed leader', not least because of its early-established infrastructure of knowledge.[101] The ordinance of 1689 remained the basis for its naval medical care system until the 1880s. The state-funded schools in Brest, Toulon and Rochefort continued to be centres of naval medical education and expertise. Curricula were standardized and examinations were held according to rules laid down in government regulations. All three towns still boasted large naval hospitals, which also served as sites for instruction of local medical schools. Professors affiliated with these institutions wrote authoritative texts on hygiene and medical practice. The entire system was supervised by an inspector general. The main changes to the system were the introduction of port councils of health, which supervised all hygienic medical matters in the port, and some improvements to the status and career prospects of surgeons serving on-board naval vessels from the 1830s.[102]

Britain made a catch-up effort of sorts in strengthening its knowledge infrastructure relating to medical care. The duties of the navy's Sick and Hurt Board, including the selection and supervision of naval surgeons, were first transferred to the Transport Board, then to the Victualling Board and eventually, from 1832, became the responsibility of a newly created head manager of the navy's medical service, the physician general of the navy. The first physician general, William Burnett, was the initiator of the annual statistical survey on the health of the navy, compiled from surgeons' journals and naval hospital records. It represented a major step forward in the study of the incidence and causes of diseases and deaths.[103] Although the British Admiralty, unlike the French navy, still lacked 'in-house' training schools for naval surgeons, it *did* encourage what Katherine Foxhall has called 'a confident naval culture of scientific and medical experimentation'. Medical libraries were established at Plymouth and Haslar hospitals in 1827, as well as a medical museum in Haslar, and a full-time lecturer was appointed at the latter hospital to teach naval surgeons, although the position was discontinued after 1840. And the surgeons of the Royal Navy, like their French colleagues, managed to achieve an improvement in their professional status, which 'contributed materially to improvement in health from the 1850s'.[104]

Merchant marines generally lagged behind the development in naval services. Imperial machines long continued to be less concerned with the welfare of seamen on merchant ships than of those on naval vessels. When governments *did* make regulations to improve health on merchant ships, and established institutions to take care of their implementation, their prime target group was that of passengers rather than crews, and especially passengers travelling on ships chartered by governments themselves. The first act for the protection of passengers was passed in the British Parliament in 1803. It restricted the number of passengers who might be carried to one for every two tons on British ships and one for every five tons on foreign vessels. It specified the amounts of bread, meal and pints of 'melasses' to be issued to each passenger, and the frequency with which bedding had to be aired and the space between decks fumigated. It also stipulated that all vessels with fifty passengers or more should carry a qualified surgeon and should be provided with a 'properly supplied' medicine chest. No ship would be allowed to leave a British port before all passengers had been mustered by government officials.[105] Yet, this first attempt at regulation ended in failure, because the rules were too complex and impractical and enforcement was inadequate. Neither custom officials nor naval officers nor justices of the peace, charged with supervising their implementation, were sufficiently up to the task. It was not until a special corps of emigration officers was put in place in the main emigration ports in England, Scotland and Ireland between 1834 and 1840 that the enforcement of the passenger laws gradually became more effective. The expertise accumulated in this executive corps later helped to improve legislation still further.[106]

Governments intervened most actively to improve conditions on vessels that were chartered to carry passengers to Australia and Asia. From the end of the Napoleonic Wars, the British Admiralty posted naval surgeons on every ship carrying convicts from Britain and Ireland to New South Wales or Van Diemen's Land, which was a major factor in the reduction of death rates.[107] When free emigration to Australia increased in the 1830s, the supervision of conditions on government-chartered emigrant ships was entrusted to a newly created body under the Colonial Office in London, the Colonial Land and Emigration Commission (CLEC). The responsibilities of the CLEC included the enforcement of all rules and regulations relating to hygiene and medical care at sea, such as the recruitment of well-qualified and experienced surgeons and the collection of sick books and journals. The commission thus became a centre of the accumulation of data and knowledge on medical conditions on board, and it made a vital contribution to the decline of mortality on passenger ships sailing to Australia.[108] For Dutch troop transports to the East Indies after 1815, contracts between the government and shipowners stipulated that every ship should carry a qualified doctor and be provided with a well-stocked medicine chest, sufficient surgical instruments and an adequate quantity of food for the sick.[109]

Like the British Parliament, the US Congress introduced regulations for passenger transport from the early nineteenth century onwards. The British act of 1803 in a way served as a model for the first US Passenger Act, adopted in 1819. But the American passenger acts had a greater emphasis on restricting immigration than the British ones. Although the ostensible purpose of the act of 1819 was to provide 'for the safety and comfort of passengers' by imposing a maximum on the number of passengers allowed per ton of registry for all ships arriving in American ports, it raised the price of passage so much that an Atlantic crossing became less affordable for potential migrants from poorer backgrounds. A new law of 1849 included an additional requirement of minimum space per passenger expressed in feet. As a result of pressure from shipping interests, however, these rules were soon relaxed.[110]

On the other hand, the Americans were ahead of the British in building an infrastructure for the medical care of merchant seamen. From 1798, the federal government assumed the task of establishing hospitals for 'the relief of sick and disabled' seamen on the understanding that such facilities would help to maintain a supply of healthy maritime workers, which would benefit the economic expansion of the Republic. The system was funded by means of a tax on mariners' wages collected by federal custom officers on the arrival of an American ship in any US port. The first federal marine hospitals were opened in Boston, Newport (RI) and New Orleans. By the end of the 1850s, the number had risen to sixteen, spread over ports on the Atlantic seaboard as well as on inland lakes and waterways.[111]

Self-organization, infrastructure and the circulation of maritime knowledge

The Brussels conference of 1853 was a milestone in many ways. The first ever international maritime conference, it brought together men of science and naval officers and started a collaborative project that involved large numbers of seamen sailing on merchantmen and warships from many countries in the world. It was an event where two forces of globalization converged: state-sponsored machines in the service of imperial power and self-organization. On the one hand, the actual business of the conference was done by representatives of agencies of imperial machines from major seafaring nations such as Britain, France, the United States and the Netherlands. On the other hand, the conference also reflected a tendency in self-organization towards more formal organization and growing specialization. Networks were increasingly supplemented by societies, formal meetings and organized disciplines. And the success of the project launched at the Brussels conference was crucially dependent on the participation of seamen who were eager and able to improve their knowledge and skills by building their own networks and organizations. This was facilitated to no small extent by the process of professionalization among masters and mates in merchant marines, which was already under way before governments began to impose more regulations on the shipping industry. Autonomous professionalization among navigators in merchant navies became an increasingly powerful factor in the making of maritime knowledge in the Atlantic world.

Scholarly correspondence networks in the Atlantic world initially continued to flourish. A change in the organization and accounting of postal services meant that scientific correspondence in the nineteenth century became even easier than in the past. The cost of sending letters fell from the 1840s and 1850s onwards, as the old system of payment by the recipient according to the number of sheets in a letter and the distance travelled was replaced by a system of prepaid postal stamps, with the fee based on the weight of the mail.[112] Private and official correspondence networks were built and maintained. Many scientists still conducted a voluminous private correspondence. Adolphe Quetelet, the host of the Brussels conference, and William Whewell, a towering figure in British science in the middle of the nineteenth century, were quintessential examples of tireless letter-writers.[113] Other scholarly correspondence was conducted by individuals in some official capacity, such as secretary, director, governor or employee of a scientific society, or an agency of an imperial or commercial machine such as the Bureau des Longitudes, the Board of Longitude, the US Coast Survey, the KNMI, the EIC or the Hudson's Bay Company.

New elements after 1800 included the proliferation of associations and formal meetings and the emergence of organized scientific disciplines. 'Scholarly networks grew tighter with the professionalization and institutionalization of science,' Angela Schwarz has observed.[114] The number of scientific and medical associations in Britain soared from 24 in 1800, via 44 in 1820 and 95 in 1840, to 139 in 1850. In the meantime, the ratio of generic 'literary and philosophical' societies to associations with a more specialist focus changed from 80:20 to 35:65.[115] With the multiplication of societies came a certain shift from London to provincial towns, and from general to disciplinary organizations The foundation of the BAAS in York in 1831 exemplifies this shift in geographical balance. Like the London-based Royal Society, the BAAS aimed to promote science in a broad sense, but it proposed to do so, more specifically, by encouraging the exchange of knowledge between all those 'who cultivated science in different parts of Britain', by giving 'a stronger impulse and more systematic direction to scientific inquiry'. Within fifteen years, the new society had over 1,800 members.[116] The Linnean Society of London, which had promoted natural history since 1788, was joined by many other discipline-based societies after 1800. Geology, geography, astronomy, zoology, botany, statistics, chemistry – all of those specialties saw the creation of separate disciplinary associations.[117] A Society for the Diffusion of Useful Knowledge among a wider public was founded in 1826.[118] All of these associations held regular, formal meetings and adopted formal rules for their organization, membership and activities.

The rise of scientific societies, the spread of formal meetings and the rise of organized disciplines was not just a British phenomenon. The foundation of the BAAS was actually inspired by the example of a general scientific association founded in Germany in 1822, the Gesellschaft Deutscher Naturforscher und Ärzte.[119] The BAAS, in turn, provided a template for the American Association for the Advancement of Science, which was launched in 1848. 'Dozens of Americans' were present at meetings of the British association in the 1830s and 1840s.[120] Discipline-based associations likewise sprang up in many countries in the Atlantic world in the nineteenth century. The creation of a geographical society in London in 1830, for example, was preceded by the foundation of a Société de Géographie in Paris in 1821 and a Gesellschaft für Erdkunde in Berlin in 1828. These societies aimed to serve both as an institutional basis for disciplinary autonomy and as a national hub for the exchange of knowledge.[121]

A mix of competition and cooperation characterized these self-organizing national associations. On the one hand, the associational movement cannot be separated from a growing belief among 'cultivators of science', especially in Britain after 1820, that new, concerted initiatives were necessary to prevent their own country being left behind in the advance of science. The foundation of the BAAS had much to do with the outcry caused by the publication of Charles Babbage's *Reflections on the Decline of Science in England* a few months previously, which had vigorously attacked those who in his view had 'mismanaged' the long-established bastion of British science, the Royal Society.[122] If nothing was done, the 'declinists' argued, Britain ran the risk of being overtaken by France and Germany. The BAAS also formed the heart of the lobby that launched the 'Magnetic Crusade', which purported to 'boost the prestige of British science and to add to national glory'. Apart from Sabine and Beaufort, all of the leading advocates of this campaign were members of the new national association.[123] On the other hand, 'intercourse … with foreign philosophers' was an objective of the BAAS from the very beginning, too. International cooperation was a distinct feature of the 'Magnetic Crusade'.

The fledgling geographical societies in European capitals after 1820 similarly aimed to combine a strong national profile with a 'universalist' ideal of the transnational exchange of knowledge.[124]

Meanwhile, relations between different social groups engaged in inquiries on the maritime environment grew tenser, in some respects. Men of science became keener to assert supremacy in the hierarchy of those who claimed to embody knowledge. In 1833, William Whewell introduced the term 'scientist' to describe the collectivity of the 'cultivators of science'.[125] Scientists as a group professed to possess a higher authority in the study of nature than mere 'practical' men, although they often relied on the cooperation of these very people to supply them with valuable data. In tidology, theorists such as Whewell were eager to get access to observations made by local tide calculators in ports and dockyards, while claiming the highest recognition for themselves as purveyors of scientific discoveries.[126] In meteorology, academically-trained scientists forcefully asserted their superiority over naval officers, who had been of critical importance in making the study of winds and currents into a distinct, legitimate discipline in the first place. Bache clashed with Maury, Buys Ballot with Jansen and Herschel with Fitzroy.[127]

Naval officers in Britain, for their part, tried to assert supreme authority in ship design against rival claims from shipwrights and naval architects. In this prolonged struggle, as we have seen, naval officers managed to gain the upper hand for a while. The contest grew more and more intense, because naval architects became increasingly assertive, too. The propaganda campaign of the Society for the Improvement of Naval Architecture in the late 1790s and the training programme at the School for Naval Architecture at Portsmouth dockyard inaugurated in 1811 led to the emergence of a new, self-confident group of experts who claimed to possess a special ability to take a scientific approach to ship construction. Although the improving society disappeared in 1801 and the school was abolished in 1832, naval architects succeeded in mobilizing substantial support for their cause among politicians and men of science in the 1830s and 1840s. John Scott Russell, a shipbuilder who combined a solid training in mechanical trades with a thorough education in mathematics and natural philosophy, received lavish grants from the BAAS for his investigations on the characteristics of waves and the optimal forms of ship hulls.[128] It was Russell who eventually took the initiative to form an organization of naval architects, which would be 'a most powerful body for the protection of the true interest of naval architects', as distinct from practical shipwrights who had learned their trade through experience. This new society, the Institution of Naval Architects (INA), founded in 1860, would serve as a platform for the exchange of knowledge between shipbuilders, engineers and naval officers, promote experimental and other investigations and examine new inventions in naval architecture. The INA, for its part, initiated the establishment of a Royal School of Naval Architecture by the Admiralty, which opened in 1864.[129]

Perhaps the most striking new phenomenon in self-organization after 1800 was the growing professionalization among navigating officers in merchant marines. It was no accident that key innovations in navigation technology, such as position-line navigation and a new solution for the double-altitude problem, were devised by an American and a Dutch merchant captain, Thomas Sumner and Abraham Hazewinkel. Masters and mates in mercantile marines became better educated, better organized and better informed about the latest developments in their field than before. This change was not primarily effected from above, as with naval officers and naval architects, but was a result of initiatives at a local level. The drive for professionalism mainly originated from below.

Local shipmasters' societies, which arose in the eighteenth century, played an important role in this process. The spread of these associations continued after 1800. No fewer than fifteen new societies, called *zeemanscolleges*, were founded in the Netherlands after the Napoleonic Wars, most of them before the 1850s.[130] Like marine societies in American ports, *zeemanscolleges* aimed to provide relief to shipmasters and their families. Each *college* established a fund that paid benefits to widows and children of deceased members, or to members living in straitened circumstances due to accident, illness or old age. The original membership – called the 'effective' or 'ordinary' members – consisted solely of shipmasters; mates and common seamen were rarely admitted. Effective members supplied the bulk of the payments to the mutual insurance fund. Later on, the societies also received contributions from non-seafaring citizens from local elites, known as 'honorary' or 'extraordinary' members. By the 1860s, most of the shipmasters in the Netherlands were members of such associations.[131]

In addition to offering assistance to their members, shipmasters' societies also fulfilled a variety of other functions after 1800. They promoted the circulation of knowledge relevant for the improvement of navigation by collecting ships' journals and making them available for public inspection. The East India Marine Society in Salem thus made sixty-seven journals of voyages to various parts of the world publicly accessible between 1800 and 1820. In 1842, the Liverpool Shipmasters' Association opened a register for 'recording such extracts from the log-books as may relate to any new discoveries or the confirmation of previous observations'. American societies were concerned with the maintenance of lighthouses.[132]

Some shipmasters' societies on both sides of the Atlantic founded libraries and reading rooms provided with newspapers, journals and professional literature. The East India Marine Society in Salem in 1825 opened a museum housing the society's collection of 'natural and artificial curiosities'. In 1829, the Amsterdam *zeemanscollege* 'Zeemanshoop' established a lectureship in navigation. In 1842, the Liverpool Shipmasters' Association started a series of lectures on 'subjects interesting to navigators'. The *Nautical Magazine* reported that 'many shipmasters [were] present' at the first lecture, given by a Mr Livingstone, 'on that most intricate and mysterious subject – Oceanic Currents'.[133] Many shipmasters' societies in the 1850s supported the advancement of science by encouraging their members to assemble masses of data on winds, currents and other marine phenomena for the benefit of meteorological and oceanographic research and, at one remove, the improvement of shipping itself. After Maury's lecture tour of the Netherlands, 'Zeemanshoop' in Amsterdam formed a 'committee for scientific seafaring' and the *zeemanscollege* 'Maatschappij tot Nut der Zeevaart' in Rotterdam installed a 'committee for the advancement of the study of oceanic phenomena', or 'Ocean committee' for short.[134]

The growth of shipmasters' societies was both a product of the collective ambition of shipmasters to achieve a measure of social security for their own group and an expression of a sustained drive to attain higher professional standards. Although professionalization among navigating officers in the merchant navies primarily originated from below, their efforts were often supported in various ways by shipowners, merchants, insurers and other members of the propertied and educated classes. Aside from helping shipmasters' societies by making contributions as 'honorary' or 'extraordinary' members, local elites also sponsored schools of navigation, encouraged the collection of data by seamen for the benefit of scientific research, and instituted (and partly manned) local boards for the examination of masters and mates.[135]

The rise in the educational level of merchant seamen was further promoted by a proliferation of nautical schools. In contrast with France and Spain, nautical schools in Britain, the Netherlands and the United States were rarely financed or regulated by the national government before the middle of nineteenth century. Most of the navigation schools in these countries were established and maintained by private individuals, local organizations or local governments. In Britain, masters and mates in the mercantile marine usually acquired their skills and knowledge in mathematics and navigation at a private navigation school or at an endowed school, such as the Liverpool Marine Free School, founded in 1815. The number of these non-state facilities only gradually diminished from the 1850s, once the role of the national government in the education and qualifications of navigators in the merchant navy had begun to expand.[136]

In the Netherlands, numerous new facilities for nautical instruction were created between 1815 and 1860, without any involvement of the national government at all. In addition to private teachers and long-established lectureships and institutes sponsored by municipal authorities or private organizations such as the Kweekschool voor de Zeevaart, a variety of other provisions emerged. New schools of navigation sponsored by local governments or associations of private citizens came into being in towns and villages all over the country, ranging from big cities such as Amsterdam, Rotterdam and Dordrecht and small ports such as Harlingen, Delfzijl and Veendam, to modest villages such as Alblasserdam or Krimpen aan de Lek. Some of these schools were planned as schools of navigation from the very start, others evolved from a kind of facility often found in seafaring communities in Dutch maritime provinces: nautical instruction in primary schools. In many such communities, it was not at all uncommon to find a master at a primary school who was able to teach pupils the basics of navigation. The 1850s also showed a shift in the orientation of the curriculum of navigation schools. Whereas the curriculum of several schools founded before 1850 was attuned to the examination requirements in the state regulations of 1823, after 1850, navigation schools primarily aimed to prepare their pupils for tests of competence, which were conducted by examining boards appointed by local authorities.[137]

Unlike the organization of medical care, nautical education for the merchant marine in the United States long remained purely a matter of self-organization by seamen and private entrepreneurs. Masters and mates normally acquired the knowledge and skills required for sailing the ocean at a private navigation school or on-board ship. When, in the 1830s, Richard Dana wished to 'qualify [himself] for an officer's berth', he used his hours of leisure during his stay in California 'for reading and studying navigation', while looking forward to enlisting on a ship for the return voyage to Boston to learn 'practical seamanship'.[138] The first state nautical schools were not established until well after the Civil War, namely in New York (1874), Pennsylvania (1889) and Massachusetts (1890). And from 1861, the first certificates for qualified masters and mates in the merchant navy were issued by a private organization, the American Shipmasters' Association. The exams were conducted by the association itself. Certificates of competence were not required, but they could serve as recommendations to shipowners.[139]

The United States represented an extreme case of the organization of examinations 'from below'. But in Britain and the Netherlands, too, central authorities initially had limited influence over the regulations of examinations for merchant seamen. The Mercantile Marine Act of 1850 in Britain could only be passed in Parliament because it left room for local involvement and control. While the exam requirements were laid down by the state and the general supervision of the system was entrusted to the Board of Trade, shipowners were allowed to elect half of the members of the local examining boards.[140] Voluntary state exams in the Netherlands attracted few candidates before the middle of the nineteenth century. Of the 168 captains of ships chartered by the NHM in 1851, only 44 (less than 25 per cent) had taken an exam before a board that had been appointed by the state under the regulation of 1823.[141] The examining boards established by local authorities in the middle of the 1850s, on the other hand, were a great success. These boards consisted of experienced shipmasters, scientists and teachers of navigation, as well as representatives of local shipping interests. The numbers of candidates for examinations soared, especially after a certificate of examination was made obligatory by the NHM in 1858. The state-sponsored examination facilities, meanwhile, were abolished in 1856.[142]

In medical care for seafarers, too, self-organization and the creation of the infrastructure that went with it increased after the Napoleonic Wars. Britain spearheaded this movement. It was private British citizens, not government agencies, who first took concerted initiatives to improve the health of seamen in the mercantile marine, although quite a few of them admittedly worked in the state apparatus themselves and more than once called on the help of the state to realize their goals. During the harsh winter of 1817–18, a committee was formed in London for the relief of the masses of 'distressed [destitute] seamen' who roamed the streets of the capital. Among the seventy members of the committee were six MPs, seven naval officers and fifteen captains in the merchant navy. In no time, the new committee managed to arrange the supply of food and lodgings for poverty-stricken sailors, by raising funds among the general public and persuading the Admiralty to loan a number of its ships.[143] Out of this temporary committee arose a permanent association in 1821, the Seamen's Hospital Society, which aimed to provide medical aid to merchant seamen in London on a lasting basis by fitting out a hospital ship moored near Deptford. The Admiralty supported this citizens' initiative by offering the society a decommissioned naval vessel. The society employed its own medical staff, which kept a meticulous record of patients and cases. A large legacy from a prominent shipowner put the society's finances on a firm footing from 1832 onwards.[144]

The movement for the improvement of the health of merchant seamen gathered momentum in the 1860s, after the Mercantile Marine Act finally laid down standards for the accommodation of crews and there had been a massive general increase in public pressure for social and institutional reform in British society. The sheer scale of this mid-Victorian drive for reform was nowhere more evident than in the Social Science Association (SSA), founded in 1857. The annual meetings of the SSA, 'held in all the major cities of Britain, and attended by thousands', 'captured national attention for a generation'. The discussions at the meetings addressed five areas of reform: jurisprudence, education, penal policy and moral improvement, public health and 'social economy' (including labour relations and the condition of the working classes). Among the topics discussed under 'public health' was also the subject of the health of merchant mariners. It was at the Dublin meeting of the SSA in 1861 that James McWilliam first presented his findings on disease and deaths among seamen in the mercantile marine.[145] Six years later, a society was founded 'in the rooms of the Social Science Association in London', dedicated to improving 'the condition of merchant seamen'. The main achievement of this short-lived society, nearly all of whose participants were 'professionally connected with sea', was the composition of a report with detailed recommendations for maritime reforms. In a sense, this report set the agenda for action in the field of health care for seamen up until the end of the century.[146]

Conclusion

Capabilities and limitations

Infrastructure and social networks underpinned the globalization of maritime knowledge relating to the maritime environment. At the same time, the capabilities for the development of maritime knowledge itself were further developed by significant advances in techniques, instruments and resources to collect, classify and interpret data and to reproduce and transmit information.

Enter the explorer and polymath Alexander von Humboldt. In the nineteenth century, it was Humboldt, first and foremost, who made the visual representation of data a widely accepted practice. Although he did not invent global distribution maps or pioneer the use of isolines, to use Nicolaas Rupke's words, he was the man who 'revolutionized' the graphical method. This he accomplished by expanding the use of graphical techniques to represent all sorts of natural phenomena on the earth's surface and inside the earth. It was Humboldt who demonstrated that the technique of isolines, introduced by Edmond Halley to portray magnetic declination, could be employed to depict a wide range of other parameters. In 1817, Humboldt himself made a map showing the distribution of heat across the globe by means of 'lignes isothermes', or lines of equal temperatures.[1] Isolines proved to be a highly effective device to order and reproduce the spatial distribution of large amounts of data in a clear, accessible way. When the 'Magnetic Crusade' and the collaborative projects on tides, winds and currents in the 1830s began to produce masses of observations on magnetic, marine and meteorological phenomena, isolines became a 'veritable craze'. Whewell and Maury adopted Humboldt's isolines for their path-breaking tidal and oceanic maps.[2]

Moreover, the production costs of maps and charts fell thanks to the spread of lithographic printing. Lithography was faster and cheaper than copper etching and engraving; stones could be used for larger printing runs than copper plates, and fewer sales were needed in the former case to recover the production costs. Invented in Bavaria in the 1790s, within thirty years the new technology had reached Britain, France, Spain, the Netherlands, the United States and other countries. However, its use in cartographic production did not become common until about 1850. Notably, the British Admiralty stuck to the printing of engraved maps and charts for many decades. The Dépôt of the US Navy produced its first lithographed charts in the late 1830s. It was not until Alexander Dallas Bache began to promote the use of lithography by the US Coast Survey in the 1850s and 1860s that the output of maps and charts using the new technology really took off in the United States.[3]

One technique that became increasingly important in the nineteenth century for the growth of knowledge relating to ship design was the use of models. Experiments with hull models had sometimes been performed in France, Britain and the Netherlands before 1800. The most systematic and comprehensive series of trials had been conducted under the auspices of the Society for the Improvement of Naval Architecture in England in the 1790s, with the results becoming fully known in the 1830s. The decisive push for the adoption of experiments with models in ship design was given by John Scott Russell in the 1840s. With financial support from the BAAS, Russell tested his wave theory on more than a hundred hulls on different scales built between 1837 and 1844, and publicized his findings widely in reports and lectures. By the mid-1850s, he was confidently claiming that naval architects could achieve superior designs when they 'consulted and cross-questioned nature' by means of experimentation. With a grant from the British Admiralty, a special tank for conducting experiments with scale models was constructed at the end of the 1860s.[4]

Advances in instrument-making helped to increase the capabilities for the growth of maritime knowledge, too. The tidal research programme in the 1830s, the Magnetic Crusade in the 1830s and early 1840s and the large collaborative project launched at the Brussels conference of 1853 could hardly have succeeded without a sufficient supply of appropriate instruments. Michael Reidy has pointed out that 'the improved accuracy needed in tidal observations' was facilitated by the introduction of self-registering tide gauges in the early 1830s, which made 'short-term observations of the tides dependable enough … to use them to perfect theory'.[5] Key instruments in the Magnetic Crusade were magnetometers for measuring magnetic intensity and Gambey circles for measuring inclination, which were relatively recent inventions.[6] To implement the programme of the Brussels conference, navigators could use a variety of instruments for making meteorological and oceanographic observations. Each captain of a Dutch merchantman who cooperated with the 'Ocean committee' of the *zeemanscollege* in Rotterdam, for example, received from shipowners not just aids for navigation such as sextants, chronometers, azimuth compasses and steering compasses but also a barometer, three thermometers, a tube for deep-sea sounding and sometimes a psychrometer and a hydrometer for making measurements of humidity.[7] New instruments were invented or improved in many different places. Marine barometers and tide gauges were perfected in England, sounding equipment in the United States, and magnetometers and Gambey circles in Norway, France and Germany.[8]

Information about new techniques, instruments and observations was circulated far more swiftly and widely than before. One of the reasons for this was the sharp reduction in the cost of sending mail, thanks to the introduction of prepaid postage after 1840, as discussed earlier.[9] Another was the rise in the number of international scientific meetings and conferences, which began slowly in the 1840s and accelerated markedly at the end of the nineteenth century. Over 3,000 such meetings were held between 1840 and 1914.[10]

Communication was also facilitated greatly by the proliferation of scientific journals and the growth of a periodical press for seamen and other interested parties in the shipping industry. As well as long-established publications such as the *Transactions* of the Royal Society, the nineteenth century saw a vast expansion in the circulation of both popular science journals and specialized scholarly journals, especially in Britain, France and Germany. Some of these serial publications appeared as 'annals' or 'transactions' of disciplinary organizations, others were produced by commercial publishers. Journals of the latter kind contained 'a variety of reviews, news, letters and meteorological observations', which were not primarily intended to report new research findings, but 'to offer observations that would be new to their readers'.[11] The medical journal *The Lancet*, founded in 1823, played a prominent role in debates in the 1830s and 1840s about the improvement of medical care in the Royal Navy, by providing a forum for the concerns and aspirations of naval medical officers. French naval physicians started their own professional journal in 1864, *Archives de médecine navale*.[12]

Britain formed the heart of a burgeoning periodical press specifically aimed at the reading public in the shipping industry. The *Nautical Magazine* started to appear in 1832, and soon became a highly influential mouthpiece for reform measures to improve the protection of life and property at sea. The *Mercantile Marine Magazine*, founded in 1854, covered a more or less similar field. The London-based *Shipping and Mercantile Gazette*, established in 1838, and the *Liverpool Journal of Commerce*, founded in 1861, were newspapers that offered a wealth of freight market reports, law reports and all sorts of news items relevant to shipmasters, shipowners, brokers and insurers. These periodicals were widely read both in Britain and abroad, and their subscribers included the libraries of shipmasters' societies.[13]

The speed of communication across the seas could hardly increase any further, however, as long as technologies for making and laying submarine telegraph cables were not yet fully developed. While long-distance communication by electric telegraph over land had become feasible by the 1840s, attempts to connect both sides of the Atlantic by laying a telegraph cable on the ocean floor initially encountered all sorts of problems. The first permanent transatlantic cable did not become operational until 1866. Transmission times then dropped dramatically; messages no longer took nearly a fortnight to reach the other side of the Atlantic, but arrived in less than a day. The increase in communication speed meant, among other things, that shipping news and weather reports could now travel to distant places much faster than had been possible in the past.[14] On the other hand, the presence of cables on the ocean floor also implied that transatlantic communication no longer depended on ships.

Apart from the challenges of finding adequate materials for insulating the cables and devising feasible methods for laying them securely on the ocean floor, entrepreneurs in submarine telegraphy initially also faced the problem of the sheer lack of knowledge about the bottom of the ocean itself. 'It is difficult to express adequately human ignorance of the ocean's depths up to the mid-nineteenth century,' Helen Rozwadowski has observed.[15] Knowledge about the shape of the ocean floor did not really begin to improve until more effective deep-sea sounding technologies had been developed and state support for deep water hydrography in the United States and in Britain increased in the 1840s and 1850s. The research programme of Maury's observatory played a crucial role in this process. As more bathymetric charts and cross-sections of the sea-bed became available for a wider public, by the 1860s, cable companies no longer considered insufficient knowledge of the ocean floor an obstacle for their projects.[16]

Vast submarine areas of the ocean nevertheless remained virtual *terra incognita*. Little was known about the properties of the sea, about life under water and about the nature of the ocean floor beyond the narrow corridors of submarine cables. The advance of oceanography and marine biology before 1860 had its limitations. Margaret Deacon has remarked that most of the 'people engaged in the physical sciences were [still] completely indifferent to the sea and its problems'.[17] Unlike many seamen and hydrographers, almost all students of natural history were convinced that life in the depths of the ocean was impossible.[18] Surely, naturalists *did* increasingly make use of dredges, derived from tools commonly wielded by fishermen, to gather samples of creatures from the sea, but their activities long remained largely restricted to areas close to the shore.[19] The systematic study of fish similarly made great strides in the first half of the nineteenth century, especially in France, but there continued to be heavy emphasis on classification and morphology, rather than on the understanding of behaviour and living conditions of underwater creatures. Despite the appearance of the twenty-two-volume *Histoire naturelle des poissons*, in which Georges Cuvier and Achille Valenciennes described over 4,000 species of fish between 1828 and 1850, 'fisheries science' 'barely existed' in the middle of the nineteenth century.[20]

The scientific exploration of the deep sea did not truly take off until after 1860, when scientists finally *did* begin to take a keen interest in the oceans. This upsurge of interest was spawned both by new, unexpected discoveries of living creatures from the depths and by the emergence of a vivid debate about the evolution of life on Earth, triggered by the publication of Charles Darwin's *Origin of Species* in 1859.[21] One of the results of this was the launching of a scientific expedition under the auspices of the British Admiralty and the Royal Society aboard the naval vessel *Challenger*, specifically devoted to collecting data for marine research. During the *Challenger*'s circumnavigation of the globe between 1872 and 1876, scientists gathered a huge number of marine animals, seawater samples, birds, plants and rocks which provided a wealth of material for further investigation.[22] Marine science moved to a new level as a result.

Changes

The Atlantic world underwent a thorough transformation in the first half of the nineteenth century. With the contraction or dissolution of Atlantic empires and the decline in the transatlantic slave trade, many long-established maritime and commercial links were loosened or severed. Yet, this very period also saw the emergence and growth of multiple new networks of shipping, trade and fishing across the Atlantic Ocean. The Atlantic world in 1860 looked very different from that of 1800, but it was clearly composed of a distinct, wide-ranging, tightly knit web of connections. It comprised the entire space from the Arctic to the southern tips of Africa and South America, from the Caribbean to the North Sea and from the Bight of Biafra to the Gulf of Saint Lawrence. Judging by criteria such as the extensity of networks, intensity of interconnectedness and the velocity of flows of ships, people and goods, globalization in the Atlantic undoubtedly continued to advance in the period between 1800 and 1860.

As before, the advance of globalization was aided by the growth of maritime knowledge, and the growth of maritime knowledge was in turn supported by the advance of globalization. But in both respects, this relationship became much more complicated than in the period up until 1800. The evidence in this chapter revealed several kinds of discrepancies that are crucial to our understanding of the relationship between globalization and the growth of maritime knowledge in general.

During some periods and in some places, globalization – as defined in terms of the growth of extensity of networks or the intensity of maritime traffic – outpaced the expansion of maritime knowledge. One indicator of the seriousness of the problem was the rise in the frequency of shipwrecks. When more and more ships were lost due to failures in ship construction, errors in stowage, deficiencies in cartographic materials or shortcomings in navigational skills or instruments, this can be taken as a sure sign that the pool of available knowledge was insufficient to keep pace with the ongoing expansion of shipping and commerce. Shipwrecks are thus a plain signal of a discrepancy between globalization and the growth of maritime knowledge.

However, such a discrepancy did not occur in all spheres of maritime knowledge. In this period, the medical care of those on board was less affected by this problem than bodies of knowledge relating to the design, loading, steering or navigating of ships themselves. The expansion and intensification of shipping in the Atlantic after the Napoleonic Wars was not accompanied by a deterioration in mortality and morbidity; death and disease rates did not rise. The improvement in one's chances of surviving on board, which had already begun in the eighteenth century, continued more or less unabatedly in most branches of shipping after 1800. In this domain, the growth of maritime knowledge clearly did *not* lag behind the pace of globalization.

Moreover, occupying an advanced position in the development of maritime knowledge did not automatically translate into a leading role in globalization – and the reverse did not hold, either. Although the Spanish hydrographic office was still a model of its kind in 1820, and the reputation of the Bureau des Longitudes and the naval medical infrastructure in France was second to none in the mid-nineteenth century, these countries trailed behind Britain in the shaping of globalization. On the other hand, American whalers and merchantmen were in the forefront of globalization in the Atlantic world from the end of the Napoleonic Wars, but the United States did not become a first-class centre in the development of ocean-related knowledge until after 1850.

At the root of these discrepancies lay the fact that after 1815, self-organized networks of entrepreneurs and imperial machines, especially in Britain, were pushing globalization in the Atlantic forward with a power that had never been seen before. It took a while for the development of maritime knowledge to catch up with the shifting frontiers, and for institutional infrastructures of knowledge to attune the creation, certification and transmission of knowledge to changing conditions in the field. Long-distance trading companies and religious organizations now played only a marginal role in the building, adaptation and maintenance of these underlying structures. The key forces in the shaping and sustaining of infrastructures of knowledge in this period were – as in the process of globalization itself – imperial machines and self-organization.

In all major Atlantic seafaring nations (albeit to varying degrees, and at different times), central governments became increasingly active in building institutions and drawing up regulations for the creation, certification and dissemination of knowledge related to the ocean. Governments intervened in an ever-wider spectrum of fields, ranging from ship construction, map-making and navigation to medical care, accommodation, stowage and storm warnings. While this growing state intervention was initially mainly focused on navies, it was later extended to merchant marines and other branches of shipping as well. Imperial machines thus became more inclusive and elaborate than ever before. States created and supported hydrographic offices, coast surveys, observatories, meteorological departments, nautical schools, examination boards, hospitals and emigration commissions; they vested sweeping supervisory powers over broad domains of knowledge in positions such as surveyors, constructor-generals, physician-generals and hydrographers of the navy; they laid down specific rules and prescriptions in government contracts, model logs and passenger acts.

This sustained expansion of the imperial machine, which was clearly visible from the second quarter of the nineteenth century onwards, was partly a consequence of a mixture of cooperation and rivalry between nation states themselves, but it was also, especially in Britain, promoted to some extent by growing pressure from self-organized reform movements that arose from below. British state agencies were propelled into action by the twin forces of competition or collaboration with France, Germany and the United States (witness the Magnetic Crusade and Whewell's and Beaufort's tidal project) as well as by the more or less subtle domestic manoeuvres of the BAAS, *The Lancet* and the SSA. While leading roles in specific fields of maritime knowledge could shift back and forth between nations (as the relationship between the Board of Longitude and the Bureau des Longitudes illustrates), after the peace of 1815, collaboration and exchange between institutes and individuals from different countries increased to the extent that disparities in knowledge did not persist for long. The Brussels conference of 1853 exemplified this trend. Maritime knowledge was shared across national borders ever more easily and quickly.

The 'collectivization' of maritime knowledge also increased between social groups. The exchange of knowledge between different social networks after 1800 grew more frequent and dense. Flows of knowledge between naval officers, men of science, shipmasters and mates in merchant marines and the whaling industry, map-makers, instrument-makers, tide calculators, publishers, teachers at nautical schools, naval architects, master shipwrights, surgeons, physicians, professors of medicine, shipowners, insurers and government administrators became more regular and intensive than in the past. Many of these groups also developed formal organizational structures. The rise of the General Shipowners' Society in Britain and the proliferation of shipmasters' societies on both sides of the Atlantic are cases in point. Like the circulation of maritime knowledge between nation states after the Napoleonic Wars, these relations between social groups were characterized by a mixture of cooperation and competition. Maury's great collaborative project of the 1850s is a perfect example of the former, but examples of frictions and rivalries are not hard to find, either. Men of science more than once clashed with naval officers, naval officers with naval architects and shipwrights, surgeons with government administrators and professors of medicine and so on; and members of these groups frequently clashed with each other, too. Underlying these tensions were struggles for power, status and autonomy. All sorts of groups – from men of science and naval officers to surgeons and shipmasters – were simultaneously claiming their identity and asserting their influence as professions, disciplines or interest groups.

The actions and aspirations of these social groups were a powerful force in the massive growth of knowledge relating to the ocean after 1800. This vast expansion of knowledge was naturally very useful for the further expansion of networks of entrepreneurs and imperial machines in the Atlantic world. On the other hand, it could also help to bolster and legitimize the positions of the social groups themselves. Advances in techniques, instruments and resources to collect, classify and interpret data and to reproduce and transmit information facilitated this sustained development of maritime knowledge. Despite the impressive advance in maritime knowledge and the striking increase in capabilities, however, large parts of the ocean remained an unexplored domain, even by the last quarter of the nineteenth century. Crossing the Atlantic had almost become easy; probing its depths was an entirely different matter.

Conclusion

The relationship between knowledge and the ocean is a complex one. Melville's Ishmael, the sole survivor of the whaling ship *Pequod*, observed that 'of books' about whales 'there [were] a plenty', but 'of real knowledge there [was] little'. Of all the landsmen and seamen who had written about those great creatures of the ocean, only a few had ever seen living whales, and just one had been 'a professional harpooner and whaleman' himself, namely William Scoresby. As a modest step to improvement, Ishmael offered his own outline for a comprehensive classification of whales, in which whales were divided, according to magnitude, into books, subdivisible into chapters. There were 'folio', 'octavo' and 'duodecimo' whales. Chapter 1 of book I (Folio) was the monarch of the seas, the sperm whale.[1]

Understanding our knowledge of the ocean has been the purpose of this book, too, and more specifically the connection between globalization and knowledge of the Atlantic Ocean. There is no dearth of literature about globalization, or about Atlantic history. Studies on knowledge relating to the ocean itself, however, and in particular its interaction with globalization, are much scarcer. This book analysed how globalization influenced the growth of knowledge relating to the Atlantic Ocean and, conversely, how the growth of maritime knowledge affected globalization. It covered a period of 200 years, including the heyday of the Atlantic world as a 'distinct regional entity' or even as an 'Atlantic system', and the time of its sweeping transformation in the first half of the nineteenth century, before the Age of Sail eventually made way for the Age of Steam.

Globalization, in the sense of the increasing intensity of interconnectedness, extensity of networks and velocity of flows of ships, people and goods, does not just 'happen'; it was, and still is, driven by a variety of forces both from above and from below. Globalizing forces in the period between 1660 and 1860 did not only consist of coordinated sets of state-supported institutions, which were described in this book as 'imperial machines'. There were trading companies and religious organizations, too, which contributed to the advance of globalization in a similar way to imperial machines. By analogy to imperial machines, these were called 'commercial machines' and 'religious machines'. In addition to these forces 'from above', globalization could also be promoted by a force 'from below', namely self-organization. 'Self-organization' refers to the emergence of patterns through numerous interactions between individual entities without any form of direct, centralized control. Thus, individuals could enter into 'bottom-up', decentralized networks both *inside* and *beyond* imperial, commercial and religious machines, which could act as a powerful force for globalization as well.

To understand the impact of these globalizing forces on the development of maritime knowledge, this book has taken a broad perspective, by making comparisons and looking at the connections between the British, Spanish and French Atlantic 'empires' as well as the Dutch and American Atlantic. This comprehensive perspective is not only useful, I argued, because it allows us to make a more nuanced assessment of the impact of the different globalizing forces than a comparison between a smaller number of cases would permit; but it is also necessary, because globalizing forces did not function independently in separate national orbits, but were interlinked across national boundaries, and more so over time, as the circulation of knowledge grew. Different 'national' spheres thus became increasingly entangled.

Knowledge has been conceived in a broad sense, too. Knowledge could mean different things to different people and the relations between these different meanings could change in the course of time. The knowledge I examined in this book could be 'raw', that is, specific and practical, but also 'cooked', that is, processed or systematized. It included both 'real knowledge' and 'books', as Ishmael would say. The only restriction that I applied here was that all knowledge should be closely related to the ocean itself; that is, it should be maritime knowledge. Some of the bodies specializing in maritime knowledge that were considered in this book were concerned with the ways in which humans dealt with the natural environment for their own ends, others concerned the maritime environment itself. The spectrum of maritime knowledge thus covers an entire range of knowledge from knowledge about ship construction, map-making, navigation, health care, stowage, fishing and whaling to knowledge about the geography and physical features of the ocean, about winds, tides, currents, weather and climate and about fishes, birds and other creatures living in, above and around the waters.

All these bodies of knowledge relating to the Atlantic Ocean expanded over time. However, the relationship between globalization and the growth of maritime knowledge changed significantly between the mid-seventeenth and mid-nineteenth centuries. In fact, the connection between globalization and changes in the cognitive domain was relatively variable. These mechanisms and the variations in these changes were examined in Parts I, II and III of this book.

While Spain's imperial machine in the sixteenth and early seventeenth centuries led the way in the creation of an infrastructure of ocean-related knowledge, the build-up of such infrastructures in the Atlantic world expanded markedly in the period between 1660 and 1730. As Chapter 1 showed, the most elaborate system of the time existed in Bourbon France. But the Spanish and French 'imperial machines' were far from being the only globalizing forces that established and maintained institutional infrastructures of knowledge. In fact, these machines could hardly have functioned without the aid of religious orders such as the Jesuits, Franciscans and Dominicans, which supplied expert personnel for state-supported institutions and maintained a worldwide network of facilities for the creation and transmission of their own knowledge. 'Imperial machines' thus had a counterpart in 'religious machines', which operated both within and beyond the organizations of the Spanish and French states. In the British and Dutch Atlantic, the emerging imperial machines, which were admittedly not yet as complex as the Spanish or French ones, were flanked by 'commercial machines' that were built and maintained by long-distance trading companies such as the EIC, the Hudson's Bay Company and the VOC and WIC. All of these companies contributed to the growth of infrastructures of knowledge and facilitated the circulation of ideas, information and data relating to the ocean.

In addition to these various forces from above, there arose a globalizing force from below consisting of self-organized networks created by actors both inside and outside the imperial, religious and commercial machines. Self-organization emerged not only among the scholars who corresponded in the Republic of Letters but also in networks of seamen, fishermen, whalers and traders. Self-organized networks facilitated the transmission of knowledge both within and between different social networks in the Atlantic orbit, including Europeans as well as Africans and Amerindians.

While globalizing forces thus contributed to the expansion of infrastructures and the circulation of knowledge, the growth of knowledge in turn had an impact of globalization, too, as Chapter 2 showed. This was most evident from practices of chart-making, navigation and medical care. The increasing output of charts, books, sailing directions, manuals on medical care at sea and the like helped people to cross the ocean with more precision and a somewhat greater chance of survival than before, and thus eased interaction between different parts of the Atlantic world. On the whole, however, the effects of the growth of maritime knowledge on globalization were not yet very pronounced.

This clearly changed in the period between 1730 and 1800, as Chapter 3 in Part II demonstrated. The growth of maritime knowledge became a major aid for globalization in the Atlantic. Advances in knowledge relating to ship design, navigation, cartography and the maritime environment significantly helped to reduce the duration of voyages. One's chances of surviving the journey improved thanks to the growth of knowledge, too. In the latter half of the eighteenth century, mortality at sea declined almost across the board. Although death rates on slave ships and naval vessels remained higher on other ships that crossed the ocean, by 1800, enslaved people and naval crews had a better chance of surviving a transatlantic voyage than they had done seventy years previously. Mortality did not decline thanks to a breakthrough in medical science; the key to this improvement was the gradual advance in the prevention and cure of disease, based on an accumulation of experience and empirical observations, as well as on the growing use of mechanical devices such as ventilators and distillation machines. Compared to the period before 1730, the Atlantic world increasingly became a single space for the exchange of knowledge on best medical practices at sea. Know-how travelled easily between the British, French, Dutch and Spanish Atlantic in the form of medical writings, personal contacts and on-site observations.

However, the growth of maritime knowledge itself cannot be isolated from the impact of globalizing forces, which supported the continued expansion of infrastructures and the sustained circulation of data, information and ideas. These were analysed in Chapter 4. There was a slow but sure change, meanwhile, in the relative weight of these forces. While the importance of religious machines decreased between 1730 and 1800, imperial machines and long-distance trading companies persisted to become powerful drivers of globalization. And there was a further rise in the density of self-organized, cross-imperial networks among many different social groups. This advance in self-organization eased the circulation of knowledge, which in turn helped ships to sail across the ocean more quickly and enhanced the chances of survival on board.

The first decades of the nineteenth century saw a continuing increase in the intensity of interconnectedness, extensity of networks and velocity of flows of ships, people and goods in the Atlantic orbit. While the patterns of shipping, trade and fishing changed, the web of connections grew unceasingly. After 1800, the Atlantic world was both reshaped and expanded; and this formed the subject of Part III. Again, one of the factors that carried this process of globalization forward was the growth of maritime knowledge, as Chapter 5 made clear. Thanks to this growth in knowledge, the speed of shipping further increased, one's chances of surviving on board rose and harvests from the sea became more abundant. In all of these ways, advances in maritime knowledge facilitated an increase in contact, interaction and exchange, which led to greater interdependence between different parts of the Atlantic world.

As in the previous period, these advances were stimulated by globalizing forces from above and below, which supported infrastructures of knowledge and facilitated the circulation of the data, information and ideas. Yet, there were some changes as well, and these changes were analysed in Chapter 6. Imperial machines and self-organization now became by far the most powerful forces driving the expansion of infrastructures and circulation of knowledge; trading companies and religious organizations, by contrast, receded into the background. In all major Atlantic seafaring nations, central governments became increasingly active in building institutions and drawing up regulations for the creation, certification and dissemination of knowledge related to the ocean. Governments intervened in an ever-broader spectrum of fields, ranging from ship construction, map-making and navigation to medical care, accommodation, stowage and storm warnings. Among the imperial machines, the United States took its place next to Britain, France and the Netherlands, while Spain fell back. Self-organization, meanwhile, became more institutionalized and specialized than ever before. Informal networks were supplemented by societies, formal meetings and organized disciplines. The growth of maritime knowledge increasingly became a collective undertaking. Making knowledge became more and more 'collectivized', and knowledge was shared across national borders increasingly easily and quickly. The international conference in Brussels of 1853 perfectly exemplified this trend. All of these advances in knowledge and all of these changes in the infrastructures and circulation of knowledge were already well under way before the Age of Sail made way for the Age of Steam. In this regard, steam did not revolutionize the Atlantic world.

The growth of maritime knowledge never proceeded evenly, however. Throughout the period between 1660 and 1860, there were often phase differences between changes in various fields or subjects. Navigation technology, map-making or the study of winds, tides and currents, for example, could develop at a different pace from ship construction, stowage, medical care or the study of fish, birds and other living creatures. Such phase differences were related to variations in capabilities and limitations for the development of knowledge of the ocean. On the one hand, capabilities could increase in the form of advances in techniques, instruments and resources to collect, classify and interpret data and to reproduce and transmit information. On the other hand, the growth of knowledge could be hampered by a lack of financial means, imperfections in techniques and instruments, lacunae in institutional infrastructures and gaps in communication between different social networks. The balance between these capabilities and limitations shifted over time, as the conclusions of Parts I, II and III showed. On all counts, by the 1860s, the capabilities for the development of maritime knowledge had grown massively as compared to the mid-seventeenth century. Yet, little was known about the properties of the ocean itself, about life under water and about the nature of the ocean floor. The depths of the ocean still largely remained *terra incognita*.

Even though the capabilities for the development of maritime knowledge generally increased, discrepancies could emerge between the growth of knowledge and globalization. On the one hand, discrepancies sometimes arose because the search for power or profit trumped safety or health considerations, even when knowledge was sufficiently available. On the other hand, globalization outpaced the advance of maritime knowledge in some periods and locations. For example, the expansion of maritime traffic gave rise to demand that could not be met by the existing pool of knowledge and skills. One of the reasons for this was that technologies – to use Daniel Headrick's words – can be environment specific.[2] Technologies that are adequate in one region are not automatically effective in another. For Britain, the largest seafaring nation at that time, the gap between the progress of globalization and the supply of knowledge became particularly evident in the second quarter of the nineteenth century. Self-organized networks of British entrepreneurs carried globalization in the Atlantic to new extremes, as Chapter 4 demonstrated. The vastly expanded merchant fleet suffered so many shipwrecks, however, that contemporaries identified an urgent need for a thorough upgrading of maritime knowledge and skills.

The growth of maritime knowledge did not only involve more cooperation; it was also accompanied by rivalry between countries and social groups. Major maritime powers in the Atlantic world, in particular Britain and France, made considerable efforts to develop institutions and arrangements that would allow them to keep up with, and if possible gain an advantage over, their competitors in the production and distribution of knowledge. Both emulation and innovation were recurrent features of this interstate rivalry. Leading roles in specific fields of maritime knowledge could shift back and forth between nations (witness the alternate leadership of Britain and France in medical science, hydrography and the determination of longitude), but disparities in knowledge did not persist for long. Relations between the social groups involved in the creation and circulation of knowledge of the ocean demonstrated a mixture of cooperation and rivalry, too. While the projects on winds and currents started by Matthew Maury, for example, showed a high degree of collaboration, there were also many instances of tensions, all the more so after the end of the Napoleonic Wars. Men of science repeatedly clashed with naval officers, naval officers had disputes with naval architects and shipwrights, and surgeons argued with government administrators and professors of medicine. All sorts of groups – from men of science and naval officers to surgeons and shipmasters – were simultaneously claiming their identity and asserting their influence as professions, disciplines or interest groups. Nevertheless, in the long run, such rivalries between countries and social groups did not obstruct the growth of knowledge relating to the ocean.

Much of the maritime knowledge discussed in this book emerged and initially circulated in the Atlantic world. This does not imply, however, that all of this knowledge was specific to that particular area. Some bodies of maritime knowledge were indeed 'environment specific', to some extent, such as knowledge on winds and currents, geography, diseases or bird life. But large parts of this knowledge were not; knowledge about map-making, navigation, instrument-making, ship construction, stowage and medical care was certainly not limited to the Atlantic context. It could, and did, travel to other environments as well. Connections between the Atlantic, the Indian Ocean and the Pacific – for example, via trading companies, scientific expeditions and whaling ventures – have been discussed at length in this book. As Chris Bayly argued, globalization processes occurred at several times and places in history.[3] The question of the extent to which, when and how the relationship between globalization and maritime knowledge developed in other regions of the world thus presents a fascinating topic for further research. The Atlantic is by no means the only 'blue hole' that deserves study by global historians. By focusing on the Atlantic as a prime case, *Global Ocean of Knowledge* has aimed to make a plausible case for how maritime history and the history of knowledge can improve our understanding of global history, and conversely, for how global history can contribute to our understanding of maritime history and the history of knowledge.

Notes

Introduction

1. Harrison's story is told by, among others, Gould, *Marine Chronometer*, 40–70, Quill, *John Harrison*, Sobel, *Longitude*, Andrewes (ed.), *Quest*.
2. Fauque, 'Testing Longitude', 161–3, Gould, *Marine Chronometer*, 83–100.
3. Renn (ed.), *Globalization*, 16–9, 69–70.
4. Ibid., 28–37.
5. Ibid., 29, 33, 234–5, 562.
6. Ibid., 370, 376, 386, 392, 577.
7. Ibid., 22–3.
8. Headrick, *Power*, 3, 6.
9. Headrick, *Information*, 4.
10. Headrick, *Power*, idem, *Tools*, idem, *Information*.
11. Headrick, *Tentacles*.
12. Headrick, *Power*, 6–9, 370–2.
13. Heidbrink, 'Closing the "Blue Hole"', 326, 329.
14. Ibid., 332.
15. Kelly and O'Grada, 'Speed'; despite this, as the same article shows, ingrained views among economic historians about the 'technological conservatism of the VOC', for example, die hard, in disregard of the other findings of maritime historians.
16. Heidbrink, 'Closing the "Blue Hole"', 331, Paine, *Sea*, Mann, *1491*, idem, *1493*.
17. See for example, Fernández-Armesto, *Civilizations*, idem, *Pathfinders*, Dunn and Higgitt (eds), *Navigational Enterprises*.
18. See for instance Delbourgo and Dew (eds), *Science and Empire*, Bleichmar et al. (eds), *Science in the Spanish and Portuguese Empires*, Cañizares-Esguerra, *Nature, Empire, and Nation,* Navarro Brotóns and Eamon (eds), *Más allá de la Leyenda Negra*, Schiebinger, *Plants*, Grove, *Green Imperialism*, Drayton, *Nature's Government*, Raj, *Relocating Modern Science*, Friedrich, Brendecke and Ehrenpreis (eds), *Transformations*.
19. De Vries, 'Limits of Globalization'. For a recent summary of various concepts on globalization, see also Van Zanden and De Zwart, *Origins*, 2–4.
20. Held et al., *Global Transformations*, 14–28; the fourth spatial–temporal dimension in the framework, 'impact propensity of global interconnectedness', will not be considered.

21 See, for example, O'Flynn and Giraldez, 'Path Dependence', idem, 'Born again', cf. O'Rourke and Williamson, 'When Did Globalisation Begin?'
22 Cf. Bayly, '"Archaic" and "Modern" Globalization'.
23 Gunn, *First Globalization*; cf. also Van Zanden and De Zwart, *Origins*, 8–10, 17–20.
24 Renn (ed.), *Globalization*, 20.
25 Ibid., 22–3.
26 Burke, *Social History*, 11–14.
27 Cook, *Matters*, 15, 20.
28 Inkster, 'Potentially Global', 238, Mokyr, *Enlightened Economy*, 35.
29 Mokyr, *Gifts of Athena*, 4–21.
30 Brendecke, *Imperium*, 12–14, 16–19.
31 Ibid., 22–9, 335–45.
32 Ibid., 12–14, 16–19, Soll, *Information Master*, 12, 72–3, 100–2, 164, Bayly, *Empire and Information*, 3–6, 366–7, 372–4.
33 Burke, *Social History*, 11.
34 Blair, *Too Much to Know*, 1–2.
35 Secord, 'Knowledge', 655.
36 Renn (ed.), *Globalization*, 370, 376, 386, 392, 577.
37 Latour, *Science in Action*, 215–57.
38 Secord, 'Knowledge', 664, Roberts, 'Centres', 6, Raj, *Relocating Modern Science*, 226, Morgan, 'Travelling Facts', 13–16.
39 Morgan, 'Travelling Facts', 16–17, 36.
40 Appadurai, *Modernity at Large*, 17. Cf. also Safier, 'Global Knowledge' and Mignolo, *Local Histories*, 12–13.
41 Cooper, *Inventing*, esp. 179.
42 O'Rourke and Williamson, *Globalization*, De Vries, 'Limits of Globalization', Gilroy, *Black Atlantic*, Inikori, *Africans*, Thornton, *Africa*, Leonard and Pretel, 'Experiments', 1–3.
43 Bailyn, *Atlantic History*, 111, Canny and Morgan, 'Introduction', esp. 16, Pietschmann, 'Introduction', 38–9.
44 Scammell, *World Encompassed*, 1–37, Cunliffe, *Facing the Ocean*, 503–5, Winroth, *Vikings*, 51–70, Pye, *Edge*, 68–95.
45 Fernández-Armesto, *Pathfinders*, Fernández-Armesto, *Before Columbus*, Russell, *Prince Henry*, Elliott, *Empires*, Benjamin, *Atlantic World*, Godinho, 'Carreira da India', Subrahmanyam, *L'empire portugais*, Schwartz, 'Iberian Atlantic'.
46 Godinho, 'Carreira da India', 32–3.
47 Chaunu, *Séville et l'Atlantique*, 6.
48 Bailyn, *Atlantic History*, 81–3, 91–2, Canny and Morgan, 'Introduction', 10–12, 16, Pietschmann, 'Introduction', 38; see also Bailyn and Denault (eds), *Soundings*, Benjamin, *Atlantic world*, esp. xxvi–xvii, Greene and Morgan (eds), *Atlantic History*, Pietschman (ed.), *Atlantic History*.

49 O'Rourke and Williamson, *Globalization*, 33–6.
50 Cunliffe, *Facing the Ocean*, 6–15, 155, 554. Cf. also Steinberg, *Social Construction*, 41–60, 98–135.
51 Chaplin, 'Atlantic Ocean', 39, 43, 45, Edney, 'Knowledge', 98–101, Lewis, 'Dividing the Ocean Sea'.
52 Reidy and Rozwadowski, 'Spaces in between', 339–41, Deacon, *Scientists*, chapters 11–16.
53 Chaunu, *Séville et l'Atlantique*, 5–6, Mauro, *Portugal*, 11–88, Klein and Mackenthun, 'Introduction', Wigen, 'Oceans of History'.
54 Bolster, 'Putting the Ocean', 21, Games, 'Atlantic History', 746.
55 Reidy and Rozwadowski, 'Spaces in between', 348–51, Lambert, Martins and Ogborn, 'Currents', Hornsby, 'Geographies'.
56 Van Zanden and De Zwart, *Origins*, 20–4.
57 Greene and Morgan (eds), *Atlantic History*, section one, Elliott, *Empires*, Canny and Morgan (ed.), *Oxford Handbook*, part II, Benjamin, *Atlantic World*, parts I and II, Van Zanden and De Zwart, *Origins*, 20–4.
58 See for example Brendecke, *Imperium*, McClellan and Regourd, *Colonial Machine*, Drayton, *Nature's Government*, Schiebinger, *Plants*, Lafuente, 'Enlightenment', Grove, *Green Imperialism*.
59 McClellan and Regourd, 'Colonial Machine', idem, *Colonial Machine*, 15, 482.
60 McClellan and Regourd, *Colonial Machine*, 21–5.
61 Ibid., part II.
62 Ibid., 25–32, 429–77, 484–5.
63 Ibid., 19–21.
64 Charles and Cheney, 'Colonial Machine Dismantled', 130–3, 159–62, Roberts, 'Centre', 320–2, 334–5.
65 Liebersohn, *Traveler's World*, 77–114, Harris, *Essays*, 171, Davids, *Rise and Decline*, 50, 86, 264, 318, 473.
66 Konvitz, *Cartography in France*, Headrick, *Information*, 99–106.
67 Harris, 'Long-distance Corporations', 272, 279; Harris 'Networks', 356–7, 360–1.
68 Harris, 'Long-distance Corporations', 285–300; Guennou, *Missions Étrangères*, 3–76, 119–34, 161–83.
69 See Harris, 'Long-distance Corporations', idem, 'Networks', Binnema, *Enlightened Zeal*, Clossey, *Salvation*, Wendt, *Missionarische Gesellschaft*.
70 Allen, *Institutional Revolution*, 19, North, *Institutions*, 3.
71 Hancock, *Oceans of Wine*, esp. xvi–xxv, Jarvis, *Bermuda*, Polónia and Owen, 'Cooperation-based Self-organizing', Antunes, 'Free Agents', Antunes and Polónia, 'Introduction', Safier, 'Itineraries', 358–9.
72 Green, 'Beyond Imperial Atlantic', Havik and Green, 'Introduction', 8, 24–6, Sparks, *Where the Negroes Are Masters*, 187, 209–10, 243–4.
73 See for example Rediker, *Between the Devil*.

74 Harris, 'Networks', 360–1.
75 Cf. Gould, 'Entangled Histories'.
76 Krohn et al., (eds), *Self-organization*, Krugman, *Self-organizing Economy*, Camazine et al., *Self-organization*.
77 Drayton, 'Knowledge', 236–7, 238, 243.
78 McClellan and Regourd, *Colonial Machine*, 433, Clossey, *Salvation*, 207–12, Cook, *Matters*, 317–29.

Part I

Introduction

1 Roggeveen, *Brandende Veen*.
2 Davids, *Zeewezen*, 400, Paesie, *Zeeuwse kaarten*, 47, Van Gelder, *Aards paradijs*, 35–7, 43–5.
3 Roggeveen, *Brandende Veen*.
4 Koeman, *Atlantes Neerlandici*, vol. IV, 450, Paesie, *Zeeuwse kaarten*, 57.
5 Steele, *English Atlantic*, 92.
6 Steele, *English Atlantic*, esp. 275, Menard, 'Transport Costs', 259.
7 Hague and Christie, *Lighthouses*, 27–9, 38–9, 121–2.
8 Steele, *English Atlantic*, 168–88, 275–6.
9 Banks, *Chasing Empire*, 164–171; the number of slave voyages is based on the Trans-Atlantic Slave Trade Database, http://www/slavevoyages.org/tast/database (accessed 1 May 2013).
10 Enthoven, 'Assessment', 406–10, Klooster, 'Overview', 378–9, Borucki, Eltis and Wheat, 'Atlantic History', 443–4.
11 Parry, *Spanish Seaborne Empire*, 249, Grahn, 'Cartagena', 170; Borucki, Eltis and Wheat, 'Atlantic History', 440, 442–3; Kuethe and Andrien, *Spanish Atlantic World*, 10; the number of slave voyages is based on, http://www/slavevoyages.org/tast/database (accessed 1 May 2013; see also Eltis, 'Volume and Structure', 23 and table I.
12 Candido, *African Slaving Port*, 156.
13 Klooster, *Illicit Riches*, Altman, 'Spanish Atlantic', 189–91, Borucki, Eltis and Wheat, 'Atlantic History', 436–8, 440, Murphy, 'Collecting Slave Traders', 660.
14 Bolster, *Mortal Sea*, 34–40, Starkey and Haines, 'Newfoundland Fisheries', 6–7, Robinson and Starkey, 'Sea Fisheries', 130, Richards, *Unending Frontier*, 554–5, Zorgdrager, *Bloeyende opkomst*, 378.
15 Vickers, *Young Men*, 45–7, 52, Magra, *Fisherman's Cause*, 32, 55, 57–60, Bolster, *Mortal Sea*, 64, Richards, *Unending Frontier*, 556–7, 563.

16 Vickers, 'First Whalemen', 565–6, idem, 'Nantucket Whalemen', 281, Bolster, *Mortal Sea*, 69–71, Jackson, *British Whaling Trade*, 48, 50.
17 Leinenga, *Arctische walvisvangst*, 49–64, 150–1, appendix III, Bolster, *Mortal Sea*, 71.
18 Based on the Trans-Atlantic Slave Trade Database, http://www/slavevoyages.org/tast/database (accessed 1 May 2013).
19 Sánchez-Albornoz, 'First Transatlantic Transfer', 27–8, 32–3, O'Reilly, 'Movements', 312–13, Belich, *Replenishing the Earth*, 32.
20 O'Reilly, 'Movements', 315–18, Canny, 'English Migration', 48–60, 64, Belich, *Replenishing the Earth*, 34–6.
21 Moogk, 'Manon's Fellow Exiles', 249–57, Marzagalli, 'French Atlantic World', 240–1.
22 Lucassen, 'The Netherlands', 173–80, Enthoven, 'Dutch Crossings', 165, Oostindie and Roitman, 'Repositioning', 140.

Chapter 1

1 Elliott, *Empires*, 109–10, Brendecke, *Imperium*, 109–76.
2 Goodman, *Power*, chapter 2, Portuondo, *Secret Science*, 4, 60–1, Sandman, 'Controlling Knowledge', 34–46, Barrera-Osorio, *Experiencing Nature*, 35–55, Barrera-Osorio, 'Knowledge', 220–4.
3 Goodman, *Power*, 242, 245–7.
4 Barrera-Osorio, 'Knowledge', 230–1, Portuondo, *Secret Science*, 82–6.
5 Portuondo, 'Cosmography', 74.
6 Jonkers, 'Rewards', 434.
7 Portuondo, *Secret Science*, 274–6.
8 Studnicki-Gizbert, *Nation*, 30–9, 108–9, 114–20, 153, Elliott, *Empires*, 108–11.
9 Cañizares-Esguerra, *Nature, Empire, and Nation*, 9, 19.
10 Pimentel, 'Iberian Vision', 26.
11 Ibid., 26, Portuondo, *Secret Science*, 86.
12 Alvarez Peláez, 'Un Nuevo Mundo', 151, Vicente Maroto, 'Cosmógrafos españoles', 351, Esteban Piñero, 'Institucionalización', 430, Goodman, *Power*, 234–6, Portuondo, 'Cosmography', 74.
13 Sandman, 'Controlling Knowledge', 33–41, Esteban Piñero, 'Institucionalización', 430, Goodman, *Power*, 245, 250, 262, Kagan, 'Arcana Imperii', 57–70, Portuondo, *Secret Science*, 7–9, 103–7, 258, Barrera-Osorio, *Experiencing Nature*, 133.
14 García Garralón, 'Formación', 12–15, González, 'Del "arte de marear"', 150–1, Tikoff, 'Saint Elmo's Orphans', 4–7.
15 González, 'Del "arte de marear"', 155–9, García Garralón, 'Formación', 15–16.

16 López Piñero, *Ciencia*, 454–5, Goodman, 'Science', 17.
17 Ferreiro, *Measure*, 31–2, Safier, *Measuring*, 7.
18 Safier, *Measuring*, 6, Ferreiro, *Measure*.
19 Safier, *Measuring*, 7, Engstrand, *Spanish Scientists*.
20 Juan and Ulloa, *Relación histórica*.
21 Kuethe and Serrano, 'Astillero', 764, 766–7, Serrano, 'Inicios', 291, 293–5.
22 McClellan and Regourd, *Colonial Machine*, 15, 21–5, Regourd, 'Capitale savante', 135 note 39.
23 Regourd, 'Capitale savante', 135–40, Regourd, 'French Science Overseas', 25–8, Marzagalli, 'French Atlantic World', 238, 242–3.
24 Banks, *Chasing Empire*, 9.
25 Soll, *Information Master*, 113, 115, 118.
26 Ibid., 12, 72–3, 100–2, 164.
27 Regourd, 'Lieux de savoir', 38–9, idem, 'Capitale savante', 137.
28 Soll, *Information Master*, 113–18.
29 McClellan and Regourd, 'Colonial Machine', 36, Regourd, 'Capitale savante', 139–40, idem, 'French Science Overseas', 26–7.
30 Chapuis, *A la mer*, 159–60, Van Egmond, *Covens en Mortier*, 128–9.
31 Chapuis, *A la mer*, 160, Konvitz, *Cartography in France*, 73, Headrick, *Information*, 113, Briggs, 'Académie Royale', 43–4.
32 Olmsted, 'Expedition', esp. 122, idem, 'Voyage', Harris, 'Networks', 344, Richer, *Observations*.
33 Dew, 'Vers la ligne', 57–60, Richer, *Observations*.
34 Cassini, *Traité de la grandeur*, 1, quoted in Vogel, 'Cosmography', 493.
35 Dew, 'Scientific Travel', 5, Cassini, *Elemens*.
36 Pinault Sørensen, 'Voyageurs artistes', 49, McClellan and Regourd, 'Colonial Machine', 41.
37 Anthiaume, *Évolution*, Book II, chapter 5, Aman, *Officiers bleus*, 31–3, Russo, 'L'hydrographie', passim.
38 Osborne, *Emergence*, 20–3.
39 *Ordonnance de Louis XIV pour les armées navales*, 347.
40 Osborne, *Emergence*, 21–3, Suberchichot, 'Corps', 322.
41 McClellan and Regourd, *Colonial Machine*, 67, 247–51, Buchet, 'Quantification', 179.
42 According to Glete, *Navies*, vol. I, 287–8, little is known about private shipyards in France in this period.
43 Pritchard, 'Shipwright', 6–7, 16, Ferreiro, *Aristotelian Heritage*, 20–1, idem, *Ships*, chapter 4, McGee, 'Craftsmanship', 230–2.
44 As McClellan and Regourd themselves also acknowledge, see, 'Colonial Machine', 44–5, idem, *Colonial Machine*, 413–29. Cf. Charles and Cheney, 'Colonial Machine Dismantled', Roberts, 'Centre'.

45 Suberchichot, 'Corps', 322.
46 Rodger, *Command*, 222.
47 Banks, *Chasing Empire*, 13, Pritchard, *In Search of Empire*, 254–63.
48 Dew, 'Scientific Travel', 8–11, 16.
49 McClellan and Regourd, *Colonial Machine*, 80, Jonkers, 'Rewards', 435–6.
50 McClellan and Regourd, *Colonial Machine*, 152.
51 Anthiaume, *Évolution*, vol. II, Russo, 'L'hydrographie', passim, Chartier c.s., *L'Éducation*, 228, Banks, *Chasing Empire*, 72, Ferreiro, *Aristotelian Heritage*, 18.
52 Banks, *Chasing Empire*, 72, McClellan and Regourd, *Colonial Machine*, 151.
53 Osborne, *Emergence*, 21–3.
54 McClellan and Regourd, 'Colonial Machine', 44–5.
55 Cuvier, *Historical Portrait*, 84, 89–90, McClellan and Regourd, *Colonial Machine*, 149–50.
56 Chapuis, *A la mer*, 161–2.
57 Ibid., 164–5, 183, 943 note 49.
58 Davis, *Shipping Industry*, 294–9, Elliott, *Empires*, 122–3, 149, 222, Koot, *Empire*, 90–1, Steele, *English Atlantic*, 230–5.
59 Iliffe, 'Mathematical Characters', 121–7, 133–40, 144.
60 Rodger, *Command*, 121–2, 519–20.
61 Sullivan, 'Naval Schoolmaster', 311, Dickinson, *Educating*, 9–32.
62 Dickinson, *Educating*, 33–56.
63 Rodger, *Command*, 195–6.
64 Buchet, 'Quantification', 179, Crimmin, 'Naval Health', 183–6, Keevil et al., *Medicine*, vol. I, 140–1, Rodger, *Command*, 214, 309.
65 'Directions for Observations and Experiments', 433–8.
66 Thrower, *Three Voyages*, vol. I, 35–41, 56–60, Waters, 'English Pilot', 339–42, Konvitz, *Cartography*, 70.
67 Forbes, *Greenwich Observatory*, vol. I, 22, Jonkers, 'Rewards', Forbes, 'Index', Dunn and Higgitt, 'Bureau and the Board', 222.
68 Rodger, *Command*, 187, 218, 220–21, Lemmers, *Techniek op schaal*, 24.
69 Rodger, *Command*, 187–8, 217–18, 297–8.
70 Cf. Glete, *Navies*, vol. I, 288, Ferreiro, *Ships*, 296–8, *Marine Architecture*, Introduction, 19, Chapelle, *Search for Speed*, 7–8.
71 Catesby, *Natural History*, vol. I, preface.
72 *Account of Several Late Voyages*, 'The bookseller's preface and introduction', xxix, Iliffe, 'Science', 621.
73 Binnema, *Enlightened Zeal*, 49.
74 Waters, *Art of Navigation*, 287, 320–1.
75 Appleby, 'New Light', 254–6.
76 Zahedieh, *Capital*, 251–2, 280, 283, 289.

77 Schnurmann, *Atlantische Welten*, esp. 372–3, Koot, *Empire*, 212–13, 224–7.
78 Davids, 'Amsterdam', 309–13.
79 Pop, *Geneeskunde*, 27–8, Leuftink, *Geneeskunde*, 35, Bruijn, *Ship's Surgeons*, 60–2.
80 SA Amsterdam PA 366 Gildenarchieven nr. 233 f. 54–5 keur chirurgijnsgilde 25 January 1709, f. 58–9, keur chirurgijnsgilde 26 January 1722, *Handvesten*, vol. II, 963, keur chirurgijnsgilde 26 January 1685, keur chirurgijnsgilde 31 March 1685.
81 Leuftink, *Geneeskunde*, 32–4, 46, 68–9.
82 Ibid., 17–18, 21–2, 87, 118–19.
83 Davids, *Zeewezen*, 297–9.
84 Ibid., 69.
85 Ibid., 294–6, 398–9, Zandvliet, *Mapping*, 86–9, 101, 165, 183, Paesie, *Zeeuwse kaarten*, 47–51.
86 Davids, *Zeewezen*, 296–7, 403.
87 Van Dam, *Beschrijvinge*, Eerste boek, deel I, 397, Bruijn, *Ship's Surgeons*, 59–64, 87–91, Pel, *Chirurgijns*, 112.
88 Cook, *Matters*, 213, Fleischer, 'Company's Garden', 11–13.
89 Cook, *Matters*, 213–18, Piso and Marcgraf, *Historia naturalis Brasiliae*.
90 Rookmaker, *Zoological Exploration*, 17–18, 21–6, Fleischer, 'Company's Garden', 125.
91 Davids, *Zeewezen*, 135–8.
92 Van Dam, *Beschryvinge*, Eerste boek, deel II, 673–4, Doorman, *Octrooien*, nr. 252 18 August 1692, NA 1.04.02 VOC 156 res. H XVII 12 July 1695, 26 December 1696, 244 res. directors Amsterdam Chamber 244 res. directors Amsterdam Chamber 11 April 1695, 245 res. directors Amsterdam Chamber 22 April 1697, 1.10.48 Collectie Hudde 24, De Jong, *Navigating*, 100–2.
93 Unger, *Dutch Shipbuilding*, chapters II and VI, Van Duivenvoorde, *Shipbuilding*, Bruijn, *Dutch Navy*, 73–4, 101–2, Hoving, *Nicolaes Witsens' scheeps-bouw-konst*.
94 Binnema, *Enlightened Zeal*, 49.
95 Bolster, *Black Jacks*, 47–50.
96 Schiebinger, 'Prospecting', 125–6; cf. Pratt, *Imperial Eyes*, 6–7.
97 Schiebinger, 'Prospecting', 121, 129, Hollstein, *Knowing Nature*, 137, Barrera-Osorio, *Experiencing Nature*, 126.
98 Schiebinger, 'Prospecting', 126–30, Hollstein, *Knowing Nature*, 164–5, Snelders, *Vrijbuiters*, 18–19, 70–97, 166–7.
99 Murphy, 'Translating', 29–40.
100 McNeill, *Mosquito Empires*, 74.
101 Houstoun, 'Account', esp. 198.
102 Quoted in Murphy, 'Translating', 34.
103 Hollstein, *Knowing Nature*, 138–9, 152–3, Snelders, *Vrijbuiters*, 13–14, 75, 82–94, 166–7, Schiebinger, 'Prospecting', 123, Murphy, 'Translating', 34, 37.

104 Bosman, *Nauwkeurige beschryving*, part II, 8, 58–60, 70–1.
105 Bosman, *Nauwkeurige beschryving*, Mulert, 'Willem Bosman'.
106 Bosman, *Nauwkeurige beschryving*, 'Missive geschreeven aan den Heere Willem Bosman', and dedication to the company.
107 Clossey, *Salvation*, 45–67.
108 McClellan and Regourd, *Colonial Machine*, 152–5, McClellan and Regourd, 'Capitale savante', 139–41, idem, 'French Science Overseas', 26–7.
109 Enthoven, 'Assessment', 391–2, especially footnote 18, and 403, Antunes and Ribeiro da Silva, 'Amsterdam Merchants', 7–8, 29, Paesie, *Lorrendrayen*, 329–30.
110 Rediker, *Between the Devil*, 10.
111 Baron, 'Sailors' Scurvy', 315–16, Snelders, *Vrijbuiters*, 57–62, Guerra, 'Hispanic-American Contributions'.
112 Boyle, *Observations and Experiments*, advertisement.
113 Zorgdrager, *Bloeijende opkomst*, idem, *Alte und neue Grönländische Fischerei*.
114 Ibid., 'Aan de heeren gecommitteerden der Hollandsceh Groenlandsche visschery', 'Aan den lezer'.
115 Ibid., 'Aan de heeren gecommitteerden der Hollandsceh Groenlandsche visschery', esp. p. 1r.
116 Cuvier, *Historical Portrait*, 75.
117 *Encyclopédie méthodique*, 413, 415, 444, 470, Van Musschenbroek, *Essai*, 445.
118 Ultee, 'Republic of Letters', 96–8, Daston, 'Ideal and Reality'.
119 Harris, 'Networks', 347–53.
120 Ibid., 360–1, Ogilvie, 'Correspondence Networks', 360–2, Fyfe, 'Journals and Periodicals', 388–9.
121 Etienne François Geoffroy to Hans Sloane, 7 March 1699, https://drc.usask.ca/projects/sloaneletters/doku.php?id=letterletterid=676 (accessed 21 September 2013).
122 The Sloane manuscripts contain several letters between Sloane and Cassini and dozens of letters between Sloane and Bignon, Jussieau and Tournefort; see https://drc.usask.ca/projects/sloaneletters/.
123 Jorink, 'Sloane', 58–69.
124 See http://ckcc.huygens.knaw.nl/epistolarium/ and Van Meerkerk, 'Correspondence Network Huygens'.
125 Stearns, *Science*, 107, 115–16, 118, 708–11.
126 Frederik Ruysch to Hans Sloane, 26 August 1706, https://drc.usask.ca/projects/sloaneletters/doku.php?id=letterletterid=1270 (accessed 1 March 2013).
127 Daniel à Loenen to Hans Sloane, 30 July 1713, https://drc.usask.ca/projects/sloaneletters/doku.php?id=letterletterid=1870 (accessed 1 March 2013), Jorink, *Boeck*, 258.
128 Vittu, 'Henry Oldenburg', 202–9.

129 Camarasa and Ibáñez, 'Salvador and Petiver: Correspondence', idem, 'Salvador and Petiver: Last Years', https://drc.usask.ca/projects/sloaneletters/doku.php, letters Juan Salvador to Hans Sloane, 22 August 1712, 10 September 1715, 16 June 1716, 14 October 1717 and 13 November 1717 (accessed 9 May 2013).
130 Van Meerkerk, 'Correspondence Network Huygens', 221 and http://ckcc.huygens.knaw.nl/epistolarium/ under Huygens and Van Leeuwenhoek; Huygens did exchange letters with visitors to Spain, such as Sébastien Chièze, see http://ckcc.huygens.knaw.nl/epistolarium/.
131 See the introductory text on 'An intellectual map of science in the Spanish empire, 1600-1810', http://republicofletters.stanford.edu.
132 Murphy, 'Collecting', 661–4.
133 Murphy, 'Collecting', 641, note 1.
134 Ibid., 640, 643, esp. note 14.
135 Ibid., 653–7.
136 Murphy, 'Translating', 15.

Chapter 2

1 Rönnbäck, 'Speed', 476, 482–3, 489.
2 Steele, *English Atlantic*, 49–50, Rodger, *Command*, 222, Parry, *Trade and dominion*, 207.
3 Koeman, *Sea on Paper*, 12–13, 18–19, 40–1, Kok, 'Cartografie', 25–7.
4 Waters, 'English Pilot', 336.
5 Banks, *Chasing Empire*, 72–3.
6 Kok, 'Cartografie', 26.
7 Ibid., 31–2.
8 Burstyn, 'Theories', Deacon, *Scientists*, chapters 4, 5, 6, Reidy, *Tides*, 20–41.
9 Vossius, *Treatise*, 'The Author to the Reader'.
10 Deacon, *Scientists*, 74–5, 79, 83.
11 Ibid., chapter 8, Reidy, *Tides*, 41–2.
12 See the map included in Halley, 'Historical Account', Robinson, *Early Thematic Mapping*, 46–8.
13 Reidy, *Tides*, 37, 40.
14 Jonkers, *Earth's Magnetism*, 83–98.
15 Fara, *Sympathetic Attractions*, 102.
16 Thrower, *Three Voyages*, vol. I, 35–41, 56–60, Waters, 'English Pilot', 339–42, Konvitz, *Cartography in France*, 70, Fara, *Sympathetic Attractions*, 109.
17 Fara, *Sympathetic Attractions*, 109.
18 Waters, 'English Pilot', 337, 339–42.

19 Juan and Ulloa, *Relación histórica*, 19–22.
20 Van Helden and Van Gent, 'Lens Production', 70–1.
21 Davids, *Zeewezen*, 135–7, Mahoney, 'Christiaan Huygens', Leopold, 'Longitude Timekeepers', Olmsted, 'Voyage', 619–25.
22 Deacon, *Scientists*, 80–3, 163–5, McConnell, 'Marine Barometer', 87–8, idem, *No Sea Too Deep*, 6–10.
23 'Directions for Observations and Experiments', 448.
24 Deacon, *Scientists*, 160–4, esp. 164, McConnell, *No Sea Too Deep*, 11.
25 Feldman, 'Late Enlightenment Meteorology', 146–8, Golinski, *British Weather*, 83–4, Zuidervaart, 'Medical–Meteorological Society', 381–2.
26 Davids, *Zeewezen*, 173–5, Van Breen, *Stiermans gemack*, De Hilster, *Navigation*, 312–37.
27 Clifton, 'Adoption', 87–8.
28 Ibid., 87–90, Bedini, *Thinkers*, 213, 299, 352, 368–9.
29 Stearns, *Science*, 514, 535–6, Warner, 'American Octants', 97, Clifton, 'Adoption', 89.
30 Stearns, *Science*, 514, note 27.
31 Clifton, 'Adoption', 89–90. Warner, 'American Octants', 97–8.
32 Juan and Ulloa, *Relación histórica*, 196–213, esp. 196.
33 Fauque, 'Introduction', 96.
34 Thrower (ed.), *Three Voyages*, Appendix D, 376–67.
35 Steele, *English Atlantic*, chapters 2, 3 and 5, Meinig, *Atlantic America*, 56–60, Banks, *Chasing Empire*, 69–87.
36 Steele, *English Atlantic*, 45–9, Menard, 'Transport Costs', 259–60.
37 Ibid, 47–8.
38 Davids, *Zeewezen*, 100–1.
39 Dampier, 'Discourse', 49–57, 108.
40 Neill, 'Buccaneer Ethnography', 173.
41 Dampier, *Discourse*, Preface and 49–57.
42 Juan and Ulloa, *Relación histórica*, 114–17.
43 Wheeler, 'Peter Artedi', 3.
44 Piso and Marcgraf, *Historia naturalis Brasiliae*, Part II book IV, Cuvier, *Historical Portrait*, 47.
45 Kusukawa, 'Historia Piscium', 182–3.
46 Cuvier, *Historical Portrait*, 84–5, Sloane, *Voyage*, vol. II, 275–93 and Tab. 246–53; for medicinal properties, see 288–9 on 'The Gurnet'.
47 Kusukawa, 'Historia Piscium', 179, 191–3.
48 Ray, *Ornithology*, 330.
49 Birkhead, *Wisdom*, 25–8, Egerton, 'History', esp. 304–8.
50 Birkhead, *Wisdom*, 41.
51 Sloane, *Voyage*, vol. II, 293–325.

52 Ibid., vol. II, 322.
53 Catesby, *Natural History*, vol. I, 72.
54 Stearns, *Science*, 318–20.
55 Magra, *Fisherman's Cause*, 63.
56 Bolster, *Mortal Sea*, 61–4.
57 See for example Zorgdrager, *Bloeijende opkomst*, part II, chapters IX and XX, part III, chapters V and VI.
58 Berry, *Path*, 119–20, 124–6, 132.
59 NA 2.21.183.16 Familie Delprat 106 a.
60 Cf. the careful observations of birds near the northeast coast of Brazil recorded by Antonio de Ulloa on his return trip in 1745, Juan and Ulloa, *Relación histórica*, 395–7.
61 Verbrugge/Schlichting, *Heel-konstige examen*, 143–4.
62 Martens, *Spitzbergische oder groenlandische Reise Beschreibung*, 62, Vaughan, *Arctic Birds*, 54–5.
63 The geographical references in the section on the cod fisheries in the Zorgdrager, *Bloeijende opkomst*, 377–92, are to France rather than to the Netherlands.
64 Zorgdrager, *Bloeijende opkomst*, 382–4.
65 http://www/slavevoyages.org/tast/database (accessed 5 June 2013).
66 Postma, *Dutch*, 244, 257, Snelders, *Vrijbuiters*, 112–5.
67 Feinberg, 'New Data', 362–3, Behrendt, 'Crew Mortality', 52–3, Klein et al., 'Transoceanic Mortality', 105–6, Snelders, *Vrijbuiters*, 30–43.
68 Bosman, *Nauwkeurige beschryving*, vol. II, 105.
69 Berry, *Path*, 232–3.
70 Kiple and Ornelas, 'Race', 67–71, McNeill, *Mosquito Empires*, 47–55, 86, Buchet, 'Quantification', 177–81.
71 Kiple and Ornelas, 'Race', 71–3, McNeill, *Mosquito Empires*, 142–4.
72 Juan and Ulloa, *Relación histórica*, 129–31.
73 Bruijn, *Ship's Surgeons*, 61.
74 Verbrugge/Schlichting, *Heel-konstige examen*, 141–53, idem, *Examen van land- en zeechirurgie*.
75 Van de Voorde, *Lichtende fakkel*, idem, *Nieuwe lichtende fakkel*, idem, *Nieuw chirurgijns zee-compas*.
76 Cockburn, *Account*, Dedication and 1–4.
77 Aubrey, *Sea-surgeon*, chapter XIV, Atkins, *Navy-surgeon*, Preface, ix, Appendix, Advertisement.
78 McNeill, *Mosquito Empires*, 69–70, Snelders, *Vrijbuiters*, 27–30.
79 Cockburn, *Account*, part III, 6–11.
80 McNeill, *Mosquito Empires*, 71.
81 Buchet, 'Quantification', 181, Kiple and Ornelas, 'Race', 66.

82 Carpenter, *History*, 40–2.
83 Cockburn, *Account*, 74–84. Cf. Carpenter, *History*, 42.
84 Verbrugge, *Heel-konstige examen*, 156, Verbrugge, *Nieuw hervormde examen*, 457, Van de Voorde, *Nieuwe lichtende fakkel*, 785–6.
85 Rutten, *Medicine Trade*, 47, 51.
86 Baron, 'Sailors' Scurvy', 317–18, Snelders, *Vrijbuiters*, 119–20, Carpenter, *History*, 34. Cf. Bosman, *Nauwkeurige beschryving*, vol. II, 68–71, on orange and lemon trees on the West African coast.
87 McNeill, *Mosquito Empires*, 82–5.
88 De Jong, *Navigating*, 102–6.
89 NA 1.04.02 VOC 156 res. H XVII 13 July 1695, 10 December 1695.
90 De Jong, *Navigating*, 107–21.

Conclusion

1 Cook, 'Time Bodies', 229–41, Margócsy, 'Advertising Cadavers', 187–90.
2 Kusukawa, 'Historia Piscium', 187, 191–3.
3 Egerton, 'History', 305, Catesby, *Natural History*, title page.
4 Chapuis, *A la mer*, 164–5, 183, 943 note 49.
5 Feldman, 'Late Enlightenment Meteorology', 148–9, Zuidervaart, 'Medical-Meteorological Society', 382, McConnell, 'Marine Barometer', 88–91.
6 Ratcliff, 'Trembley's Strategy', 557, Cook, *Matters*, 325–6.
7 Ogilvie, *Science*, Jorink, *Boeck*.
8 Cf. Catesby, *Natural History*, Preface, xi.
9 Deacon, *Scientists*, 87.
10 Boyle, *Observations and Experiments*, advertisement.

Part II

Introduction

1 Descriptions of these devices in Bicker, 'Verhandeling', 4–57, and Duhamel, *Moyens*, 91–129. See also De Jong, *Navigating*, 128–35.
2 De Vries, 'Connecting Europe and Asia', 91–3, De Vries, 'Dutch Atlantic Economies', 19 table 3.
3 See the data in the transatlantic slave trade database: http://www.slavevoyages.org/, consulted March 2017.

4 Inikori, *Africans*, 305.
5 Hornsby, 'Geographies', 18.
6 Fatah-Black, *Suriname*, 202–19 and graph 1.
7 Steele, *English Atlantic*, 76–7, Hornsby, 'Geographies', 33–8.
8 Vickers, *Young Men*, 69, 72.
9 Magra, *Fisherman's Cause*, 86–7, 98.
10 Ibid., 79, 86–90.
11 Starkey and Haines, 'Newfoundland Fisheries', 8–10, Richards, *Unending Frontier*, 559–60, Hornsby, 'Geographies', 26.
12 Starkey and Haines, 'Newfoundland Fsheries', 8–9, Robinson and Starkey, 'Sea Fisheries', 129–30, Myers, 'Testing', 33–4.
13 Liss, *Atlantic Empires*, 28.
14 Ibid., 28–32, Magra, *Fisherman's Cause*, 92–3.
15 Vickers, 'Nantucket Whalemen', 281, Liss, *Atlantic Empires*, 31, Davis, Gallman and Gleiter, *Leviathan*, 35–6.
16 Vickers, 'Nantucket Whalemen', 281, Dolin, *Leviathan*, 139, Morral and White, *Hidden History*, 80.
17 Leinenga, *Arctische walvisvangst*, 18, 144, 156–8, 164 and appendix III.
18 Gruber, 'Atlantic Warfare', 428–31, Canny and Morgan, 'Introduction', 13.
19 Bruijn, *Dutch Navy*, 152.
20 Bleichmar, 'Visible and Useful Empire', 297–8, Rodger, *Command*, 327–8, Liebersohn, *Traveler's World*, chapter 2, McClellan and Regourd, *Colonial Machine*, 197–206, Drayton, 'A l'école des Français', 96.
21 O'Reilly, 'Movements', 312–18, Belich, *Replenishing the Earth*, 32–6.
22 Dolin, *Leviathan*, 139, Magra, *Fisherman's Cause*, 7.
23 De Vries, 'Connecting Europe and Asia', 69 table 2.5.
24 Canny, 'English Migration', 48–60, 64, Enthoven, 'Dutch Crossings', 165, Galenson, 'Indentured Servitude', 12–13.
25 Canny and Morgan, 'Introduction', 10.

Chapter 3

1 Menard, 'Transport Costs', 253–69.
2 Ibid., 275.
3 North, 'Sources', Walton, 'Obstacles', 'Measure', Shepherd and Walton, *Shipping*, 77–90, French, 'Atlantic Shipping', 630–1, Menard, 'Transport Costs', 262, Wing, 'Shipping Productivity', 230–2, 236–9.
4 Craig, 'Printed Guides', 24–5.
5 Shepherd and Walton, *Shipping*, 78–9, 122–3, French, 'Atlantic Shipping', 623–4.

6   Menard, 'Transport Costs', 259, 271, Eltis and Richardson, 'Productivity', table 6, Rönnbäck, 'Speed', 483.
7   Shepherd and Walton, *Shipping*, 80.
8   Rönnbäck, 'Speed', esp. 489, Shepherd and Walton, *Shipping*, 77–8.
9   Ferreiro, *Ships*, 25–6, 304–5, Pritchard, 'Shipwright', McGee, 'Craftsmanship', 230–6.
10 Davis, *Shipping Industry*, 72–4, Parry, *Trade and Dominion*, 207–9.
11 Rodger, *Command*, 221, Cock, 'Finest Invention', 447–8, 456.
12 Rodger, *Command*, 344, 375, Solar and Rönnbäck, 'Copper Sheathing', 811.
13 Solar and Rönnbäck, 'Copper Sheathing', 810–12, 817–18, Solar, 'Merchant Ships', 58, Kelly and O'Grada, 'Speed'.
14 Rodger, *Command*, 344, 350, 374–5.
15 Rönnbäck, 'Speed', 485.
16 French, 'Atlantic Shipping', 625–8.
17 Davis, *Shipping Industry*, 123.
18 Hogerzeil and Richardson, 'Slave Purchasing Strategies', 162 footnote 5 and Appendix Table 1.
19 Davids, *Zeewezen*, 232–40.
20 Mendoza y Ríos, 'Recherches', 45–6.
21 Davids, *Zeewezen*, 233, Crone, *Cornelis Douwes*, 217–26, Douwes, 'Verhandeling'.
22 Crone, *Cornelis Douwes*, 264–5, Pemberton, 'Some Considerations'.
23 RGO 14/5, Confirmed minutes of the Board of Longitude, 11 April 1767, 2 May 1767 and 18 June 1768, http://cudl.lib.cam.ac.uk/collections/longitude (accessed 26 December 2013).
24 Crone, *Cornelis Douwes*, 266–9, 271–6, 284–5, 287–90.
25 Clifton, 'Adoption', 93–4.
26 Mörzer Bruyns, 'Trade Labels', Warner, 'American Octants', 86.
27 Davids, *Zeewezen*, 231, Mörzer Bruyns, *Schip recht door zee*, 96–7.
28 Fauque, 'Introduction', 95–101.
29 Juan and Ulloa, *Relación histórica*, 196–213, esp. 196, Sellés, 'Intrumentos', 139, 141.
30 See, for example, Forbes, *Birth*, Gould, *Marine Chronometer*, 40–70, Cotter, *History*, chapter VI, Sobel, *Longitude*, McClellan and Regourd, *Colonial Machine*, 237–43.
31 Pimentel, 'Southern Meridian', 22–3, Gascoigne, 'Navigating', 184–6.
32 Wess, 'Navigation', 211–15.
33 Davids, *Zeewezen*, 190–1, 255–7.
34 Wess, 'Navigation', 215.
35 Miller, 'Longitude Networks', 225, May, 'How the Chronometer', 646, 648.
36 Boistel, 'Training Seafarers', 162.
37 Davids, *Zeewezen*, 184–6, 259–62, Lafuente and Sellés, 'Problem'.
38 Davids, 'Finding Longitude', 281, Jonkers, *Earth's Magnetism*, 48–61.
39 Pumfrey, 'O tempora', Jonkers, *Earth's Magnetism*, 75–8.

40 Thrower (ed.), *Three Voyages*, 29–30, 35–41, 49, 56–60.
41 Ibid., appendix D, 365–7, Murray, *Construction*, 6.
42 See, for example, McClellan and Regourd, *Colonial Machine*, 234–5.
43 Jonkers, *Earth's Magnetism*, 189–90, Thrower (ed.), *Three Voyages*, vol. I, 368–9, Hitchens and May, *Lodestone*, 46–8, Fanning, *Steady*, 71.
44 Davids, *Zeewezen*, 206–7.
45 Juan, *Compendio*, 'Carta de las variaciones', included at the back of the volume.
46 Ibid., 35.
47 Hitchins and May, *Lodestone*, 50; cf. Jonkers, *Earth's Magnetism*, 191–5.
48 Davids, *Zeewezen*, 207.
49 NA 1.04.02 VOC nr. 5036 Verbeeterde instructive van de eygenschap der winden en de courssen te houden in het vaarwater tusschen Nederland en Java, Amsterdam 1768, 8–9.
50 Steenstra, *Openbaare lessen*, 43.
51 Davids, *Zeewezen*, 196.
52 Chapuis, *A la mer*, 164–5, 183, 943 note 49.
53 Davids, *Zeewezen*, 224.
54 McClellan and Regourd, *Colonial Machine*, 177–9, Chias and Abad, 'Nautical Charts', Lafuente and Sellés, 'Problem'.
55 Tofiño, *Atlas maritimo*, part I, Carta esfericá Islas de las Azores o Terceras.
56 Davids, *Zeewezen*, 147, Juan and Ulloa, *Relación histórica*, 428–45.
57 Chaplin, *First Scientific American*, 196–9, 304–5, 310–11, Chaplin, 'Knowing the Ocean', 86–91, Konvitz, *Cartography in France*, 63–6, Robinson, *Early Thematic Mapping*, 81.
58 Deacon, *Scientists*, 220–2.
59 *Waarnemingen*, esp. Introduction, A 3 (and footnote) and Appendix.
60 NA 1.01.46 Admiraliteitscolleges 1170, journal Castor 13 July 1769.
61 Dampier, *Discourse*, 100.
62 Duquette, 'Ship Crowding', Appendix Table 2, 545.
63 Haines and Shlomowitz, 'Mortality Decline', 263 table 1. The mean crude death rate is 'the number of deaths, divided by the average population at risk, with the resulting quotient divided by the average length of voyage (in thirty day months) and expressed as a rate per 1000'; see Haines, Shlomowitz and Brennan, 'Maritime Mortality Revisited', 136.
64 Behrendt, 'Crew Mortality', 51–5, Klein et al., 'Transoceanic Mortality', 105.
65 Buchet, 'Quantification', 182–6, 189–91.
66 Blane, *Select Dissertations*, 4–5 and 40, Table II.
67 Rodger, *Command*, 486.
68 Groustra and Bruijn, 'Kentering', 30, 40.
69 Klein et al., 'Transoceanic Mortality', 112 table III.

70 Earle, *Sailors*, 130.
71 McNeill, *Mosquito Empires*, 155–67.
72 Ibid., 185–6.
73 Curtin, *Death*, 2, Kiple and Ornelas, 'Race', 69–71.
74 Jackson, *Treatise*, 392–6, idem, *Outline*, vi–vii, chapter I.
75 See, for example, Rodschied, *Medizinische und Chirurgische Bemerkungen*, 195, and *Dritter Abschnitt*, Bajon, *Mémoires*, IV–V, Jackson, *Treatise*, 247–51.
76 Haines and Shlomowitz, 'Mortality Decline', 264, 270, 273–80.
77 Crimmin, 'Naval Health', 194–5.
78 Groustra and Bruijn, 'Kentering', 36–40.
79 Sheridan, *Doctors*, 28–35, McClellan and Regourd, *Colonial Machine*, 255. See, for example, Bajon, *Mémoires*, Dazille, *Observations*, Jackson, *Treatise*, Rodschied, *Bemerkungen*.
80 Gallandat, *Noodige onderrichting*.
81 De Monchy, *Essay*, Lardizabal, *Consideraciones*.
82 Poissonnier-Desperrières, *Traité* (1780), 'Avertissement', v.
83 Blane, *Observations*, Preface.
84 Titsingh, *Konst-broederlyke lessen, passim*.
85 De Monchy, *Essay*, Preface, vi–vii.
86 Lardizabal, *Consideraciones*, Prologo, paragraphs 3 and 4.
87 Pringle, *Discourse*, 19, 21–35.
88 Haines and Shlomowitz, 'Mortality Decline', 278.
89 Monchy, *Essay*, Preface, v, chapters II and V.
90 Lind, *Treatise* (1772), 474–83 and 484–4.
91 Blane, *Observations*, 206–7.
92 Gonzalez, *Tratado*, xix.
93 Pringle, *Observations*, Pringle, *Discourse*, Lind, *Treatise*, Lind, *Health*, Duhamel, *Moyens*, De Monchy, 'Verhandeling', Rouppe, *De morbis navigantium*.
94 Rouppe, *Observations*, Preface, iii, v.
95 Jackson, *Treatise*, 395–6.
96 Harrison, 'Tender Frame of Man', 79–86.
97 Huxham, *Essay*, 261–2.
98 See, for example, Titsingh, *Geneeskonst*, 159, Rouppe, *Observations*, Preface, xxi–xxiii, 60–99, Lind, *Essay*, 12–13, 20, 23–6, 35, 38, De Monchy, *Essay*, 4–20, Poissonnier-Desperrières, *Traité* (1767), 'Épitre dédicatoire', 6, *Traité* (1780), xxvi–xxxvi.
99 For example, Huxham, *Essay*, 122.
100 Trotter, *Medicina Nautica*, vol. I, 128, De Monchy, *Essay*, 157–62, Rodger, *Command*, 484–5.
101 Duhamel, *Moyens*, 192–4, Poissonnier-Desperrières, *Traité* (1780), 416–17.

102 Rodger, *Command*, 484–5.
103 Solar and Hens, 'Ship Speeds', 73–4.
104 NA 1.04.02 VOC 170 res. H. XVII 16 March 1750.
105 NA 1.04.02 VOC 197 res. H XVII 8 May 1788, Pop, *Geneeskunde*, 118.
106 NA 1.04.02 VOC 169 res. H XVII 3 November 1746.
107 Bicker, 'Verhandeling', 55–8.
108 Hales, 'Account', 334–8, Clark-Kennedy, *Stephen Hales*, 169, Rodger, *Wooden World*, 107.
109 McClellan and Regourd, *Colonial Machine*, 224–6.
110 De Jong, *Navigating*, 136–7.
111 Kiple and Ornelas, 'Race', 70–1.
112 Gallandat, *Noodige onderrichtinge*, 24.
113 Van Manen, 'Preventive Medicine', 168, 171, 175–7, 182, 184.
114 De Jong, *Navigating*, 134–5.
115 Pringle, *Discourse*, 31–2.
116 Bicker, 'Verhandeling', 50.
117 Solar and Rönnbäck, 'Copper Sheathing', 826.
118 Dillo, *Nadagen*, 182–5, Solar and De Zwart, 'Dutch East Indiamen', 742–3.
119 Solar, 'Merchant Ships', 58.
120 Buchet, 'Quantification', 191.
121 Klein et al., 'Transoceanic Mortality', 94, 99, 101, 109.
122 Hogerzeil and Richardson, 'Slave Purchasing Strategies', 183.
123 Behrendt, 'Crew Mortality', 61.

Chapter 4

1 McClellan and Regourd, *Colonial Machine*, 58–9, Boistel, 'Training Seafarers'.
2 Garralón, 'Formación', 187–95.
3 Kuethe and Andrien, *Spanish Atlantic World*, 243–6, 281, 290–5, Ruiz-Zorrilla, *Apunte*, 91–108.
4 Davids, *Zeewezen*, 327–9, Warnsinck, *Kweekschool*, 17–25.
5 Miller, 'Longitude Networks', 232–3.
6 Davids, *Zeewezen*, 302–3.
7 Ruiz-Zorrilla, *Apunte*, 101, García, 'Losing Professional Identity', 457–8.
8 Wess, 'Navigation', 207–8, Miller, 'Longitude Networks', 234.
9 Miller, 'Longitude Networks', 232–5, Harries, 'Pre-Greenwich Sea Longitudes', 317.
10 Warnsinck, *Kweekschool*, 38–41, 52, 74, Davids, *Zeewezen*, 328.
11 Salazar, *Discurso*, 46–7.
12 Lafuente and Sellés, 'Problem', 245–6, Pimentel, 'Southern Meridian', 21–2.

13 Boistel, 'Training Seafarers', 153-7.
14 Chapuis, *A la mer*, 222-5, Chapuis, 'Hydrographical Departments'.
15 Chapuis, *A la mer*, 191, 483-4.
16 McClellan and Regourd, *Colonial Machine*, 189-90.
17 Salazar, *Discurso*, 85-7.
18 Ibid., 47-8, 52-7, Pimentel, 'Southern Meridian', 20-3.
19 Salazar, *Discurso*, 49-50, Tofiño, *Atlas maritimo*.
20 Salazar, *Discurso*, 51-2, 95, 163-70, Lamb, 'Martín Fernández de Navarrete', 32-3.
21 Waters, 'English Pilot', 348-50, Cook, 'Dalrymple', 55, Chapuis, *A la mer*, 198-201, Chapuis, 'Hydrographical Departments', 164-5, Chaplin, 'Knowing the Ocean', 77.
22 Binnema, *Enlightened Zeal*, 106-15.
23 Chapuis, *A la mer*, 236-40, 271-3, Widmalm, 'Accuracy', 186-9.
24 Waters, 'English Pilot', 350, Cook, 'Dalrymple', 53-4, Chapuis, 'Hydrographical Departments', 165.
25 Cook, 'Dalrymple', 60-2.
26 Van der Krogt (ed.), *Advertenties*, 123 no. 631, 214 no. 1136, 255 no. 1379, 258 no. 1395.
27 Bom, *Bijdragen*, 61-2, Davids, *Zeewezen*, 188, 342, 354-5.
28 Mörzer Bruyns, 'Octant en sextant', 35-6.
29 Bom, *Bijdragen*, 62, Lauts, 'Iets', 764-7.
30 Bom, *Bijdragen*, 62, Davids, *Zeewezen*, 342.
31 Sadler, 'Lunar Distances', Croarken, 'Providing Longitude', 112-22.
32 Boistel, 'Lacaille to Lalande', 52-60.
33 Lafuente and Sellés, 'Problem', 245-6, Sellés, 'Instrumentos', 152.
34 Davids, 'Longitude Committee', 33-5.
35 Bedini, *Thinkers*, 213, 299, 352, 368-9, Mörzer Bruyns, 'Trade Labels', Warner, 'American Octants', Delbourgo, *Scene of Wonder*, 47-8.
36 Glick, 'Imperio', Pimentel, 'Southern Meridian', 18, 22, 25, Salazar, *Discurso*, 52.
37 Alejandro Malaspina, 'Introducción', in David et al. (eds.), *Malaspina Expedition*, vol. I, xcv.
38 Appendix 5 in David et al. (eds.), *Malaspina Expedition*, vol. III, 363-5.
39 See, for example, Morrison-Low, *Making Scientific Iinstruments*, 160, Mörzer Bruyns, *Schip Recht door Zee*, 130, Leopold, 'Some Notes', Cohen and Cohen-de Meester, 'Fahrenheit', Hackmann, *Cuthbertson*, 14.
40 Morrison-Low, *Making Scientific Instruments*, 147, Clifton, 'Growth', Zuidervaart, *Van 'konstgenoten'*, 304-8, Van Zuylen, 'Van Deijl'.
41 McConnell, 'Craft Workshop', 41-3.
42 Ibid., 43, Morrison-Low, *Making Scientific Instruments*, 177-8.
43 Bedini, *Thinkers*, 192-5, 213, Brooke Hindle, *Rittenhouse*, 344, 352.
44 Bedini, *Thinkers*, 213-4, 268.

45 McConnell, 'Craft Workshop', 50.
46 Ibid., 36, 38, 41, 45, Morrison-Low, *Making Scientific Instruments*, 147–9, 155–6, 287, Sorrenson, *Perfect Mechanics*, 107–9.
47 De Clercq, *Oriental Lamp*, 55–62.
48 Mörzer Bruyns, *Schip Recht door Zee*, 119–21, 123–5.
49 Ibid., 123–7.
50 NA 2.01.12 Binnenlandse Zaken 1795-1813, nr. 1233 'État des fabriques en Hollande', f. 147, Davids, *Zeewezen*, 252–5, Maclean, *Bijdrage*, 4–5, 9.
51 Turner, 'Mathematical Instrument-making', 83–7.
52 Sellés, 'Instrumentos', 146–7, 153–4, Lafuente and Sellés, 'Problem', 247–9.
53 *Diario de las Córtes. Estraordinarias*, vol. IV, 19 November 1821, 12.
54 McClellan and Regourd, *Colonial Machine*, 239–41.
55 Sorrenson, 'State Demand', passim.
56 Gould, *Marine Chronometer*, 40–74, 83–100, 116–30, Mercer, *John Arnold Son*, 15–39, 79–81, 133, 209–12, 217–18.
57 Davids, *Zeewezen*, 260–1, Leopold, 'Third Seafaring Nation', Mörzer Bruyns, 'Astronomical Clocks', 456.
58 Henwood, 'Académie de Marine', Chapuis, *A la mer*, 154–8, Konvits, *Cartography*, 73.
59 Le Page, 'Bibliothèque'.
60 Henwood, 'Académie de Marine', 132–4, Konvits, *Cartographye*, 73.
61 Pritchard, 'Shipwright', 6–7, 16, Ferreiro, *Ships*, 74–9, 164–71 and chapter 4, McGee, 'Craftsmanship', 230–2, McClellan and Regourd, *Colonial Machine*, 228–9.
62 Pritchard, 'Shipwright', 11–12, 15–23, Ferreiro, *Ships*, 59–62, 259–72, McGee, 'Craftsmanship', 230–2, Gillispie, *Science Old Regime*, 23, 340.
63 Ferreiro, *Ships*, 272, 291, Salazar, *Discurso*, 39, Rodger, *Command*, 411, 418.
64 Ferreiro, *Ships*, 292–3.
65 Ibid., 273–5. The French translation of Juan's *Examen maritimo* was published in 1783, see Juan, *Examen maritime*.
66 Schaffer, 'Charter'd Thames', 298–9.
67 Rodger, *Command*, 410.
68 Pritchard, 'Shipwright', 6, 9, 13–14, 24.
69 Rodger, *Command*, 415–16.
70 Kuethe and Serrano, 'Astillero', 774, Serrano, 'Él poder y la gloria', 104, Wing, *Roots*, 197–8.
71 Rodger, *Command*, 408, 411–15.
72 Ibid., 418.
73 Ibid., 409.
74 Schaffer, 'Charter'd Thames', 288; cf. also Chapelle, *Search for Speed*, 79.
75 McGee, 'Craftsmanship', 222–7, Hoving and Lemmers, *In tekening gebracht*, chapters II and III, Bruijn, Gaastra and Schöffer (eds.), *Dutch-Asiatic Shipping*, vol. I, 44–7, De Jong, 'Drawings', 182–4, 188–90.

76 Hoving and Lemmers, *In tekening gebracht*, 102–3, 183–8.
77 Bossut, 'Mémoire', Euler, 'Traité'.
78 Hutchinson, *Treatise*, 25.
79 Bossut, 'Mémoire', 1, 4–5.
80 Bruijn, *Commanders*, 197.
81 Cf. Falola and Warnock, *Encyclopedia*, sub 'Plans and Diagrams', 304.
82 Clarkson, *History*, 377, 379; cf. Rediker, *Slave Ship*, 308–42. Garland and Klein, 'Allotment', 247, only mention drawings for the *Brookes* and the *Vigilante* (borrowed from a booklet published in 1823). Early nineteenth-century 'storage plans' for French slave ships were partly based on the *Brookes* plan, see http://slaveryimages.org.
83 McClellan and Regourd, *Colonial Machine*, 67–9, Osborne, *Emergence*, 27–32, Romieux, 'Histoire', 498, Suberchichot, 'Corps', 322–5.
84 McClellan and Regourd, *Colonial Machine*, 129–31.
85 Poissonnier-Desperrières, *Traité* (1767), 427–8.
86 Lomas Salmonte et al., *Historia*, 465–8, 'Historia del real colegio de cirugía de Cádiz', http://proyectoargantonio2.blogspot.nl/2011/02/historia-del-real-colegio-de-cirugia-de.html.
87 García-Cubillana, 'Salud', Saiz Carrero, 'Real Colegio'.
88 Gonzalez, *Tratado*.
89 Lloyd and Coulter, *Medicine*, vol. III, 8–13, 29, Rodger, *Command*, 487, Crimmin, 'Naval Health', 184, idem, 'Sick and Hurt Board', 91, 102–3, Crumplin, 'Surgery', 67–70.
90 Lloyd and Coulter, *Medicine*, vol. III, 13, Lloyd (ed.), *Health*, 2.
91 Lloyd and Coulter, *Medicine*, vol. III, 11.
92 Cardwell, 'Royal Navy Surgeons', 46–51.
93 Lloyd and Coulter, *Medicine*, vol. III, 187–95, 207–12, 261–5, Crimmin, 'Naval Health', 184–6, idem, 'Sick and Hurt Board', 99–102.
94 Lloyd and Coulter, *Medicine*, vol. III, 217–27, 265–78, Lloyd (ed.), *Health*, 3, 132–3, 214–15, Crimmin, 'Naval health', 185–7, Lind, *Essay*, Blane, *Observations*, Trotter, *Medicina Nautica*.
95 Crimmin, 'Sick and Hurt Board', 101–2.
96 Pop, *Geneeskunde*, 22, 29.
97 SA Amsterdam, Archief 366 nr. 216 f. 136, 143, 210, 244, 266, nr. 233 Reglement voor het chirurgijnsgilde 1796, Kan, 'Illustre School', 70, GA Rotterdam Gildearchieven nr. 23 articles 63–7.
98 Pop, *Geneeskunde*, 20–2.
99 Titsingh, *Konst-broederlyke lessen*, idem, *Geneeskonst*, Verbrugge/Schlichting, *Nieuw hervormde examen*, 'Approbatie'.
100 Pop, *Geneeskunde*, 131, Groustra and Bruijn, 'Kentering', 45 note 65.

101 Pop, *Geneeskunde*, 106–16, NA Collectie VerHuell nr. 198 Nota Pieter van Woensel 1806, nr. 199 Bijlage A.
102 See for this distinction Delbourgo, *Scene of Wonders*, 18–20.
103 Davids, 'Scholarly Atlantic', 243.
104 Cf. Winterer, 'Where Is America', 603–4, Ogilvie, 'Correspondence Networks', 365.
105 *List of the Linnean Society 1798*, 3–4, Charters and bye-laws of the Linnean Society, 'List of the Linnean Society', 6–7.
106 Chaplin, *First Scientific American*, 196.
107 Davids, 'Scholarly Atlantic', 238–9, Franklin, Brownrigg and Farrish, 'Stilling of Waves'.
108 Mertens, 'Honour', 6–9.
109 Van Lelyveld, *Berichten en Prijs-vragen*, 1–4, 14, 22, 40–2 and appendices A–K. Mertens, 'Honour', 7, Davids, 'Scholarly Atlantic', 239.
110 Ferreiro, *Ships*, 153, Wright, 'Beaufoy's Experiments', Schaffer, 'Charter'd Thames', 298–300.
111 De Jong, *Navigating*, 186–210.
112 Davids, 'Seamen's Organisation', 155, Davids, 'Technological Change', 289.
113 Morris, *Government*, 199, Gilje, *Liberty*, 282 note 87.
114 See for example *Laws of the Marine Society at Salem*, 3, *History of the Marine Society of Newburyport*, 14, 18, Boston: www.bostonmarinesocety.org, New York: http://www.marinesocietyny.org/about.htm.
115 *East India Marine Society of Salem*, 3.
116 *Laws of the Marine Society at Salem*, 3–4.
117 http://marinesocietysalem.org/letterbook.html, Letter Book Salem Marine Society, 2 and 25 February, 17 December 1792, 10, 30 and 31 January, 2 February and 28 November 1793, 18 January, 3 February 1796, 23 November 1797.
118 *East India Marine Society of Salem*, 3–4.
119 Earle, 'Political Economy', 94–8.
120 Bolster, *Black Jacks*, 17–26.
121 Ibid., 48–51, 60–1.
122 Sheridan, *Doctors*, 72, 329.
123 Murphy, 'Translating', esp. 30, 41.
124 Sheridan, *Doctors*, 292.
125 Ibid., 72–3, 269–70, 292–309, Harrison, 'Tender Frame of Man', 83.
126 Gallandat, *Noodige onderrichtinge*, 41.
127 McClellan and Regourd, *Colonial Machine*, 287–94.
128 Voeks, 'African Medicine', 74–5, Newson, 'Medical Practice', 378.
129 Bravo, 'Mission Gardens', 54–9, Fatah-Black, *Suriname*, 150.
130 Bravo, 'Mission Gardens', 51–4.
131 Cranz, *Historie*.

132 Leinenga, *Arctische walvisvangst*, 18, 144, 156–8, 164 and appendix III.
133 Ibid., 166–9.
134 Groot, *Beknopt en getrouw verhaal*, 16.
135 Leinenga, *Arctische walvisvangst*, 23, 165, Groot, *Beknopt en getrouw verhaal*, 36–8, Kat, *Dagboek*, 42.
136 Scoresby, *Arctic Regions*, vol. I, 510, Leinenga, *Arctische walvisvangst*, 157.

Conclusion

1 Gould, *Marine Chronometer*, 72, McClellan and Regourd, *Colonial Machine*, 224–5.
2 Bleichmar, *Visible Empire*, 18, 84, 191.
3 Hales, *Description*, 12–15, 38, 42–4, Morogues, 'Mémoire', 400–2.
4 Lind, *Treatise*, 191–6.
5 Trotter, *Observations*, 75–6.
6 Lind, *Essay*, 133–40.
7 McClellan and Regourd, *Colonial Machine*, 68, 256; Pierre-Isaac Poissonnier also wrote a textbook on anatomy for naval surgeons, see Poissonnier, *Abrégé*.
8 Blane, *Observations*, 179–204.
9 Sorrenson, *Perfect Mechanics*, 13–30, 106–24, McConnell, 'Craft Workshop', Zuidervaart, 'Medical–Meteorological Society', 49–60, Bennett, 'Shopping'.
10 Sorrenson, *Perfect Mechanics*, 45–58, appendix A.
11 Zuidervaart, 'Medical–Meteorological Society', 59.
12 Van Swinden, *Dissertation*, especially VI and VII.
13 Charters, 'Intention', 28–34. Crimmin, 'Naval Health', 187–8.
14 De Jong, *Navigating*, 124–32, McClellan and Regourd, *Colonial Machine*, 224–5.
15 De Jong, *Navigating*, 179–91, 225–9, 234.
16 Ibid., 233–4, Dillo, *Nadagen*, 17–18, 183, Solar and De Zwart, 'Dutch East Indiamen', 742–3.
17 Cf. Solar and De Zwart, 'Dutch East Indiamen', 743, who oddly enough call this 'further evidence' of the 'conservatism' of the VOC.
18 Rodger, *Command*, 344, 375.
19 Davids, 'Scholarly Atlantic', 241–2.
20 Steele, *English Atlantic*, 10, 114.
21 Kuethe and Andrien, *Spanish Atlantic World*, 10, Stangl, *Authentizität*, 188–9, Moya, *Cousins*, 68.
22 McClellan and Regourd, *Colonial Machine*, 417–18.
23 Bartram to Gronovius, 6 December 1745, in Darlington (ed.), *Memorials*, 352–4, esp. 353, Colden to Gronovius, 30 May 1747, in Gray (ed.), *Selections*, 19–20. Cf. Parsons and Murphy, 'Ecosystems', 531.

24 Salazar, *Discurso*, 86, 87.
25 Lamb, 'Felipe Bauzá', 321, Pimentel, 'Southern Meridian', 26.
26 Crimmin, 'Naval Health', 195–6.
27 Marsigli, *Histoire*, McConnell, 'L.F. Marsigli', McConnell, 'Profitable Visit'.
28 Deacon, *Scientists*, 181–94, 202–15, Reidy, *Tides*, 42–58.
29 McConnell, *No Sea Too Deep*, 14–30, Deacon, *Scientists*, 181–94.
30 Reidy, *Tides*, 48–50.
31 Ibid., 42–3, 47–6.
32 McClellan and Regourd, *Colonial Machine*, 279–80.
33 Feldman, 'Late Enlightenment Meteorology', 153–5, McClellan and Regourd, *Colonial Machine*, 273–9.
34 Zuidervaart, 'Medical–Meteorological Society', 392–3, 61, and Appendix.
35 Reidy, *Tides*, 43–6, 57–8.
36 Quoted in Zuidervaart, 'Medical–Meteorological Society', 410; Feldman, 'Late Enlightenment Meteorology', 174.
37 Reidy, *Tides*, 46–54.
38 Zuidervaart, 'Medical–Meteorological Society', 410, McClellan and Regourd, *Colonial Machine*, 280, Feldman, 'Late Enlightenment Meteorology', 177.
39 Cuvier, *Historical Portrait*, 95–104.
40 Wheeler, 'Peter Artedi', idem, 'Gronovius Fish Collection', Hendrik Engels' *Alphabetical List*, 104–5, 249–50.
41 Pietsch (ed.), *Fishes, Crayfishes, and Crabs*, 18–36, 60–1.
42 Cuvier, *Historical Portrait*, 99, 105–7, Gronovius, *Museum ichthyologicum*, idem, *Zoophylacium Gronovianum*, Seba, *Locupletissimi rerum naturalium*.
43 Anderson, *Nachrichten*, 51–95, 173–227.
44 Ibid., 213–15, 229.
45 Ibid., 'Vorrede'.
46 Ibid., 177–83, 204–7.
47 Parsons and Murphy, 'Ecosystems', 524–6, 528.
48 Gronovius, 'Method'.

Part III

Introduction

1 FitzRoy, *Narrative*, vol. II, 66–72.
2 Benjamin, *Atlantic World*, 661–63.
3 Canny and Morgan, 'Introduction', 16, Rothschild, 'Late Atlantic History', 636–7.
4 Marshall, *Making*, Bayly, *Imperial Meridian*.

5 See the data on voyages and numbers of slaves embarked in the transatlantic slave trade database, http://www.slavevoyages.org/.
6 Eltis and Jennings, 'Trade', 945.
7 Bowen, *Business*, 269.
8 Guennou, *Missions Étrangères*, 241, 248–9, Kilpatrick, *Fathers*, 6.
9 Bayly, *Birth*, 345–51, Law, 'Africa', 599–600.
10 Eltis and Jennings, 'Trade', 942, 946, Lynn, *Commerce*, 12–20, 33, 51–2.
11 Beckert, *Empire*, 67–73, 85–7, 104, North, *Growth*, 31.
12 Beckert, *Empire*, 104, 200–1.
13 Llorca-Jaña, 'Impact', 46–51, Llorca-Jaña, *Textile Trade*, chapter 2.
14 Rosal, 'Exportación', Schmit and Rosal, 'Exportaciones', Llorca-Jaña, *Textile Trade*, 75, 209.
15 Davis, Gallman and Gleiter, *Leviathan*, 19, 461.
16 Ibid., 6, 40–1, 43–4.
17 Ibid., 39, 42.
18 Headland, *South Georgia*, 35.
19 Cushman, *Guano*, 26–7, 40–8.
20 Igler, *Great Ocean*, 181–3.
21 Fichter, *So Great a Profit*, 150–1, 156, 208, 284–5.
22 Solar, 'Opening', 626, 630–2.
23 Hughes, *Fatal Shore*, 143–4, 151.
24 Van Zanden and Van Riel, *Strictures*, 112–16.
25 Broeze, *Stad Schiedam*, 6–12, Horlings, *Economic Development*, 174–81, 385–92, 401, Davids, 'Technological Change', 282–3, De Jonge, *Industrialisatie*, 132–4.
26 Bossenbroek, *Van Holland*, 47–54, 193, 198.
27 Broeze, 'International Diffusion', 82–7.
28 Moch, *Moving Europeans*, 147–9, Hatton and Williamson, *Age of Mass Migration*, 7–9.
29 Moya, *Cousins*, 46, 56.
30 Cushman, *Guano*, 43.
31 De Jonge, *Industrialisatie*, 134, Horlings, *Economic Development*, 183.
32 Horlings, *Economic Development*, 177–81, 190, Broeze, 'International Diffusion', 82–6.
33 Davis, Gallman and Gleiter, *Leviathan*, 460–1.
34 See for example Beckert, *Empire*, 200–18, Beckert, *Monied Metropolis*, 19–24, Earle, *Earles of Liverpool*, 249–58, Lynn, *Commerce*, 26–7, Llorca-Jaña, *Textile Trade*, 75, Cassis, *Capitals*, 15–24, Davis, Gallman and Gleiter, *Leviathan*, 381–45, Gaastra, 'Zeilende kustvaart', 156–9.
35 Rodger, *Command*, 483.
36 Lewis, *Navy*, 69.
37 Ibid., 12, McAleer, *Britain's Maritime Empire*, esp. chapter 2.
38 Wilcox, 'Peaceable Times', 480–7.

Chapter 5

1. Rönnbäck, 'Speed', 476, 481–2, 489, Solar and Hens, 'Ship Speeds', 66–71.
2. Bossenbroek, *Van Holland*, 62.
3. SA Rotterdam Archief Oceaancommissie no. 7, Jaarverslag over 1867, 2, Jaarverslag over 1876, 2, Jaarverslag over 1880, 3; the average duration of voyages in 1845–1855 was 103 days, see Van der Hoeven, *Voorlezing*, 23.
4. Llorca-Jaña, *Textile Trade*, 213.
5. Albion, *Rise New York Port*, 51–2, 54, 334–5, Albion, *Square-riggers*, 77, 189–92, 317, Taylor, *Transportation Revolution*, 145–6, Keeling, 'Transportation Revolution', 44, Kelly and O'Grada, 'Speed'.
6. Grocott, 'Shipwrecks', 151.
7. 'Report from a Select Committee', 132.
8. Ibid., 135.
9. McGowan, *Century*, 5.
10. Rodger, *Command*, 422, Knight, *Britain against Napoleon*, 360, 369, Seppings, 'Great Strength'.
11. 'Report from a Select Committee', 134–5.
12. Llorca-Jaña, *Textile Trade*, 211–14.
13. Chapelle, *Search for Speed*, 278–9, Davis, Gallman and Gleiter, *Leviathan*, 271.
14. Albion, *Square-riggers*, 190.
15. Ferreiro and Pollara, 'Contested Waterlines', 417–20.
16. Ibid., 429–31, Chapelle, *Search for Speed*, 364–5.
17. Davis, Gallman and Gleiter, *Leviathan*, 268–9.
18. '*Report from Select Committee on Shipwrecks of Timber Ships*', 5, Sjostrom, 'Safety Regulation'.
19. Glascock, *Naval Service*, 138–40, Murphy and Jeffers, *Nautical Routine*, part III, 1–2, 'Statistics of stowage', 116.
20. Murphy and Jeffers, *Nautical Routine*, part III, 1; Thompson, *Working*.
21. Edwards, *Practical Guide*, 26.
22. Stevens, *Stowage*, Preface to the first edition, and 10–12.
23. Ibid., 11; Stevens's book was reprinted six times between 1859 and 1894; Craig, 'Printed Guides', 32–3.
24. Webb, *Expansion*, 349–50.
25. Ritchie, *Admiralty Chart*, 189, David, 'Emergence', 5.
26. Webb, *Expansion*, 349 figure 8.2 and 426 appendix 17.
27. Llorca-Jaña, *Textile Trade*, 214–15.
28. Ibid., 215–16.
29. An example in Maury, *Explanations* (1858), 486–7, see also http://icoads.noaa.gov/maury.pdf; Wallbrink, Koek and Brandsma, *The US Maury Collection*.

30 Houvenaghel, 'Conference Maritime', 43, 47.
31 See Maury's explanation of these different types of charts in Maury, *Explanations* (1853), 249–92.
32 Smith, 'Maury; Pathfinder', 417–18.
33 Quoted in Smith, 'Maury; Pathfinder', 418.
34 The eighth edition, published in 1858, was more than four times as long as the third edition, published in 1851, see Maury, *Explanations*, 1851 and 1858.
35 Review of A. G. Findlay's 'Chart of the North-Atlantic Ocean' in *The Nautical Magazine and Naval Chronicle for 1858*, 685; *Maandelijkse zeilaanwijzing van het Kanaal naar Java*.
36 Maury, *Explanations* (1858), vol. I, iv–vi, vol. II, 368, 459.
37 SA Rotterdam, Archief Oceaancommisssie, nr. 7, Jaarverslag over 1863, 11, Jaarverslag over 1866, 2; *Koninklijk Nederlands Meteorologisch Instituut*, 206–7; *Mededeelingen*, iii–iv.
38 Woodruff, Worley and Reynolds, 'Early Ship Observations', 170 figure 1, Maury, *Explanations* (1858), vol. I, 375.
39 Maury, *Explanations* (1858), vol. I, iv.
40 Davids, 'Vrijheid', 10.
41 Maury, *Explanations* (1858), vol. I, iv.
42 Ibid., vol. II, 594, and see note 13.
43 Ibid., vol. II, 594.
44 Ibid., vol. I, 318.
45 Ibid., vol. I, viii, Achbari, *Rulers*, 91–24.
46 Reidy, *Tides*, 88–9.
47 Ibid., 84–5, 94, 98, 102.
48 Ibid., 228, 232, Day, *Hydrographic Service*, 47, 87, Cartwright, *Tides*, 92.
49 Miller, 'Longitude Networks', 225.
50 May, 'How the Chronometer', 644, 646, 648.
51 Ibid., 654–5, Webb, *Expansion*, 303–5.
52 Chapuis, *A la mer*, 85.
53 Dick, 'U.S. Naval Observatory', 168, Dick, 'Centralizing', 491–2, 495.
54 Davids, *Zeewezen*, 259–60, Spek, *Tijdmeters*.
55 'Report from a Select Committee', 137, cf. Sobel, *Longitude*, 152–63.
56 May, 'How the Chronometer', 643–4.
57 Chapuis, *A la mer*, 85.
58 Hazewinkel, *Handleiding*, Warnsinck, *Kweekschool*, 248–50, Cotter, *History*, 155–62.
59 Vanvaerenbergh and Ifland, *Line of Position Navigation*, 9–15, Cotter, *History*, 275–82, 292, Warnsinck, *Kweekschool*, 251–9.
60 Fanning, *Steady*, 71; see, for example, 'A chart of magnetic curves of equal variation' by Peter Barlow (Edinburgh 1833 and subsequent editions) and the 'Chart of the variation of the magnetic needle', by Thomas Yeates (London 1817, 1824^2).

61 Day, *Hydrographic Service*, 73, Fanning, *Steady*, 72, Cawood, 'Magnetic Crusade', passim.
62 Fanning, *Steady*, xxx–xxx1, 1–3, Vasey, 'Emergence', 143.
63 Fanning, *Steady*, 6–7, Thomson, *Mathematical and Physical Papers*, vol. VI, 320, *Admiralty Manual*, 81.
64 Fanning, *Steady*, xxii–xlii, 14–27, Poisson, 'Mémoire', *Practical Rules*, passim, *The Nautical Magazine and Naval Chronicle for 1865*, 539.
65 Blane, *Brief Statement*, 11–12.
66 Ellis, 'Health', 192, Harrison, 'Important and Truly National Subject', 112.
67 Dutton, 'Royal Naval Data'.
68 *Statistical reports on the health of the Navy for the years 1831 ... 1836*, 80, 138, 199, Milroy, 'Health', 551.
69 Milroy, 'Health', 551–4.
70 Harrison, 'Important and Truly National Subject', 126–7, Rasor, *Reform*, 103, Balfour, 'Comparative Health', esp. 17–19, Keevil, Lloyd and Coulter, *Medicine*, vol. IV, 271.
71 Curtin, *Death*, 35–9.
72 Haines, Shlomowitz and Brennan, 'Maritime Mortality Revisited', 135–7.
73 Ibid., 135, Stewart and Shlomowitz, 'Mortality and Migration', 130–1, Cohn, 'Mortality', 291–6.
74 Carter, *Merchant Seamen's Health*, 36–7, Solar and Hens, 'Ship Speeds', 75.
75 Harrison, 'Important and Truly National Subject', 115, 119.
76 McWilliam, 'On the Health', 544–6.
77 Milroy, 'Health', 551, McWilliam, 'On the Health', 545, Steinthal, 'Report of the Liverpool Committee', 555.
78 Bossenbroek, *Van Holland*, 90.
79 Klein et al., 'Transatlantic Mortality', 114, table V.
80 Cohn, 'Death', 689, Haines, Shlomowitz and Brennan, 'Maritime Mortality Revisited', 134–8.
81 Solar and Hens, 'Ship Speeds', 76.
82 Smith, 'Cleanse', 179–80, 196, Harrison, 'Important and Truly National Subject', 118–20, 126, Haines, Shlomowitz and Brennan, 'Maritime Mortality Revisited', 143.
83 Smith, 'Cleanse', 181, Foxhall, *Health*, 68.
84 Smith, 'Cleanse', 180–3, 191, 195, Keevil, Lloyd and Coulter, *Medicine*, vol. IV, 83–7, Haines, Shlomowitz and Brennan, 'Maritime Mortality Revisited', 143, 151, 153, 155, 161–2, Haines, 'Migrant Voyages', 183–92, Foxhall, *Health*, 67–73, Curtin, 'White Man's Grave', 105–9, Osborne, *Emergence*, 59, 61, Masson, *Mort*, 281–4, Bossenbroek, *Van Holland*, 87.
85 Macdonagh, *Pattern*, 75, 147–8, 200, 294, 341, Haines, Shlomowitz and Brennan, 'Maritime Mortality Revisited', 152, Haines, 'Migrant Voyages', 177, Foxhall, *Health*, 61, Zolberg, *Nation*, 110–13, Northrup, *Indentured Labor*, 83–4.

86 Haines, 'Migrant Voyages', 182, Stewart and Shlomowitz, 'Mortality and Migration', 131, Haines, Shlomowitz and Brennan, 'Maritime Mortality Revisited', 147–51.
87 Smith, 'Cleanse', 184.
88 Dompeling, *Handboek*, 'Voorrede', vi–vii, 627–31, Forget, *Médecine navale*, Johnston, *Influence*.
89 Horner, *Diseases*, vii–viii, 18, 46.
90 Masson, *Mort*, 281–2.
91 Fonssagrives, *Traité*, 550, Osborne, *Emergence*, 63–4, 70.
92 Smith, 'Cleanse', 184.
93 Foxhall, *Health*, 121–6.
94 Masson, 'Révolution sanitaire', 408, Osborne, *Emergence*, 70.
95 Steinthal, 'Report of the Liverpool Committee', 555, 559.
96 Starkey and Haines, 'Newfoundland Fisheries', 10, Robinson and Starkey, 'Sea Fisheries', 132–6, Christensen and Nielsen, 'Norwegian Fsheries', 157–9, Bolster, *Mortal Sea*, 122–5 and 285.
97 Bolster, *Mortal Sea*, 102–3, 106–7, 125–9, 145–50, 197–206.
98 Ibid., 104–8, 146–8, 163–7, 200, Cadigan and Hutchings, 'Expansion', 45–6, Robinson and Starkey, 'Sea Fisheries', 135.
99 Cadigan and Hutchings, 'Expansion', 36–7, 40, 64.
100 Ryan, *Ice Hunters*, 47, 54, 104, 143, Sanger, 'Sail versus Steam', figure 1 and conclusion.
101 Ryan, *Ice Hunters*, 65, 74, 82–5.
102 Headland, *South Georgia*, 24–6, 45–51, Burton, 'South Georgia', 914.
103 Davis, Gallman and Gleiter, *Leviathan*, 7, 16–17, 461, 478–86.
104 Ibid., 268–70.
105 Ibid., 270–94.
106 Cushman, *Guano*, 45.
107 Bolster, *Mortal Sea*, 121–3.
108 Cadigan and Hutchings, 'Expansion', 36–7, 40, Ryan, *Ice Hunters*, 111–17, Headland, *South Georgia*, 35–6, 45–51, Burton, 'South Georgia', 914.
109 Davis, Gallman and Gleiter, *Leviathan*, 131.
110 Cf. ibidem, 135–6, 148 and Bolster, *Mortal Sea*, 123–35.

Chapter 6

1 Day, *Hydrographic Service*, 334–5, Cook, 'Dalrymple', 53–4, 58.
2 Cook, 'Dalrymple', 66, David, 'Admiralty Chart', 5.
3 Cook, 'Dalrymple', 65, Ritchie, *Admiralty Chart*, 93, 159.
4 Day, *Hydrographic Service*, 29, David, 'Admiralty Chart', 7–8, Ritchie, *Admiralty Chart*, 101.

5   Day, *Hydrographic Service*, 42, David, 'Admiralty Chart', 8, Webb, *Expansion*, 296–06.
6   Chapuis, *Á la mer*, 415.
7   Lamb, 'London Years', 324–8, David, 'Admiralty Chart', 8–9, 11.
8   Day, *Hydrographic Service*, 31, 47, 73.
9   Ibid., 48, 51, 75.
10 Ibid., 31, 33, David, 'Admiralty Chart', 13–14.
11 David, 'Admiralty Chart', 12–13.
12 Day, *Hydrographic Service*, 31, Webb, *Expansion*, 155–6, 296, 301–5, May, 'How the Chronometer', 647, 650.
13 Day, *Hydrographic Service*, 35–6, Webb, *Expansion*, 260–6 and Appendix 15.
14 Reidy, Kroll and Conway, *Exploration*, 82, Day, *Hydrographic Service*, 46–7, 56.
15 Day, *Hydrographic Service*, 67, Morrell and Thackray, *Gentlemen*, 338, 524, Lambert, *Franklin*, 81, Reidy, *Tides*, 122–32, 169.
16 Reidy, *Tides*, 210–11.
17 Ibid., 133, 140, 147, 161–93, Morrell and Thackray, *Gentlemen*, 513–17.
18 Reidy, *Tides*, 191.
19 *The Nautical Magazine*, 1 (1832), 1–2, 'Address to the public' and 'Prospectus', Day, *Hydrographic Service*, 46.
20 *Manual of Scientific Enquiry*, iii–iv, Reidy, *Tides*, 254.
21 Fanning, *Steady*, 13–15.
22 Binnema, *Enlightened Zeal*, 132–3, 138–9, 152 158, 168–9.
23 Dunn and Higgitt, 'Bureau and the Board', 203–16, Gascoigne, *Science*, 29–30, Barr, 'Exploration Voyages', 111–13, Howse, 'Britain's Board of Longitude', 401, Williams, *Arctic Labyrinth*, part III.
24 Day, *Hydrographic Service*, 45–6, Barr, 'Exploration Voyages', 113, Reidy, Kroll and Conway, *Exploration*, 82.
25 Vaughan, *Arctic Birds*, 58–9, 62, Sabine, 'Memoir', 527.
26 Quoted in Vaughan, *Arctic Birds*, 63.
27 https://cudl.lib.cam.ac.uk/collections/longitude, RGO 14/8 Confirmed minutes of the Board of Longitude 1823–1829 f. 2 3 April 1823, f. 20 1 April 1824, f. 23 4 November 1824.
28 Morrell and Thackray, *Gentlemen*, 520–3, Reidy, *Tides of History*, 289, http://www.royalobservatorygreenwich.org/articles.php?article=997.
29 Day, *Hydrographic Service*, 56–7.
30 Anderson, *Predicting*, 117, Achbari, *Rulers*, 92–7, Reidy, *Tides*, 288, Deacon, *Scientists*, 292.
31 Chapuis, *A la mer*, 477–8.
32 Ibid., 494.
33 Chapuis, *A la mer*, 404–8, 416, Gascoigne, 'Navigating', 186–7, 190–4.
34 Chapuis, *A la mer*, 480, 482.

35 Ibid., 504–5.
36 Pouvreau, 'Mesures', 125–7, 132–5, Reidy, *Tides*, 180.
37 Dick, 'Centralizing', 508 note 89.
38 Schiavon, 'Bureau', 70, Schiavon and Rollet, 'Pour une histoire', 15–16.
39 http://www.bureau-des-longitudes.fr/histoire.htm, Loi relative à la formation d'un Bureau des Longitudes, 7 messidor An III (25 June 1795), Débarbat, 'Évolution administrative', 25–8, Gillispie, *Science Revolutionary and Napoleonic Years*, 304, 455–7.
40 See also Drayton, 'A l'école des Français'.
41 http://www.bureau-des-longitudes.fr/histoire.htm, 'Rapport fait à la Convention nationale dans sa séance du 7 messidor an III (25 Juin 1795), par le Représentant du Peuple Grégoire, sur l'établissement du Bureau des Longitudes'.
42 Dunn and Higgitt, 'Bureau and the Board', 209–12.
43 Cawood, 'Magnetic Crusade', 494.
44 Ibid., 502, 507, Binnema, *Enlightened Zeal*, 210–13. Cf. Malin and Barracough, 'Humboldt', 282–4, Carter, *Magnetic Fever*, 8–27, 43–69.
45 Schiavon, 'Bureau', 68, 71–2, 78.
46 http://bdl.ahp-numerique.fr/, Procès-verbaux Bureau des Longitudes, 28 May 1851, 21 September 1853, 11 May 1859, Houvenaghel, 'Conférence', 45, Achbari, *Rulers*, 54.
47 Achbari, *Rulers*, 15–16, 80, 86–7.
48 Dick, 'Centralizing', 468, 470, 474.
49 Ibid., 495–7.
50 Ibid., 507–8.
51 Ibid., 496–7.
52 Ibid., 500–3, 509, Dick, 'How the Observatory Began', 172–3, 175–7, Bruce, *Modern American Science*, 208–9.
53 Dick, 'Centralizing', 498, 503, Dick, 'How the Observatory Began', 179.
54 Slotte, *Patronage*, 43–4.
55 Ibid., 99–100, 137–9, Deacon, *Scientists*, 291.
56 Slotte, *Patronage*, 44.
57 Ibid., 99–100, 113–28.
58 Ibid., 1, 62–71, 144.
59 Lamb, 'London Years', 320–1, 324–5, Lamb, 'Martin Fernandez de Navarrete', 34–8.
60 Maury, *Explanations* (1858), vol. I, vi.
61 NA 2.01.29.01 Departement van Marine 1795–1813, Aanhangsel 1 nr. 55 Instructie voor den mathematicus en examinateur-generaal van 's Lands zee-officieren, articles IV and V; Davids, 'Florijn', 176.
62 NA 1.01.47.08 Admiraliteitscolleges XII Florijn) nr. 3 letter Jacob Florijn to the Minister van Marine en Koloniën 27 January 1808, *Instructie voor den Directeur van het Depot der Marine*, 23 March 1808.

63 Davids, 'Longitude Committee', 40–1, Davids, 'Zeevaartkundig onderwijs', 169, Dekker, 'Frederik Kaiser', 26–7, Warnsinck, *Kweekschool*, 183–6.
64 Davids, 'Longitude Committee', 32.
65 Schilder and Mörzer Bruyns, 'Navigatie', 197–8, 208–11, Jansen and L' Honoré Naber, *Leven*, 127, 137–43, Achbari, *Rulers*, 33, Acda, *Deining*, 127–8.
66 Davids, 'Longitude Committee', 41, Dekker, 'Frederik Kaiser', 26–7, Acda, *Deining*, 128.
67 Van Lunteren, 'Oprichting', Achbari, *Rulers*, 32–45, 51–2, 59–63, 74–9.
68 Vasey, 'Emergence', 47, 91, 171, 329–31.
69 García, *Mundo del trabajo*, 224–8.
70 NA 2.02.01 Algemene Staatssecretarie 1813-1840 nr. 1783 KB 12 October 1823 no. 65, Davids, 'Technological Change', 285.
71 Davids, 'Technological Change', 288, 295.
72 Mansvelt, *Geschiedenis*, vol. 2, 149; SA Rotterdam, Archief Kamer van Koophandel no.44/18 minute letter to Minister van Binnenlandse Zaken, 14 January 1851.
73 Vasey, 'Emergence', 19–20, 90–1, Williams, 'Buckingham', 118–19.
74 Rodger, *Command*, 511–12, Lewis, *Navy*, 102, 108.
75 Williams, 'Buckingham', 120, 123, Vasey, 'Emergence', 105–11, 116, 297–301.
76 Vasey, 'Emergence', 203–8, 308–15, 347, Jeans, 'First Statutory Qualifications', Kennerley, 'Navigation', 53–62, Kennerley, 'Merchant Marine Education', 106, Course, *Merchant Navy*, 210–13.
77 Vasey, 'Emergence', 242–71, Williams, 'James Silk Buckingham', 120–2.
78 Kennerley, 'Merchant Marine Education', 106.
79 Ibid., 111–12.Kennerley, 'Early State Support', 213–16.
80 Kennerley, 'Early State Support', 219–21.
81 Leeman, *Long Road to Annapolis*, 6–8, 31, 81, 236–7.
82 Witt, 'Education', 644, Speelman, 'United States Navy'.
83 Slotten, *Patronage*, 121.
84 Dick, 'Centralizing', 497–8.
85 Mörzer Bruyns, 'Trade Labels', 1–2, 21, 24–5.
86 Davids, 'Longitude Committee', 37.
87 Miller, 'Longitude Networks', 227, Dekker, 'Frederik Kaiser', 29–35.
88 Leggett, *Shaping*, 20, 26–9.
89 Knight, *Britain against Napoleon*, 359–60, 363–5.
90 Ibid., 361–2, 366–7.
91 Ibid., 362–3.
92 Packard, 'Seppings', 145.
93 Seppings, 'Great Strength', Seppings, 'New Principle', 'Obituary. Sir Robert Seppings', Leggett, *Shaping*, 49.
94 Schaffer, 'Charter'd Thames', 280, 298–302, Leggett, *Shaping*, 40, 47.

95 Leggett, *Shaping*, 30–5, 39–58.
96 Ibid., 76–83.
97 Lemmers, *Techniek op schaal*, 25–7, 85–91, 127–9, 145–6, Ferreiro, *Ships*, 298.
98 Lemmers, *Techniek op schaal*, 148–59, 170–1, 174–89.
99 Speck Obreen, *Aanleiding*, 91–4, 106, 116, 161–3, Tideman, *Verhandeling*, 2, 54–62, 67, 73. Speck Obreen and Tideman referred to a French translation of Jorge Juan's *Examen maritimo* (1771), first published in 1783.
100 Ferreiro, *Ships*, 293.
101 Smith, 'Cleanse', 184.
102 Osborne, 'Emergence', 32–3, 117–26, 217–18.
103 Crimmin, 'Sick and Hurt Board', 102–6, Cardwell, 'Royal Navy Surgeons', 44–53, 5–59, Smith, 'Cleanse', 182–3, Keevil, Lloyd and Coulter, *Medicine*, vol. IV, 2–5.
104 Foxhall, *Health*, 70–1, Harrison, 'Important and Truly National Subject', 108, 110, 126, Keevil, Lloyd and Coulter, *Medicine*, vol. IV, 26–9.
105 Macdonagh, *Pattern*, 58–61.
106 Ibid., 61–4, 77–82, 91–137, 342–46.
107 Foxhall, *Health*, 15, 26, 44.
108 Haines, 'Migrant Voyages', 177–82, Haines, Shlomowitz and Brennan, 'Maritime Mortality Revisited', 142, 152–4, Foxhall, *Health*, 33–4.
109 Bossenbroek, *Van Holland*, 88, 194–5 appendix F.
110 Zolberg, *Nation*, 105, 110–13, 145–7.
111 Rao, 'Sailor's Health'.
112 Ogilvie, 'Correspondence Networks', 363–4.
113 Wellens-De Donder, *Correspondance Quetelet*, Yeo, *Defining Science*, 23–4.
114 Schwarz, 'Intersecting Anglo-German Networks', 69.
115 Morrell and Thackray, *Gentlemen*, 12–14, 546–7.
116 Ibid., 52–94, 543, 548–9.
117 Ibid., 27–9.
118 Reidy, *Tides*, 80–1.
119 Morrell and Thackray, *Gentlemen*, 44–5, 64, 76, 541, Schwarz, 'Intersecting Anglo-German Networks', 70.
120 Morrell and Thackray, *Gentlemen*, 418–22, Bruce, *Modern American Science*, 256.
121 Phillips, 'Academies', 230–1, Péaud, 'Premières sociétés'.
122 Morrell and Thackray, *Gentlemen*, 47–52, Babbage, *Reflections*, xiii–xiv.
123 Cawood, 'Magnetic Crusade', 498–500, 518. The quote is from John Herschel.
124 Péaud, 'Premières sociétés'.
125 Yeo, *Defining Science*, 338, 110, 215.
126 Reidy, *Tides*, 198–271.
127 Achbari, *Rulers*, 64–8.
128 Leggett, *Shaping*, 44–7, 64–5, Morrell and Thackray, *Gentlemen*, 505–8, Ferreiro and Pollara, 'Contested Waterlines', 417–20.

129 Leggett, *Shaping*, 113–23.
130 Davids, 'Seamen's Organizations', 155–6, Burton, 'Making', 112–16, Craig, 'Printed Guides', 27.
131 Davids, 'Technological Change', 289–90, 296.
132 See, for example, *History Marine Society Newburyport*, 107.
133 *The Nautical Magazine for 1842*, 11 (1842), 787, *East India Marine Society of Salem*, 3–4; Davids, 'Zeevaartkundig onderwijs', 172–3, Davids, 'Technological Change', 289–91.
134 Davids, 'Technological Change', 289–91.
135 Ibid., 289–93, 303, Burton, 'Making', 98–9.
136 Kennerley, 'Merchant Marine Education', 105–7, Kennerley and Seymour, 'Aids', 165, Gavine, 'Navigation', 9–10.
137 Davids, 'Zeevaartkundig onderwijs', 182–5, Davids, 'Technological Change', 286–7.
138 Dana, *Two Years before the Mast*, 164.
139 Speelman, 'United States Navy', https://research.mysticseaport.org/item/l006405/l006405-c030/. Master's certificate (1861).
140 Vasey, 'Emergence', 242, 256, 262–3.
141 Davids, 'Technological Change', 286.
142 Ibid., 287–8.
143 Cook, 'Committee', *Address to the Honourable Committee for the Relief of Distressed Seamen*.
144 Cook, 'Disease', idem, 'Medical Disease', idem, 'Health'.
145 Goldman, *Science*, 1–2, Carter, *Merchant Seamen's Health*, 89–90, McWilliam, 'On the Health', 544.
146 Williams, 'Mid-Victorian Attitudes', 102–3, 122–3.

Conclusion

1 Rupke, 'Humboldtian Distribution Networks', 93–4, 97, 99, 103, Reidy, *Tides*, 7–8, 194, Livingstone, *Geographical Tradition*, chapter 4.
2 Rupke, 'Humboldtian Distribution Networks', 107, Reidy, *Tides*, 162, 196, Sachs, *Humboldt Current*, 93 and note 64, Malin and Barraclough, 'Humboldt', 285–6.
3 Ristow, 'Lithography', 77–9, 92–3, 100–1, 110–11, Hentschel, *Mapping*, 171–2, Holden, 'Development', Lamb, 'Early Spanish Plans', 324–9, Van Lente, 'Illustratietechniek', 274, 'NOAA's paper nautical charts get a needed update – literally', https://noaacoastsurvey.wordpress.com/2013/12/10/paper-nautical-charts-get-a-needed-update-literally/.

4　Ferreiro and Pollara, 'Contested Waterlines', 417–20, Leggett, *Shaping*, 105–7, 176–80.
5　Reidy, *Tides*, 141.
6　Cawood, 'Terrestrial Magnetism', 568, 573, 576–8, Enebakk, 'Hansteen's Magnetometer'.
7　*Overzicht vijf en dertig jaar bestaan Vereeniging Oceaan*, Appendix A.
8　McConnell, 'Origins', 92–3, 97, Reidy, *Tides*, 141, Deacon, *Scientists*, 234–43, Rozwadowski, *Fathoming*, 76, 94, Ritchie, 'Brief History', 7–9, McConnell, *No Sea Too Deep*, 25–30, 50–4, Cawood, 'Terrestrial Magnetism', 568–9, 576, Enebakk, 'Hansteen's Magnetometer'.
9　Ogilvie, 'Correspondence Networks', 363–4.
10　Schwarz, 'Intersecting Anglo-German Networks', 70.
11　Fyfe, 'Journals and Periodicals', 34–5, Bruce, *Modern American Science*, 243–5.
12　Harrison, 'Important and Truly National Subject', 109–10, Osborne, 'Emergence', 53.
13　Craig, 'Printed Guides', 29–32.
14　Headrick, *Tools*, 158–9, Osterhammel, *Verwandlung*, 74, 1023–6, McConnell, *No Sea Too Deep*, 49.
15　Rozwadowski, *Fathoming*, 73.
16　Ibid., 80–90, 94, McConnell, *No Sea Too Deep*, 49–59.
17　Deacon, *Scientists*, 298.
18　Ibid., 281, 296–8, Rozwadowski, *Fathoming*, 138, Schlee, *History*, 81, 88–9, 92.
19　Rozwadowski, *Fathoming*, 100–3, 111–32, Deacon, *Scientistsa*, 298–9.
20　Bauchot et al., *l'Ichtyologie*, 5–30, Bolster, *Mortal Sea*, 122.
21　Schlee, *History*, 92–3, 98, Deacon, *Scientists*, 298–9.
22　Deacon, *Scientists*, 332–70, Schlee, *History*, 126–8, McConnell, *No Sea Too Deep*, 106–16.

Conclusion

1　Melville, *Moby-Dick*, chapter 32 'Cetology'.
2　Headrick, *Powers*, 370.
3　Bayly, '"Archaic" and "Modern" Globalization'.

Sources and bibliography

Archives

Nationaal Archief, The Hague (NA)
Stadsarchief Amsterdam (SA Amsterdam)
Stadsarchief Rotterdam (SA Rotterdam)

Manuscripts

Koninklijke Bibliotheek, The Hague
Universiteitsbibliotheek Amsterdam
Universiteitsbibliotheek Leiden

Websites

http://ckcc.huygens.knaw.nl/epistolarium/
http://cudl.lib.cam.ac.uk/collections/longitude
http://drc.usask.ca/projects/sloaneletters/
http://www.e-enlightenment.com/
http://icoads.noaa.gov/
http://bibliotheek.knmi.nl/knmipuboud.html
http://linnaeus.c18.net
http://www.bureau-des-longitudes.fr/
http://www.maritiemdigitaal.nl/
http://republicofletters.stanford.edu
http://slaveryimages.org
http://stuyvesant.library.uu.nl
http://tempo.idcpublishers.info.access.authkb.kb.nl
http://www.slavevoyages.org/
http://www.marinesocietyny.org
http://www.bostonmarinesociety.org
http://marinesocietysalem.org/letterbook.html

Published primary sources

An Account of Several Late Voyages & Discoveries to the South and North. London: S. Smith & B. Walford, 1694.

An Address to the Honourable Committee for the Relief of Distressed Seamen. London: May Dennis, 1818.

Admiralty Manual for Ascertaining and Applying the Deviations of the Compass, edited by F. J. Evans and A. Smith, 2nd edn. London: HMSO, 1863.

Almanak ten dienste der zeelieden voor het jaar 1828. The Hague: Algemeene Landsdrukkerij, 1827.

Anderson, Johann. *Nachrichten von Island, Grönland und der Strasse Davis: zum wahren Nutzen der Wissenschaften und der Handlung.* Hamburg: G.C. Grund, 1746.

Arthy, Elliott. *The Seamen's Medical Advocate.* London: Richardson & Egerton, 1798.

Atkins, John. *The Navy-Surgeon or a Practical System of Surgery.* London: J. Hodges, 1734 [1737^2 1742^3].

Aubrey, T. *The Sea-Surgeon or the Guinea Man's Vademecum.* London: John Clarke, 1729.

Babbage, Charles. *Reflections on the Decline of Science in England, and on Some of Its Causes.* London: B. Fellowes, 1830.

Bajon, Bertrand. *Mémoires pour servir a l'histoire de Cayenne, et de la Guiane françoise*, 2 vols. Paris: Grangé, 1777–1778.

Balfour, T. Graham. 'Comparative Health of Seamen and Soldiers, as Shown by the Naval and Military Statistical Reports'. *Journal of the Statistical Society of London* 35 (1872): 1–24.

Bicker, L. 'Verhandeling over de nuttigheid der ventilators op onze oorlog-, oostindische en andere schepen'. *Natuurkundige Verhandelingen van de Bataafsche Maatschappij der Wetenschappen te Haarlem*, Eerste deel, tweede stuk (1801): 1–152.

Blane, Gilbert. *Observations on the Diseases Incident to Seamen.* London: Joseph Cooper, 1785.

Blane, Gilbert. *Select Dissertations on Several Subjects of Medical Science.* London: Underwood, 1822.

Blane, Gilbert. *A Brief Statement of the Progressive Improvement of the Health of the Royal Navy.* London: W. Nicol, 1830.

Bosman, Willem. *Nauwkeurige beschryving van de Guinese Goud- Tand- en Slavenkust.* Amsterdam: Isaac Stokmans, 1704.

Bossut, Charles. 'Mémoire sur l'arrimage des vaisseaux'. *Recueil des pièces qui ont remporté les prix de l'Académie Royale des Sciences* 7 (Paris, 1769): 1–76.

Boyle, Robert. *Observations and Experiments about the Saltness of the Sea.* Oxford: R. Davis, 1674.

Breen, Joost van. *Stiermans gemack, ofte een korte beschryving van de konst der stierlieden.* The Hague: Iohannes Rammazeyn, 1662.

Camper, Petrus. 'Verhandeling over het gehoor van den cachelot, of pot-walvisch'. *Verhandelingen Hollandsche Maatschappij der Wetenschappen te Haarlem* IX (1766): 193–229.

Cassini, Gian-Domenico. *Les Elemens de l'astronomie verifiez par Monsieur Cassini par le rapport de ses tables aux observations de M. Richer faites en l'isle de Caïenne*. Paris: Imprimerie Royale, 1684.

Catesby, Mark. *The Natural History of Carolina, Florida, and the Bahama Islands*, 2 vols. London: For the Author, 1731–1743.

Charter and Bye-laws of the Linnean Society of London. London: Richard and Joh Taylor, 1802.

Clarkson, Thomas. *The History of the Rise, Progress and Accomplishment of the Abolition of the African Slave Trade by the British Parliament*. London: Longman, 1839[2].

Cockburn, William. *An Account of the Nature, Causes, Symptoms and Cure of the Distempers that are Incident to Seafaring People*, 2 vols. London: Hugh Newman, 1696–1697 [1710[2], 1736[3]].

Cranz, David. *Historie von Grönland enthaltend die Beschreibung des Landes und der Einwohner*, 3 vols. Barby: Heinrich Detlev Ebers, 1765–1770.

Cuvier, Georges. *Historical Portrait of the Progress of Ichthyology from Its Origins to Our Own Time*, edited by Theodore W. Pietsch, translated by Abby J. Simpson. Baltimore: Johns Hopkins University Press, 1995 [1828].

Dam, Pieter van. *Beschrijvinge van de Oostindische Compagnie*, 7 vols, edited by F. W. Stapel. The Hague: Martinus Nijhoff, 1927–1954.

Dampier, William. *A Discourse of Trade- winds, Breezes, Storms, Seasons of the Year, Tides and Currents of the Torrid Zone throughout the World*. London: James Knapton, 1700.

Dana, Richard Henry. *Two Years before the Mast: A Personal Narrative of Life at Sea*. New York: Harper & Brothers, 1840.

Darlington, William. *Memorials of John Bartram and Humphry Marshall, with Notices of their Botanical Contemporaries*. Philadelphia: Lindsay & Blakiston, 1849.

David, Andrew, Felipe Fernández-Armesto, Carlos Novi and Glyndwr Williams, eds. *The Malaspina Expedition 1789–1794: Journal of the Voyage by Alejandro Malaspina*, 3 vols. London: Routledge, 2001–2004.

Dazille, Jean-Barthélemy. *Observations sur les maladies des nègres*. Paris: Didot le Jeune, 1786.

Diario de las actas y discusiones de las Córtes, vol. 4, *Estraordinarias del año 1821*. Madrid: Minerva Española, 1821.

Dieperink, A. J. *Handboek voor zeevarenden*. Amsterdam: Gebr. Kraay, 1862.

'Directions for Observations and Experiments to be made by Masters of Ships, Pilots, and Other Fit Persons in their Sea-voyages'. *Philosophical Transactions of the Royal Society* 2, no. 24 (1667): 433–48.

Dompeling, J. B. *Handboek voor scheeps-geneeskundigen*. Amsterdam: L. van Bakkenes, 1844.

Doorman, G., ed. *Octrooien voor uitvindingen in de Nederlanden uit de 16e-18e eeuw*. The Hague: Martinus Nijhoff, 1940.

Douwes, Cornelis. 'Verhandeling om buiten den middag op zee de waare middagsbreedte te vinden'. *Verhandelingen Hollandsche Maatschappij der Wetenschappen te Haarlem* I (1754): 127–256.

Duhamel du Monceau, Henri-Louis. *Moyens de conserver la santé aux équipages des vaisseaux*. Paris: Guerin & Delatour, 1759.

Duhamel du Monceau, Henri-Louis. *Baak der gezondheid voor zeevarenden ofte verhandeling over de middelen om de gezondheid van het scheeps-volk te bewaren*. Leiden: Abraham Honkoop, 1760.

East India Marine Society of Salem. Salem: W. Palfray, 1821.

Edwards, Pierrepont. *A Practical Guide for British Shipmasters to the United States Coast*. London: Longmans, Green & Co., 1866.

Encyclopédie méthodique par ordre des matières. Paris: Veuve Agasse, 1819.

Euler, JohanAlbert. 'Traité de l'arrimage des vaisseaux'. *Recueil des pièces qui ont remporté les prix de l'Académie Royale des Sciences* 7 (Paris, 1769): 1–56.

FitzRoy, Robert. *Narrative of the Surveying Voyages of His Majesty's ships Adventure and Beagle, between the Years 1826 and 1836*, vol. II. London: Henry Colburn, 1839.

Fonssagrives, Jean-Baptiste. *Traité de hygiène navale*. Paris: J.-B. Baillière & Fils, 1856.

Forget, Charles-Polydore. *Médecine navale ou Nouveaux éléments d'hygiène, de pathologie et de thérapeutique médico-chirurgicales, à l'usage des officiers de santé de la marine de l'Etat et du commerce*. Paris: J.-B. Baillière, 1832.

Franklin, Benjamin, William Brownrigg and Mr. Farish. 'Of the Stilling of Waves by Means of Oil'. *Philosophical Transactions of the Royal Society* 64 (1774): 445–60.

Gallandat, D. H. *Noodige onderrichtinge voor de slaafhandelaren*. Middelburg: Pieter Gillissen, 1769.

Glascock, William Nugent. *The Naval Service, or Officer's Manual for Every Grade in His Majesty's Ships*. London: Saunders & Otley, 1836.

Gonzalez, Pedro Maria. *Tratado de las enfermedades de la gente de mar*. Madrid: Imprenta Real, 1805.

Gray, Asa, ed. *Selections from the Scientific Correspondence of Cadwallader Colden with Gronovius, Linnaeus, Collinson and other Naturalists*. New Haven: B. L. Hamlen, 1843.

Gronovius, Johan Frederik. 'A Method of Preparing Specimens of Fish by Drying their Skins, as practised by John. Frid. Gronovius, M.D. at Leyden'. *Philosophical Transactions of the Royal Society* 42 (1742): 57–8.

Gronovius, Laurens Theodorus. *Museum ichthyologicum*, 2 vols. Leiden: Theodoor Haak, 1754–1756.

Gronovius, Laurens Theodorus. *Zoophylacium Gronovianum*, 3 vols. Leiden: Theodoor Haak, 1763–1781.

Groot, Jeldert Jansz. *Beknopt en getrouw verhaal van den reys van commandeur Jeldert Jansz Groot uit Texel na en in Groenland*. Amsterdam: Voor den autheur, 1778.

Hadley, John. 'The Description of a New Instrument for Taking Angles'. *Philosophical Transactions of the Royal Society* 37, no. 420 (1731): 147–57, 356.

Hales, Stephen. 'An Account of the Great Benefit of Ventilators in Many Instances, in Preserving the Health and Lives of People, in Slave and Other Ships'. *Philosophical Transactions of the Royal Society* 49 (1755–1756): 332–39.

Hales, Stephen. *A Description of Ventilators*. London: W. Innys, 1743.

Halley, Edmond. 'An Account of the Cause of the Change of the Variation of the Magnetic Needle, with an Hypothesis of the Structure of the Internal Parts of the Earth'. *Philosophical Transactions of the Royal Society* 17, no. 195 (1692): 563–78.

Halley, Edmond. 'An Historical Account of the Trade Winds, and Monsoons, Observable in the Seas Between and Near the Tropicks, with an Attempt to Assign the Physical Case of the Said Winds'. *Philosophical Transactions of the Royal Society* 16, no. 179–91 (1686): 153–68.

Hazewinkel, A. C. *Handleiding om op verschillende wijzen de breedte buiten den middag of meridiaan te vinden, door waarnemingen aan de zon of starren*. Groningen: R.J. Schiebeeck, 1827.

'Health and Lives of People, in Slave and Other Ships'. *Philosophical Transactions of the Royal Society* 49 (1755–1756): 332–9.

Heywood, Peter. *A Memoir of the late Captain Peter Heywood R.N. with Extracts from his Diaries and Correspondence, by Edward Tagart*. London: Effgingham Wilson, 1832.

Hoeven, W. van der. *Voorlezing gehouden op de openbare vergadering der commissie ter bevordering van het onderzoek naar de verschijnselen op den oceaan te Rotterdam*. Rotterdam, 1867.

Horner, G. R. B. *Diseases and Injuries of Seamen with Remarks on their Enlistment, Naval Hygiene and the Duties of Medical Officers*. Philadelphia: Lippingcott, Grambo & Co., 1854.

Horsburgh, James. *Directions for Sailing to and from the East Indies, China, New Holland, Cape of Good Hope, and the Interjacent Ports*, 2 vols. London: Black, Parbury & Allen, 1809–1811 [1819^2, 1826^3, 1841–1843, 5th edn].

Horsburgh, James. *Zeemans-gids naar, en uit Oost-Indiën, China, Japan, Australiën, de Kaap de Goede Hoop, Braziliën en tusschenliggende havens volgesn de vierde Engelsche uitgave ... . In het Nederduitsch overgebragt, en met vele aantekeningen en opnemingen vermeerderd door G. Kuyper Hz*. Amsterdam: C.F. Stemler, 1841.

Houstoun, William. 'An Account of the Contrayerva'. *Philosophical Transactions of the Royal Society* 37 (1731–1732): 195–8.

Hutchinson, William. *A Treatise on Practical Seamanship*. Liverpool: Cowburne, 1777.

Huxham, John. *Essay on Fevers*. London: S. Austen, 1750.

Jackson, Robert. *A Treatise on the Fevers of Jamaica, with Some Observations on the Intermitting Fever of America*. London: J. Murray, 1791.

Jackson, Robert. *An Outline of the History and Cure of Fever*. Edinburgh: Mundell & Son, 1798.

Jansen, Marin Henri. *Het leven van een vloothouder. Gedenkschriften*, edited by S. P. L'Honoré Naber. Utrecht: Kemink, 1925.

Johnston, James. *The Influence of Tropical Climates on European Constitutions*. Portsmouth: Mottley & Harrison, 1818.

Juan, Jorge. *Compendio de navegación*. Cádiz: Acadêmia, 1757.

Juan, Jorge. *Examen maritimo theorico-práctico o Tratado de mechanica aplicado á la construccion, conocimiento, manejo de los nauios y demas embarcaciones*. Madrid: Francisco Manuel de Mena, 1771.

Juan, Jorge. *Examen maritime, théorique-pratique, ou traité de méchanique, appliqué à la construction et à la manoeuvre des vaisseaux et autres bâtiments*. Nantes: Malassis & Despilly, 1783.

Juan, Jorge and Antonio de Ulloa. *Relación histórica del viage à la America meridional hecho de orden de S. Mag.*, 5 vols. Madrid: Antonio Marin, 1748.

Kat, Hidde Dirks. *Dagboek eener reize ter walvisch- en robben-vangst gedaan in de jaren 1777 en 1778*. Haarlem: Wed. A. Loosjes Pz., 1818.

Krogt, Peter van der, ed. *Advertenties voor kaarten, atlassen, globes e.d. in Amsterdamse kranten, 1621–1811*. Amsterdam: Hes & De Graaf, 1985.

Lardizabal, Vicente de. *Consideraciones polito-médicas sobre la salud de las navegantes*. Madrid: Antionio Sanz, 1769.

Laws of the Marine Society at Salem. Salem: Marine Society, 1936.

Lelyveld, Frans van, *Berichten en Prijs-vragen over het storten van olie, traan, teer, of andere dryvende stoffen, in zee-gevaren*. Leiden: Johannes le Mair, 1775.

Lind, James. *Treatise of the Scurvy*. Edinburgh: A. Kincaid & A. Donaldson, 1753.

Lind, James. *An Essay on the Most Effectual Means of Preserving the Health of Seamen in the Royal Navy*, 2nd edn. London: D. Wilson, 1762.

Lind, James, *An Essay on Diseases Incidental to Europeans in Hot Climates with the Method of Preventing their Fatal Consequences*. London: J. Murray, 1768.

List of the Linnean Society 1798. London, 1798.

Lloyd, Christopher, ed. *The Health of Seamen. Selections from the Works of dr. James Lind, Sir Gilbert Blane and Thomas Trotter*. Greenwich: Navy Records Society, 1965.

Maandelijkse zeilaanwijzing van het Kanaal naar Java, als uitkomsten van wetenschap en ervaring, aangaande winden en zeestroomingen in sommige gedeelten van de oceaan. De Bilt: KNMI, 1859 [1860^3].

Manual of Scientific Enquiry, edited by John Herschel. London: John Murray, 1849.

Marine Architecture, or Directions for Carrying on a Ship (1739), facsimile edition. New York: Scholar Facsimilies, 1993.

Marsigli, Luigi-Fernando. *Histoire physique de la mer*. Amsterdam, 1725.

Martens, Friedrich. *Spitzbergische oder groenlandische Reise Beschreibung getahn im Jahr 1671*. Hamburg: Gofftfried Schultzen, 1675.

Maury, Matthew Fontaine. *Explanations and Sailing Directions to Accompany the Wind and Current Charts*. Philadelphia: E.C. and J. Biddle, 1851³ [1853 5th edn, 1858–1859 8th edn].

McWilliam, J. 'On the Health of Our Merchant Seamen'. *Transactions of the National Association for the Promotion of Social Science, London Meeting 1862*, 544–7. London, 1863.

Mededeelingen uit de journalen aangaande bijzondere meteorologische verschijnselen. Utrecht: KNMI, 1867.

Melville, Herman. *Moby-Dick; or, The Whale*. New York: Harper & Brothers, 1851.

Mendoza y Ríos, José de. 'Recherches sur les principaux problèmes de l'astronomie nautique'. *Philosophical Transactions of the Royal Society* 87 (1797): 43–122.

Milroy, Gavin. 'The Health of the Army and Navy compared with Each Other'. *Transactions of the National Association for the Promotion of Social Science, London Meeting 1862*, 547–54. London, 1863.

Monchy, Salomon de. 'Verhandeling van de oorzaaken, genezing en voorbehoeding der gewoone ziekten van ons scheepsvolk dat naar de West-Indiën vaart'. *Verhandelingen Hollandsche Maatschappij der Wetenschappen te Haarlem* VI (1761): 1–185.

Monchy, Salomon de. *An Essay on the Causes and Cure of the Usual Diseases in Voyages to the West Indies*. London: T. Becket & P.A. de Hondt, 1762.

Morogues, Sébastien-François Bigot de. 'Mémoire sur la corruption de l'air dans les vaisseaux'. *Mémoires de mathématiques et de physique presentés à l'Académie Royale des Sciences par les savants étrangers* I (1748): 394–410.

Murphy, John McLeod. *Nautical Routine and Stowage with Short Rules in Navigation*. New York: H. Spear, 1849.

Musschenbroek, Petrus van. *Essai de physique*. Leiden: Samuel Luchtmans, 1739.

Nautical Magazine, later *The Nautical Magazine and Naval Chronicle*, 1 (1832) – .

Noordkerk, Hermanus, ed. *Handvesten ofte privilegien ende octroyen (…) der Stad Amsterdam*, 4 vols. Amsterdam: Hendrik van Waesberghe, 1748.

Norrie, J. W. *Directions for Sailing to and from the coast of Brazil, River Plate, Cape of Good Hope, &c.* London, 1819.

Northcote, William. *The Marine Practice of Physics and Surgery*, 2 vols. London: W. & J. Richardson, 1770.

'Obituary. Sir Robert Seppings F.R.S.'. *Gentleman's Magazine* 14 (1840): 97.

Ordonnance de Louis XIV pour les armées navales et arsenaux de marine. Paris: Estienne Michallet, 1689.

Overzicht van het vijf en dertig jaar bestaan van de Vereeniging ter bevordering van het onderzoek naar de verschijnselen op den oceaan te Rotterdam. Rotterdam, 1889.

The Papers of Benjamin Franklin, vol. 2 and 3, edited by Leonard W. Labaree, vol. 21, edited by William B. Wilcox et al. New Haven: Yale University Press, 1960, 1961, 1978.

Pemberton, Henry, 'Some Considerations on a Late Treatise intituled, A New Set of Logarithmic Solar Tables etc. intended for a More Commodious Method of Finding

Latitude at Sea, by two Observations of the Sun'. *Philosophical Transactions of the Royal Society* 51 (1759): 910–29.

Pietsch, Theodore W., ed. *Fishes, Crayfishes, and Crabs: Louis Renard's Natural History of the Rarest Curiosities of the Seas of the Indies*. Baltimore: Johns Hopkins University Press, 1995.

Piso, Willem and Georg Marcgraf. *Historia Naturalis Brasiliae*. Amsterdam: Elzevier, 1648.

Poisson, Siméon Denis. 'Mémoire sur les deviations de la boussole produites par le fer des vaisseaux'. *Mémoire de l'Académie des Sciences de l'Institut Imperial de France* 14 (1838): 479–555.

Poissonnier, Pierre-Isaac. *Abrégé d'anatomie à l'usage des Élèves en Chirurgie dans les Écoles royales de marine*, 2 vols. Paris: Ph.-D. Pierres, 1783.

Poissonnier-Desperrières, Antoine. *Traité des maladies des gens de mer*. Paris: Imprimerie Royale, 1767 [1780^2].

Practical Rules for Ascertaining the Deviations of the Compass which Are Caused by the Ship's Iron. London: Hydrographic Office Admiralty, 1892.

Pringle, John. *Observations on the Diseases of the Army in Camp and Garrison*. London: A. Millar & D. Wilson, 1752.

Pringle, John. *A Discourse upon some Improvements of the Means for Preserving the Health of Mariners*. London: Royal Society, 1776.

Ray, John. *The Ornithology [of Francis Willughby] in Three Books. Wherein All the Birds Hitherto Known, Being Reduced into a Method Suitable to Their Natures*. London: John Martyn, 1678.

Rennell, James. *Waarnemingen over een stroom welke dikwyls stand grypt ten westen van Scilly ... door James Rennell... uit het Engelsch vertaald, en met eenige Aantekeningen vermeerderd door Jacob Florijn*. Amsterdam: G. Hulst van Keulen, 1794.

'Report from a Select Committee appointed to Inquire into the Causes of Shipwrecks 1836'. *The Monthly Review* II (May 1838): 132–47.

Report from Select Committee on Shipwrecks of Timber Ships with the Minutes of Evidence, Appendix, and Index, Ordered to be printed 2nd August 1839. London: Parliamentary Reports and Papers, 1839.

Richer, Jean. *Observations astronomiques et physiques faites en l'isle de Caïenne*. Paris: Imprimerie Royale, 1679.

Rodschied, Ernst Karl. *Medizinische und chirurgische Bemerkungen über das Klima, die Lebensweise und Krankheiten der Einwohner der Hollaendischen Kolonie Rio Essequebo*. Frankfurt: Jaergeschen Buchhandlung, 1796.

Roggeveen, Arent. *Het eerste deel van het Brandende Veen, verlichtende geheel West-Indien, de vaste kust en de eylanden*. Amsterdam: Pieter Goos, 1675.

Roggeveen, Arent. *La primera parte del monte de turba ardiente*. Amsterdam: Pieter Goos, 1680.

Rouppe, Lewis. *Observations on Diseases Incidental to Seamen*. London: T. Carnan & F. Newbery, 1772.

Rouppe, Lodewijk. *De morbis navigantium*. Leiden: Theodorus Haak, 1764.
Sabine, Edward. 'A Memoir on the Birds of Greenland'. *Transactions of the Linnean Society of London* 12, no. 2 (1819): 527–59.
Salazar, Luis María de. *Discurso sobre los progresos y estado actual de la hidrografia en España*. Madrid: Imprenta Rela, 1809.
Scoresby, William. *An Account of the Arctic Regions*, 2 vols. Edinburgh: Archibald Constable & Co., 1820.
Seba, Albertus. *Locupletissimi rerum naturalium Thesauri accurata descriptio*, 4 vols. Amsterdam: J. Wetstein & W. Smith, 1735–1765.
Seppings, Robert. 'On the Great Strength given to Ships of War by the Application of Diagonal Braces'. *Philosophical Transactions of the Royal Society* 108 (1818): 1–8.
Seppings, Robert. 'On a New Principle of Constructing Ships in the Mercantile Navy'. *Philosophical Transactions of the Royal Society* 110 (1820): 133–43.
Sloane, Hans. *A Voyage to the Islands Madera, Barbados, Nieves, St. Christopher's and Jamaica*, 2 vols. London: B.M., 1707–1725.
Speck Obreen, H. A. van der. *Aanleiding tot de kennis van het beschouwende gedeelte der scheepsbouwkunde*. Amsterdam: G.C. Sulpke, 1840.
Statistical Reports on the Health of the Navy for the years 1830, 1831, 1832, 1833, 1834, 1835, and 1836. South American, West Indian and North- American, Mediterranean and Peninsular Commands. London: William Clowes & Sons, 1841.
'Statistics of Stowage'. *The Nautical Magazine and Naval Chronicle* 12 (1843): 116.
Steenstra, Pybo. *Openbaare lessen over het vinden der lengte op zee*. Amsterdam: Yntema & Tieboel, 1770.
Steinthall, S. A. 'Report of the Liverpool Committee on "The Health of Merchant Seamen"'. *Transactions of the National Association for the Promotion of Social Science, London Meeting 1862*, 555–61. London, 1863.
Stevens, Robert White. *On the Stowage of Ships and their Voyages*. London: Longmans, 1858 [1863, 1867, 1869].
Swinden, Jan Hendrik van. *Dissertation sur la comparaison des thermomètres*. Amsterdam, 1778.
Thrower, N. J. W., ed. *The Three Voyages of Edmond Halley in the Paramore 1698–1701*, 2 vols. London: Hakluyt Society, 1981.
Tideman, Bruno Johannes. *Verhandeling over de scheepsbouwkunde als wetenschap*. Amsterdam: Wed. G. Hulst van Keulen, 1859.
Titsingh, Abraham. *Konst-broederlyke lessen of noodige aanmerkingen, wegens de koortsen op schepen van oorlog, tot nut der heelmeesteren*. Amsterdam: Gerrit de Groot, 1742.
Titsingh, Abraham. *Geneeskunst der heelmeesters tot dienst van de zeevaart*. Amsterdam: Adriaan Wor, 1752.
Tofiño de San Miguel, Vicente. *Atlas maritimo de España*. Madrid, 1789.
Trotter, Thomas. *Observations on the Scurvy*. Edinburgh: Charles Elliott, 1786.
Trotter, Thomas. *Medicina Nautica. An Essay on the Diseases of Seamen*, 2 vols. London: T. Cadell & W. Davies, 1797–1799 [1804^2].

Verbrugge, Johannes. *Heel-konstige examen ofte instructie der chirurgie*, 2nd edn. Amsterdam: Jan Claesz. Ten Hoorn, 1677.

Verbrugge, Johannes. *Examen van land- en zeechirurgie*, 4th edn. Amsterdam: Jan ten Hoorn, 1696.

Verbrugge, Johannes. *De nieuw hervormde examen van land- en zeechirurgie ... eertijds opgesteld door Johannes Verbrugge ... en met aantekeningen ... verklaart en vermeerdert door Johannes Daniel Schlichting*, 7th edn. Amsterdam: Jacob Graal, 1734 [10th edn, 1768].

Voorde, Cornelis van de. *Lichtende fakkel der chirurgie*. Middelburg: Krook, 1664 [2nd edn, 1668].

Voorde, Cornelis van de. *Nieuwe lichtende fakkel der chirurgie, ofte hedendaagze heel-konst ... van nutte en noodige aantekeningen ... voorzien door Anthonius de Heyde ... verrijkt met een Chirurgijns- of heel-meesters zee-compas*. Middelburg: Wilhelmus Goeree, 1680.

Voorde, Cornelis van de. *Nieuw chirurgijns zee-compas ... nieuwlyks overzien ... door P. Boon*. Amsterdam: Andries van Damme, 1719.

Vossius, Isaac. *A Treatise Concerning the Motion of the Seas and Winds*. London: Henry Brome, 1677.

Waarnemingen over een stroom welke dikwyls stand grypt ten westen van Scilly ... door James Rennell ... uit het Engelsch vertaald, en met eenige Aantekeningen vermeerderd door Jacob Florijn. Amsterdam: Gerard Hulst van Keulen, 1794.

Wellens-De Donder, Liliane. *La correspondence d'Adolphe Quetelet*. Brussels: Centre National d'Historie des Sciences, 1964.

Zorgdrager, Cornelis Gijsbertsz. *Alte und neue Grönländsiche Fischerei und Wallfischfang*. Leipzig: Peter Conrad Monath, 1723.

Zorgdrager, Cornelis Gijsbertsz. *Bloeijende opkomst der aloude en hedendaagsche Groenlandsche visschery*, 2 edn, by Abraham Moubach. The Hague: P. van Thol & R.C. Alberts, 1727.

Bibliography

Acda, Gerard. *Op de deining van de wetenschap. Leven en werk van Gustaaf Frederik Tydeman (1858-1939), zeeofficier en hydrograaf*. Leiden: Van Wijnen, 2019.

Achbari, Azadeh. *Rulers of the Winds: How Academics came to Dominate the Science of the Weather*. Amsterdam: For the author, 2017.

Albion, R. G. *Square-riggers on Schedule: The New York Sailing Packets to England, France, and the Cotton Ports*. Princeton: Princeton University Press, 1938.

Albion, R. G. *The Rise of New York Port 1815–1860*. New York: Scribner's, 1939.

Alfonsi, Liliane. 'Un successeur de Bouguer: Étienne Bézout (1730–1783) commissaire pour la marine à l'Académie royale des sciences'. *Revue d'Histoire des Sciences* 63, no. 1 (2010): 161–87.

Allen, Douglas W. *The Institutional Revolution: Measurement and the Economic Emergence of the Modern World*. Chicago: University of Chicago Press, 2012.

Altman, Ida. 'The Spanish Atlantic, 1650–1780'. In *The Oxford Handbook of the Atlantic World*, edited by Nicholas Canny and Philip Morgan, 183–200. Oxford: Oxford University Press, 2011.

Alvarez Peláez, Raquel. 'Un Nuevo Mundo para la ciencia: el descubrimiento de la naturleza americana'. In *Más allá de la Leyenda Negra. España y la Revolución Científica*, edited by Victor Navarro Brotóns and William Eamon, 147–54. Valencia: CSIC, 2007.

Aman, Jacques. *Les Officiers bleus dans la marine française au XVIIIe siècle*. Geneva: Droz, 1976.

Anderson, Katharine. *Predicting the Weather: Victorians and the Science of Meteorology*. Chicago: University of Chicago Press, 2005.

Andrewes, William J. H., ed. *The Quest for Longitude*. Cambridge, MA: Harvard University Press, 1996.

Anthiaume, A. *Évolution et enseignement de la science nautique en France et principalement chez les Normans*, 2 vols. Paris: Ernest Dumont, 1920.

Antunes, Cátia. 'Free Agents and Formal Institutions in the Portuguese Empire. Towards a Framework of Analysis'. *Portuguese Studies* 28, no. 2 (2012): 173–86.

Antunes, Cátia and Amélia Polónia. 'Introduction'. In *Beyond Empires: Global, Self-organizing, Cross-Imperial Networks 1500–1800*, edited by Cátia Antunes and Amélia Polónia, 1–12. Leiden: Brill, 2016.

Antunes, Cátia and Filipa Ribeiro da Silva. 'Amsterdam Merchants in the Slave Trade and African Commerce, 1580s-1670s'. *Tijdschrift voor Sociale en Economische Geschiedenis* 9, no. 4 (2012): 3–30.

Appadurai, Arjun. *Modernity at Large: Cultural Dimensions of Globalization*. Minneapolis: University of Minnesota Press, 1996.

Appleby, John H. 'New Light on John Woodall, Surgeon and Adventurer'. *Medical History* 25, no. 3 (1981): 251–68.

Archila, Ricardo. *Historia de la medicina en Venezuela: Epoca colonial*. Caracas: Vargas, 1961.

Bailyn, Bernard. *Atlantic History: Concept and Contours*. Cambridge, MA: Harvard University Press, 2005.

Bailyn, Bernard. 'Introduction: Reflections on Some Major Themes'. In *Soundings in Atlantic History: Latent Structures and Intellectual Currents, 1500–1830*, edited by Bernard Bailyn and Patricia L. Denault, 1–43. Cambridge, MA: Harvard University Press, 2009.

Banks, Kenneth J. *Chasing Empire across the Sea: Communications and the State in the French Atlantic, 1713–1763*. Montreal and Kingston: McGill-Queen's University Press, 2002.

Bannet, Eve. *Empire of Letters: Letter Manuals and Transatlantic Correspondence, 1680–1820*. Cambridge: Cambridge University Press, 2006.

Baron, Jeremy Hugh. 'Sailors' Scurvy before and after James Lind – A Reassessment'. *Nutrition Reviews* 67, no. 6 (2009): 315–32.

Barr, William. 'Exploration Voyages, 1815 to the Present'. In *The Oxford Encyclopedia of Maritime History*, vol. III, edited by John B. Hattendorf, 111–16. Oxford: Oxford University Press, 2007.

Barrera-Osorio, Antonio. *Experiencing Nature: The Spanish American Empire and the Early Scientific Revolution*. Austin: University of Texas Press, 2006.

Barrera-Osorio, Antonio. 'Knowledge and Empiricism in the Sixteenth-Century Spanish Atlantic World'. In *Science in the Spanish and Portuguese Empires, 1500–1800*, edited by Daniela Bleichmar, Paula de Vos, Kristin Huffine and Kevin Sheehan, 219–32. Stanford: Stanford University Press, 2009.

Bauchot, M. L., J. Dachet and R. Bauchot. *l'Ichtyologie en France au début du XIXe siècle*. Paris: Museum National d'Histoire Naturelle, 1990.

Bayly, Chris A. *Imperial Meridian: The British Empire and the World, 1780–1830*. London: Routledge, 1989.

Bayly, Chris A. *Empire and Information: Intelligence Gathering and Social Communication in India, 1780–1870*. Cambridge: Cambridge University Press, 1996.

Bayly, Chris A. '"Archaic" and "Modern" Globalization in the Eurasian and African Arena, c. 1750–1850.' In *Globalization in World History*, edited by A. G. Hopkins, 47–73. London: Pimlico, 2002.

Bayly, Chris A. *The Birth of the Modern World 1780–1914*. Oxford: Oxford University Press, 2004.

Beckert, Sven. *The Monied Metropolis: New York City and the Consolidation of the American Bourgeoisie, 1850–1896*. Cambridge: Cambridge University Press, 2001.

Beckert, Sven. *Empire of Cotton: A Global History*. New York: Vintage Books, 2014.

Bedini, Silvio A. *Thinkers and Tinkers: Early American Men of Science*. New York: Scribner's, 1975.

Behrendt, S. D. 'Crew Mortality in the Transatlantic Slave Trade in the Eighteenth Century'. *Slavery and Abolition* 18, no. 1 (1997): 49–71.

Belich, James. *Replenishing the Earth: The Settler Revolution and the Rise of the Anglo-World, 1783–1939*. Oxford: Oxford University Press, 2009.

Benjamin, Thomas. *The Atlantic World: Europeans, Africans, Indians and Their Shared History, 1400–1900*. Cambridge: Cambridge University Press, 2009.

Bennett, James A. 'Shopping for Instruments in Paris and London'. In *Merchants and Marvels: Commerce, Science, and Art in Early Modern Europe*, edited by Pamela H. Smith and Paula Findlen, 370–95. New York: Routledge, 2002.

Berry, Stephen R. *A Path in Mighty Waters: Shipboard Life and Atlantic Crossings to the New World*. New Haven: Yale University Press, 2015.

Binnema, Ted. *Enlightened Zeal: The Hudson's Bay Company and Scientific Networks, 1670–1870*. Toronto: University of Toronto Press, 2014.

Birkhead, Tim. *The Wisdom of Birds: An Illustrated History of Ornithology*. London: Bloomsbury, 2011.

Blair, Ann, *Too Much to Know: Managing Scholarly Information before the Modern Age*. New Haven: Yale University Press, 2010.

Bleichmar, Daniela. 'A Visible and Useful Empire: Visual Culture and Colonial Natural History in the Eighteenth-Century Spanish World'. In *Science in the Spanish and Portuguese Empires, 1500–1800*, edited by Daniela Bleichmar, Paula de Vos, Kristin Huffine and Kevin Sheehan, 290–310. Stanford: Stanford University Press, 2009.

Bleichmar, Daniela. *Visible Empire: Botanical Expeditions and Visual Culture in the Hispanic Enlightenment*. Chicago: University of Chicago Press, 2012.

Boistel, Guy. 'Training Seafarers in Astronomy. Methods, Naval Schools and Naval Observatories in 18th- and 19th Century France'. In *The Heavens on Earth: Observatories and Astronomy in Nineteenth-Century Science and Culture*, edited by David Aubin, Charlotte Bigg and Heinz Otto Sibum, 148–73. Durham, NC: Duke University Press, 2010.

Boistel, Guy. 'From Lacaille to Lalande: French Work on Lunar Distances, Nautical Ephemerides and Lunar Tables, 1742–1785'. In *Navigational Enterprises in Europe and Its Empires, 1730–1880*, edited by Richard Dunn and Rebekah Higgitt, 47–64. London: Palgrave Macmillan, 2015.

Bolster, W. Jeffrey. *Black Jacks: African American Seamen in the Age of Sail*. Cambridge, MA: Harvard University Press, 1997.

Bolster, W. Jeffrey. 'Putting the Ocean in Atlantic History: Maritime Communities and Marine Ecology in the Northwest Atlantic, 1500–1800'. *American Historical Review* 113, no.1 (2008): 19–47.

Bolster, W. Jeffrey. *The Mortal Sea: Fishing in the Atlantic in the Age of Sail*. Cambridge, MA: Harvard University Press, 2012.

Bom, G. D. *Bijdragen tot eene geschiedenis van het geslacht 'Van Keulen'*. Amsterdam: Bom, 1885.

Borucki, Alex, David Eltis and David Wheat. 'Atlantic History and the Slave Trade to Spanish America'. *American Historical Review* 120, no. 2 (2015): 433–61.

Bossenbroek, M. P. *Van Holland naar Indië. Het transport van koloniale troepen voor het Oost-Indische leger 1815–1909*. Amsterdam: De Bataafsche Leeuw, 1986.

Bowen, H. V. *The Business of Empire: The East India Company and Imperial Britain, 1756–1833*. Cambridge: Cambridge University Press, 2006.

Bravo, Michael T. 'Geographies of Exploration and Improvement: William Scoresby and Arctic Whaling, 1782–1822'. *Journal of Historical Geography* 32, no. 3 (2006): 512–38.

Bravo, Michael T. 'Mission Gardens: Natural history and Global Expansion'. In *Colonial Botany: Science, Commerce, and Politics in the Early Modern World*, edited by Londa Schiebinger and Claudia Swan, 49–65. Philadelphia: University of Pennsylvania Press, 2007.

Brendecke, Arndt. *Imperium und Empirie. Funktionen des Wissens in der spanischen Kolonialherrschaft*. Cologne: Böhlau Verlag, 2009.

Briggs, Robin. 'The Académie Royale des Sciences and the Pursuit of Utility.' *Past and Present*, no. 131 (1991): 38–88.

Broeze, Frank J. A. *De Stad Schiedam. De Schiedamsche Scheepsreederij en de Nederlandse vaart op Oost-Indië omstreeks 1840*. The Hague: Martinus Nijhoff, 1978.

Broeze, F. J. A. 'The International Diffusion of Ocean Steam Navigation. The Myth of the Retardation of Netherlands Steam Navigation to the East Indies'. *Economisch- en Sociaal-Historisch Jaarboek* 45 (1982): 77–95.

Brown, Vincent. *The Reaper's Garden: Death and Power in the World of Atlantic Slavery*. Cambridge, MA: Harvard University Press, 2008.

Bruce, Robert V. *The Launching of Modern American Science 1846–1876*. New York: Alfred A. Knopf, 1987.

Bruijn, Iris. *Ship's Surgeons of the Dutch East India Company, Commerce and the Progress of Medicine in the Eighteenth Century*. Leiden: Leiden University Press, 2009.

Bruijn, Jaap R. *The Dutch Navy of the Seventeenth and Eighteenth Centuries*. Columbia, SC: University of South Carolina Press, 1993.

Bruijn, Jaap R. *Commanders of Dutch East India Ships in the Eighteenth Century*. Woodbridge: Boydell Press, 2011.

Bruijn, Jaap R., Femme S. Gaastra and Ivo Schöffer, eds. *Dutch-Asiatic Shipping in the 17th and 18th Centuries*, 3 vols. The Hague: Martinus Nijhoff, 1979–1987.

Buchet, Christian. 'Quantification des pertes dans l'espace caraïbe et retombées stratégiquees'. In *Le homme, la santé et la mer*, edited by Christian Buchet, 177–94. Paris: Honoré Champion, 1997.

Burke, Peter. *A Social History of Knowledge from Gutenberg to Diderot*. Cambridge: Cambridge University Press, 2000.

Burstyn, Harold. 'Theories of Winds and Ocean Currents from the Discoveries to the End of the Seventeenth Century'. *Terrae Incognitae* 3, no. 1 (1971): 7–31.

Burton, Jim. 'Robert Fitzroy and the Early History of the Meteorological Office'. *British Journal for the History of Science* 19, no. 2 (1986): 147–76.

Burton, M. Diane and Tom Nicholas. 'Prize, Patents and the Search for Longitude'. *Explorations in Economic History* 64, no. 3 (2017): 21–36.

Burton, Robert. 'South Georgia.' In *Encyclopedia of the Antarctic*, edited by Beau Riffenburgh, 911–14. London: Routledge, 2007.

Burton, Valerie. 'The Making of a Nineteenth-Century Profession: Shipmasters and the British Shipping Industry'. *Journal of the Canadian Historical Association* 1, no. 1 (1990): 97–118.

Cadigan, Sean T. and Jeffrey A. Hutchings. 'Nineteenth-Century Expansion of the Newfoundland Fishery for Atlantic Cod: An Exploration of the Underlying Causes'. In *The Exploited Seas. New Directions for Marine Environmental History*, edited by Poul Holm, Tim D. Smith and David J. Starkey, 31–65. Liverpool: Liverpool University Press, 2001.

Camarasa, Josep M. and Neus Ibáñez. 'Joan Salvador and James Petiver: A Scientific Correspondence (1706–1714) in Time of War'. *Archives of Natural History* 34, no. 1 (2007): 140–73.

Camarasa, Josep M. and Neus Ibáñez. 'Joan Salvador and James Petiver: The Last Years (1715–1718) of their Scientific Correspondence'. *Archives of Natural History* 39, no. 2 (2012): 191–216.

Camazine, Scott et al. *Self-organization in Biological Systems*. Princeton: Princeton University Press, 2001.

Candido, Mariana P. *An African Slaving Port and the Atlantic World: Benguela and Its Hinterland*. Cambridge: Cambridge University Press, 2013.

Cañizares-Esguerra, Jorge. *Nature, Empire, and Nation: Explorations in the History of Science in the Iberian World*. Stanford: Stanford University Press, 2006.

Canny, Nicholas. 'English Migration into and across the Atlantic during the Seventeenth and Eighteenth Centuries'. In Nicholas Canny, *Europeans on the Move: Studies on European Migration, 1500–1800*, 39–75. Oxford: Oxford University Press, 1994.

Canny, Nicholas and Philip Morgan. 'Introduction: The Making and Unmaking of an Atlantic World'. In *The Oxford Handbook of the Atlantic World 1450–1800*, edited by Nicholas Canny and Philip Morgan, 1–17. Oxford: Oxford University Press, 2011.

Cardwell, M. John. 'Royal Navy Surgeons, 1793–1815: A Collective Biography'. In *Health and Medicine at Sea, 1700–1900*, edited by David Boyd Haycock and Sally Archer, 38–62. Woodbridge: Boydell Press, 2009.

Carpenter, Kenneth J. *The History of Scurvy and Vitamin C*. Cambridge: Cambridge University Press, 1988.

Carter, Christopher. *Magnetic Fever: Global imperialism and Empiricism in the Nineteenth Century*. Philadelphia: American Philosophical Society, 2009.

Carter, Tim. *Merchant Seamen's Health, 1860–1960: Medicine, Technology, Shipowners, and the State in Britain*. Woodbridge: Boydell Press, 2014.

Cartwright, David Edgar. *Tides: A Scientific History*. Cambridge: Cambridge University Press, 1999.

Cassis, Youssef. *Capitals of Capital: The Rise and Fall of International Financial Centres 1780-2009*. Cambridge: Cambridge University Press, 2010.

Cawood, John. 'Terrestrial Magnetism and the Development of International Collaboration in the Early Nineteenth Century'. *Annals of Science* 34, no. 6 (1977): 551–87.

Cawood, John. 'The Magnetic Crusade: Science and Politics in Early Victorian Britain'. *Isis* 70, no. 4 (1979): 493–518.

Chapelle, Howard I. *The Search for Speed under Sail 1700–1850*. New York: W. W. Norton, 1967.

Chaplin, Joyce E. *The First Scientific American: Benjamin Franklin and the Pursuit of Genius*. New York: Basic Books, 2006.

Chaplin, Joyce E. 'Knowing the Ocean: Benjamin Franklin and the Circulation of Atlantic Knowledge'. In *Science and Empire in the Atlantic World*, edited by James Delbourgo and Nicholas Dew, 73–96. London: Routledge, 2008.

Chaplin, Joyce E. 'The Atlantic Ocean and Its Contemporary Meanings, 1492–1808'. In *Atlantic History: A Critical Appraisal*, edited by Jack P. Greene and Philip D. Morgan, 35–51. New York: Oxford University Press, 2009.

Chapuis, Olivier. *A la mer comme au ciel. Beautemps-Beaupré et la naissance de l'hydrographie moderne (1700–1850)*. Paris: Presses de l'Úniversité de Paris-Sorbonne, 1999.

Chapuis, Olivier. 'Hydrographical Departments'. In *The Oxford Encyclopedia of Maritime History*, edited by John B. Hattendorf, vol. II, 162–67. Oxford: Oxford University Press, 2007.

Charles, Loïc and Paul Cheney. 'The Colonial Machine Dismantled: Knowledge and Empire in the French Atlantic'. *Past and Present*, no. 219 (2013): 127–63.

Charters, Erica M. '"The Intention Is Certainly Noble": The Western Squadron, Medical Trials, and the Sick and Hurt Board during the Seven Year's War (1756–1763)'. In *Health and Medicine at Sea*, 1700–1900, edited by David Boyd Haycock and Sally Archer, 19–37. Woodbridge: Boydell Press, 2009.

Chaunu, Pierre. *Séville et l'Atlantique (1504–1650)*, vol. VIII. Paris: S.E.V.P.E.N., 1959.

Chias, P. and T. Abad. 'The Nautical Charts of the Spanish Mediterranean Coasts in the 18th and 19th Centuries'. *e-Perimetron* 5, no. 2 (2010): 58–74.

Christensen, Pål and Alf Ranar Nielssen. 'Norwegian Fisheries 1100–1970. Main Developments'. In *The North Atlantic Fisheries, 1100–1976. National Perspectives on a Common Resource*, edited by Poul Holm, David J. Starkey and Jón Th. Thór, 145–67. Esbjerg: Fiskeri- of Søfartsmuseet, 1996.

Clark-Kennedy, Charles Edmund. *Stephen Hales*. Cambridge: Cambridge University Press, 1929.

Clercq, Peter de. *At the Sign of the Oriental Lamp: The Musschenbroek Workshop in Leiden, 1660–1750*. Rotterdam: Erasmus Publishing, 1997.

Clifton, Gloria. 'The Spectaclemakers' Company and the Origins of the Optical Instrument-Making Trade in London'. In *Making Scientific Instruments Count. Essays on Historical Instruments Presented to Gerard L'Estrange Turner*, edited by R. W. G. Anderson, J. A. Bennett and W. F. Ryan, 341–64. Aldershot: Variorum, 1993.

Clifton, Gloria. 'The Growth of the British Scientific Instrument Trade, 1600–1850'. In *Proceedings of the Eleventh Scientific Instrument Symposium in Bologna, 1991*, edited by G. Dragoni et al., 61–70. Bologna: Grafis 1994.

Clifton, Gloria. 'The Adoption of the Octant in the British Isles'. In *Koersvast. Vijf eeuwen navigatie op zee*, edited by Remmelt Daalder, Frits Looijmeijer and Diederick Wildeman, 85–94. Zaltbommel: Aprilis, 2005.

Clossey, Luke. *Salvation and Globalization in the Early Jesuit Missions*. Cambridge: Cambridge University Press, 2008.

Cock, Randolph. '"The Finest Invention in the World": The Royal Navy's Early Trials of Copper Sheathing, 1708–1770'. *The Mariner's Mirror* 87, no. 4 (2001): 446–59.

Cohen, E. and W. A. T. Cohen-de Meester. 'Daniel Gabriel Fahrenheit'. *Proceedings of the Royal Academy of Science of Amsterdam* 16, no. 2 (1936): 1–37 and 17, no. 8 (1937): 682–9.
Cohn, Raymond L. 'Mortality on Immigrant Voyages to New York, 1838–1853'. *Journal of Economic History* 44, no. 2 (1984): 289–300.
Cohn, Raymond L. 'Death of Slaves in the Middle Passage'. *Journal of Economic History* 45, no. 3 (1985): 685–92.
Cohn, Raymond L. 'Maritime Mortality in the Eighteenth and Nineteenth Centuries: A Survey'. *International Journal of Maritime History* 1, no. 1 (1989): 159–91.
Cook, Andrew. 'Alexander Dalrymple and the Hydrographic Office'. In *Pacific Empires. Essays in Honour of Glyndwr Williams*, edited by Alan Frost and Jane Samson, 53–68. Carlton, South and Victoria: Melbourne University Press, 1999.
Cook, G. C. 'Disease in the Nineteenth-Century Merchant Navy: The Seamen's Hospital Society's experience'. *The Mariner's Mirror* 87, no. 4 (2001): 460–71.
Cook, G. C. 'Scurvy in the British Mercantile Marine in the 19th Century and the Contribution of the Seamen's Hospital Society'. *Postgraduate Medical Journal* 80, no. 942 (2004): 224–9.
Cook, G. C. 'Medical Disease in the Merchant Navies of the World in the Days of Sail: The Seamen's Hospital Society's Experience'. *The Mariner's Mirror* 91 no. 1 (2005): 46–51.
Cook, G. C. 'Committee for the Relief of Distressed Seamen: Correspondence from the Admiralty in 1818–19'. *Postgraduate Medical Journal* 83, no. 975 (2007): 54–8.
Cook, G. C. 'Health of the British Seafarer in the Nineteenth and Early Twentieth Centuries'. http://www.semm.org/m1eng/pdf/XXBritishseafarer.pdf.
Cook, Harold J. 'Time's Bodies: Crafting the Preparation and Preservation of Naturalia'. In *Merchants and Marvels. Commerce, Science, and Art in Early Modern Europe*, edited by Pamela H. Smith and Paula Findlen, 233–47. New York: Routledge, 2002.
Cook, Harold J. *Matters of Exchange: Commerce, Medicine, and Science in the Dutch Golden Age*. New Haven: Yale University Press, 2007.
Cooper, Alix. *Inventing the Indigenous: Local Knowledge and Natural History in Early Modern Europe*. Cambridge: Cambridge University Press, 2007.
Cotter, Charles H. *A History of Nautical Astronomy*. London: Hollis & Carter, 1968.
Course, A. G. *The Merchant Navy: A Social History*. London: Frederick Muller, 1963.
Craig, Robin. 'Printed Guides for Master Mariners as a Source of Productivity Change in Shipping, 1750–1914'. *Journal of Transport History* 3, no. 3 (1982): 23–35.
Crimmin, Patricia Kathleen. 'British Naval Health, 1700–1800: Improvement over Time?'. In *British Military and Naval Medicine, 1600–1830*, edited by Geoffrey L. Hudson, 183–200. Amsterdam: Rodopi, 2007.
Crimmin, Patricia Kathleen. 'The Sick and Hurt Board: Fit for Purpose?' In *Health and Medicine at Sea 1700-1900*, edited by David Boyd Haycock and Sally Archer, 90–107. Woodbridge: Boydell Press, 2009.
Croarken, Mary. 'Providing Longitude for All: The Eighteenth Century Computers of the Nautical Almanac'. *Journal for Maritime Research* 4, no. 1 (2002): 106–26.

Crone, Ernst. *Cornelis Douwes 1712-1773. Zijn leven en werk*. Haarlem: Tjeenk Willink & Zoon, 1941.
Crumplin, Michael. 'Surgery in the Royal Navy during the Republican and Napoleonic Wars (1793-1815)'. In *Health and Medicine at Sea 1700-1900*, edited by David Boyd Haycock and Sally Archer, 63-89. Woodbridge: Boydell Press, 2009.
Cunliffe, Barry. *Facing the Ocean: The Atlantic and Its Peoples 8000 BC – AD 1500*. Oxford: Oxford University Press, 2001.
Curtin, Philip D. *Death by Migration: Europe's Encounter with the Tropical World in the Nineteenth Century*. Cambridge: Cambridge University Press, 1989.
Curtin, Philip D. 'White Man's Grave: Image and Reality, 1780-1850'. *Journal of British Studies* 1, no. 1 (1961): 94-110.
Cushman, Gregory T. *Guano and the Opening of the Pacific World: A Global Ecological History*. Cambridge: Cambridge University Press, 2013.
Daston, Lorraine. 'The Ideal and Reality of the Republic of Letters in the Enlightenment'. *Science in Context* 4, no. 2 (1991): 367-86.
Daumas, Maurice. *Les instruments scientifiques au XVIIe et XVIIIe siècles*. Paris: Presses Universitaires de France, 1953.
David, Andrew. *The Voyage of Alejandro Malaspina to the Pacific, 1789-1794*. London: Routledge, 2000.
David, Andrew. 'The Emergence of the Admiralty Chart in the Nineteenth Century'. In *Symposium on 'Shifting Boundaries: Cartography in the 19th and 20th Centuries'*, 1-16. Portsmouth: Portsmouth University, 2008.
Davids, Karel. 'Het zeevaartkundig onderwijs voor de koopvaardij in Nederland tussen 1795 en 1875'. *Tijdschrift voor Zeegeschiedenis* 4, no. 3 (1985): 165-90.
Davids, Karel. *Zeewezen en wetenschap. De wetenschap en de ontwikkeling van de navigatietechniek in Nederland tussen 1585 en 1815*. Amsterdam/Dieren: De Bataafsche Leeuw, 1986.
Davids, Karel. 'Finding Longitude at Sea by Magnetic Declination on Dutch East Indiamen, 1596/1795'. *The American Neptune* 50, no. 4 (1990): 280-90.
Davids, Karel. 'Van vrijheid naar dwang. Over de relatie tussen zeewezen en wetenschap in Nederland in de 19e en vroege 20e eeuw'. *Tijdschrift voor de Geschiedenis der Geneeskunde, Natuurwetenschappen, Wiskunde en Techniek* 13, no. 1 (1990): 5-22.
Davids, Karel. 'Technological Change and the Professionalism of Masters and Mates in the Dutch Mercantile Marine, 1815-1914'. *Collectanea Maritima* V (1991): 282-303.
Davids, Karel. 'Seamen's Organisations and Social Protest in Europe, c. 1300-1825'. *International Review of Social History* 39, no. 4 (1994): 145-69.
Davids, Karel. 'Amsterdam as a Centre of Learning in the Dutch Golden Age, c. 1580-1700'. In *Urban Achievement in Early Modern Europe: Golden Ages in Antwerp, Amsterdam and London*, edited by Patrick O'Brien, Derek Keene, Marjolein 't Hart and Herman van der Wee, 305-23. Cambridge: Cambridge University Press, 2001.

Davids, Karel. *The Rise and Decline of Dutch Technological Leadership. Technology, Economy and Culture in the Netherlands, 1350-1800*. Leiden: Brill, 2008.

Davids, Karel. *Religion, Technology and the Great and Little Divergences: China and Europe Compared, c.700-1800*. Leiden: Brill, 2013.

Davids, Karel. 'The Scholarly Atlantic: Circuits of Knowledge between Britain, the Dutch Republic and the Americas in the Eighteenth Century'. In *Dutch Atlantic Connections 1680-1800: Linking Empires, Bridging Borders*, edited by Gert Oostindie and Jessica V. Roitman, 224-48. Leiden: Brill, 2014.

Davids, Karel. 'The Longitude Committee and the Practice of Navigation in the Netherlands, c. 1750-1850'. In *Navigational Enterprises in Europe and its Empires, 1730-1880*, edited by Richard Dunn and Rebekah Higgitt, 32-46. London: Palgrave Macmillan, 2015.

Davids, Karel. 'Florijn, Van Swinden and the Longitude Committee (1787-1818)'. In *Pour une histoire du Bureau des Longitudes (1795-1932)*, edited by Martina Schiavon and Laurent Rollet, 175-94. Nancy: Presses Universitaires de Lorraine, 2017.

Davis, Lance E., Robert E. Gallman and Karin Gleiter, *In Pursuit of Leviathan: Technology, Institutions, Productivity, and Profits in American Whaling, 1816-1906*. Chicago: University of Chicago Press, 1997.

Davis, Ralph. *The Rise of the English Shipping Industry in the Seventeenth and Eighteenth Centuries*, 2nd edn. St. John's: Marquis, 2012.

Day, Archibald. *The Admiralty Hydrographic Service 1795-1919*. London: HMSO, 1967.

Deacon, Margaret. *Scientists and the Sea 1650-1900: A Study of Marine Science*. London: Academic Press, 1971.

Débarbat, Suzanne. 'L'évolution administrative du Bureau des longitudes: une approche par les textes officielles'. In *Pour une histoire du Bureau des longitudes (1795-1932)*, edited by Martina Schiavon and Laurent Rollet, 23-40. Nancy: Presses Universitaires de Lorraine, 2017.

Dekker, Elly. 'Frederik Kaiser en zijn pogingen tot hervorming van "het sterrekundig deel van onze zeevaart"'. *Tijdschrift voor de Geschiedenis der Geneeskunde, Natuurwetenschappen, Wiskunde en Techniek* 13, no. 1 (1990): 23-41.

Delbourgo, James. *A Most Amazing Scene of Wonders: Electricity and Enlightenment in Early America*. Cambridge, MA: Harvard University Press, 2006.

Deveau, Jean-Michel. 'Le problème sanitaire à bord des navires négriers'. In *Le homme, la santé et la mer*, edited by Christian Buchet, 139-64. Paris: Honoré Champion 1997.

Dew, Nicholas. '*Vers la ligne*. Circulating Measurements around the French Atlantic'. In *Science and Empire in the Atlantic World*, edited by James Delbourgo and Nicholas Dew, 53-72. London: Routledge, 2008.

Dew, Nicholas. 'Scientific Travel in the Atlantic World: the French Expedition to Gorée and the Antilles, 1681-1683'. *British Journal for the History of Science* 43, no. 1 (2009): 1-17.

Dick, Steven J. 'How the U.S. Naval Observatory began, 1830–1865'. In *Sky with Ocean Joined. Proceedings of the Sesquicentennial symposium of the U.S. Naval Observatory*, edited by Steven J. Dick and LeRoy E. Doggett, 167–81. Washington DC: The Observatory, 1983.

Dick, Steven J. 'Centralizing Navigational Technology in America: The U.S. Navy's Depot of Charts and Instruments, 1830–1842'. *Technology and Culture* 33, no. 3 (1992): 469–85.

Dickinson, Harry W. *Educating the Royal Navy: Eighteenth and Nineteenth-Century Education for Officers*. London: Routledge, 2007.

Dillo, Ingrid G. *De nadagen van de Verenigde Oostindische Compagnie 1783–1795. Schepen en zeevarenden*. Amsterdam: De Bataafsche Leeuw, 1992.

Dirkzwager, Jan M. *Bernard Johannes Tideman*. Leiden: Brill, 1970.

Dolin, Eric Jay. *Leviathan: The History of Whaling in America*. New York: W. W. Norton, 2007.

Drayton, Richard. 'À l'école des Français: Les sciences et le deuxième empire britannique (1780–1830)'. *Revue Française d'Histoire d'Outre-mer* 86, no. 322–3 (1999): 91–118.

Drayton, Richard. *Nature's Government: Science, Imperial Britain, and the 'Improvement' of the World*. New Haven: Yale University Press, 2000.

Drayton, Richard. 'Maritime Networks and the Making of Knowledge'. In *Empire, The Sea and Global History: Britain's Maritime World, c. 1760 – c. 1840*, edited by David Cannadine, 72–82. New York: Palgrave Macmillan, 2007.

Duivenvoorde, Wendy van. *Dutch East India Company Shipbuilding: The Archaeological Study of the Batavia and Other Seventeenth-century VOC Ships*. College Station: Texas A & M University Press, 2015.

Dunn, Richard and Rebekah Higgitt. 'The Bureau and the Board: Change and Collaboration in the Final Decades of the British Board of Longitude'. In *Pour une histoire du Bureau des longitudes (1795–1932)*, edited by Martina Schiavon and Laurent Rollet, 195–219. Nancy: Presses Universitaires de Lorraine, 2017.

Duquette, Nicolas J. 'Revealing the Relationship between Ship Crowding and Slave Mortality'. *Journal of Economic History* 74, no. 2 (2014): 535–52.

Dutton, Vaughan. 'Royal Navy Data in the 19th Century: Factors Affecting Data Quality'. http://doc.ukdataservice.ac.uk/doc/7390/mrdoc/pdf/guide.pdf.

Earle, Peter. *Sailors: English Merchant Seamen 1650–1775*. London: Methuen, 1998.

Earle, Peter. *The Earles of Liverpool: A Georgian Merchant Dynasty*. Oxford: Oxford University Press, 2015.

Earle, Rebecca. 'The Political Economy of Nutrition in the Eighteenth Century'. *Past and Present*, no. 242 (2019): 79–117.

Edney, Matthew H. 'Knowledge and Cartography in the Early Atlantic'. In *The Oxford Handbook of the Atlantic World 1450–1800*, edited by Nicholas Canny and Philip Morgan, 87–112. Oxford: Oxford University Press, 2011.

Egerton, Frank N. 'Á History of the Ecological Sciences, part 18: John Ray and His Associates Francis Willughby and William Derham'. *Bulletin of the Ecological Society of America* 86, no. 4 (2003): 301–13.

Egmond, Marco van. *Covens en Mortier. Productie, organisatie en ontwikkeling van een commercieel-kartografisch uitgevershuis in Amsterdam (1685–1866)*. Utrecht: HES & De Graaf Publishers, 2005.

Elliott, John H. *Empires of the Atlantic World: Britain and Spain in America 1492–1830*. New Haven: Yale University Press, 2006.

Ellis, F. P. 'The Health of the Navy: The Changing Pattern'. *British Journal of Industrial Medicine* 26, no. 3 (1969): 190–201.

Eltis, David. *Economic Growth and the Ending of the Transatlantic Slave Trade*. Oxford: Oxford University Press, 1987.

Eltis, David. 'The Volume and Structure of the Transatlantic Slave Trade: A Reassessment'. *The William and Mary Quarterly* 58, no. 1 (2001): 17–46.

Eltis, David and David Richardson. 'Productivity in the Transatlantic Slave Trade'. *Explorations in Economic History* 32, no. 4 (1995): 465–84.

Eltis, David and Lawrence C. Jennings. 'Trade between Western Africa and the Atlantic World in the Pre-colonial Era'. *American Historical Review* 93, no. 4 (1988): 936–59.

Emmer, Pieter C. *The Dutch in the Atlantic Economy, 1580–1800: Trade, Slavery and Emancipation*. Aldershot: Variorum, 1998.

Emmer, Pieter C. 'In Search of a System: The Atlantic Economy, 1500–1800'. In *Atlantic History: History of the Atlantic System, 1580–1830*, edited by Horst Pietschmann, 169–78. Göttingen: Vandenhoeck & Ruprecht, 2002.

Enebakk, Vidar. 'Hansteen's Magnetometer and the Origin of the Magnetic Crusade'. *British Journal for the History of Science* 47, no. 4 (2014): 587–608.

Engstrand, Iris H. W. *Spanish Scientists in the New World: The Eighteenth-Century Expeditions*. Seattle: University of Washington, 1981.

Enthoven, Victor. 'An Assessment of Dutch Transatlantic Commerce, 1585–1817'. In *Riches from Atlantic Commerce: Dutch Transatlantic Trade and Shipping, 1585–1817*, edited by Johannes Postma and Victor Enthoven, 385–444. Leiden: Brill, 2003.

Enthoven, Victor. 'Dutch Crossings: Migration between the Netherlands and the New World, 1600–1800'. *Atlantic Studies* 2, no. 2 (2005): 153–76.

Esteban Piñero, Mariano. 'La institucionalización de la ciencia aplicada en España del siglo XVI. Un modelo cuestionado'. In *Más allá de la Leyenda Negra. España y la Revolución Científica*, edited by Victor Navarro Brotóns and William Eamon, 427–42. Valencia: CSIC, 2007.

Falola, Toyin and Amanda Warnock. *Encyclopedia of the Middle Passage*. Westport: Greenwood Publishing, 2007.

Fanning, A. E. *Steady as She Goes: A History of the Compass Department of the Admiralty*. London: HMSO, 1986.

Fara, Patricia. *Sympathetic Attractions: Magnetic Practices, Beliefs, and Symbolism in Eighteenth Century England*. Princeton: Princeton University Press, 1996.

Fatah-Black, Karwan. *Suriname and the Atlantic World 1650–1800*. Leiden: Fatah-Black, 2013.

Fauque, Danielle. 'The Introduction of the Octant in Eighteenth-century France'. In *Koersvast. Vijf eeuwen navigatie op zee*, edited by Remmelt Daalder, Frits Looijmeijer and Diederick Wildeman, 95–104. Zaltbommel: Aprilis, 2005.

Fauque, Danielle. 'Testing Longitude Methods in Mid-eighteenth century France'. In *Navigational Enterprises in Europe and Its Empires, 1730–1880*, edited by Richard Dunn and Rebekah Higgitt, 159–79. London: Palgrave Macmillan, 2015.

Feinberg, H. M. 'New Data on European Mortality in West Africa: The Dutch on the Gold Coast, 1714–1760'. *Journal of African History* 15, no. 3 (1974): 357–71.

Feldman, Th. S. 'Late Enlightenment Meteorology'. In *The Quantifying Spirit in the Eighteenth Century*, edited by Tore Frängsmyr, John L. Heilbron and Robin E. Rider, 143–77. Berkeley: University of California Press, 1990.

Fernández-Armesto, Felipe. *Before Columbus, Exploration and Colonization from the Mediterranean to the Atlantic, 1229–1492*. Philadelphia: University of Pennsylvania Press, 1987.

Fernández-Armesto, Felipe. *Civilizations*, 2nd edn. London: Pan Books, 2001.

Fernández-Armesto, Felipe. *Pathfinders: A Global History of Exploration*. Oxford: Oxford University Press, 2006.

Fernández-Armesto, Felipe. *1492. The Year Our World Began*. London: Bloomsbury, 2009.

Ferreiro, Larrie D. *Ships and Science: The Birth of Naval Architecture in the Scientific Revolution, 1600–1800*. Cambridge: Cambridge University Press, 2007.

Ferreiro Larrie D. *The Aristotelian Heritage in Early Naval Architecture, from the Venetian Arsenal to the French Navy, 1500 –1700*. Berlin: Max Planck Institut für Wissenschaftsgeschichte, 2009.

Ferreiro, Larrie D. *Measure of the Earth: The Enlightenment Expedition that Reshaped our World*. New York: Basic Books, 2011.

Ferreiro, Larrie D. and Alexander Pollara. 'Contested Waterlines: The Wave-line Theory and Shipbuilding in the Nineteenth Century'. *Technology and Culture* 57, no. 2 (2016): 414–44.

Fichter, James R. *So Great a Profit: How the East Indies Trade transformed Anglo-American Capitalism*. Cambridge, MA: Harvard University Press, 2010.

Fleischer, Alette. 'The Company's Garden and the (Ex)change of Nature and Knowledge at the Cape of Good Hope (1652–1700)'. In *Centres and Cycles of Accumulation in and around the Netherlands in the Early Modern Period*, edited by Lissa Roberts, 101–27. Zürich: LIT Verlag, 2011.

Flynn, Dennis O. and Arturo Giráldez. 'Path Dependence, Time Lags and the Birth of Globalization: A Critique of O'Rourke and Williamson'. *European Review of Economic History* 8, no. 1 (2004): 81–108.

Flynn, Dennis O. and Arturo Giráldez. 'Born Again: Globalization's Sixteenth-Century Origins'. *Pacific Economic Review* 13, no. 3 (2008): 359–87.

Forbes, Eric G. 'Index of the Board of Longitude Papers at the Royal Greenwich Observatory'. *Journal for the History of Astronomy* 1, no. 2 (1970): 169–79, 2 (1971), no. 1: 58–70 and no. 2: 133–45.

Forbes, Eric G. *The Birth of Scientific Navigation: The Solving in the Eighteenth Century of the Problem of Finding Longitude at Sea*. London: National Maritime Museum, 1974.

Forbes, Eric G. *Greenwich Observatory*, vol. I *Origins and Early History (1675–1835)*. London: Taylor & Francis, 1975.

Foxhall, Katherine. *Health, Medicine and the Sea: Australian Voyages c. 1815–1860*. Manchester: Manchester University Press, 2012.

Fraser Harris, D. 'Stephen Hales, the Pioneer in the Hygiene of Ventilation'. *The Scientific Monthly* 3, no. 5 (1916): 440–54.

French, Christopher. 'Productivity in the Atlantic Shipping Industry: A Quantitative Study'. *Journal of Interdisciplinary History* 17, no. 3 (1987): 613–38.

Friedrich, Susanne, Arndt Brendecke and Stefan Ehrenpreis, eds. *Transformations of Knowledge in Dutch Expansion*. Berlin: De Gruyter, 2015.

Frijhoff, Willem. *La société néerlandaise et ses gradués, 1575–1814*. Maarssen: APA, 1981.

Fyfe, Aileen. 'Journals and Periodicals'. In *A Companion to the History of Science*, edited by Bernard Lightman, 387–99. Oxford: Oxford University Press, 2016.

Gaastra, Femme. 'Zeilende kustvaart van circa 1750 tot circa 1720. Het fenomeen van de Groninger zeevaart in de negentiende eeuw'. *Tijdschrift voor Zeegeschiedenis* 26, no. 2 (2007): 154–65.

Galenson, David W. 'The Rise and Fall of Indentured Servitude in the Americas: An Economic Analysis'. *Journal of Economic History* 44, no. 1 (1984): 1–26.

Games, Alison. 'Atlantic History: Definitions, Challenges, and Opportunities'. *American Historical Review* 111, no. 3 (2006): 740–57.

Garcia, Enric. 'Losing Professional Identity? Deck Officers in the Spanish Merchant Marine, 1868–1914'. *International Journal of Maritime History* 26, no. 3 (2014): 451–70.

Garcia, Enric. *El mundo del trabajo en la marina mercante española (1834–1914)*. Barcelona: Icaraia Editorial, 2017.

García-Cubillana de la Cruz, J. M. 'La salud y la enfermedad en el Real Hospital de la Armada del Arsenal de la Carraca (1756–1821)'. *Sanidad Militar* 71, no. 3 (2015): 158–78.

García Garralón, Marta. 'The Education of Pilots for the Indies Trade in Spain during the Eighteenth Century'. *International Journal of Maritime History* 21, no. 2 (2009): 189–220.

García Garralón, Marta. 'La formación de los pilotos de la Carrera de India en el siglo XVIII'. *Anuario de Estudios Atlánticos* 55 (2009): 159–228.

García Garralón, Marta. 'The Seamen of the Indies Trade and the University of Seafarers of Seville'. *International Journal of Maritime History* 25, no. 1 (2013): 91–102.

Garland, Charles and Herbert S. Klein. 'The Allotment of Space for Slaves aboard Eighteenth-Century British Slave Ships'. *William and Mary Quarterly* 42, no. 2 (1985): 238–48.

Gascoigne, John. *Science in the Service of Empire. Joseph Banks, the British State and the Uses of Science in the Age of Revolution.* Cambridge: Cambridge University Press, 1998.

Gascoigne, John. 'Navigating the Pacific from Bougainville to Dumont d'Urville: French Approaches to Determining Longitude, 1766–1840'. In *Navigational Enterprises in Europe and Its Empires, 1730–1880*, edited by Richard Dunn and Rebekah Higgitt, 180–97. London: Palgrave Macmillan, 2015.

Gaskell, Jeremy. *Who Killed the Great Auk?* Oxford: Oxford University Press, 2000.

Gavine, David. 'Navigation and Astronomy Teachers in Scotland Outside the Universities'. *The Mariner's Mirror* 76, no. 1 (1990): 5–12.

Gelder, Roelof van. *Naar het aards paradijs. Het rusteloze leven van Jacob Roggeveen, ontdekker van het Paaseiland (1659–1729)*. Amsterdam: Balans, 2012.

Gilje, Paul. *Liberty on the Waterfront. American Maritime Culture in the Age of Revolution.* Philadelphia: University of Pennsylvania Press, 2004.

Gillispie, Charles C. *Science and Polity in France at the End of the Old Regime.* Princeton: Princeton University Press, 1980.

Gillispie, Charles C. *Science and Polity in France: The Revolutionary and Napoleonic Years.* Princeton: Princeton University Press, 2004.

Gilroy, Paul. *The Black Atlantic: Modernity and Double Consciousness.* Cambridge, MA: Harvard University Press, 1995.

Glete, Jan. *Navies and Nations. Warships, Navies and State-building in Europe and America, 1500–1860.* Stockholm: Almqvist & Wiksell International, 1993.

Glick, Thomas F. 'Imperio y dependencia científica en el XVIII español e inglés: La provisión de los instrumentos científicos'. In *Ciencia, vida y espacio en Iberoamerica*, vol. III, edited by José L. Peset, 49–63. Madrid: CSIC, 1989.

Godinho, V. Magalhaes, 'The Portuguese and the "Carreira da India", 1497–1810'. In *Ships, Sailors and Spices: East India Companies and their Shipping in the 16th, 17th and 18th Centuries*, edited by Jaap R. Bruijn and Femme S. Gaastra, 1–47. Amsterdam: NEHA, 1993.

Goldgar, Anne. *Impolite Learning. Conduct and Community in the Republic of Letters, 1680–1750.* New Haven: Yale University Press, 1995.

Goldman, Lawrence. *Science, Politics and Reform in Victorian Britain: The Social Science Association 1857–1886.* Cambridge: Cambridge University Press, 2004.

Golinski, Jan. *British Weather and the Climate of Enlightenment.* Chicago: University of Chicago Press, 2007.

González González, Francisco José. 'Del "Arte de marear" a la navegación astronómica: Técnicas e instrumentos de navegación en la España de la Edad Moderna'. *Cuadernos de Historia Moderna. Anejos* V (2006): 135–66.

Goodman, David C. *Power and Penury: Government, Technology and Science in Philip II's Spain*. Cambridge: Cambridge University Press, 1988.

Goodman, David C. 'Science, Medicine, and Technology in Colonial Spanish America: New Interpretations, New Approaches'. In *Science in the Spanish and Portuguese Empires, 1500-1800*, edited by Daniela Bleichmar, Paula de Vos, Kristin Huffine and Kevin Sheehan, 9-34. Stanford: Stanford University Press, 2009.

Goodman, Dena. *The Republic of Letters: A Cultural History of the French Enlightenment*. Ithaca: Cornell University Press, 1994.

Goslinga, C. Ch. *The Dutch in the Caribbean and on the Wild Coast 1580-168*. Assen: Van Gorcum, 1971.

Gould, Eliga H. 'Entangled Histories, Entangled Worlds: The English-speaking Atlantic as a Spanish Periphery'. *American Historical Review* 112, no. 3 (2007): 764–86.

Gould, Rupert T. *The Marine Chronometer: Its History and Development*, 2nd edn. London: Holland Press, 1976.

Grahn, Lance R. 'Cartagena and Its Hinterland in the Eighteenth Century'. In *Atlantic Port Cities: Economy, Culture, and Society in the Atlantic World (1650-1750)*, edited by Franklin W. Knight and Peggy K. Liss, 168-95. Knocksville: University of Tennessee Press, 1991.

Green, Toby. 'Beyond Imperial Atlantic: Trajectories of Africans from Upper Guinea and West-Central Africa in the Early Atlantic World'. *Past and Present*, no. 230 (2016): 91–122.

Grocott, D. F. C. 'Shipwrecks in the Revolutionary and Napoleonic Eras 1793-1815. Causal Factors and Comments'. *Journal of Navigation* 52, no. 2 (1999): 149–62.

Groustra, F. N. and Jaap R. Bruijn. 'Een kentering in de gezondheid aan boord. Bataafse vloten naar Oost- en West-Indië, 1802'. *Tijdschrift voor Zeegeschiedenis* 14, no. 1 (1995): 25–50.

Grove, Richard. *Green Imperialism: Colonial Expansion, Tropical Island Edens and the Origins of Environmentalism*. Cambridge: Cambridge University Press, 1995.

Gruber, Ira D. 'Atlantic Warfare, 1440-1763'. In *The Oxford Handbook of the Atlantic World*, edited by Nicholas Canny and Philip Morgan, 417-32. Oxford: Oxford University Press, 2011.

Guennou, Jean. *Missions Étrangères de Paris*. Paris: Fayard, 1986.

Guerra, F. 'Hispanic-American Contributions to the History of Scurvy'. *Centaurus* 1, no. 1 (1950): 12–23.

Gunn, Geoffrey C. *First Globalization: The Eurasian Exchange, 1500-1800*. Lanham: Rowman & Littlefield, 2003.

Gurney, Alan. *Compass: A Story of Exploration and Innovation*. New York: W. W. Norton, 2004.

Hackmann, William D. *John and Jonathan Cuthbertson: The Invention and Development of the Eighteenth Century Plate Electrical Machine*. Leiden: Rijksmuseum Geschiedenis der Natuurwetenschappen, 1973.

Hague, Douglas B. and Rosemary Christie. *Lighthouses: Their Architecture, History and Archaeology*. Cardiff: Gomer Press, 1975.

Haines, Robin. 'Ships, Families and Surgeons: Migrant Voyages to Australia in the Age of Sail'. In *Health and Medicine at Sea, 1700–1900*, edited by David Boyd Haycock and Sally Archer, 172–94. Woodbridge: Boydell Press, 2009.

Haines, Robin, John McDonald and Ralph Shlomowitz. 'Mortality and Voyage Length in the Middle Passage Revisited'. *Explorations in Economic History* 38, no. 4 (2001): 503–33.

Haines, Robin and Ralph Shlomowitz. 'Explaining the Mortality Decline in the Eighteenth-Century British Slave Trade'. *Economic History Review* 53, no. 2 (2000): 262–83.

Haines, Robin, Ralph Shlomowitz and Lance Brennan. 'Maritime Mortality Revisited'. *International Journal of Maritime History* 8, no. 1 (1996): 133–71.

Hallema, A. 'Olie op de golven in de 18de eeuw'. *Marineblad* 62, no. 3 (1952): 269–85.

Hancock, David. *Oceans of Wine: Madeira and the Emergence of American Trade and Taste*. New Haven: Yale University Press, 2009.

Hardenberg, H. 'Benjamin Franklin en Nederland'. *Bijdragen voor de Geschiedenis der Nederlanden* 5, no. 3–4 (1950–1951): 213–30.

Harding, Richard. *Seapower and Naval Warfare 1650–1830*. London: Taylor & Francis, 1999.

Hardy, Penelope. 'Matthew Fontaine Maury: Scientist'. *International Journal of Maritime History* 28, no. 2 (2016): 402–10.

Harley, C. Knick. 'Ocean Freight Rates and Productivity, 1740–1913: The Primacy of Mechanical Invention Reaffirmed'. *Journal of Economic History* 48, no. 4 (1988): 503–33.

Harries, Henry. 'Pre-Greenwich Sea Longitudes'. *The Observatory* 50, no. 10 (1927): 315–19.

Harris, John R. *Essays in Industry and Technology in the Eighteenth Century*. Aldershot: Ashgate, 1992.

Harris, Steven J. 'Long-Distance Corporations, Big Sciences, and the Geography of Knowledge'. *Configurations* 6, no. 2 (1998): 269–304.

Harris, Steven J. 'Networks of Travel, Correspondence, and Exchange'. In *The Cambridge History of Science*, vol. 3, *Early Modern Science*, edited by Katharine Park and Lorraine Daston, 341–62. Cambridge: Cambridge University Press, 2006.

Harrison, Mark. '"The Tender Frame of Man". Disease, Climate, and Racial Difference in India and the West Indies, 1760–1860'. *Bulletin of the History of Medicine* 70, no. 1 (1996): 68–93.

Harrison, Mark. 'An "Important and Truly National Subject": The West-Africa Service and the Health of the Royal Navy in the Mid Nineteenth Century'. In *Health and Medicine at Sea, 1700–1900*, edited by David Boyd Haycock and Sally Archer, 108–27. Woodbridge: Boydell Press, 2009.

Hatton, Timothy J. and Jeffrey G. Williamson. *The Age of Mass Migration: Causes and Economic Impact*. New York: Oxford University Press, 1998.

Haudrère, Philippe. 'The "Compagnie des Indes" and Maritime Matters (c. 1725-1770)'. In *Ships, Sailors and Spices: East India Companies and their Shipping in the 16th, 17th and 18th Centuries*, edited by Jaap R. Bruijn and Femme S. Gaastra, 81–98. Amsterdam: NEHA, 1993.

Haudrère, Philippe. 'Santé et voyages au long cours: la route du Cap au XVIIe siècle'. In *Le homme, la santé et la mer*, edited by Christian Buchet, 223–30. Paris: Honoré Champion, 1997.

Havik, Philip J. and Toby Green. 'Introduction: Brokerage and the Role of Western Africa in the Atlantic World'. In *Brokers of Change. Atlantic Commerce and Cultures in Precolonial Western Africa*, edited by Toby Green, 1–26. Oxford: Oxford University Press, 2012.

Headland, Robert. *The Island of South Georgia*, 2nd edn. Cambridge: Cambridge University Press, 1992.

Headrick, Daniel R. *The Tools of Empire: Technology and European Imperialism in the Nineteenth Century*. Oxford: Oxford University Press, 1981.

Headrick, Daniel R. *The Tentacles of Progress: Technology in the Age of Imperialism, 1850–1940*. Oxford: Oxford University Press, 1988.

Headrick, Daniel R. *When Information Came of Age: Technologies in the Age of Reason and Revolution, 1700–1850*. Oxford: Oxford University Press, 2000.

Headrick, Daniel R. *Power over Peoples: Technology, Environments and Western Imperialism, 1400-Present*. Princeton: Princeton University Press, 2010.

Heidbrink, Ingo. 'Closing the "Blue Hole": Maritime History as a Core Element of Historical Research'. *International Journal of Maritime History* 29, no. 2 (2017): 325–32.

Held, David, Anthony McGrew, David Goldblatt and Jonathan Perraton. *Global Transformations: Politics, Economic and Culture*. Cambridge: Polity Press, 1999.

Helden, Anne C. van and Rob H. van Gent. 'The Lens Production by Christiaan and Constantijn Huygens'. *Annals of Science* 56, no. 1 (1999): 69–79.

Hendrik Engels' Alphabetical List of Dutch Zoological Cabinets and Menageries, edited by Pieter Smit, 2nd edn. Amsterdam: Rodopi, 1986.

Hentschel, Klaus. *Mapping the Spectrum: Techniques of Visual Representation in Research and Teaching*. Oxford: Oxford University Press, 2002.

Henwood, Philippe. 'L'Académie de Marine à Brest au XVIIIe siècle'. In *La mer au siècle des Encyclopédistes*, edited by Jean Balcou, 125–34. Paris: Champion-Slatkine, 1987.

Hilaire-Perez, Liliane and Cathérine Verna. 'Les circulations techniques: hommes, produits, savoirs au Moyen Âge et à l'époque moderne (Orient, Occident)'. In *Circulations techniques en amont de l'innovation: hommes, objets et idées en movement*, edited by Michel Cotte, 11–35. Belfort: Presses Universitaires de Franche-Comté, 2004.

Hilster, Nicolàs de. *Navigation on Wood: Wooden Navigational Instruments 1590–1731*. Castricum: De Hilster, 2018.

Hindle, Brooke. *David Rittenhouse*. Princeton: Princeton University Press, 1964.

Hindley, Meredith. 'Mapping the Republic of Letters'. http://www.neh.gov/humanities/2013novemberdecember/feature.
History of the Marine Society of Newburyport. Newburyport: Press of the Daily News, 1906.
Hitchins, H. L. and W. E. May. *From Lodestone to Gyro-Compass.* London: Hutchinson's, 1955.
Hogerzeil, Simon J. and David Richardson. 'Slave Purchasing Strategies and Shipboard Mortality: Day to day Evidence from the Dutch African Trade, 1751–1797'. *Economic History Review* 67, no. 1 (2007): 160–90.
Holden, Maria S. 'The Development of Lithographic Cartography and the Conservation Treatment of a Large Varnished Map'. http://cool.conservation-us.org/coolaic/sg/bpg/annual/v03/bp03-08.html.
Hollstein, Laura. *Knowing Nature: Knowledge of Nature in French and English Travel Accounts of the Caribbean.* Åbo: Åbo University Press, 2006.
Horlings, Edwin. *The Economic Development of the Dutch Service Sector 1800–1850. Trade and Transport in a Premodern Economy.* Amsterdam: NEHA, 1995.
Hornsby, Stephen. 'Geographies of the British Atlantic World'. In *Britain's Oceanic Empire. American and Indian Ocean Worlds, c. 1550–1850*, edited by H. V. Bowen, Elizabeth Mancke and John G. Reid, 15–44, 2nd edn. Cambridge: Cambridge University Press, 2015.
Houvenaghel, G. 'La conférence maritime de Bruxelles en 1863: première conférence océanographique internationale'. *Tijdschrift voor de Geschiedenis der Geneeskunde, Natuurwetenschappen, Wiskunde en Techniek* 13, no. 1 (1990): 42–9.
Hoving, Ab J. *Nicolaes Witsens Scheeps-bouw-konst open gestelt.* Franeker: Van Wijnen, 1994.
Hoving, Ab J. and Alan A. Lemmers. *In tekening gebracht. De achttiende-eeuwse scheepsbouwers en hun ontwerpmethoden.* Amsterdam: De Bataafsche Leeuw, 2001.
Howse, Derek. 'Britain's Board of Longitude: The Finances, 1714–1828'. *The Mariner's Mirror* 84, no. 4 (1998): 400–17.
Hughes, Paul and Alan D. Wall. 'The Dessiou Hydrographic Work: Its Authorship and Place'. *International Journal of Maritime History* 17, no. 2 (2005): 167–92.
Hughes, Robert. *The Fatal Shore: A History of the Transportation of Convicts to Australia 1787–1868.* London: Vintage Books, 1988.
Hugill, P. *World Trade since 1431: Geography, Technology and Capitalism.* Baltimore: Johns Hopkins University Press, 1991.
Igler, David. *The Great Ocean: Pacific Worlds from Captain Cook to the Gold Rush.* Oxford: Oxford University Press, 2013.
Iliffe, Rob. 'Mathematical Characters: Flamsteed and Christ's Hospital Royal Mathematical School'. In *Flamsteed's Stars: New Perspectives in the Life and Work of the First Astronomer Royal 1646–1719*, edited by Frances Willmoth, 115–44. Woodbridge: Boydell Press, 1997.

Iliffe, Rob. 'Science and Voyages of Discovery'. In *The Cambridge History of Science*, vol. 4, *Eighteenth-Century Science*, edited by Roy Porter, 618–45. Cambridge: Cambridge University Press, 2003.

Inikori, Joseph. *Africans and the Industrial Revolution in England: A Study of International Trade and Economic Development*. Cambridge: Cambridge University Press, 2002.

Inkster, Ian. 'Potentially Global: "Useful and Reliable Knowledge" and Material Progress in Europe, 1474–1914'. *The International History Review* 28, no. 2 (2006): 237–86.

Israel, Jonathan I. *Dutch Primacy in World Trade, 1585–1740*. Oxford: Oxford University Press, 1989.

Jackson, Gordon. *The British Whaling Trade*. London: A. & C. Black, 1978.

Jarvis, Michael J. *In the Eye of All Trade. Bermuda, Bermudians, and the Maritime World, 1680–1783*. Chapel Hill: University of North Carolina Press, 2010.

Jeans, C. 'The First Statutory Qualifications for Seafarers'. *Transport History* 6, no. 2 (1973): 248–67.

Johnson, Peter. 'The Board of Longitude 1714–1828'. *Journal of the British Astronomical Association* 99, no. 2 (1989): 63–9.

Johnston, Katherine. 'The Constitution of Empire: Place and Bodily Health in the Eighteenth-Century Atlantic'. *Atlantic Studies* 10, no. 4 (2013): 443–66.

Jong, Johan de. 'Drawings, Ships and Spices. Accumulation at the Dutch East India Company'. In *Centres and Cycles of Accumulation in and around the Netherlands during the Early Modern Period*, edited by Lissa Roberts, 177–204. Zürich: LIT Verlag, 2011.

Jong, Johan de. *Navigating through Technology: Technology and the Dutch East India Company VOC in the Eighteenth Century*. Zutphen: Wöhrmann, 2016.

Jonge, Jan Aart de. *De industrialiatie in Nederland tussen 1850 en 1914*. Amsterdam: Scheltema & Holkema, 1968.

Jonkers, Art. *Earth's Magnetism in the Age of Sail*. Baltimore: Johns Hopkins University Press, 2003.

Jonkers, Art. 'Rewards and Prizes'. In *The Oxford Encyclopedia of Maritime History*, vol. III, edited by John Hattendorf, 433–6. Oxford: Oxford University Press, 2007.

Jorink, Eric. *Het Boeck der Natuere. Nederlandse geleerden en de wonderen van Gods schepping 1571–1715*. Leiden: Primavera Press, 2006.

Jorink, Eric. 'Sloane and the Dutch Connection'. In *From Books to Bezoars: Sir Hans Sloane and His Collections*, edited by Alison Walker, Arthur MacGregor and Michael Hunter, 57–70. London: British Library, 2013.

Kagan, Richard L. 'Arcana Imperii: Mapas, ciencia y poder en la corte de Felipe IV'. In *El atlas del rey planeta: La 'descripción de España y de las costas y puertos de sus reinos' de Pedro Teixeira (1634)*, edited by Felipe Pereda and Fernando Marias, 49–70. Madrid: Nerea Editorial, 2002.

Kan, J. B. 'De Illustre School te Rotterdam'. *Rotterdams Jaarboekje* 1 (1888): 1–96.

Keeling, Drew. 'The Transportation Revolution and Transatlantic Migration, 1850–1914'. *Research in Economic History* 19 (1999): 39–74.

Keevil, J. J., Christopher Lloyd and Jack L. S. Coulter. *Medicine and the Navy 1200–1900*, 4 vols. Edinburgh: E & S. Livingstone, 1957–1963.

Kelly, Morgan and Cormac O'Grada. 'Speed under Sail during the Early Industrial Revolution (c. 1750–1830)'. *Economic History Review* 72, no. 2 (2019): 459–80.

Kennerley, Alston. 'Navigation and Training Ship: Educational Provision in Plymouth for the Mercantile Marine in the Nineteenth Century'. In *West Country Maritime and Social History: Some Essays*, edited by Stephen Fisher, 53–78. Exeter: University of Exeter, 1980.

Kennerley, Alston. 'Merchant Marine Education in Liverpool and the Nautical College of 1892'. *International Journal of Maritime History* 5, no. 2 (1993): 103–34.

Kennerley, Alston. 'Early State Support of Vocational Education: The Department of Science and Art Navigation Schools, 1853–1863'. *Journal of Vocational Education & Training* 52, no. 2 (2000): 211–24.

Kennerley, Alston and Percy Seymour. 'Aids to the Teaching of Navigation of Nautical Astronomy and Its History from 1600'. *Paedagogica Historica* 36, no. 1 (2000): 151–78.

Kilpatrick, Jane. *Fathers of Botany: The Discovery of Chinese Plants by European Missionaries*. Chicago: University of Chicago Press, 2014.

Kiple, K. F. and K. C. Ornelas. 'Race, War, and Tropical Medicine in the Eighteenth-Century Caribbean'. In *Warm Climates and Western Medicine: The Emergence of Tropical Medicine, 1500–1900*, edited by David Arnold, 65–79. Amsterdam: Rodopi, 1996.

Klein, Bernhard and Gesa Mackenthun. 'Introduction: The Sea is History'. In *Sea Changes: Historicizing the Ocean*, edited by Bernhard Klein and Gesa Mackenthun, 1–12. New York: Routledge, 2003.

Klein, Herbert S., Stanley S. Engerman, Robin Haines and Ralph Shlomowitz. 'Transoceanic Mortality: The Slave Trade in Comparative Perspective'. *The William and Mary Quarterly* 58, no. 1 (2001): 93–118.

Klooster, Wim. *Illicit Riches: Dutch Trade in the Caribbean, 1647–1795*. Leiden: KITLV, 1998.

Klooster, Wim. 'An Overview of Dutch Trade with the Americas, 1600–1800'. In *Riches from Atlantic Commerce. Dutch Transatlantic Trade and Shipping, 1585–1817*, edited by Johannes Postma and Victor Enthoven, 365–83. Leiden: Brill, 2003.

Knight, Roger. *Britain against Napoleon: The Organization of Victory 1793–1815*. London: Penguin, 2013.

Koehler, Peter, Stanley Finger and Marco Piccolino. 'The "Eels" of South America: Mid-18th Century Dutch Contributions in the Theory of Animal Electricity'. *Journal of the History of Biology* 42, no. 4 (2009): 715–63.

Koeman, Cornelis. *Atlantes Neerlandici. Bibliography of Terrestrial, Maritime and Celestial Atlases and Pilot Books, published in the Netherlands up to 1880*, 4 vols. Amsterdam: Theatrum Orbis Terrarum, 1967-1985.

Koeman, Cornelis. *The Sea on Paper: The Story of the Van Keulens and Their Sea Torch*. Amsterdam: Theatrum Orbis Terrarum, 1972.

Kok, M. 'Cartografie van de firma Van Keulen'. In '*In de Gekroonde Lootsman'. Het kaarten-, boekuitgevers en instrumentmakershuis Van Keulen te Amsterdam 1680-1885*, edited by E. O. van Keulen, Willem F. J. Mörzer Bruyns and Elsiabeth K. Spits, 15-43. Utrecht: HES, 1989.

Koninklijk Nederlands Meteorologisch Instituut 1854-1954. The Hague: SDU, 1954.

Konvitz, Josef W. *Cartography in France. Science, Engineering and Statecraft*. Chicago: University of Chicago Press, 1987.

Koot, Christian J. *Empire at the Periphery: British Colonists, Anglo-Dutch Trade, and the Development of the British Atlantic, 1621-171*. New York: New York University Press, 2011.

Krohn, Wolfgang et al., eds. *Self-organization. Portrait of a Scientific Revolution*. Dordrecht: Kluwer, 1990.

Krugman, Paul. *The Self-Organizing Economy*. Cambridge, MA: Wiley & Blackwell, 1996.

Kuethe, Allen J. and José Manuel Serrano. 'El astillero de La Habana y Trafalgar'. *Revista de Indias* 67, no. 241 (2007): 763-76.

Kuethe, Allan J. and Kenneth J. Andrien. *The Spanish Atlantic World in the Eighteenth Century: War and the Bourbon Reforms, 1713-1796*. Cambridge: Cambridge University Press, 2014.

Kuile, Sybrich ter and Willem F. J. Mörzer Bruyns, *Amsterdamse kompasmakers, ca. 1580-ca. 1850. Bijdrage tot de kennis der instrumentmakerij in Nederland*. Amsterdam, 1999.

Kupperman, Karen Ordahl. 'Fear of Hot Climates in the Anglo-American Colonial Experience'. *The William and Mary Quarterly* 41, no. 2 (1984): 213-40.

Kupperman, Karen Ordahl. *The Atlantic in World History*. Oxford: Oxford University Press, 2012.

Kurlansky, Mark. *Cod: A Biography of the Fish that Changed the World*. London: Vintage, 1997.

Kusukawa, Sachiko. 'The "Historia Piscium" (1686)'. *Notes and Records of the Royal Society of London* 54, no. 2 (2000): 179-97.

Lafuente, Antonio. 'Enlightenment in an Imperial Context: Local Science in the Late Eighteenth-Century Hispanic World'. *Osiris* 2nd series 15, no. 1 (2000): 155-73.

Lafuente, Antonio and Manuel A. Sellés. 'The Problem of Longitude at Sea in the 18th Century in Spain'. *Vistas in Astronomy* 28 (1985): 243-50.

Lamb, Ursula. 'Martín Fernández de Navarrete Clears the Deck: The Spanish Hydrographic Office (1809-1824)'. *Centro de estudos de História e Cartografia Antiga*, Série Separatas 81, 29-45. Coimbra: Junta de Investigações Cientificicas do Ultramar, 1980.

Lamb, Ursula. 'The London Years of Felipe Bauzá: Spanish Hydrographer in Exile, 1823-34'. *The Journal of Navigation* 34, no. 3 (1981): 319-40.

Lamb, Ursula. 'Early Spanish Plans for Lithographic Reproduction of Maps: A Fruitful Failure'. In Ursula Lamb, *Homenaje a Luis de Albuquerque, Revista da Universidade de Coimbra* 35 (Coimbra, 1990): 323-31.

Lambert, Andrew. *Franklin: Tragic Hero of Polar Navigation*. London: Faber & Faber, 2009.

Lambert, David, Luciana Martins and Miles Ogborn. 'Currents, Visions and Voyages: Historical Geographies of the Sea'. *Journal of Historical Geography* 32, no. 3 (2006): 479-93.

Lamikiz, Xabier. *Trade and Trust in the Eighteenth-Century Atlantic World: Spanish Merchants and their Overseas Networks*. Woodbridge: Boydell Press, 2010.

Latour, Bruno. *Science in Action: How to Follow Scientists and Engineers through Society*. Cambridge, MA: Harvard University Press, 1987.

Law, Robin. 'Africa in the Atlantic World, c. 1760 – c. 1840'. In *The Oxford Handbook of the Atlantic World 1450-1800*, edited by Nicholas Canny and Philip Morgan, 585-601. Oxford: Oxford University Press, 2011.

Leeman, William P. *The Long Road to Annapolis: The Founding of the Naval Academy and the Early American Republic*. Chapel Hill: University of North Carolina Press, 2010.

Leggett, Don. *Shaping the Royal Navy: Technology, Authority and Naval Architecture 1830-1906*. Manchester: Manchester University Press, 2015.

Leinenga, Jurjen R. *Arctische walvisvangst in de achttiende eeuw. De betekenis van Straat Davis als vangstgebied*. Amsterdam: De Bataafsche Leeuw, 1995.

Lemmers, Alan. *Techniek op schaal. Modellen en het technologiebeleid van de Marine 1725-1885*. Amsterdam: De Bataafsche Leeuw, 1996.

Lente, Dick van. 'Illustratietechniek'. In *Techniek in Nederland. De wording van een moderne samenleving 1800-1890*, edited by H. W. Lintsen et al., 255-5. Zutphen: Walburg Pers, 1993.

Leonard, Adrian B. and David Pretel. 'Experiments in Modernity: The Making of the Atlantic World Economy'. In *The Caribbean and the Atlantic World Economy. Circuits of Trade, Money and Knowledge*, edited by A. B. Leonard and David Pretel, 1-14. London: Palgrave Macmillan, 2016.

Leopold, J. H. 'The Longitude Timekeepers of Christiaan Huygens'. In *The Quest for Longitude*, edited by William J. Andrewes, 101-15. Cambridge, MA: Harvard University Press, 1993.

Leopold, J. H. 'Some Notes on Benjamin Ayres'. In *Making Scientific Instruments Count: Essays on Historical Instruments Presented to Gerard L'Estrange Turne*, edited by R. W. G. Anderson, J. A. Bennett and W. F. Ryan, 395-402. Aldershot: Variorum, 1993.

Leopold, J. H. 'The Third Seafaring Nation. The Introduction of the Marine Chronometer in the Netherlands'. *Antiquarian Horology* 22, no. 6 (1996): 486-500.

Le Page, Rémi. 'La bibliothèque de l'Académie de Marine de Brest'. In *La mer au siècle des Encyclopédistes*, edited by Jean Balcou, 135–46. Paris: Champion-Slatkine, 1987.
Leuftink, Arnold E. *De geneeskunde bij 's Lands oorlogsvloot in de 17ᵉ eeuw*. Assen: Van Gorcum, 1953.
Leuftink, Arnold E. *Harde heelmeesters. Zeelieden en hun dokters in de 18de eeuw*. Zutphen: Walburg Pers, 1991.
Lewis, Martin W. 'Dividing the Ocean Sea'. *Geographical Review* 89, no. 2 (1999): 188–214.
Lewis, Michael. *The Navy in Transition, 1814–1864: A Social History*. London: Hodder & Stoughton, 1965.
Liebersohn, Harry. *The Traveler's World: Europe to the Pacific*. Cambridge, MA: Harvard University Press, 2006.
Liss, Peggy K. *Atlantic Empires: The Network of Trade and Revolution*. Baltimore: Johns Hopkins University Press, 1983.
Livingstone, David N. *The Geographical Tradition: Episodes in the History of a Contested Enterprise*. London: John Wiley & Sons, 1992.
Llorca-Jaña, Manuel. *The British Textile Trade in South America in the Nineteenth Century*. Cambridge: Cambridge University Press, 2012.
Llorca-Jaña, Manuel. 'The Impact of Early Nineteenth-Century Globalization on Foreign Trade in the Southern Cone: A Study of British Trade Statistics'. *Investigaciones de Historia Económica* 10, no. 1 (2014): 46–56.
Lomas Salmonte, Francisco Javier et al. *Historia de Cádiz*. Madrid: Silex, 2005.
López Piñero, José María. *Ciencia y técnica en la sociedad española de los siglos XVI y XVII*. Barcelona: Labor, 1979.
Lucassen, Jan. 'The Netherlands, the Dutch, and Long-distance Migration in the Late Sixteenth to Early Nineteenth-Century'. In *Europeans on the Move: Studies on European Migration, 1500–1800*, edited by Nicholas Canny, 153–91. Oxford: Oxford University Press, 1994.
Lucassen, Jan and Richard Unger. 'Labour Productivity in Ocean Shipping, 1450–1875'. *International Journal of Maritime History* 12, no. 2 (2000): 127–41.
Lunteren, Frans van. 'De oprichting van het Koninklijk Nederlands Meteorologisch Instituut: Humboldtiaanse wetenschap, internationale samenwerking en praktisch nut'. *Gewina* 21, no. 2 (1998): 216–43.
Lux, David S. and Harold J. Cook 'Closed Circles or Open Networks? Communicating at a Distance during the Scientific Revolution'. *History of Science* 36, no. 2 (1998): 179–211.
Lynn, Martin. *Commerce and Economic Change in West-Africa: The Palm Oil Trade in the Nineteenth Century*. Cambridge: Cambridge University Press, 1997.
Macdonagh, Oliver. *A Pattern of Government Growth 1800-60: The Passenger Acts and their Enforcement*. London: MacGibbon & Kee, 1961.
Maclean, J. *Bijdrage tot de geschiedenis der Nederlandse instrumentmakerijen in de periode 1781–1880*. Leiden: Museum Geschiedenis der Natuurwetenschappen, 1976.

Magra, Christopher P. *The Fisherman's Cause: Atlantic Commerce and the Maritime Dimension of the American Revolution*. Cambridge: Cambridge University Press, 2009.

Mahoney, M. S. 'Christiaan Huygens: The Measurement of Time and Longitude at Sea'. In *Studies on Christiaan Huygens*, edited by H. J. M. Bos et al., 234–70. Lisse: Swets & Zeitlinger, 1980.

Malin, S. R. C. and D. R. Barraclough. 'Humboldt and the Earth's Magnetic Field'. *Quarterly Journal of the Royal Astronomical Society* 32, no. 3 (1991): 279–93.

Manen, Niels van. 'Preventive Medicine in the Dutch Slave Trade, 1747–1797'. *International Journal of Maritime History* 18, no. 2 (2006): 129–85.

Mann, Charles C. *1491. New Revelations of the Americas before Columbus*. New York: Vintage, 2005.

Mann, Charles C. *1493. How Europe's Discovery of the Americas Revolutionized Trade, Ecology and Life on Earth*. London: Granta, 2011.

Mansvelt, W. F. *Geschiedenis van de Nederlandsche Handel-Maatschappij*, 2 vols. Haarlem: Joh. Enschedé & Zonen, 1924.

Marchena Fernández, Juan. *Oficiales y soldados en el Ejército de América*. Seville: Escuela de Estudios Hispanoamericanos, 1983.

Margócsy, Dániel. 'Advertising Cadavers in the Republic of Letters: Anatomical Publications in the Early Modern Netherlands'. *British Journal for the History of Science* 42, no. 2 (2009): 187–210.

Marshall, Peter J. *The Making and Unmaking of Empires: Britain, India, and America, c. 1750–1783*. Oxford: Oxford University Press, 2005.

Marzagalli, Silvia. 'The French Atlantic World in the Seventeenth and Eighteenth Centuries'. In *The Oxford Handbook of the Atlantic World 1450-1800*, edited by Nicholas Canny and Philip Morgan, 235–51. Oxford: Oxford University Press, 2011.

Masson, Philippe. *La mort et les marins*. Grenoble: Glénat, 1995.

Masson, Philippe. 'La revolution sanitaire au XIXe siècle'. In *Le homme, la santé et la mer*, edited by Christian Buchet, 407–15. Paris: Honoré Champion, 1997.

Mathias, Peter. 'Swords and Ploughshares: The Armed Forces, Medicine and Public Health in the Late Eighteenth Century'. In Peter Mathias, *The Transformation of England: Essays in the Economic and Social History of England in the Eighteenth Century*, 265–85. London: Methuen, 1979.

Mauro, Frederico. *Le Portugal et l'Atlantique au XVIIe siècle 1570–1670*. Paris: Université de Paris, 1957.

May, W. E. 'How the Chronometer Went to Sea'. *Antiquarian Horology* 9, no. 6 (1976): 646–64.

Maya Restrepo, Luz Adriana. 'Botánica y medicinas africanas en la Nueva Granada, siglo XVII'. *Historia crítica* 19, no. 1 (2000): 27–47.

McAleer, John. *Britain's Maritime Empire: Southern Africa, the South Atlantic and the Indian Ocean, 1763–1820*. Cambridge: Cambridge University Press, 2017.

McClellan III, James E. *Colonialism and Science: Saint Domingue in the Old Regime*, 2nd edn. Chicago: University of Chicago Press, 1992.

McClellan III, James E. and François Regourd. 'The Colonial Machine: French Science and Colonization in the Ancien Régime'. *Osiris* 15, no. 1 (2000): 31–50.

McClellan III, James E. and François Regourd. *The Colonial Machine: French Science and Overseas Expansion in the Old Regime*. Turnhout: Brepols, 2011.

McConnell, Anita. *No Sea Too Deep: The History of Oceanographic Instruments*. Bristol: Hilger, 1982.

McConnell, Anita. 'A Profitable Visit: Luigi Fernando Marsigli's Studies, Commerce and Friendships in Holland, 1722-23'. In *Italian Scientists in the Low Countries in the XVIIth and XVIIIth Centuries*, edited by Cesare S. Maffioli and Lodewijk C. Palm, 189–206. Amsterdam: Rodopi, 1989.

McConnell, Anita. 'From Craft Workshop to Big Business – The London Scientific Instrument Trade's Response to Increasing Demand'. *The London Journal* 19, no. 1 (1994): 36–53.

McConnell, Anita. 'L.F. Marsigli (1658–1730): Early Contributions to Marine Science and Hydrography'. *International Hydrographic Review* 5, no. 2 (2004): 6–15.

McConnell, Anita. 'Origins of the Marine Barometer'. *Annals of Science* 62, no. 1 (2005): 83–101.

McGee, David. 'From Craftsmanship to Draftsmanship: Naval Architecture and the Three Traditions of Early Modern Design'. *Technology and Culture* 40, no. 2 (1999): 209–36.

McGowan, A. P. *The Century before Steam: The Development of the Sailing Ship 1700–1820*. Greenwich: HMSO, 1980.

McNeill, John R. *Mosquito Empires: Ecology and War in the Greater Caribbean, 1620–1914*. Cambridge: Cambridge University Press, 2010.

Meerkerk, Edwin van. 'The Correspondence Network of Christiaan Huygens (1629–1695)'. In *Les grands intermédiaires culturels de la république des letters: etudes des réseaux de correspondances du XVIe au XVIIIe siècles*, edited by Christiane Berkvens-Stevelinck, Hans Bots and Jens Häseler, 211–28. Paris: Honoré Champion, 2005.

Meinig, D. W. *The Shaping of America: A Geographical Perspective on 500 Years of History*, vol. I, *Atlantic America, 1492–1800*. New Haven: Yale University Press, 1986.

Menard, Russell. 'Transport Costs and Long-Range Trade 1300–1800: Was there a European "Transport Revolution" in the Early Modern Era?'. In *The Political Economy of Merchant Empires: State Power and World Trade 1350–1750*, edited by James Tracy, 228–75. Cambridge: Cambridge University Press, 1991.

Mercer, Vaudrey. *John Arnold & Son Chronometer Makers 1762-184*. London: Antiquarian Horological Society, 1972.

Mertens, Joost. 'The Honour of Dutch Seamen: Benjamin Franklin's Theory of Oil on Troubled Waters and Its Epistemological Aftermath'. *Physics Today* 59, no. 1 (2006): 36–41.

Mignolo, Walter D. *Local Histories/Global Designs: Coloniality, Subaltern Knowledges and Border Thinking*. Princeton: Princeton University Press, 2000.
Miller, David Philip. 'Longitude Networks on Land and Sea: The East India Company and Longitude Measurement "in the Wild"'. In *Navigational Enterprises in Europe and Its Empires, 1730–1880*, edited by Richard Dunn and Rebekah Higgitt, 223–47. London: Palgrave Macmillan, 2015.
Moch, Leslie Page, *Moving Europeans: Migration in Western Europe since 1650*. Bloomington: Indiana University Press, 1992.
Mokyr, Joel. *The Gifts of Athena: Historical Origins of the Knowledge Economy*. Princeton: Princeton University Press, 2002.
Mokyr, Joel. *The Enlightened Economy: An Economic History of Britain 1700–1850*. New Haven: Yale University Press, 2009.
Moogk, Peter. 'Manon's Fellow Exiles: Emigration from France to North America before 1763'. In *Europeans on the Move: Studies on European Migration, 1500–1800*, edited by Nicholas Canny, 236–60. Oxford: Oxford University Press, 1994.
Morgan, Mary. 'Travelling Facts'. In *How Well do Facts Travel? The Dissemination of Reliable Knowledge*, edited by Peter Howlett and Mary Morgan, 3–39. Cambridge: Cambridge University Press, 2011.
Morral, Frank and Barbara Ann White. *Hidden History of Nantucket*. Charleston: History Press, 2015.
Morrell, Jack and Arnold Thackray. *Gentlemen of Science: Early Years of the British Association for the Advancement of Science*. Oxford: Oxford University Press, 1981.
Morris, Richard B. *Government and Labor in Early America*. New York: Columbia University Press, 1946.
Morrison-Low, Alison D. *Making Scientific Instruments in the Industrial* Revolution. Aldershot: Ashgate, 2007.
Mörzer Bruyns, Willem F. J. 'Een octant en sextant van de firma Van Keulen'. *Jaarverslag Nederlands Historisch Scheepvaartmuseum 1980*, 33–7. Amsterdam: NHSM, 1981.
Mörzer Bruyns, Willem F. J. 'The Astronomical Clocks of Andreas Hohwü: A Checklist'. In *Making Scientific Instruments Count: Essays on Historical Instruments Presented to Gerard L'Estrange Turner*, edited by R. W. G. Anderson, J. A. Bennett and W. F. Ryan, 454–70. Aldershot: Variorum, 1993.
Mörzer Bruyns, Willem F. J. *Schip Recht door Zee. De octant in de Republiek in de achttiende eeuw*. Amsterdam: Edita, 2003.
Mörzer Bruyns, Willem F. J. 'Trade Labels: Evidence of English Octants and Sextants in America up to about 1860'. *Rittenhouse* 23, no. 1 (2009): 1–37.
Moya, Jose C. *Cousins and Strangers: Spanish Immigrants in Buenos Aires, 1850–1950*. Berkeley: University of California Press, 1998.
Mulert, F. E. 'Willem Bosman'. *Nieuw Nederlandsch Biografisch Woordenboek*, vol. 2, 229. The Hague: Martinus Nijhoff, 1912.
Murphy, Kathleen S. 'Translating the Vernacular: Indigenous and African Knowledge in the Eighteenth-Century British Atlantic'. *Atlantic Studies* 8, no. 1 (2011): 29–48.

Murphy, Kathleen S. 'Collecting Slave Traders: James Petiver, Natural History, and the British Slave Trade'. *The William and Mary Quarterly* 70, no. 4 (2013): 637–70.

Murray, Lori L. 'The Construction of Edmond Halley's 1701 Map of Magnetic Declination'. MA diss., School of Graduate and Postdoctoral Studies, University of Western Ontario, London, 2012.

Myers, Ransom A. 'Testing Ecological Models: The Influence of Catch Rates on Settlement of Fishermen in Newfoundland'. In *The Exploited Seas: New Directions for Marine Environmental History*, edited by Poul Holm, Tim D. Smith and David J. Starkey, 13–29. Liverpool: Liverpool University Press, 2001.

Neill, Anna. 'Buccaneer Ethnography: Nature, Culture, and Nation in the Journals of William Dampier'. *Eighteenth-Century Studies* 33, no. 2 (2000): 165–80.

Newson, Linda. 'Medical Practice in Early Colonial Spanish America: A Prospectus'. *Bulletin of Latin American Research* 25, no. 3 (2006): 367–91.

North, Douglass C. *Growth and Welfare in the American Past: A New Economic History*. Englewood Cliffs: Prentice-Hall, 1974.

North, Douglass C. 'Sources of Productivity Change in Ocean Shipping'. *Journal of Political Economy* 76, no. 5 (1968): 953–70.

North, Douglass C. *Institutions, Institutional Change and Economic Performance*. Cambridge: Cambridge University Press, 1990.

Northrup, David. *Indentured Labor in the Age of Imperialism, 1834–1922*. Cambridge: Cambridge University Press, 1995.

O'Flanagan, Patrick. *Port Cities of Atlantic Iberia, c. 1500–1900*. Aldershot: Ashgate, 2008.

Ogilvie, Brian. *The Science of Describing: Natural History in Renaissance Europe*. Chicago: University of Chicago Press, 2006.

Ogilvie, Brian. 'Correspondence Networks'. In *A Companion to the History of Science*, edited by Bernard Lightman, 358–71. Oxford: Oxford University Press, 2016.

Olmsted, John W. 'The Expedition of Jean Richer in Cayenne (1672–1673)'. *Isis* 34, no. 2 (1942): 117–28.

Olmsted, John W. 'The Voyage of Jean Richer in Acadia in 1670: A Study in the Relations of Science and Navigation under Colbert'. *Proceedings of the American Philosophical Society* 104 (1960): 612–35.

Oostindie, Gert and Jessica Vance Roitman. 'Repositioning the Dutch in the Atlantic, 1680–1800'. *Itinerario* 36, no. 2 (2012): 129–60.

O'Reilly, William. 'Movements of People in the Atlantic World, 1450–1850'. In *The Oxford Handbook of the Atlantic World 1450–1800*, edited by Nicholas Canny and Philip Morgan, 305–23. Oxford: Oxford University Press, 2011.

Ormrod, David. *The Rise of Commercial Empires: England and the Netherlands in the Age of Mercantilism, 1660–1770*. Cambridge: Cambridge University Press, 2003.

O'Rourke, Kevin H. and Jeffrey G. Williamson. *Globalization and History: The Evolution of a Nineteenth-Century Atlantic Economy*. Cambridge, MA: Harvard University Press, 2000.

O'Rourke, Kevin H. and Jeffrey G. Williamson. 'When Did Globalisation Begin?' *European Review of Economic History* 6, no. 1 (2002): 23–50.

Osborne, Michael A. *The Emergence of Tropical Medicine in France*. Chicago: University of Chicago Press, 2014.

Osterhammel, Jürgen. *Die Verwandlung der Welt. Eine Geschichte des 19.Jahrhunderts.* Munich: C.H. Beck, 2009.

Packard, J. J. 'Sir Robert Seppings and the Timber Problem'. *The Mariner's Mirror* 64, no. 2 (1978): 145–56.

Paesie, Ruud. *Lorrendrayen op Africa. De illegale goederen- en slavenhandel op West-Afrika tijdens het achttiende-eeuwse handelsmonopolie van de West-Indische Compagnie, 1700-1734*. Amsterdam: De Bataafsche Leeuw, 2008.

Paesie, Ruud. *Zeeuwse kaarten voor de VOC. Het kaartenmakersbedrijf van de kamer Zeeland in de 17de en 18de eeuw*. Zutphen: Walburg Pers, 2010.

Paine, Lincoln. *The Sea and Civilization: A Maritime History of the World*. New York: Vintage, 2013.

Parry, John H. *Trade and Dominion: The European Overseas Empires in the Eighteenth Century*. New York: Praeger Publishers, 1971.

Parry, John H. *The Spanish Seaborne Empire*, 3rd edn. London: Hutchinson, 1977.

Parsons, Christopher M. and Kathleen S. Murphy. 'Ecosystems under Sail: Specimen Transport in the Eighteenth-Century French and British Atlantics'. *Early American Studies: An Interdisciplinary Journal* 10, no. 3 (2012): 503–39.

Pearson, Michael. *The Indian Ocean*. London: Routledge, 2003.

Péaud, Laura. 'Les premières sociétés de géographie (Paris, Berlin, Londres). Entre coopération universaliste et concurrence nationale (1820–1860)'. *Terra Brasilis (Nova Série). Revista de rede Brasilieira de História da Geographia e Geografia Histórica* 5, no. 1 (2015). https://journals.openedition.org/terrabrasilis/1394.

Pel, J. Z. S. *Chirurgijns, doctoren, heelmeesters en artsen op het eiland Walcheren 1700–2000*. Middelburg: Koninklijk Zeeuwsch Genootschap der Wetenschappen, 2006.

Phillips, Denise. 'Academies and Societies'. In *A Companion to the History of Science*, edited by Bernard Lightman, 224–37. Oxford: Oxford University Press, 2016.

Pietschmann, Horst. 'Introduction: Atlantic History – History between European History and Global History'. In *Atlantic History: History of the Atlantic System, 1580–1830*, edited by Horst Pietschmann, 11–54. Göttingen: Vandenhoeck Ruprecht, 2002.

Pimentel, Juan. 'The Iberian Vision: Science and Empire in the Framework of a Universal Monarchy, 1500–1800', *Osiris* 15, no. 1 (2000): 17–30.

Pimentel, Juan. 'A Southern Meridian: Astronomical Undertakings in the Eighteenth-Century Spanish Empire'. In *Navigational Enterprises in Europe and Its Empires, 1730–1880*, edited by Richard Dunn and Rebekah Higgitt, 13–31. London: Palgrave Macmillan, 2015.

Pinault Sørensen, Madeleine. 'Les voyageurs artistes en Amérique du Sud au XVIIIe siècle'. In *Les naturalistes français en Amerique du Sud XVIe – XIXe siècles*, edited by Yves Laissus, 43–55. Paris: Éditions du Comité des travaux historiques et scientifiques, 1995.

Plumley, N. 'The Royal Mathematical School within Christ's Hospital'. *Vistas in Astronomy* 20, no. 1 (1976): 51–9.

Polónia, Amélia and Jack B. Owen. 'Cooperation-based Self-organizing Networks in Portuguese Expansion in the First Global Age, 1400–1800'. http://www.dyncoopnet-pt.org/working-papers/.

Pop, G. F. *De geneeskunde bij het Nederlandsche zeewezen*. Batavia: G. Kloff & Co., 1922.

Portuondo, María M. 'Cosmography at the Casa, Consejo, and Corte during the Century of Discovery'. In *Science in the Spanish and Portuguese Empires, 1500–1800*, edited by Daniela Bleichmar, Paula de Vos, Kristin Huffine and Kevin Sheehan, 57–77. Stanford: Stanford University Press, 2009.

Portuondo, María M. *Secret Science: Spanish Cosmography and the New World*. Chicago: University of Chicago Press, 2009.

Postma, Johannes. *The Dutch in the Atlantic Slave Trade* 1600–1815. Cambridge: Cambridge University Press, 1990.

Pouvreau, Nicolas. 'Les mesures du niveau de la mer à Brest d'hier à aujourd'hui'. In *Pour une histoire du Bureau des Longitudes (1795–1932)*, edited by Martina Schiavon and Laurent Rollet, 119–44. Nancy: Presses Universitaires de Lorraine, 2017.

Pratt, Mary Louise. *Imperial Eyes: Travel Writing and Transculturation*. London: Routledge, 1992.

Pritchard, James. 'From Shipwright to Naval Constructor: The Professionalization of 18th-Century French Naval Shipbuilders'. *Technology and Culture* 28, no. 1 (1987): 1–25.

Pritchard, James. *Louis XV's Navy 1748–1762: A Study of Organization and Administration*. Montreal: McGill – Queen's University Press, 1987.

Pritchard, James. *In Search of Empire: The French in the Americas, 1670–1730*. Cambridge: Cambridge University Press, 2004.

Pumfrey, Stephen. '"O tempora, O magnes!" A Sociological Analysis of the Discovery of Secular Magnetic Variation in 1634'. *British Journal for the History of Science* 22, no. 2 (1989): 181–214.

Pye, Michael. *The Edge of the World. How the North Sea Made Us Who We Are*. London: Penguin, 2014.

Quill, Humphrey. *John Harrison: The Man Who Found Longitude*. London: John Baker, 1966.

Raj, Kapil. *Relocating Modern Science: Circulation and the Construction of Knowledge in South Asia and Europe, 1650–1900*. London: Palgrave Macmillan, 2007.

Rao, Gautham. 'Sailor's Health and National Wealth: Marine Hospitals in the Early Republic'. *Common-place* 9, no. 10 (2008). www.commonplace.org.

Rasor, E. L. *Reform in the Royal Navy: A Social History of the Lower Deck 1850–1880*. Hamden: Archon Books, 1976.

Ratcliff, Marc J., 'Abraham Trembley's Strategy of Generosity and the Scope of Celebrity in the Mid-Eighteenth Century'. *Isis* 95 (2004): 555-75.

Rediker, Marcus. *Between the Devil and the Deep Blue Sea: Merchant Seamen, Pirates, and the Anglo-American Maritime World, 1700-1750*. Cambridge: Cambridge University Press, 1987.

Rediker, Marcus. *The Slave Ship: A Human History*. New York: Viking, 2007.

Regourd, François. 'French Science Overseas'. In *Imperialism and Science: Social Impact and Interaction*, edited by George N. Vlahakis et al., 19-49. Santa Barbara: ABC-CLIO, 2006.

Regourd, François. 'Capitale savante, capitale coloniale: Sciences et savoirs coloniaux à Paris aux XVII et XVIIIe siècles'. *Revue d'Histoire Moderne et Contemporaine* 55, no. 2 (2008): 121-51.

Regourd, François. 'Les lieux de savoir et d'expertise coloniale à Paris au XVIIIe siècle: institutions et enjeux savants'. In *Les mondes coloniaux à Paris au XVIIIe siècle. Circulation et enchevêtrement des savoirs*, edited by Anja Bandau, Marcel Dorigny and Rebekka von Mallinckrodt, 31-48. Paris: Karthala, 2010.

Reidy, Michael S. *Tides of History: Ocean Science and Her Majesty's Navy*. Chicago: University of Chicago Press, 2008.

Reidy, Michael S., Gary Kroll and Erik M. Conway. *Exploration and Science: Social Impact and Interaction*. Santa Barbara, 2007.

Reidy, Michael S. and Helen M. Rozwadowski. 'The Spaces in Between: Science, Ocean, Empire'. *Isis* 105, no. 2 (2014): 338-51.

Renn, Jürgen, ed. *The Globalization of Knowledge*. Berlin: Max Planck Institut für Wissenschaftsgeschichte, 2012.

Richards, John F. *The Unending Frontier: An Environmental History of the Early Modern World*, 2nd edn. Berkeley: University of California Press, 2005.

Ristow, Walter W. 'Lithography and Maps, 1796-1850'. In *Five Centuries of Map Printing*, edited by David Woodward, 77-112. Chicago: University of Chicago Press, 1975.

Ritchie, George S. *The Admiralty Chart: British Naval Hydrography in the Nineteenth Century*. London: Hollis & Carter, 1967.

Ritchie, Steve. 'A Brief History of 19th Century Deep Sea Sounding'. *International Hydrographic Review* 1, no. 1 (2000): 6-14.

Robert, Rudolph. *Chartered Companies and Their Role in the Development of Overseas Trade*. London: G. Bell & Sons, 1969.

Roberts, Lissa. 'Centres and Cycles of Accumulation'. In *Centres and Cycles of Accumulation in and around the Netherlands in the Early Modern Period*, edited by Lissa Roberts, 3-27. Zürich: LIT Verlag, 2011.

Roberts, Lissa. '"Le centre de toutes choses": Constructing and Managing Centralization on the Isle de France'. *History of Science* 52, no. 3 (2014): 319-42.

Robinson, Arthur H. *Early Thematic Mapping in the History of Cartography*. Chicago: University of Chicago Press, 1982.

Robinson, Robb and David J. Starkey. 'The Sea Fisheries of the British Isles, 1376–1976: A Preliminary Survey'. In *The North Atlantic Fisheries, 1100–1976: National Perspectives on a Common Resource*, edited by Poul Holm, David J. Starkey and Jón Th. Thór, 121–43. Esbjerg: Fiskeri- of Søfartsmuseet, 1996.

Rodger, Nicholas A. M. *The Command of the Sea: A Naval History of Britain, 1649–1815*. London: Penguin, 2004.

Romieux, Yannick. 'Histoire de l'École d'anatomie et de chirurgie navale de Rochefort (1722–1964)'. *Revue d'histoire de la pharmacie* 89, no. 332 (2001): 489–500.

Rönnbäck, Klas. 'The Speed of Ships and Shipping Productivity in the Age of Sail'. *European Review of Economic History* 16, no. 4 (2012): 469–89.

Rookmaker, Kees. *The Zoological Exploration of Southern Africa, 1650–1790*. Rotterdam: CRC Press, 1989.

Rosal, Miguel A. 'La exportación de cureros, lana y tasajo a través del Puerto de Buenos Aires entre 1835 y 1854'. *Anuario de studios Americanos* 55, no. 2 (1998): 565–88.

Rothschild, Emma. 'Late Atlantic History'. In *The Oxford Handbook of the Atlantic World 1450–1800*, edited by Nicholas Canny and Philip Morgan, 634–48. Oxford: Oxford University Press, 2011.

Rozwadowski, Helen M. *Fathoming the Ocean: The Discovery and Exploration of the Deep Sea*. Cambridge, MA: Harvard University Press, 2005.

Ruiz-Zorrilla, Ricardo Arroyo. *Apunte para una historia de la enseñanza de la nautica en España*. Madrid: Direccion General de la Marina Mercante, 1989.

Rupke, Nicholaas. 'Humboldtian Distribution Maps: The Spatial Ordering of Scientific Knowledge'. In *The Structure of Knowledge: Classifications of Science and Learning since the Renaissance*, edited by Tore Frängsmyr, 93–116. Berkeley: University of California Press, 2001.

Russell, Peter. *Prince Henry 'the Navigator': A Life*. New Haven: Yale University Press, 2001.

Russo, F. 'L' hydrographie en France au XVIIe et XVIIIe siècles: écoles et ouvrages d' enseignement'. In *Enseignement et diffusion des sciences en France au XVIIIe siècle*, edited by René Taton, 419–40. Paris: Hermann, 1964.

Rutten, Alfons M. G. *Dutch Transatlantic Medicine Trade of the Eighteenth Century under Cover of the West India Company*. Rotterdam: Erasmus Publishing, 2000.

Ryan, Shannon. *The Ice Hunters: A History of Newfoundland Sealing to 1914*. St. Johns: Breakwater Books, 1994.

Sachs, Aaron. *The Humboldt Current: Nineteenth-Century Exploration and the Roots of American Environmentalism*. New York: Viking, 2006.

Sadler, Donald H. 'Lunar Distances and the *Nautical Almanac*'. *Vistas in Astronomy* 20, no. 1 (1976): 113–21.

Safier, Neil. *Measuring the New World: Enlightenment Science and South America*. Chicago: University of Chicago Press, 2008.

Safier, Neil. 'Global Knowledge on the Move: Itineraries, Amerindian Narratives, and Deep Histories of Science'. *Isis* 101, no. 1 (2010): 133–45.

Saiz Carrero, A. 'Real Colegio de Cirugiá de San Carlos'. http://www.icomem.es/verD
ocumento.ashx?Id=35.
Sánchez-Albornoz, Nicolás. 'The First Transatlantic Transfer: Spanish Migration
to the New World, 1493–1810'. In *Europeans on the Move: Studies on European
Migration, 1500–1800*, edited by Nicholas Canny, 26–36. Oxford: Oxford
University Press, 1994.
Sandman, Alison. 'Controlling Knowledge, Navigation, Cartography, and Secrecy in the
Early Modern Spanish Atlantic'. In *Science and Empire in the Atlantic World*, edited
by James Delbourgo and Nicholas Dew, 31–51. New York: Routledge, 2008.
Sanger, Chesley W. 'Sail versus Steam: Post 1863 Technological and Spatial Adaptation
in the Newfoundland Seal Fishery'. *Newfoundland and Labrador Studies* 23, no. 2
(2008): 139–69.
Scammell, Geoffrey V., *The World Encompassed: The First European Maritime Empires
c. 800–1650*. London: Methuen, 1981.
Schaffer, Simon. '"The Charter'd Thames": Naval Architecture and Experimental Spaces
in Georgian Britain'. In *The Mindful Hand. Inquiry and Invention from the Late
Renaissance to Early Industrialization*, edited by Lissa Roberts, Simon Schaffer and
Peter Dear, 279–305. Amsterdam: Edita, 2007.
Schaffer, Simon. 'Instruments, Surveys and Maritime Empire'. In *Empire, the Sea
and Global History: Britain's Maritime World, c. 1760 –c. 1840*, edited by David
Cannadine, 83–104. London: Palgrave Macmillan, 2007.
Schiavon, Martine. 'The Bureau des Longitudes: An Institutional Study'. In *Navigational
Enterprises in Europe and Its Empires, 1730–1880*, edited by Richard Dunn and
Rebekah Higgitt, 63–85. London: Palgrave Macmillan, 2015.
Schiavon, Martine and Lauret Rollet. 'Pour une histoire du Bureau des longitudes
(1795–1932)'. In *Pour une histoire du Bureau des longitudes (1795–1932)*, edited
by Martine Schiavon and Lauret Rollet, 11–22. Nancy: Presses Universitaires de
Lorraine, 2017.
Schiebinger, Londa. *Plants and Empire: Colonial Bioprospecting in the Atlantic World*.
Cambridge, MA: Harvard University Press, 2004.
Schiebinger, Londa. 'Prospecting for Drugs: European Naturalists in the West Indies'.
In *Colonial Botany: Science, Commerce, and Politics in the Early Modern World*,
edited by Londa Schiebinger and Claudia Swan, 119–33. Philadelphia: University of
Pennsylvania Press, 2007.
Schilder, Günther and Willem F. J. Mörzer Bruyns. 'Navigatie'. In *Maritieme
Geschiedenis der Nederlanden*, edited by Frank J. A. Broeze, Jaap R. Bruijn and
Femme S. Gaastra, 191–225, Vol. 3. Bussum: De Boer Maritiem, 1977.
Schlee, Susan. *The Edge of an Unfamiliar World: A History of Oceanography*. New York:
Dutton, 1973.
Schmidt, Benjamin. *Innocence Abroad: The Dutch Imagination and the New World,
1570–1670*. Cambridge: Cambridge University Press, 2001.

Schmit, Roberto and Miguel A. Rosal. 'Las exportaciones del Litoral Argentino al Puerto de Buenos Aires entre 1783 y 1850'. *Revista de Historia Economica* 13, no. 3 (1995): 581–607.
Schnurmann, Claudia. *Atlantische Welten: Engländer und Niederländeer im amerikanisch-atlantischen Raum, 1648–1713*. Cologne: Böhlau, 1998.
Schnurmann, Claudia. 'Atlantic Trade and Regional Identities: The Creation of Supranational Atlantic Systems in the 17th Century'. In *Atlantic History: History of the Atlantic System, 1580–1830*, edited by Horst Pietschmann, 179–97. Göttingen: Vandenhoeck & Ruprecht, 2002.
Schwartz, Stuart B. 'The Iberian Atlantic to 1650'. In *The Oxford Handbook of the Atlantic World*, edited by Nicholas Canny and Philip Morgan, 147–64. Oxford: Oxford University Press, 2011.
Schwarz, Angela. 'Intersecting Anglo-German Networks in Popular Science and their Functions in the Late Nineteenth Century'. In *Anglo-German Scholarly Networks in the Long Nineteenth-Century*, edited by Heather Ellis and Ulrike Kirchberger, 65–83. Leiden: Brill, 2014.
Secord, James A. 'Knowledge in Transit'. *Isis* 95, no. 4 (2004): 654–72.
Sellés, Manuel. 'Los instrumentos y su contexto. El caso de la marina Española en el siglo XVIII'. *Éndoxa: Series Filosóficas* 10 (2005): 137–58.
Serrano Ávarez, José Manuel. 'Los inicios del astillero de La Habana en el siglo XVIII y la influencia francesa'. *História* 30, no. 1 (2011): 287–304.
Serrano Ávarez, José Manuel. 'Él poder y la gloria: Élites y asientos militares en el astillero de La Habana durente el siglo XVIII'. *Studia Histórica: Historia moderna* 35 (2013): 99–125.
Shannon Baker, Alexi. 'The London Instrument Trade, from Culpeper to Cole'. In *Who Needs Scientific Instruments? Conference on Scientific Instruments and Their Users 20-22 October 2005*, edited by Bart Grob and Hans Hooijmaijers, 99–105. Leiden: Museum Boerhaave, 2006.
Sheehan, Jonathan and Dror Wahrman. *Invisible Hands: Self-organization and the Eighteenth Century*. Chicago: University of Chicago Press, 2015.
Shepherd, James F. and Gary M. Walton. *Shipping, Maritime Trade, and the Economic Development of Colonial North America*. Cambridge: Cambridge University Press, 1972.
Sheridan, Richard B. *Doctors and Slaves: A Medical and Demographic History of Slavery in the British West Indies, 1680–1834*. Cambridge: Cambridge University Press, 1985.
Sjostrom, W. 'Safety Regulation at Sea: Deck Load Laws and the 19th Century Timber Trade'. *International Journal of Transport Economics* 27, no. 3 (2000): 303–13.
Slotten, Hugh Richard. *Patronage, Practice and the Culture of American Science: Alexander Dallas Bache and the U.S. Coast Survey*. Cambridge: Cambridge University Press, 1994.
Smith, Elise Juzda. '"Cleanse or Die": British Naval Hygiene in the Age of Steam, 1840–1900'. *Medical History* 62, no. 2 (2018): 177–98.

Smith, Jason W. 'Matthew Fontaine Maury: Pathfinder'. *International Journal of Maritime History* 28, no. 2 (2016): 411-20.
Snelders, Stephen. *Vrijbuiters van de heelkunde. Op zoek naar medische kennis in de tropen, 1600-1800.* Amsterdam: Atlas, 2012.
Sobel, Dava. *Longitude: The True Story of a Lone Genius Who Solved the Greatest Scientific Problem of His Time.* London: Walker, 1995.
Solar, Peter M. 'Opening to the East: Shipping between Europe and Asia, 1770-1830'. *Journal of Economic History* 73, no. 3 (2013): 625-61.
Solar, Peter M. 'Late Eighteenth-Century Merchant Ships in War and Peace'. *International Journal of Maritime History* 28, no. 1 (2016): 36-63.
Solar, Peter M. and Klas Rönnbäck. 'Copper Sheathing and the British Slave Trade'. *Economic History Review* 68, no. 3 (2015): 806-29.
Solar, Peter M. and Luc Hens. 'Ship Speeds during the Industrial Revolution: East India Company Ships, 1770-1828'. *European Review of Economic History* 20, no. 1 (2015): 66-78.
Solar, Peter M. and Pim de Zwart. 'Why Were Dutch East Indiamen So Slow?' *International Journal of Maritime History* 29, no. 4 (2017): 738-51.
Soll, Jacob. *The Information Master: Jean-Baptiste Colbert's Secret State Intelligence System.* Ann Arbor: University of Michigan Press, 2009.
Sorrenson, Richard. 'The State's Demand for Accurate Astronomical and Navigational Instruments in Eighteenth-Century Britain'. In *The Consumption of Culture 1600-1800*, edited by Ann Bermington and John Brewer, 263-71. London: Routledge, 1995.
Sorrenson, Richard. *Perfect Mechanics: Instrument Makers at the Royal Society of London in the Eighteenth Century.* Boston: Docent Press, 2013.
Sparks, Randy J. *Where the Negroes are Masters: An African Port in the Era of the Slave Trade.* Cambridge, MA: Harvard University Press, 2014.
Speelman, Jennifer L. 'The United States Navy and the Genesis of Maritime Education'. *Transactions of the American Philosophical Society* 97, no. 4 (2007): 65-82.
Spek, H. *Tijdmeters en waarnemingshorloges van de Departementen van Marine en Koloniën in de negentiende eeuw.* Oegstgeest: MEOB, 1982.
Stack, Margaret. 'Matthew Fontaine Maury: Scientist'. *International Journal of Maritime History* 28, no. 2 (2016): 394-401.
Stangl, Werner. *Zwischen Authentizität und Fiktion. Die private Korrespondenz Spanischer Emigranten aus Amerika, 1492-1824.* Vienna: Böhlau, 2012.
Starkey, David J. and Michael Haines. 'The Newfoundland Fisheries, c. 1500-1900: A British Perspective'. In *The Exploited Seas: New Directions for Marine Environmental History*, edited by Poul Holm, Tim D. Smith and David J. Starkey, 1-11. Liverpool: Liverpool University Press, 2001.
Stearns, Raymond Phineas. *Science in the British Colonies of America.* Urbana: University of Illinois Press, 1970.

Steckel, Richard H. and Richard A. Jensen. 'New Evidence on the Causes of Slave and Crew Mortality in the Atlantic Slave Trade'. *Journal of Economic History* 46, no. 1 (1986): 57–77.

Steele, Ian K. *The English Atlantic 1675–1740: An Exploration of Communication and Community*. New York: Oxford University Press, 1986.

Steinberg, Philip E. *The Social Construction of the Ocean*. Cambridge: Cambridge University Press, 2001.

Stewart, Hamish Maxwell and Ralph Shlomowitz. 'Mortality and Migration: A Survey'. In *Health and Medicine at Sea, 1700–1900*, edited by David Boyd Haycock and Sally Archer, 128–42. Woodbridge: Boydell Press, 2009.

Storr, Christopher. 'Health, Sickness and Medical Services in Spain's Armed Forces c. 1665–1700'. *Medical History* 50, no. 3 (2006): 325–50.

Studnicki-Gizbert, Daviken. *A Nation upon the Ocean Sea: Portugal's Atlantic Diaspora and the Crisis of the Spanish empire, 1492–1640*. Oxford: Oxford University Press, 2007.

Suberchichot, Jean-Luc. 'Le corps des officiers de santé de la Marine'. In *Le homme, la santé et la mer*, edited by Christian Buchet, 317–31. Paris: Honoré Champion, 1997.

Subrahmanyam, Sanjay. *L'empire portugais d'Asie 1500-1700*. Paris: Éditions Points, 2013.

Sullivan, F. B. 'The Naval Schoolmaster during the Eighteenth and Early Nineteenth Century'. *The Mariner's Mirror* 62, no. 4 (1976): 311–26.

Taylor, George R. *The Transportation Revolution 1815-1860*. London: Routledge, 1977.

Thompson, Michael D. *Working on the Dock of the Bay: Labor and Enterprise in an Antebellum Southern Port*. Columbia: University of South Carolina Press, 2015.

Thompson, William. *Mathematical and Physical Papers*, vol. VI. Cambridge: Cambridge University Press, 1911.

Thornton, John K. *Africa and Africans in the Making of the Atlantic world, 1400–1800*. Cambridge: Cambridge University Press, 1998.

Tikoff, Valentina K. 'Saint Elmo's Orphans: Navigation Education and Training at the Royal School of San Telmo in Seville during the Eighteenth Century'. *International Journal of Maritime History* 20, no. 1 (2008): 1–32.

Turner, A. J. 'Mathematical Instrument-Making in Early Modern Paris'. In *Luxury Trades and Consumerism in Ancien Régime Paris: Studies in the History of the Skilled Workforce*, edited by Robert Fox and Anthony Turner, 63–96. Aldershot: Ashgate, 1998.

Ultee, Maarten. 'The Republic of Letters: Learned Correspondence, 1680–1720'. *Seventeenth Century* 2, no. 1 (1987): 95–112.

Unger, Richard W. *Dutch Shipbuilding before 1800*. Assen: Van Gorcum, 1978.

Valverde, Nuria and Antonio Lafuente. 'Space Production and Spanish Imperial Policies'. In *Science in the Spanish and Portuguese Empires*, edited by Daniela Bleichmar, Paula de Vos, Kristin Huffine and Kevin Sheehan, 198–215. Stanford: Stanford University Press, 2009.

Vanvaerenbergh, Michel and Peter Ifland. *Line of Position Navigation: Sumner and Saint Hilaire, the Two Pillars of Modern Celestial Navigation*. Bloomington: Unlimited Publishing, 2003.
Vasey, Thomas Watson Cornforth. 'The Emergence of Examinations for British Shipmasters and Mates, 1830 – 1850'. PhD diss. Durham University, Durham, 1980. http://etheses.dur.ac.uk/7567/.
Vaughan, Richard. *In Search of Arctic Birds*. London: T & A D Poyser, 1992.
Vicente Maroto, Ma. Isabel. 'Los cosmógrafos españoles del siglo XVI: del humanista al técnico'. In *Más allá de la Leyenda Negra. España y la Revolución Científica*, edited by Victor Navarro Brotóns and William Eamon, 347–69. Valencia: CSIC, 2007.
Vickers, Daniel. 'The First Whalemen of Nantucket'. *The William and Mary Quarterly* 40, no. 4 (1983): 560–83.
Vickers, Daniel. 'Nantucket Whalemen in the Deep-sea Fishery: The Changing Anatomy of an Early American Labor Force'. *The Journal of American History* 72, no. 2 (1985): 277–96.
Vickers, Daniel. *Young Men and the Sea: Yankee Seafarers in the Age of Sail*. New Haven: Yale University Press, 2005.
Ville, Simon. 'Total Factor Productivity in the English Shipping Industry: The North-East Coal Trade, 1700–1850'. *Economic History Review* 20, no. 3 (1986): 355–70.
Vittu, Jean-Pierre. 'Henry Oldenburg, "Grand Intermédiaire"'. In *Les grands intermédiaires culturels de la république des letters: etudes des réseaux de correspondances du XVIe au XVIIIe siècles*, edited by Christiane Berkvens-Stevelinck, Hans Bots and Jens Häseler, 183–209. Paris: Honoré Champion, 2005.
Voeks, Robert. 'African Medicine and Magic in the Americas'. *Geographical Review* 83, no. 1 (1993): 66–78.
Vogel, Klaus A. 'Cosmography'. In *The Cambridge History of Science*, vol. 3, *Early Modern Science*, edited by Katharine Park and Lorraine Daston, 469–96. Cambridge: Cambridge University Press, 2006.
Vries, Jan de. 'Connecting Europe and Asia: A Quantitative Analysis of the Cape-Route Trade, 1497–1795'. In *Global Connections and Monetary History, 1470–1800*, edited by Dennis O. Flynn, Arturo Giráldez and Richard von Glahn, 35–106. Aldershot: Ashgate, 2003.
Vries, Jan de. 'The Dutch Atlantic Economies'. In *The Atlantic Economy during the Seventeenth and Eighteenth Centuries*, edited by Peter A. Coclanis, 1–29. Columbia: University of South Carolina Press, 2005.
Vries, Jan de. 'The Limits of Globalization in the Early Modern World'. *Economic History Review* 63, no. 3 (2010): 710–33.
Walbrink, Henk, Frits Koek and Theo Brandsma. *The US Maury Collection Metadata 1796 – 1861*. De Bilt: KNMI, 2009.
Walton, Gary M. 'A Measure of Productivity Change in American Colonial Shipping'. *Economic History Review* 21, no. 2 (1968): 268–82.

Walton, Gary M. 'Obstacles to Technical Diffusion in Ocean Shipping'. *Explorations in Economic History* 8, no. 2 (1970): 123–40.

Warner, Deborah J. 'American Octants and Sextants: The Early Years'. *Rittenhouse* 3, no. 3 (1989): 86–112.

Warnsinck, J. C. M. *De Kweekschool voor de Zeevaart en de stuurmanskunst 1785–1935*. Amsterdam: Vaderlandsch Fonds, 1935.

Waters, David W. *The Art of Navigation in England in Elizabethan and Early Stuart Times*. London: Hollis & Carter, 1958.

Waters, David W. 'The English Pilot: English Sailing Directions and Charts and the Rise of English Shipping, 16th to 18th Centuries'. *Journal of Navigation* 42, no. 3 (1989): 317–55.

Webb, Adrian. 'The Expansion of British Naval Hydrographic Administration, 1808–1829'. PhD diss., University of Exeter, Exeter, 2010.

Wendt, Helge. *Die Missionarische Gesellschaft. Mikrostrukturen einer kolonialen Globalisierung*. Wiesbaden: Frans Steiner Verlag, 2011.

Wess, Jane. 'Navigation and Mathematics: A Match Made in the Heavens?' In *Navigational Enterprises in Europe and Its Empires, 1730–1880*, edited by Richard Dunn and Rebekah Higgitt, 201–22. London: Palgrave Macmillan, 2015.

Wheeler, Alwyne C. 'The Gronovius Fish Collection: A Catalogue and Historical Account'. *Bulletin of the British Museum (Nat.Hist.)* Hist.Ser. 1, no. 5 (1958): 185–249.

Wheeler, Alwyne C. 'Peter Artedi, Founder of Modern Ichthyology'. In *Proceedings V Congress of European Ichthyology*, 3–10. Stockholm, 1985.

Widmalm, Sven. 'Accuracy, Rhetoric, and Technology: The Paris-Greenwich Triangulation, 1784-1788'. In *The Quantifying Spirit in the 18th Century*, edited by Tore Frängsmyr, John L. Heilbron and Robin E. Rider, 179–206. Berkeley: University of California Press, 1990.

Widmalm, Sven. 'A Commerce of Letters: Astronomical Communication in the 18th Century'. *Science Studies* 5, no. 2 (1992): 43–58.

Wigelsworth, J. R. *Selling Science in the Age of Newton: Advertising and the Commoditization of Knowledge*. Aldershot: Ashgate, 2010.

Wigen, Kären. 'Introduction: AHR Forum Oceans of History'. *American Historical Review* 111, no. 3 (2006): 717–21.

Wilcox, Martin. '"These Peaceable Times are the Devil": Royal Navy Officers in the Post-war Slump, 1815–1825'. *International Journal of Maritime History* 26, no. 3 (2014): 471–88.

Williams, David M. 'Mid-Victorian Attitudes to Seamen and Maritime Reform: The Society for Improving the Condition of Merchant Seamen, 1867'. *International Journal for Maritime History* 3, no. 1 (1991): 101–26.

Williams, David M. 'James Silk Buckingham: Sailor, Explorer and Maritime Reformer'. In *Merchant and Mariners: Selected Writings of David M. Williams*, 109–26. St. Johns: Marquis, 2000.

Williams, Glyn. *Arctic Labyrinth: The Quest for the Northwest Passage*. Berkeley: University of California Press, 2010.
Williams, Glyn. *Naturalists at Sea: Scientific Travellers from Dampier to Darwin*. New Haven: Yale University Press, 2013.
Wing, John F. 'Shipping Productivity in Maryland's Tobacco Trade, 1689-1759'. *International Journal of Maritime History* 20, no. 2 (2008): 223-40.
Wing, John F. *Roots of Empire: Forests and State Power in Early Modern Spain, 1500-1750*. Leiden: Brill, 2015.
Winroth, Anders. *The Age of the Vikings*. Princeton: Princeton University Press, 2014.
Winterer, Caroline. 'Where Is America in the Republic of Letters?' *Modern Intellectual History* 9, no. 3 (2012): 593-623.
Witt, Jann M. 'Education and Training: Nautical Certification'. In *The Oxford Encyclopedia of Maritime History*, edited by John B. Hattendorf, vol. II, 632-48. Oxford: Oxford University Press, 2007.
Woodruff, Scott D., Steven J. Worley and Richard W. Reynolds. 'Early Ship Observational Data and Icoads'. *Climatic Change* 73, no. 1-2 (2005): 169-94.
Wright, Thomas. 'Mark Beaufoy's Nautical and Hydraulic Experiments'. *The Mariner's Mirror* 75, no. 4 (1989): 313-27.
Yeo, Richard. *Defining Science: William Whewell, Natural Knowledge, and Public Debate in Early Victorian Britain*. Cambridge: Cambridge University Press, 1993.
Zahedieh, Nuala. *The Capital and the Colonies: London and the Atlantic Economy 1660-1700*. Cambridge: Cambridge University Press, 2010.
Zanden, Jan Luiten van and Arthur van Riel. *The Strictures of Inheritance: The Dutch Economy in the Nineteenth Century*. Princeton: Princeton University Press, 2000.
Zanden, Jan Luiten van and Pim de Zwart. *The Origins of Globalization: World Trade in the Making of the Global Economy, 1500-1800*. Cambridge: Cambridge University Press, 2018.
Zandvliet, Kees. *Mapping for Money: Maps, Plans and Topographic Paintings and their Role in Dutch Overseas Expansion during the 16th and 17th Centuries*. Amsterdam: Batavian Lion, 1998.
Zolberg, Aristide R. *A Nation by Design: Immigration Policy in the Fashioning of America*. Cambridge, MA: Harvard University Press, 2006.
Zuidervaart, Huib J. *Van'konstgenoten' en hemelse fenomenen. Nederlandse sterrenkunde in de achttiende eeuw*. Rotterdam: Erasmus Publishing, 1999.
Zuidervaart, Huib J. 'An Eighteenth-Century Medical-Meteorological Society in the Netherlands: An Investigation of Early Organization, Instrumentation and Quantification'. *British Journal for the History of Science* 28, no. 4 (2005): 379-410; no. 5 (2006): 49-66.
Zuylen, Jan van. 'Jan en Harmanus van Deijl. Een optische werkplaats in de 18e eeuw'. *Tijdschrift voor de Geschiedenis der Geneeskunde, Wiskunde, Natuurwetenschappen en Techniek* 10, no. 2 (1987): 208-28.

Index

Académie Royale de Marine   15, 122
Académie Royale des Sciences   15–16, 35, 37–9, 41, 52, 55, 62, 98, 192
accommodation   180, 216, 223, 230
Admiralties (Dutch)   49, 106, 115–16, 129, 133
Admiralty (Royal Navy)   94, 103, 108, 114–15, 119, 128, 141, 167, 172, 174–5, 186–90, 193, 200–1, 204, 206–7, 212, 215, 218, 221, *see also* English/British Navy
Africa   11–12, 18, 29, 53, 58–9, 66, 69–72, 84, 90–1, 96, 103–7, 109, 114, 136, 147, 154, 178
   North   114
   South   49, 177, 221 (*see also* Cape Colony; Cape of Good Hope)
   West   18, 25, 31, 46, 51–2, 57, 60, 84, 86, 99, 135, 155–6, 159, 161, 167, 179, 186
   West Central   18
air pressure   62, 144
Airy, George Biddell   175, 188, 190
Allamand, Jean   132–3
altitude-measuring instruments   61, 63–4, 93, *see also* back-staff; cross-staff; octant; reflecting circle; sextant; *spiegelboog*
America/Americas   4, 8, 11, 18, 25, 28–9, 30–1, 33, 36–7, 46, 51–3, 56, 59, 64–7, 69, 84, 86–7, 89–90, 96, 98–100, 103, 109, 111, 118, 130–1, 137, 142, 147, 154–6, 158–9, 178, 221
   Central   11, 86, 160
   North   28, 30–1, 42, 58–9, 64–5, 84–5, 90–1, 93, 100, 108, 114–15, 118–19, 131, 134–6, 142, 154, 158–9, 167, 177 (*see also* Canada; United States)
   South   11, 61, 66, 91, 131, 153, 156, 160, 167–8, 186 (*see also* Brazil; Guiana; Spanish America; Suriname)

American Atlantic   20–1, 227
Amerindians   51–2, 57, 78, 135, 228, *see also* Inuit; Native Americans
Amsterdam   25, 47–50, 54, 56, 59, 73, 75–6, 92, 96, 99, 102, 108, 112, 115–16, 118–22, 125, 129–30, 134, 142, 145–6, 197, 199, 202, 205, 213–14
anatomy   39, 47, 56, 70, 127, 129–30
anchorage   25, 186, 195
Anderson, Johann   146
Angola   109
animals   4, 37, 55, 57, 75–6, 106, 137, 145–6, 182, 221
apothecaries   39, 129, 144
apprentices   18, 43, 45, 121, 204
D'Après de Mannevillette, Jean-Baptiste-Nicolas-Denis   98, 122, 144
Arctic   54, 157, 183–4, 189–90, 221
Argentina   156, 160, 167
armament   50, 89
Artedi, Peter   144–5
Asia   126, 144, 154–5, 158, 160, 162, 178, 200, 207
asiento   56
associations   111, 131, 133, 209–10, 212, 214
Astronomer Royal   43, 93, 116, 175, 187–8, 190
astronomers   33, 38, 63, 93–4, 116, 190, 193
astronomy   3, 25, 38, 41, 43, 47, 116, 147, 188, 193, 196, 198, 210
Atlantic history   12, 14, 18, 226
Atlantic Ocean   9, 11–13, 18, 25, 27, 42, 58, 60–1, 74, 87, 99–100, 140, 162, 221, 226–7
   Middle   111
   North Atlantic   11, 25–6, 54, 67, 130, 146, 157, 170, 182–4
   North-West Atlantic   29–30, 86, 147
   South Atlantic   49, 112, 153–4, 156–158, 160–1, 167, 182

Atlantic system   10, 46, 226
Atlantic world   3–7, 10–14, 18–21, 27, 31, 46, 50, 53, 58, 77–8, 84, 87–8, 102, 110, 117–19, 122, 126, 131, 136, 140, 143, 147, 149, 153–5, 160–2, 184–5, 202, 209–210, 221–2, 224, 226–32
  defined   13–14
atlases   25–7, 38, 59–60, 76, 78, 96–8, 114–15
Australia   158–60, 171, 177–8, 180–1, 207
Azores   59, 65, 86, 98, 114

BAAS, *see* British Association for the Advancement of Science
Bache, Alexander Dallas   196, 198, 202, 211, 218
back-staff (Davis's quadrant)   61, 93, 120
Baffin Island   30, 157, 190
Bahamas   45, 65, 67
Bailyn, Bernard   10
ballast   125, 165
Banks, Joseph   189
Barbados   65, 89, 103
Barcelona   35, 56, 111, 121, 128
barometer, marine   62–3, 140, 168, 190, 219
Barrow, John   189–90
Basques   30, 103
Batavia   48, 73, 126, 141, 158
Bayly, Chris   7–8, 232
beacons   134
Beaufort, Francis   174, 186–91, 198, 210, 223
Beautemps-Beaupré, Charles-François   191, 198
Belgium   170, 199
Bellin, Jacques-Nicolas   42, 96, 98, 122
bellows   83, 107, 139
Berlin   2–5, 7, 9, 210
Bermuda   65, 114
Berthoud, Ferdinand   1, 118–19
Bight of Benin   18, 109
Bight of Biafra   51, 109, 221
Binnema, Ted   17, 51
birds   13, 45, 66–8, 76, 79, 95, 149, 190, 221, 227, 230
Blagden, Charles   98–9, 144
Blane, Gilbert   100, 102–4, 126, 129, 140, 175–6
blocks   165

'blue hole'   5, 12, 232
Board of Longitude   1, 44, 92, 94, 121, 187, 189–90, 192–3, 209, 224
Board of Trade (UK)   42, 177, 191, 201, 215
boatmen   51, 135
Boerhaave, Herman   55, 104
Bolster, Jeffrey   135
Bosman, Willem   52, 69
Boston   63, 85, 134, 157, 159, 165, 208, 214
botanical gardens   33, 47–8, 51, 75, 78, 137, 143
botany   41, 47, 56, 210
Bougainville, Louis-Antoine de   16, 87
Bouguer, Pierre   122–3
Boyle, Robert   53, 76
braces   164, 205
Brandenburg   19, 25, 27
Brazil   11–12, 21, 30, 48–9, 52, 71, 86, 153–4, 156, 159, 178
Brendecke, Arndt   8, 14, 32, 36
Brest   15, 39, 41, 122–3, 177, 180, 192, 206
Bristol   119
Britain   1, 11, 16, 27, 42, 44–5, 51, 56–7, 64–5, 83–6, 91, 94–5, 99–100, 103–4, 107, 113–16, 118–21, 123–5, 128, 130–1, 133, 139, 148, 155–60, 162, 164, 166–8, 170–1, 174, 177–8, 181–2, 185–6, 188–9, 191, 193–7, 199–203, 205–11, 213–16, 218–20, 221–4, 230–1, *see also* British Isles; England; Ireland; Scotland
British Association for the Advancement of Science (BAAS)   188–91, 209–11, 218, 224
British Atlantic   46, 56, 77, 131, 154
British/English empire   28, 46, 137, 154
British Isles   84–5, 123, 172, 182, 188, *see also* Britain; England; Ireland; Scotland
brokers   161, 220
Brussels conference   168, 170, 191, 194, 196, 198, 208–9, 218, 224, 230
Buenos Aires   142, 156
buoys   134
Bureau des Longitudes   117, 189, 192–4, 196, 209, 222, 224
Burke, Peter   7–8
Buys Ballot, Christopher   168, 171, 198, 211

cabinets   76, 78
Cádiz   35, 98, 111, 113, 117–18, 127–8, 142, 196
Caesar's cure   57
California   158–9, 171, 214
Cambridge   102, 188, 190
Cameroons   155
Canada   31, 37–40, 59, 64, 136, 159, 165, 182–3
Canary Islands   99, 114
Canny, Nicholas   10, 87, 154
canoes   51, 135
Cape Breton   59, 85, 98, 132
Cape Colony   49, 100
Cape Horn   86, 134, 157–9, 162, 167, 170
Cape of Good Hope   11–12, 31, 46, 48, 64, 95, 98, 134, 137, 158–9, 167, 174, 187, 189, 203
Cape Verde islands   18, 106
capstans   165
captains   43, 46, 53, 60, 65, 76, 92, 94, 98–9, 101, 103–4, 106, 115, 126, 131–2, 153, 161, 166–7, 170, 172–3, 183, 190, 200, 212, 215, 218, *see also* shipmasters
cargo   57, 90, 125–6, 134, 142, 163–6
Caribbean   11, 18, 25, 28–30, 38–9, 41–2, 46, 52, 58, 64–6, 69, 72, 84–7, 90, 107, 109, 114, 135, 187, 221, *see also* West-Indies
Cartagena   26, 28, 56, 65, 100
cartographic aids   98, 113–16, 197, *see also* atlases; charts; maps; rutters; sailing directions
cartography   15, 34, 121–2, 168, 229, *see also* charts; hydrography; map-making
Casa de la Contratación   8, 32, 35
Catesby, Mark   45, 67, 75
Cayenne   52, 98
certificates of competence   201, 214, *see also* examinations
Charleston   85, 135, 156, 173
charts   25, 38, 42, 48, 59–61, 75–6, 78, 87, 96–8, 110, 113–17, 122, 139, 143–4, 147–8, 166–71, 173–4, 186–9, 191, 194–7, 217–18, 220, 228
  Admiralty   167, 187
  bathymetric   220

isogonic   61, 64, 95–6, 174
isomaps   188, 217
Mercator   25, 59, 173
thematic   60–1, 78, 168
track   168, 170
Chatham   45, 204
Chaunu, Pierre   11–12
Chesapeake   65, 85, 89, 135
Chile   38, 156–7, 159, 162, 170
China   19, 155, 157–9, 182
chronometer, marine   1, 49, 62, 64, 74, 83, 93–5, 121–2, 139, 172–3, 187, 190, 194, 197, 202
circulation of knowledge   8–9, 20–2, 26, 31–5, 50–1, 53, 57, 78–9, 104, 110, 122, 125, 127, 130, 132–4, 136, 143, 148, 161, 185, 189, 204, 212, 224, 227–31
climate   13, 54, 70, 105, 109, 144, 180, 227
clothing   102, 138, 182
coastal profiles/views   25, 95, 114
Coast Guard (UK)   188
Cockburn, William   71–2, 77, 104
coffee   84, 158
Colbert, Jean-Baptiste   8, 15, 36–42, 77–8, 123
collectivization   185, 224, 230
collectors of naturalia   55–7, 68
Collen, Caspar van   73, 75, 140
Colonial Land and Emigration Commission (UK)   207
colonial machine   14–6, 40–1, 127
colonists   15, 29–30, 51–2, 78, 131
commercial machine   14, 16–7, 50–3, 78, 110–11, 126, 130, 148, 154, 209, 227–9, *see also* long-distance corporations; trading companies
  defined   16–17
communication   4, 8, 11, 19, 27–8, 32, 37, 40–1, 50–1, 55, 58, 76, 79, 137, 141–2, 149, 160, 219–20, 231
Compagnie des Indes   19, 41, 106, 113–14, 122, 154
Compass Department (UK)   189
compasses   61, 120, 168, 189
  Admiralty Standard   175
  azimuth   219
  bearing   61
  steering   174

surveying   118
compass needle   44, 95, 174
   deviation of   175, *see also* iron
   variation of   44, 60-1, 64, 95-6,
      see also magnetic declination
computers (calculators)   116-17, 211, 224
conferences (scientific)   168, 191, 194, 198, 208-9, 218-19, 224, 230,
      see also Brussels conference
consuls   177, 199
contracting by the state   44-5, 47, 125, 128, 130, 203, 207, 223
contrayerva   52, 79
convicts   30, 100, 109, 158, 177-8, 180, 207
convoys   32
Cook, James   16, 87, 94, 103-4, 108, 114, 139
copper sheathing   91, 108, 141, 164, 178
correspondence networks   18, 55-6, 63, 78, 131, 209
cost-benefit calculations   107-8
cotton   156, 165
Council of the Indies   8, 32, 35, 143
courses (of ships)   64-5, 96, 134, 170, 195
Creoles   34, 70
crews   42, 69, 73, 89, 100-1, 105-6, 132, 135, 137, 140-1, 180, 206, 216, 229
cross-staff   61, 63, 93, 120
crowding   101, 105, 179
Cuba   36, 100, 124, 154, 156, 186
Curaçao   28, 86
cure of diseases   51-3, 57, 71-2, 102-6, 126, 136, 139, 141, 148, 202, 220-1, 229
currents   13, 65, 79, 92, 98-9, 134, 144, 147, 149, 168, 170-1, 198, 211, 213, 217, 227, 230, 232
Cuvier, Georges   54, 221

Dalrymple, Alexander   114-15, 186-7
Dampier, William   65, 98-9
Darwin, Charles   153, 221
Davis Strait   30, 54, 86, 136-7, 146-7, 190
dead reckoning   92, 95, 153, 173
death rates   69, 99-100, 108-9, 116, 176-80, 187, 207, 222, 229
decks   83, 101, 105-7, 141, 179, 207

Denmark   30, 86, 186, 188, 191, 197
density of seawater   144, 166-7
depositories of maps and charts   75,
   see also hydrographical departments
   Depósito and Dirección hidrographica   114, 186, 196
   Dépôt des cartes et plans de la Marine/Dépot general de la Marine   38, 41-2, 48, 76, 97, 113-16, 122, 144, 186, 191-2, 194
   Depot of maps and charts of the Dutch Navy   197
   Hydrographer of the EIC   186-7
   Hydrographer of the VOC   48, 116
   Hydrographic Office of the Royal Navy   115, 186-7
   US Coast Survey   218
   US Navy Depot of charts and instruments   194-5, 218
Deptford   28, 45, 125, 215
depths of the sea   44, 60, 62, 66-7, 74, 76, 92, 144-6, 168, 195, 220-1, 225, 231
Dessiou, Joseph   187-8
diet   51, 102, 106, 134, 139, *see also* food; victuals
disciplinary organizations   131, 208-10, 219, 230
diseases   39, 51, 69-73, 100-5, 108, 126, 129-30, 136, 140-1, 143-4, 148-9, 175-80, 206, 216, 222, 229, 232,
   see also cure of diseases; hygiene; morbidity; prevention of diseases
   cholera   177-9
   dysentery   52, 69, 136, 177
   elephantiasis   101
   'fevers'   69, 176-8
   Guinea-worm disease   69
   leprosy   101, 136
   malaria   51, 69, 71, 73, 101, 148, 179
   respiratory diseases   177
   scurvy   53, 68-9, 72, 104-6, 139, 148, 176-8, 180-1
   smallpox   69
   venereal diseases   57, 72, 177
   yaws   101
   yellow fever   69, 71, 100-1, 176, 178, 180
distances (sailed)   134, 195
distillation machine   49, 73-4, 106-7, 139, 141, 148, 229

dividing engine 120–1, 140, 202
doctors 47, 51–2, 55, 71–2, 101, 103, 130–1, 135–6, 143, 180, 207, *see also* physicians
Dolben's Act 101
double altitude method for finding latitude 92–3, 112, 147, 173, 212
Douwes, Cornelis 92–3, 173
draughtsmen 53, 68, 74, 113, 186
dredges 221
drinking water 49, 73
drowning 178
Dublin 128, 216
Duhamel du Monceau, Henri-Louis 83, 102–4, 106, 122–3, 180
duration of voyages 89–90, 109, 162–3, 168, 171, 179, 229
Dutch Atlantic 46, 53, 75, 104, 148, 228
Dutch colonies 28, 31, 87
Dutch East India Company (VOC) 16, 25, 46, 48–50, 65, 70–3, 75, 78, 84, 87, 94, 96, 98, 106, 108, 111–12, 115–17, 125–6, 129, 132–3, 140–1, 148, 154, 158, 197, 228
Dutch East-Indies 158–9, 198
Dutch Guianas 31, 46, *see also* Suriname; Wild Coast
Dutch Republic 131–3, 144–5, 148, 199, *see also* Netherlands
Dutch West India Company (WIC) 28, 46, 48, 52–3, 69, 154, 228

East India Company (EIC) 19, 45–6, 53, 78, 94–6, 99, 106, 112, 114, 119, 141, 155, 158, 172, 186–7, 200, 209, 228
École des Ingénieurs-Constructeurs de la Marine 123
economic historians 5, 7, 12, 14, 233 n.15
Edinburgh 128
EIC, *see* East India Company
electrometers 140
El Ferrol 35–6
emigrant ships 101, 180, 207
empires 5, 8, 11–12, 14, 18–20, 42, *see also* British/English; French; Spanish empire
engineering corps 123–4, 191, 205
engineering schools 205

England 16, 27–30, 42–3, 45–6, 48, 55–7, 59–60, 62, 64–6, 72, 75, 84, 120, 123, 131–2, 142, 145, 158, 173, 182, 202–3, 207, 218–19, *see also* Britain
English/British colonies in America 28, 42, 53, 64–5, 85–6, 91, 93, 119, 131, 135–6, 154
English Channel 60, 162, 170–1
engravers 113, 143, 186
engraving 76, 115, 218
Enkhuizen 47, 130
entrepreneurs 27–8, 46, 107, 111, 118, 148, 214, 220, 223–4, 231
Europe 3, 5, 10–11, 14, 16–7, 30, 36, 41–2, 48, 52, 56, 63–4, 69, 72, 78, 84–7, 100, 116, 137, 147, 155, 158–9, 165, 168, 177–8, 182
  Continental 38, 60, 77, 118, 130–1, 157
  Northern 183
  Northwestern 64
  Southern 85
examinations
  of engineers 123
  of masters, mates, naval officers, pilots 32, 39, 43, 47–8, 110–12, 148, 197, 199–202, 213–15, 223
  of surgeons 33, 39, 43, 46–7, 70, 127–30, 206
examiners 75, 78
  of masters, mates, naval officers, pilots 25, 48, 96, 111–12, 116, 197, 199
  of surgeons 33, 47–8, 70, 128–30
expeditions (scientific) 16, 33–6, 38, 41, 45, 49, 74, 87, 94, 114, 116, 118, 139, 143, 174, 186, 193, 195, 221, 232, *see also* exploration voyages
experience 7, 13, 25, 38, 53, 61, 65, 67, 71–2, 92, 101–3, 106–8, 124, 126, 129, 137, 141, 144, 147–9, 186, 194, 200, 204, 207, 211, 215, 229
experiments 49, 53, 60–2, 74, 101, 106, 108, 132–3, 141, 157, 218, *see also* trials
exploration voyages 49, 87, 94, 153, 189–91, 193, 221

Feuillée, Louis 38, 41
financial constraints 34–5, 75, 79, 143, 149, 231

fisheries   13, 21, 29, 49, 85, 181–3, 229
  cod   29, 54, 85–7, 147, 181–3
  halibut   181–3
  herring   68, 182
  mackerel   67, 181–3
  menhaden   181–3
fishermen   20, 29, 66–8, 76, 78, 85, 132–3, 135, 146, 149, 182–4, 221, 228
fishes, knowledge about   41, 45, 66–8, 76, 145–6, 149, 221, 227, 230, *see also* ichthyology
fishing boats   29, 68, 87
fishing grounds   29, 183
fishing techniques   182–3
Fitzroy, Robert   153, 161, 191, 211
Fleurieu, Charles-Pierre Claret de   98, 114, 122
Florijn, Jacob   116–17
Fonssagrives, Jean-Baptiste   180–1
food   68–9, 84, 86, 105, 135, 137, 179, 182, 190, 207, 215, *see also* diet; victuals
France   1, 11, 16, 28–31, 36–8, 40–6, 48, 55–7, 59, 62, 64, 72, 76–8, 83–4, 91, 93–4, 97–8, 100–1, 103–4, 107, 111, 113–16, 118, 121–31, 139–40, 144–5, 148, 158–60, 166, 170, 186, 188, 191–7, 199, 202–6, 208, 210, 213, 218–19, 221–3, 228, 230–1
Franklin, Benjamin   98, 131–3, 135, 144
Franklin, John   190
freight rates   89, *see also* transport costs
French Atlantic   28, 40, 42, 52, 77, 127, 144, 227
French colonies   31, 59
French empire   37, 142, 197
French Revolution   121, 154
fruits   53, 106, 140
fumigation   108, 179
fur   63, 137, 157, 182, 184

Gallandat, David Henri   102–3, 107, 136
Gambey, Henri Prudence   202
Gambey circles   218–19
General Shipowners' Society   200, 224
geodesy   193, 196
geography   13, 18, 32, 34, 38, 113, 193, 210, 227, 232
geology   210

Germany   30, 131, 137, 159, 210, 223
Gibraltar   38, 60
Glasgow   65, 128
glass   62–3, 118–21, 140
global history   5, 14, 22, 232
globalization, defined   6–7
globalizing forces, defined   13–19
Godfrey, Thomas   63–4
gold   14, 86, 158
Gold Coast   18, 69, 109
Gonzalez, Pedro Maria   102, 104, 126, 128
Gorée   38, 41
government administrators   37, 53, 103, 123–4, 133, 224, 232
Grand Bank   29, 68
graphical method   217
Greenland   11–12, 30, 54, 86, 136–7, 146, 149, 186
Greenwich   43, 98, 115–16, 121, 187, 190, 193, 197, 203
Gresham College   62
Gronovius, Johan Frederik   142–3, 145–6
Guadeloupe   31, 38
guaiac   72
guano   157–8, 160, 181, 183
guides for mariners   90
guilds   32, 47, 107, 121, 129–30, 133
Guinea   18, 71, 103, 136
Gulf of Maine   181
Gulf of Mexico   64, 156, 187
Gulf of Saint Lawrence   59, 186, 221
Gulf Stream   98–9, 131–2, 144, 195
gunners/gunnery   11, 35

Hadley, John   63–4, 93
Hales, Stephen   102, 104, 106–8, 139, 141
Halley, Edmond   44–5, 60–1, 64, 74–5, 95–6, 98, 168, 217
Hamburg   68, 86, 146
harpoons   183
Harris, Steven   16–18
Harrison, John   1, 83, 94, 139
Havana   28, 32, 36, 56, 86, 100, 124, 142
Hazewinkel, Abraham   173, 212
Headrick, Daniel   2, 4–5, 231
health   15, 17, 21, 53, 58, 70–3, 83, 100–1, 103–7, 109, 111, 141, 175–6, 179–81, 206, 208, 215–16, 227, 231
health care, *see* medical care

Heidbrink, Ingo 5
Held, David 6, 10, 19
hemp 165
herbal remedies 135–6
herbs 33, 52, 57, 136
Hernández, Francisco 33–4
Herrnhutters, *see* Moravians
Herschel, John 190, 193, 211
hides 156
history of knowledge 9, 22, 232
Hooke, Robert 60, 62–3
Horsburgh, James 167, 187
hospitals 33–5, 39–41, 43–4, 46–8, 51, 77, 102, 126–30, 136, 140, 148, 175–7, 206, 208, 215, 223
hospital ships 43, 129
Hoste, Paul 39, 41
hourglasses 61
Hudson's Bay Company 76, 96, 114, 117, 155, 157, 189, 209, 228
hulls 91, 108, 123, 125, 133, 141, 165, 204, 211, 218
Hulst van Keulen, Gerard 115, 197
Humboldt, Alexander von 217
humours 71, 104
hunting grounds 67–8, 157, 184
Hurd, Thomas 114, 187
Huxham, John 102, 104–5
Huygens, Christiaan 38, 49, 55–6, 62–4, 74
hydrodynamics 123, 204
hydrographic departments of trading companies
 of the Compagnie des Indes 19, 113–14, 122
 of the EIC 45, 186–7
 of the VOC 48, 116
hydrographic offices of navies, *see also* Dépôt des cartes et plans de la Marine/Dépôt general de la Marine; US Coast Survey US Navy Depot of charts and instruments
 of the Dutch navy 198
 Dirección hidrographica (Spain) 114, 186, 196
 of the Royal Navy 115, 174, 186–7, 190, 192
hydrography 113, 188, 194, 196, 220, 231, *see also* cartography; charts; map-making

hygiene 101–2, 179–80, 206–7
hygrometers 140

iatrochemistry 72
Iberian Peninsula 12, 29, 36, 85, 159, 167
icebergs 54
Iceland 11, 146
ichthyology 145–6, *see also* fishes; knowledge about
imperial machine 14, 16–17, 19–22, 32, 34, 36–7, 39–40, 42, 44, 57, 76–7, 87, 111, 113, 115–16, 122–3, 126, 142–4, 148, 185–6, 189, 199, 202, 206, 208, 223–4, 226, 228–30
 defined 16–17
indentured servants 30, 87
India 154–5, 158–9, 161
Indian Ocean 12, 15, 53, 60, 75, 113, 144, 156–7, 161, 168, 188, 232
informants 51, 114, 135, 166
infrastructure of knowledge, defined 20
injuries 39, 46–7, 129, 176, 180
instrument-makers 32, 62, 64, 93–4, 118–22, 140, 144, 148, 202, 218, 224, 231
instruments (optical, navigational, mathematical, philosophical) 22, 31, 36, 44, 56, 60–4, 69, 74–6, 79, 83, 88, 92–3, 110, 112, 114–18, 139–40, 145, 147, 149, 166, 173, 187–91, 193–5, 198, 202, 207, 217, 219, 222, 230–1
insurance 89, 133, 212
insurers 161, 171, 199–200, 213, 220, 224
Inuit 30, 136–8, 149, 157, 182, 190
ipecacuanha 52, 79
Ireland 65, 158, 188, 207
iron 91, 141, 165, 175
isolines 75, 217
Isthmus of Panama 28, 32, 158
Italy 56, 131

Jackson, Robert 101, 103, 105
Jamaica 43, 52, 84, 89, 113, 140
Jansen, Marin Henri 198, 211
Japan 157
Jardin du Roi 15, 37–8, 41
Java 159, 170
Jesuit bark, *see* Peruvian bark

Jesuits   19, 33–4, 41, 45, 51–2, 72, 111, 155, 228, *see also* Society of Jesus
journals (general, medical, scientific)   104, 140, 176, 213, 219
Juan, Jaime   33–4
Juan, Jorge   35–6, 93, 96–7, 113, 123–4, 205

kayaks   137
van Keulen, firm   59, 115–16, 120–1, 197
KNMI, *see* Koninklijk Nederlands Meteorologisch Instituut (KNMI)
knowledge, defined   7–10
Koninklijk Nederlands Meteorologisch Instituut (KNMI)   168, 198, 209
Kweekschool voor de Zeevaart   112, 214

Labrador   30, 85, 137, 182
Lacaille, Nicolas-Louis de   116
Lalande, Joseph-Jérôme de   122
La Pérouse, Jean-François   87, 94
Lardizabal, Vicente de   102–3
latitude   33, 36, 38, 61, 65, 92–3, 95–6, 112, 168, *see also* double altitude method for finding latitude
Latour, Bruno   9–10
lecturers   45, 47, 70, 75, 78, 116, 129, 197–9, 206, 213–14
Leeuwenhoek, Antonie van   55–6
Le Hâvre   39, 163
Leiden   47, 49, 75, 120, 128, 132, 142, 145–6, 198
Lelyveld, Frans van   132–3
Le Roy, Pierre   1
lighthouses   27, 134, 182, 212
lime juice/lemon juice   72, 106, 180–1
limes/lemons   53, 72, 106, 140
Lind, James   53, 102–4, 106–7, 126, 128–9, 139–40, 180–1
Linnean Society   131, 190, 210
Lisbon   19
literary and philosophical societies, *see* scientific (learned) societies
lithography   217–18
Liverpool   65, 126, 156, 159, 161, 163, 183, 213–19
Liverpool Shipmasters' Association   212–13
local knowledge   10, 51, 167

local/ municipal governments   47, 111, 129, 213–15
logbooks, *see* ship's journals/logs
logs and lines   61, *see also* distances sailed
London   19, 28, 42–4, 46, 51, 53, 56, 59, 61–5, 86, 89–93, 98, 118–21, 128, 131–2, 135, 155–6, 161, 163–4, 167, 176, 190, 196, 201–3, 207, 209–10, 215–16, 219
long-distance corporations   16–17, 117, 185, 223, 228–9, *see also* commercial machines; trading companies
longitude, methods for determining   1, 33, 38, 43–4, 47, 57, 61–2, 64, 93–8, 112, 115–18, 122, 172–3, 186, 193, 231, *see also* lunar distances; marine chronometers; variation of the compass
Longitude Acts   1, 189
Longitude Committee (Dutch Navy)   115, 117, 197–9
Louis XIV, king of France   8, 36
Louisiana   39, 41, 156
lunar distances   1, 64, 93–4, 112–13, 116, 147, 173

Madeira   29, 65
Madrid   32–3, 35–6, 128
Magnetic Crusade   174, 188, 193, 210, 217–18, 223
magnetic declination   61, 64, 75, 95, 97, 147, 174, 217, *see also* variation of the compass
magnetism   61, 69, 174, 189, 193, 196, 198, 218
magnetometers   218–19
mail   28, 55, 142, 149, 159, 209, 219
Malaspina, Alejandro   16, 87, 94, 118, 139, 143, 186
Manila   158
manuals   70–2, 77, 90, 93–4, 96, 103, 112, 117, 123, 127, 129–30, 166, 180, 188–9, 228
manufactures   84, 155–6
map-making   13, 32, 48, 59, 62, 74, 76, 78, 115, 148–9, 161, 223, 227, 230, 232, *see also* cartography; charts; hydrography
Marcgraf, Georg   49, 66

Marine, Ministère de la   37, 40
marine biology   58, 145–6, 220–1
marine boards   200
marine science   59–60, 62, 75, 143–5, 221, *see also* oceanography
marine societies, *see* shipmasters' societies
maritime environment   12–13, 20–2, 88–9, 130, 133, 137, 147, 149, 198, 211, 217, 227, 229
maritime history   5, 22, 232
maritime knowledge, defined   13
markets   6, 29, 59, 61, 64, 83, 85, 89–90, 115, 118, 154, 172, 181, 195, 202, 219
Martens, Friedrich   68, 146
Martinique   28, 31, 38, 68, 115
Maskelyne, Nevil   93
Massachusetts   29, 62, 67, 214
masters, *see* shipmasters
masts   91, 125, 165
mates   35, 39, 47, 65, 92–3, 96, 111–12, 133, 166, 199–201, 209, 212–14, 224, *see also* pilots
mathematicians   33, 38–9, 63, 92, 126, 175, 197–8
mathematics   25, 33–4, 39, 43, 47, 112, 116, 119, 123–5, 147, 199, 204, 211, 213
Mauro, Frédéric   12
Maury, Matthew Fontaine   168–71, 194–6, 198, 211, 213, 217, 220, 224, 232
McClellan, James   14–15, 36, 142
McWilliam, James O.   177–8, 216
meat   85, 156, 182
medical care   33, 39, 43, 47–8, 70, 78, 88, 102–4, 110, 127–30, 134–5, 143, 148, 161, 176, 180, 206–8, 214–15, 219, 222–3, 228, 230, 232
medical chests, *see* surgeons' chests
medical libraries   206
medical practices   49, 102, 108, 130, 136, 180, 206, 229
medical practitioners   57, 128
medical schools   126–7, 206, *see also* surgical schools
medical science   101, 148, 179, 229, 231
medical writings   102, 104–5, 126, 148, 229

medicinal plants   33, 37, 51, 135, *see also* herbal remedies; herbs
medicines   34, 39, 49, 52, 71, 73, 136
Mediterranean   42, 66, 100, 108, 144, 176, 178, 186
Mendoza y Ríos, José de   92–3, 117
Mercantile Marine Act   201–2, 215–16
Mercantile Marine Board   200–1
merchant navies/mercantile marines   167, 175, 195, 209, 212–13, 223
  American   85, 164–5, 202, 214
  British   164, 175, 177, 179, 181, 199–201, 213–16, 219
  Dutch   199–200
  French   39, 173
  Spanish   113, 143
merchants   25, 29–30, 33, 41, 46, 53–4, 57, 78, 85, 142, 156, 160–1, 171, 213
merchant ships/ merchantmen   28, 35, 47, 69, 85, 87, 89, 91, 94, 100, 102, 113, 134, 141, 158–60, 162–5, 168, 170, 177–80, 200–1, 203, 206, 208, 222
Meteorological Department (UK)   191
meteorology   144–5, 190–1, 193–6, 198, 202, 211, 213, 217–19, 223, *see also* wind; weather
Mexico   12, 19, 33–4
Middelburg   25, 47, 70
Middelburgsche Commercie Compagnie   92, 107, 109
midshipmen   166, 200, 202
migration   2, 30–1, 51, 87, 100–1, 109, 159–60, 177–8, 180, 207–8, 223
missionary societies (Protestant)   136, 155, 188, *see also* Moravians
Missions Etrangères de Paris   17, 41, 155
models (of objects)   114, 123, 125, 133, 204–5, 218
Mokyr, Joel   7–8
molasses   85
Monchy, Salomon de   102–4, 180
monopoly   33, 42, 46, 149, 155, 158–9
Moravians   136–7, 149
morbidity   69, 73, 108, 140, 176, 178–9, 222, *see also* diseases
Morgan, Philip   10, 88, 154
Morogues, Sébastien-François Bigot de   102–4, 139

mortality, *see* death rates
Moubach, Abraham   54
Mountaine & Dodson, firm   96–7, 174
Mount & Page, firm   61, 95, 98, 114
museums   134, 190, 206, 213

Nantucket   30, 86, 90, 131, 149, 157
National Association for the Promotion of Social Science, *see* Social Science Association
Native Americans   30, 136, *see also* Amerindians; Inuit
natural history   34, 38, 67, 75–6, 87, 131, 137, 145–6, 190, 196, 210, 220
nautical almanacs   93, 116–17, 147–8, 173, 187, 197
nautical education   41, 47, 94, 110–13, 133, 147, 199–202, 213–14, 223, *see also* naval academies
nautical/navigational instruments   76, 110, 117–19, 121–2, 188, 222, *see also* altitude-measuring instruments; compasses
naval academies   35, 43, 111–12, 202, *see also* nautical education
naval architects   204–5, 211, 218, 224, 237
naval architecture   41, 134, 204–5, 211–12, 218
naval cadets   111, 113
naval engineers   123–4, 205
naval officers   35, 39, 41, 47, 78, 94, 98, 111–14, 122, 139, 153, 175, 180, 186–7, 189–91, 197–8, 202, 204–5, 207–8, 211–12, 215, 224, 232
navies   70, 77, 91, 124, 126, 134, 153, 172, 175, 194, 223
  British   43–4, 47, 71, 91, 94, 96, 100–1, 106–8, 125, 128–9, 134–5, 140–1, 143, 161, 164, 167, 174–7, 181–2, 187, 189–90, 200, 203–4, 206, 219
  Dutch   47, 49–50, 100, 102, 108, 111, 115–16, 129–30, 172, 197–9, 202, 205
  French   15, 37–9, 95, 102, 111–13, 121–3, 127, 140, 172, 194
  Spanish   35–6, 111–14, 127, 143, 196, 199
  US   172, 194–5, 201–2

Navigation Acts   42, 160
navigational skills   91, 222
navigation schools, *see under* nautical education
navigators   38, 45, 48, 89–94, 96–8, 111–13, 143, 148, 167, 172, 174, 193, 199–202, 209, 213–14, 218, *see also* masters; mates; naval officers; pilots
Navy Board (UK)   43, 128–9, 187, 203–4
Nederlandsche Handel-Maatschappij (NHM)   158–60, 199–200, 215
Nentwigh, Christiaan   49, 74
Netherlands   31, 50, 55–6, 59, 64, 94–6, 98, 100, 111, 115, 119, 122, 125, 129, 131–3, 141, 144–5, 159, 168, 170–1, 173, 178, 180, 186, 188, 196–203, 205, 208, 212–15, 218, 230, *see also* Dutch Republic
New Bedford   157, 161
New England   12, 29–30, 45, 60, 64, 85–7, 114, 146, 157, 181, 183
Newfoundland   11, 25, 29–30, 54, 59, 64, 68, 85–6, 114, 137, 147, 181–4
New Orleans   156, 208
New South Wales   158, 207
Newton, Isaac   63, 144
New York   28, 59, 85, 134, 142–3, 157, 159, 161, 163, 165, 177, 180, 183, 214
NHM, *see* Nederlandsche Handel-Maatschappij
Nieuwland, Pieter   115–17
Norsemen   11
North, Douglass   17, 89
North Pole   189
North Sea   181, 188, 221
Northwest Passage   189
Norway   12, 38, 159, 170, 188, 219
Nova Scotia   106, 114

Observatoire Royal de Paris   15–16, 37–8, 41, 52, 55, 117
observatories   47, 75, 115, 148, 174, 187, 190, 193, 196, 203, 223
Observatorio Real (Cádiz)   98, 196
oceanography   12, 196, 220, *see also* marine science
octant   63–4, 93, 112, 117, 120–1, 140, 147, 173, 202

oil on water   132–3
Oldenburg, Henry   56
oranges   53, 72, 106, 140
Ordinance of 1689 (France)   39, 126, 206
ornithology   66–7, 75, 190, *see also* birds
Oxford   119, 190

Pacific Ocean   12, 16, 60, 86–7, 155–8, 168, 188–91, 195, 232
packet boats   28, 98, 142, 163, 165, 201, *see also* mail
palm oil   155–6
Paris   19, 29, 35–9, 41, 52, 55–6, 76, 98, 115, 117–19, 121, 123, 127–8, 143, 202
Parliament (UK)   1, 44, 128, 160, 163, 166, 189, 200, 207, 215
Parliamentary committees (UK)   163, 165, 173, 174
passenger acts   179, 207–8, 223
passengers   69, 87, 100, 159, 165, 177–80, 206–7
patents for inventions   64, 120
Pennsylvania   45, 59, 85, 87, 119, 142, 214
periodicals   55, 140, 146, 219–20
Peru   36, 38, 73, 157, 159–60, 170, 183
Peruvian bark (Jesuit bark, quinine)   51, 72, 105, 179
Petiver, James   55–7
pharmacies   34, 51, 136
Philadelphia   63, 85, 100, 119, 131, 134, 149, 177
Philip II, king of Spain   33–4, 37
Philip III, king of Spain   33–34, 47
Philippines   33
physicians   33, 39, 43, 47–9, 51, 70–2, 77, 102–3, 129, 133, 140, 144, 175, 219, 224, *see also* doctors
physicians-general   206, 223
physics   116, 147, 196
pilotage   134
pilot books   59, 98, 115, 166–7
pilot-major   113, 143
pilots   25, 32, 44, 47–8, 53, 60, 76, 78, 111, 113, 145, 199, 201, *see also* mates
piracy   89
Piso, Willem   49
plans for ship construction   125

plantation colonies   29, 86–7
plantations   51, 69–70, 136
planters   53, 57, 76
Plumier, Charles   38, 41, 66, 74
Plymouth   129, 206
Poissonnier, Pierre-Isaac   106–7, 127, 139–41
Poissonnier-Desperrières, Antoine   102–4, 106, 126–8
Portobello   56, 65, 70
ports/ harbours   11, 28–30, 39, 43, 46, 56, 65, 84, 86, 89–90, 111, 134, 142, 144–5, 156–7, 159–60, 163, 172, 177, 180–1, 186, 188, 192, 195, 197, 199, 201, 203, 207–8, 211–12, 214
Portsmouth   43, 45, 65, 111–12, 129, 203–4, 211
Portugal   21, 29, 170, 188, 197
position-line navigation   212
postal services, *see* mail; packet boats
preparation techniques   75, 146
prevention of diseases   102–3, 105–6, 126, 148, 229
prime meridians   93, 98, 197
Pringle, John   102–4, 108, 180
privateers   143
productivity of shipping   89–90, 110
professionalization   124, 205, 209, 212–13
professors   47, 55, 111, 122–3, 129, 144, 206, 224, 232
provincial governments   46–7
publishers   25, 54, 59, 61, 114–15, 167, 187, 219, 224
Puerto Rico   115, 186
purification   101, 105–7

Quebec   28, 39, 41, 98
Quetelet, Adolphe   209
Quiberon Bay   115
Quinine, *see under* Jesuit bark

Ramsden, Jesse   119–20
Ray, John   66–7, 75
Real Academia de Guardias Marines (Cádiz)   35
Real Colegio de Cirugía   127–8
Real Colegio Seminario de San Telmo   35, 111
Real Hospital (Cádiz)   127–8

reflecting circle   94, 121, 147
Regourd, François   14–15, 36, 142
religious machine   14, 16–18, 20, 27, 34, 41, 46, 50, 52, 78, 88, 110, 136, 155, 185, 227
   defined   16–7
religious orders   33–4, 41, 45, 50, 127, 228
Renard, Louis   96, 145
Renn, Jürgen   2–3
Rennell, James   99
Republic of Letters   15, 54–6, 66–7, 69, 78, 130, 228
resources   4, 15–16, 22, 31, 74–5, 88, 117, 139, 143, 149, 189, 217, 224, 230
rewards   1, 33, 44, 47–8, 57, 64, 92, 189, 203
rice   86, 89, 135
Richer, Jean   38, 74
rigging   58, 91, 125, 165
Rio de Janeiro   171
Río de la Plata/River Plate   86, 147, 156, 159, 167–8
Rittenhouse, David   119
Robijn, Jacobus   25, 59
Rochefort   39, 41, 122, 127, 206
Rodger, Nicholas   124–5, 164
Roggeveen, Arent   25, 48, 53, 59, 63, 77
Rome   17, 19
Rönnback, Klas   58, 90–1, 108, 162
Ross, Daniel   188
Ross, John   190
Rotterdam   50, 56, 106, 111–12, 116, 125, 129–30, 142, 199, 205, 213–14, 218
Rouillé de Meslay   41, 64
Rouppe, Lodewijk   102–5, 180
routes   11, 27, 57–9, 64–5, 89–92, 98, 158–60, 162, 167
Royal African Company   46, 96
Royal Mathematical School (London)   43, 93, 111–12
Royal Mathematics Academy (Madrid)   33–4
Royal Natural History Cabinet (Madrid)   143
Royal Naval Academy (Portsmouth)   43, 111–12
Royal Observatory (Greenwich)   43, 98, 116, 191

Royal Observatory Paris, *see* Observatoire Royal de Paris
Royal School of Naval Architecture (UK)   212
Royal Society of London   19, 43–5, 55–7, 60, 62–3, 66, 75–6, 92, 95, 98–9, 106, 115, 131, 133, 144, 187, 189, 204, 209–10, 219, 221
Rozwadowski, Helen   12, 220
Russell, John Scott   165, 211, 218
Russia   189, 200
rutters   32, *see also* sailing directions
Ruysch, Frederik   55–6, 75

Sabine, Edward   188, 190, 193, 210
safety of shipping   11, 89, 98, 126, 132–4, 141, 161, 163, 168, 171–2, 188, 199, 208, 231
sailing directions   25, 59, 65, 78, 96–8, 113, 166–71, 187–9, 228, *see also* rutters
sails   58, 61, 65, 83, 91, 125, 165
Saint-Domingue/Santo Domingo   31, 86, 98, 101, 115
Saint Lawrence river   114
Salazar, Luis María de   143
Salem   85, 134
Salem East India Marine Society   212–13
salinity of seawater   60, 62, 144, 195
sauerkraut   106
Schlichting, Joannes Daniel   129–30
scholars   1, 7, 10, 18, 20, 51–2, 54–7, 63–4, 66–7, 76, 78, 95, 131, 133, 144–6, 175, 185, 228, *see also* scientists
Scientific Branch of the Navy (UK)   187, 190
scientific/learned societies   46, 55, 62, 75, 92, 104, 122, 133, 209–10, *see also* associations
scientists   12–13, 36, 113, 124, 171, 174, 193, 196, 198, 209, 211, 215, 221, *see also* scholars
Scoresby, William   138, 226
Scotland   27, 31, 90, 114, 134, 165, 173, 207
screening/checking of medical condition   102, 107, 180
sealing/seal hunting   157, 181–4
seal oil   182

seals 86, 137, 157, 181–2, 184
sealskins 137, 182
seamanship 35, 43, 47, 145, 214
seamen/sailors 12, 15, 18, 20, 27, 33, 35, 42, 44, 46–7, 51, 53–4, 57, 59–71, 73, 76–8, 87, 92–4, 96, 98–107, 111–13, 116, 126, 128, 130, 132–6, 143–7, 167–78, 180–1, 185, 188, 196, 200, 202, 206, 208–9, 212–16, 219–20, 226, 228
Seamen's Hospital Society 215
seaweed 91
Seba, Albertus 55, 75, 145–6
secrecy 34, 51
self-organization, defined 18–19
Senegal/Senegambia 38, 41, 51, 109
Seppings, Robert 164, 204–5
Service des Marées 192
Seville 32–3, 35, 111
sextant 94, 112, 117, 120–1, 140, 147, 173, 202, 219
Shetland 11
shipbuilding/ship construction 13, 36, 39–40, 44–5, 49–50, 76, 88–90, 110, 122–5, 133, 141, 148, 161, 165, 175, 203–5, 211, 222–3, 227, 230, 232
ship design 39, 45, 58, 74, 123–5, 133, 147, 164, 203–5, 211, 218, 229
shipmasters 25, 38, 48, 53, 56–7, 90, 133, 146, 200, 212, 215, 220, 224, 232, *see also* captains
shipmasters' societies 133–4, 166, 212–14, 220, 224
shipowners 35, 107, 142, 161, 164, 166, 171, 199–200, 207, 213–15, 218, 220, 224
shipping seasons 27
ship repair 164–5, 203
ships, types of, *see also* merchant ships; packet boats; slave ships; transport ships; warships; whaling ships
  barks 183
  clippers 165
  East Indiamen 49, 91, 125, 141, 178
  frigates 124, 203
  schooners 182
ship's frame 164
ship's journals/logs 30, 38–9, 42, 48, 61, 75, 94, 96–9, 106, 113, 116, 122, 134, 168, 170–1, 194, 197, 212, 223

shipworms 91
shipwrecks 154, 163, 165, 168, 173–4, 177, 195, 200, 222, 231
shipwrights 39–40, 44–5, 49–50, 123–5, 133, 147, 204–5, 211, 224, 232
shipyards 165
  company 49, 141
  naval 36, 39–40, 44, 49, 123–5, 128, 203–5, 211
  private 45, 49, 125, 133, 165, 203–4, 211
Sick and Hurt Board (UK) 106, 128, 141, 143, 206
sickness, *see* diseases
silver 14, 86
skippers, *see* shipmasters
slave doctors 52
slave hospitals 136
slavery 11, 84, 86, 135, 147, 154, *see also* plantations
slaves (enslaved people) 15, 18, 28–30, 57, 69–72, 78, 84, 90, 99–101, 103, 107–9, 126, 135, 140, 154–5, 229
slave ships/slavers 69, 72, 91, 99–102, 106–9, 109, 126, 162, 178, 229
slave trade 11, 28–9, 46, 53, 57, 69, 84, 87, 90, 99, 101–2, 107, 147, 154–6, 161–2, 178, 221
slave voyages 28–9, 84, 154, 178
Sloane, Hans 55–6, 63, 66–7
social networks of knowledge, defined 20
social reform movements 200, 215–16, 223
Social Science Association 181, 216
Société Royale de Agriculture 15
Société Royale de Médecine 15, 127, 144–5
Society for the Diffusion of Useful Knowledge 172, 210
Society for the Encouragement of Arts, Manufacture and Commerce 133
Society for the Improvement of Naval Architecture 133, 204, 211, 218
Society of Jesus 16, 41, 52, 77, 148, 155, *see also* Jesuits
Solar, Peter 91, 108, 178
soldiers 30, 69–70, 87, 100–1, 105, 107, 159, 177–8

sounding 44, 60, 85, 134, 168, 219–20, *see also* depths of the sea
sounding instruments 44, 62
sounding lines 61–2
South Carolina 57, 85, 156, 173
South Georgia 12, 157, 182, 184
South Sea Company 56–7
Spain 15–6, 28–30, 32–7, 41–2, 45–8, 56, 64, 70, 76–8, 85–6, 91, 93, 95–6, 100, 111–14, 116–18, 121, 123–4, 127, 131, 139, 148–9, 170, 186–8, 191, 196–7, 199, 205, 213, 218, 228, 230
Spanish America 28–30, 32, 34–5, 57, 64, 78, 87, 126, 148
Spanish Atlantic 20–1, 34–5, 75, 102, 111, 229
Spanish empire 8, 11–12, 14, 33–4, 42, 56, 85, 139, 154, 227
speed of shipping 5, 11, 58, 85, 90–1, 98, 110, 160, 162–5, 172, 178, 229
spiegelboog (mirror-staff) 63
Spitsbergen 12, 30, 54, 68
states 11, 14–15, 18–19, 32–4, 75, 77–8, 94, 111, 116–18, 160, 185, 198, 223–4, 231
statistics 73, 75, 129, 140, 166, 176, 178–9, 210
steamship companies 159–60
steamships 4, 11, 159–60, 163
Steenstra, Pybo 96
steering 58, 65, 183, 222
St. Eustatius 28
Stevens, Robert White 166–7
St. Helena 53, 174, 203
storm warnings 194, 223.,230
stowage 13, 125–6, 165–7, 222–3, 227, 230, 232, 253 n.82
stowage plans 126
Strait Sunda 171
subcontracting 120–1
Suez Canal 160
sugar 69, 84, 89, 135, 158
Sumner, Thomas 173–4, 212
surgeons general 45–7, 127
surgeons 33, 39, 46–8, 56–7, 70–2, 77–8, 101–3, 108, 127–30, 135–6, 148, 179–80, 206–7, 224, 232

surgeons' chests 46, 48, 71
Surgeons' Company 43, 128
surgeons' journals 39, 73
surgeons' training 39, 43, 47, 127–9, *see also* surgical schools
surgery 47, 70
surgical schools 126, 128, 206
Suriname 46, 56, 75, 84, 87, 137
Surveyor of the Navy 44, 125, 164, 204–5
surveyors 114, 186, 223
Swart, Jacob 197
Sweden 83, 145, 159, 170, 188
Swinden, Jan Hendrik van 115, 117, 140, 145
symbols 60, 75, 170

tables
  astronomical 193
  for double-latitude method 92–3
  lunar 116–17, 197
  of morbidity and mortality 140, 176, *see also* statistics
  tide 145, 171–2, 188
tea 165
telescopes 61–3, 119, 140, 202
temperature 170, 217
  of the air 76, 140, 144
  of seawater 60, 62, 144, 168, 195
Tenerife 98, 117, 197
thermometer 62–3, 140, 144, 190, 219
tide gauges 218–19
tides 13, 60, 65, 98–9, 144, 147, 149, 171–2, 191–2, 211, 218, 227, 230
tide theories 144–5
tidology 188, 196, 211, *see also* tide tables
timber 85, 124, 137, 163, 165
time-ball 203
time constraints 143, 149
timekeeper, *see* marine chronometer
Titsingh, Abraham 102–4, 129
tobacco 27, 59, 65, 84, 89–90
Tofiño, Vicente 98, 114
ton/man ratios 89, *see also* productivity of shipping
tonnage 46, 84
Toulon 39, 41, 122–3, 127, 206
trading companies 16–18, 27, 41, 45–6, 48–53, 55–6, 58, 70, 75, 77–8, 107,

114, 117, 134, 154, 159, 185, 223, 226, 228–30, 232, *see also* long-distance corporations
transoceanic telegraph cables   160, 220
Transport Board (UK)   206
transport costs   11, *see also* freight rates
transport ships   106
travel accounts   30, 65, 75, 98, 116
trials   1, 49, 53, 62, 74–5, 123, 133, 140–1, 175, 181, 197, 204, 218, *see also* experiments
Trinity House   28, 44, 60, 188, 201
troop transports   100, 159, 162, 178, 207, *see also* soldiers
Trotter, James   102–3, 129, 140, 180
Troughton and Simms, firm   202
turnaround times   89–90

Ulloa, Antonio de   35–6, 61, 64–5, 70, 93, 96, 98
United Kingdom, *see* Britain; England; Ireland; Scotland
United Provinces, *see* Dutch Republic
United States   93, 119, 154, 156–60, 165, 168, 170–1, 182, 186, 188, 194–6, 199, 201, 208, 213–14, 218–20, 223, 230
universities   34–5, 47, 55, 102, 128, 196, 198
US Congress   134, 195, 201–2, 207
useful knowledge   7, 8, 121, 143
US Naval Academy at Annapolis   202
Utrecht   47, 198

Van Diemen's Land   158, 207
vegetables   53, 106
ventilators   83, 106–8, 139, 141, 148, 179, 229
Vera Cruz   28, 32, 56
Verbrugge, Johannes   68, 70–2, 77, 129
Victualling Board   134, 206
victuals   71, 73, 105, *see also* diet; food
Vikings, *see* Norsemen
vinegar   105
Virginia   27, 57, 65, 87
visual representation   25, 75–6, 168, 217
VOC (Verenigde Oostindische Compagnie), *see* Dutch East India Company

Voorde, Cornelis van de   70, 72, 77
Vries, Jan de   6, 84

wars   85, 91, 100, 158, 203
    of 1812   157
    American War of Independence   86, 140, 221
    of the Austrian Succession   86, 103, 142
    Civil War (US)   156, 202, 214
    Fourth Anglo-Dutch   130
    of Jenkins' Ear   86, 100
    Napoleonic   22, 94, 116, 121, 155, 158–9, 161, 163–4, 167, 172, 174, 177–8, 180, 183, 185, 189, 199–200, 202–3, 205, 207, 212, 215, 222–4, 232
    Nine Years'   45, 71
    Revolutionary   86, 103, 124, 163, 203, 205
    Second Anglo-Dutch   47
    Seven Years'   12, 29, 36, 85–6, 97, 100, 103, 108, 122, 127, 129, 142
    of the Spanish Succession   28, 46, 85, 103
warships   28, 36, 47, 69, 86–7, 103, 106, 108, 124–5, 127, 147, 161, 164, 175, 203–4, 208
Washington   194–5, 198, 203
wave line   165, 218
waves   61, 132–3, 188, 211
weather   13, 44, 60, 62, 137, 142–5, 149, 163, 171, 198, 220, 227
West Indies   28, 31, 37–8, 43, 46, 51, 59, 63–4, 69–72, 84–7, 89–91, 100–1, 103–4, 107, 135, 137, 142, 147, 158–9, 167, 176, 178, *see also* Caribbean
whale oil   86, 182
whales   30, 54, 67, 86, 131, 146, 149, 170, 181, 183, 226
whaling ships   29–30, 47, 86, 157, 165, 222, 226
whaling/whalers   13, 21, 30, 49, 54, 66–70, 76, 78, 86–7, 100, 129, 131, 137–8, 146–7, 157, 160, 165, 183–4, 190, 224, 227–8, 232
Whewell, William   188, 191, 209, 211, 217, 223
WIC (Westindische Compagnie), *see* Dutch West India Company

Wild Coast 154
Willughby, Francis 66–7, 75
winches 165, 183
winds 13, 44, 50, 60–1, 65, 74–5, 79,
  91–2, 98–9, 132, 134, 137, 144, 147,
  149, 163, 168–71, 190, 194, 198,
  211, 213, 217, 227, 230, 232
wind sails 107–8

wool 156, 166
workshops 64, 114, 120–2

Zeeland 25, 48, 63, 70, 133
zeemanscolleges 212, *see also*
  shipmasters'societies
Zorgdrager, Cornelis Gijsbertsz 65,
  67–8, 146

www.ingramcontent.com/pod-product-compliance
Lightning Source LLC
Chambersburg PA
CBHW072121290426
44111CB00012B/1732